Korean Literature Through the Korean Wave

Korean Literature Through the Korean Wave engages with the rising interest in both the Korean Wave and Korean language learning by incorporating Korean Wave cultural content, especially K-dramas, films and songs, to underline and support the teaching of Korean literature.

It combines both premodern and modern texts, including poetry, novels, philosophical treatises, and even comics, to showcase the diversity of Korean literature. Particular care has been taken to include the voices of those marginalised in the often male, elite-dominated discourse on Korean literature. In particular, this book also distinguishes itself by extending the usual breadth of what is considered modern Korean literature up until the present day, including texts published as recently as 2017. Many of these texts are very relevant for recent discourse in Korean affairs, such as the obsession with physical appearance, the #MeToo movement and multiculturalism.

This textbook is aimed at B1-B2 level and Intermediate-Mid students of Korean. On the one hand the textbook introduces students to seeing beyond Korean literature as a monolithic entity, giving a taste of its wonderful richness and diversity. On the other hand, it provides an entry point into discussions on Korean contemporary society, in which the text (and associated media extracts) provides the catalyst for more in-depth analysis and debate.

Jieun Kiaer is Young Bin Min-Korea Foundation Associate Professor in Korean Language and Linguistics at the Oriental Institute of the University of Oxford. Her research interest lies in cross-linguistic and cross-cultural aspects of translation, particularly found in Korean-English translation. She has translated and published *The Old Korean Poetry* (2014), *Jeju Language and Tales from the Edge of the Korean Peninsula* (2014) and *The Routledge Course in Korean Translation* (2017). She has also recently finished *Translation and Literature in East Asia: Between Visibility and Invisibility* (2019, Routledge) with Jennifer Guest and Amy Xiofan Li. She is the Series Editor for the *Routledge Studies in East Asian Translation*.

Anna Yates-Lu is an Associate Faculty Member at the Oriental Institute of the University of Oxford. She recently completed her PhD on the traditional Korean sung storytelling art form p'ansori, titled 'P'ansori Today: Reconciling Tradition and Creativity in Modern Society.' Her most recent research project is studying consumption and performance of p'ansori by non-Koreans, and unpacking the complexity of interlocking cultural hierarchies that emerge through this. She also works as a Korean-English translator, particularly in translating poetry as song.

Routledge Studies in East Asian Translation
Series Editors: Jieun Kiaer
University of Oxford, UK
Amy Xiaofan Li
University of Kent, UK

Routledge Studies in East Asian Translation aims to discuss issues and challenges involved in translation between Chinese, Japanese and Korean as well as from these languages into European languages with an eye to comparing the cultures of translation within East Asia and tracking some of their complex interrelationships.

Most translation theories are built on translation between European languages, with only few exceptions. However, this Eurocentric view on language and translation can be seriously limited in explaining the translation of non-European literature and scholarship, especially when it comes to translating languages outside the Indo-European family that have radically different script forms and grammatical categories, and may also be embedded in very different writing traditions and cultures. This series considers possible paradigm shifts in translation theory, arguing that translation theory and practice need to go beyond European languages and encompass a wider range of literature and scholarship.

Translingual Words
An East Asian Lexical Encounter with English
Jieun Kiaer

Translation and Literature in East Asia
Between Visibility and Invisibility
Jieun Kiaer, Jennifer Guest, and Xiaofan Amy Li

Korean Literature Through the Korean Wave
Jieun Kiaer and Anna Yates-Lu

For more information about this series, please visit: www.routledge.com/languages/series/RSEAT

Korean Literature Through the Korean Wave

Jieun Kiaer and Anna Yates-Lu

LONDON AND NEW YORK

First published 2020
by Routledge
2 Park Square, Milton Park, Abingdon, Oxon OX14 4RN

and by Routledge
52 Vanderbilt Avenue, New York, NY 10017

Routledge is an imprint of the Taylor & Francis Group, an informa business

© 2020 Jieun Kiaer and Anna Yates-Lu

The right of Jieun Kiaer and Anna Yates-Lu to be identified as authors of this work has been asserted by them in accordance with sections 77 and 78 of the Copyright, Designs and Patents Act 1988.

All rights reserved. No part of this book may be reprinted or reproduced or utilised in any form or by any electronic, mechanical, or other means, now known or hereafter invented, including photocopying and recording, or in any information storage or retrieval system, without permission in writing from the publishers.

Trademark notice: Product or corporate names may be trademarks or registered trademarks, and are used only for identification and explanation without intent to infringe.

British Library Cataloguing-in-Publication Data
A catalogue record for this book is available from the British Library

Library of Congress Cataloging-in-Publication Data
A catalog record for this book has been requested

ISBN: 978-0-367-22530-8 (hbk)
ISBN: 978-0-367-22531-5 (pbk)
ISBN: 978-0-429-27537-1 (ebk)

Typeset in Times New Roman
by Apex CoVantage, LLC

Contents

Acknowledgements viii

Introduction 1

1 Family 4

    1.1 오륜가 – 주세붕 (The Song of Five Relationships – *Chu Sebung*) 4
    1.2 심청가 (The Song of Shimch'ŏng – *Anonymous*) 6
    1.3 엄마를 부탁해 – 신경숙 (Please Look After Mother – *Shin Kyŏngsuk*) 12
    1.4 홍보가 (The Song of Hŭngbo – *Anonymous*) 15
    1.5 홍길동전 – 허균 (The Tale of Hong Kiltong – *Hŏ Kyun*) 21
    1.6 눈길 – 이청준 (A Snowy Road – *Yi Ch'ŏngjun*) 25

2 Love 30

    2.1 소나기 – 황순원 (Rain Shower – *Hwang Sunwŏn*) 30
    2.2 춘향가 (The Song of Ch'unhyang – *Anonymous*) 33
    2.3 사랑 손님과 어머니 – 주요섭 (Mother and a Guest – *Chu Yosŏp*) 39
    2.4 시조 – 황진이 (*Various* shijo – *Hwang Chini*) 42
    2.5 향가 (Hyangga – *various authors*) 43
    2.6 구운몽 – 김만중 (The Nine Cloud Dream – *Kim Manjung*) 47

3 Friendship and loyalty 51

    3.1 오우가 – 윤선도 (The Song of Five Friends – *Yun Sŏndo*) 51
    3.2 지란지교를 꿈꾸며 – 유안진 (Dreaming of a Good and Noble Friendship – *Yu Anjin*) 54
    3.3 달밤 – 이태준 (Moonlit Night – *Yi T'aejun*) 57
    3.4 우리들의 일그러진 영웅 – 이문열 (Our Twisted Hero – *Yi Munyŏl*) 61
    3.5 안민가 – 충담사 (Song of Peace to the People – *Ch'ungdamsa*) 64
    3.6 하여가 – 이방원, 단심가 – 정몽주 (Anyway Song – *Yi Pangwŏn*; and Steadfast Song – *Chŏng Mongju*) 67

4 Satire 71

    4.1 배비장전 (The Tale of Aide Pae – *Anonymous*) 71
    4.2 오적 – 김지하 (Five Bandits – *Kim Chiha*) 74
    4.3 닭을 빌려타고 돌아가다 – 서거정 (Riding Home on a Borrowed Chicken – *Sŏ Kŏjŏng*) 79
    4.4 허생전 – 박지원 (The Tale of Mr. Hŏ – *Pak Chiwŏn*) 80
    4.5 대하 – 김남천 (Scenes from the Enlightenment – *Kim Namch'ŏn*) 85
    4.6 맹진사댁경사 – 오영진 (The Happy Day of Maeng Chinsa – *O Yŏngjin*) 88

5 Han 92

    5.1 제망매가 – 월명사 (Song for a Departed Sister – *Wŏlmyŏngsa*) 92
    5.2 향수 – 정지용 (Thoughts of Home – *Chŏng Chiyong*) 95
    5.3 은세계 – 이인직 (Silver World – *Yi Injik*) 97
    5.4 한중록 – 혜경궁 홍씨 (The Memoirs of Lady Hyegyŏng – *Lady Hyegyŏng*) 101
    5.5 풀 – 김금숙 (Grass – *Keum Suk Gendry-Kim*) 106
    5.6 민요 아리랑, 가시리 (*Folk songs* Arirang, Will You Go – *Anonymous*) 111

6 Social change 115

    6.1 무정 – 이광수 (Heartless – *Yi Kwangsu*) 115
    6.2 삼포 가는 길 – 황석영 (The Road Going to Sampo – *Hwang Sŏkyŏng*) 119
    6.3 1964년 서울 – 김승옥 (Seoul: 1964, Winter – *Kim Sŭngok*) 122
    6.4 소년이 온다 – 한강 (Human Acts – *Han Kang*) 125
    6.5 바리데기 – 황석영 (Princess Pari – *Hwang Sŏkyŏng*) 128
    6.6 완득이 – 김려령 (Wandŭgi-Punch – *Kim Ryŏryŏng*) 131

7 Women in Korean society 135

    7.1 내훈 – 소혜왕후 (Instructions for Women – *Queen Sohye*) 135
    7.2 규원가 – 허난설헌 (Lament of the Inner Chamber – *Hŏ Nansŏrhŏn*) 137
    7.3 음식디미방 – 장계향, 규합총서 – 이빙허각 (Recipes for Tasty Foods – *Chang Kyehyang; and* Encyclopaedia of the Inner Chambers – *Yi Pinghŏgak*) 143
    7.4 이춘풍전 (The Tale of Yi Ch'unp'ung – *Anonymous*) 148
    7.5 탁류 – 채만식 (Turbid Rivers – *Ch'ae Manshik*) 150
    7.6 채식주의자 – 한강 (The Vegetarian – *Han Kang*) 154

8 Nature, beauty, and aesthetics   158

8.1 멋설 – 조지훈 (On Beauty – *Cho Chihun*) *158*
8.2 강호사시가 – 맹사성 (Song of Four Seasons by Rivers and Lakes – *Maeng Sasŏng*) *160*
8.3 실록예찬 – 이양하 (In Praise of Fresh Green – *Yi Yangha*) *163*
8.4 무소유 – 법정 (Non-possession – *Pŏpchŏng*) *166*
8.5 죽은 왕녀를 위한 파바느 – 박민규 (Pavane for a Dead Princess – *Pak Minkyu*) *170*
8.6 마네킹 – 최윤 (Mannequin – *Ch'oe Yun*) *173*

Appendix: English translations   178

Acknowledgements

The first author would like to acknowledge the support from the Korea Foundation Fellowship for Field Research in 2017 which enabled her to work on how the Korean Wave, particularly dramas and films, can be used in teaching Korean language and literature. The second author gratefully acknowledges the support, guidance and encouragement of Keith Howard, who first lead her to the study of the Korean Wave and *p'ansori*, as well as her co-author, Jieun Kiaer, for encouraging her to seek out ways in which this knowledge can be applied to literature. We would also like to thank our students for their input and feedback in putting together this textbook. Particular thanks go to Stacey Lui and Jing Yan for their help in proofreading and editing.

We are grateful to the following authors and scholars for kindly giving permission for us to use extracts from their work:

CH'OE Tonghyŏn (*Shimch'ŏngga, Hŭngboga, Ch'unhyangga*)
Keum Suk GENDRY-KIM (*Grass*)
SHIN Kyŏngsuk (*Please Look After Mother*)
YU Anjin (*Dreaming of a Good and Noble Friendship*)

This textbook features the translations, not just of the authors and their students (Alex Kimmon, Derek Driggs, Ben Cagan, Jing Yan, Karolina Watroba), but also of many other translators, as part of our mission to highlight the importance of translation in the spread of Korean literature. We sincerely thank the following translators for their permission in using parts of their translations in these textbooks:

Brother Anthony of Taizé (*Five Bandits*)
Sora Kim-Russell (*Princess Pari*)
Deborah Smith (Published: *Human Acts, The Vegetarian*. Unpublished: *Rain Shower, Mother and a Guest*)

In addition, we wish to extend our grateful acknowledgment to authors and translators we were unable to contact for permission, extracts from whose work we are using under the understanding of fair dealing:

CH'AE Manshik (*Turbid Rivers*)
CHO Chihun (*On Beauty*)
CH'OE Yun (*Mannequin*)
CHŎNG Chiyong (*Thoughts of Home*)

CHU Yosŏp (*Mother and a Guest*)
James GALE (*The Nine Cloud Dream*)
HWANG Sunwŏn (*Rain Shower*)
HWANG Sŏkyŏng (*The Road Going to Sampo, Princess Pari*)
JUNG Yewon (*Mannequin*)
Amber Hyun Jung KIM (*Pavane for a Dead Princess*)
KIM Chiha (*Five Bandits*)
KIM Yuna (*315360*)
JaHyun KIM HABOUSH (*The Memoirs of Lady Hyegyŏng*)
KIM Ryŏryŏng (*Wandŭgi-Punch*)
KIM Sŭngok (*Seoul: 1964, Winter*)
Charles LASHURE (*Scenes from the Enlightenment*)
Ann Sung-hi LEE (*Heartless*)
O Yŏngjin (*The Happy Day of Maeng Chinsa*)
Kevin O'ROURKE (*Shijo* by Hwang Chini)
PAK Minkyu (*Pavane for a Dead Princess*)
PAK Sŭngbae (*Shimch'ŏngga*)
Marshall PIHL (*Seoul: 1964, Winter*)
Pŏpchŏng (*Non-possession*)
YI Ch'ŏngjun (*A Snowy Road*)
YI Kwangsu (*Heartless*)
YI T'aejun (*Moonlit Night*)
YI Yangha (*In Praise of Fresh Green*)

Finally, we would like to also thank our family and friends. Without their support, this book would never have come to fruition.

Introduction

The inspiration for this book came from our observation of the rising interest in Korea and Korean culture, which has resulted in a rise of people learning the Korean language (a feature profiling this development was shown on the BBC, 11 July 2018), and a corresponding rise in university departments teaching Korean literature. As has become apparent from events such as the 7th European Association for Korean Language Education (2018), it is interest in K-dramas in particular that has sparked this rise, mainly in Europe and North America but also around the world. We have also observed a rising interest in Korean literature, as can be seen in the several instances in recent years of translated Korean literature winning prestigious awards: *Please Look After Mother* by Shin Kyung-sook won the Man Asian Literary Prize in 2011, and Han Kang's *The Vegetarian* won the Man Booker International Award in 2016. While the interest is clearly there, it has been difficult linking students' interests to what standard Korean Studies or Korean Literature courses have to offer. In addition, there is a significant lack of textbooks for teaching Korean literature, as most teachers have to develop their own class material from scratch, which tends to stay limited within a very narrow field. This textbook aims to fill this gap.

In this book, we combine both pre-modern and modern texts, including poetry, novels, philosophical treatises, even comics (*manhwa*), to showcase the diversity of Korean literature. In addition, we have aimed to include a variety of different writing styles, orthographies (Sino-Korean, middle Korean and modern Korean), and dialects (North Korean, Chŏlla province, and Kyŏngsang province). Many texts include the voices of those marginalised in the often male, elite-dominated discourse on Korean literature – women (both high and low class), commoners, foreigners, etc. In particular, this book distinguishes itself by extending the usual breadth of what is considered modern Korean literature (generally stopping sometime around the 1930s) up until the present day, including texts published as recently as 2017. The original text in classical literature is represented with the modern Korean orthography with a few exceptions for readability. Many of these texts are very relevant for recent discourse in Korean affairs, such as the obsession with physical appearance, the #MeToo movement and multiculturalism. This textbook is hence intended, on the one hand, to introduce students to see beyond Korean literature as a monolithic entity, giving a taste of its wonderful richness and diversity. On the other hand, it provides an entrypoint into discussions on Korean contemporary society, in which the text (and associated media extract) provides the catalyst for more in-depth analysis and debate. For this reason, our text selection was guided by the themes we wanted to discuss. Rather than this being an anthology of the most iconic Korean literature texts, in allowing thematic content to be our guiding principle we found the text styles we used also diversified greatly, a development we can consider to be only of benefit.

Organisation of the textbook

The book is split up into eight overarching themes, addressing family; love; friendship; satire; *han* (sorrow and resentment); social change; women in Korean society; and nature, beauty, and aesthetics. These are subdivided into six chapters, providing 48 weeks of class material in a modular fashion, so teachers can pick and choose which elements of the lesson plans they wish to use.

The first section, on family, looks at ideal family relations (*The Song of Five Relationships*); filial piety (*The Song of Shimch'ŏng*); sacrificial motherhood (*Please Look After Mother*); the relationship between siblings (*The Song of Hŭngbo*); conflict over legitimacy (*The Tale of Hong Kiltong*); and tension in the relationship between parent and child (*A Snowy Road*).

The second section, on love, addresses first love (*Rain Shower*); love that overcomes all obstacles (*The Song of Ch'unhyang*); love that goes against social norms (*Mother and a Guest*); love for sale (*shijo* by Hwang Chini); love and jealousy in *hyangga*; and jealousy between primary wives and concubines (*The Nine Cloud Dream*).

In the third section, on friendship and loyalty, we address Confucian ideals of friendship (*The Song of Five Friends*); what makes true friendship (*Dreaming of a Good and Noble Friendship*); friendship blossoming in unexpected situations (*Moonlit Night*); the absence of friendship, or bullying (*Our Twisted Hero*); loyalty to a true king (*Song of Peace to the People*); and differing definitions of loyalty (*Anyway Song and Steadfast Song*).

The fourth section looks at satirical texts, criticizing hypocritical aristocrats (*The Tale of Aide Pae*); the excesses of the Park Chung-hee government (*Five Bandits*); miserly people (*Riding Home on a Borrowed Chicken*); the prejudice of the *yangban* against mercantile activity (*The Tale of Mr Hŏ*); people overly obsessed with new trends (*Scenes From the Enlightenment*); and those overly greedy for social advancement (*The Happy Day of Maeng Chinsa*).

In the fifth section we look at the emotion of *han*, a mixture of sadness, resentment and longing that is often touted as unique to the Korean nation. We cover the loss of loved ones (*Song for a Departed Sister*); homesickness (*Thoughts of Home*); sorrow due to oppression (*Silver World*); the death of Crown Prince Sado (*The Memoirs of Lady Hyegyŏng*); the lives of comfort women (*Grass*); and using folk songs as a means to both express and overcome sorrow (Folk Songs *Arirang, Will You Go*).

The fifth section addresses social change and key moments in Korea's modern history: the Cultural Nationalist movement (*Heartless*); industrialization (*The Road Going to Sampo*); alienation in modern life (*Seoul: 1964, Winter*); the Kwangju Uprising (*Human Acts*); the North Korean diaspora (*Princess Pari*); and multiculturalism (*Wandŭgi – Punch*).

In the seventh section we look at the position of women in Korean society, moving beyond stereotypes of passivity to show a variety of womanly behaviour, demonstrating their proactive participation in society. We address proper womanly behaviour (*Instructions for Women*); the isolation felt by married women (*Lament of the Inner Chamber*); women as cooks and managers of the household (*Recipes for Tasty Foods* and *Encyclopaedia of the Inner Chambers*); women correcting their husband's flaws (*The Tale of Yi Ch'unp'ung*); the #MeToo movement (*Turbid Rivers*); and protest against the narrow confines of the female role in Korean society (*The Vegetarian*).

The final section looks at nature, beauty and aesthetics. We highlight the true nature of beauty (*On Beauty*); the joy in the turn of the seasons (*Song of Four Seasons by Rivers and Lakes*); enjoyment of the freshness that spring brings (*In Praise of Fresh Green*); the spiritual beauty of non-possession (*Musoyu*); the obsession with physical appearance in Korean society (*Pavane for a Dead Princess*); and the commodification of beauty (*Mannequin*).

For each chapter, we have also provided a number of resources with which to better understand the text and the associated thematic content. We hence first provide a general introduction to the subject matter for the students to get general idea of the issue, followed by the original text in Korean for reading and/or translation, as well as some key vocabulary and grammar points to both aid understanding and open linguistic discussion. After this, we have included basic comprehension questions related to the text, to make sure students have properly grasped the material provided, as well as a popular media extract (from a film, television drama, or song), also with comprehension questions, to help give students an entry point, particularly for more difficult texts. Due to copyright reasons, we are unable to provide access to all the extracts. However, by highlighting specific scenes or songs, we hope to spare teachers the task of trawling through countless hours of footage to find relevant material. Finally, we conclude each chapter with more in-depth discussion questions on the text and associated social issues. These are aided by a brief reference selection that has been provided for the use of both students and teachers. In this way, we hope to open a new way of teaching Korean through multimodal resources.

On romanisation and translation

In line with current Korean Studies convention, we have chosen to employ McCune-Reischauer romanisation in this textbook, with the exception of some commonly-known names (Seoul, Park Chung-hee) and instances in which the widely-known international name of a film or drama included non-standard romanisation.

Finally, we would like to highlight our treatment of the English translations of these texts. Given the purpose of Korean language education which is tied up with this textbook, we have chosen to keep the English translations separate, in an appendix at the end of the book. However, with the purpose of highlighting the not-insignificant role of the translator in transmitting a text to readers of a different language, we have chosen wherever possible to include published versions of the texts in translation. This will, on the one hand, allow those wishing to engage in discussion on the nature of Korean-English translation to have ample material available; on the other hand, it also helps raise the profile of the often-sidelined work done by translators, which we both firmly believe to worthy of more attention. We are grateful to all those who provided us access to their translations, and want to particularly thank Deborah Smith for kindly giving us access to many of her unpublished works.

1 Family

1.1 오륜가 – 주세붕 (*The Song of Five Relationships – Chu Sebung*)

Introduction to the text

The Song of Five Relationships (오륜가/五倫歌), by Shinjae Chu Sebung (1495–1554), teaches the five traditional values that make up the basis of Confucian moral standards. These are listed below, in the order they are presented in the poem:

부자유친 (*pujayuch'in* 父子有親) means *Father and son have an intimate relationship*. This refers to the duty of the child to the parents, springing from respect, debt, and gratitude for birthing and raising him or her.

군신유의 (*kunshinyuŭi* 君臣有義) means *Master and servant have order*. This refers to the unbreakable hierarchical structure between servant and master, subject and ruler.

부부유별 (*pubuyubyŏl* 夫婦有別) means *Husband and wife are different*. This refers to the complementary duties of a husband and a wife, but also implies a hierarchy within the married relationship, where a wife is expected to serve the husband.

형제우애 (*hyŏngje'u'ae* 兄弟友愛) means *Love and affection of siblings*. This refers to the respect and affection which should be present between brothers.

장유유서 (*changyuyusŏ* 長幼有序) means *Old and young have order*. This refers to the hierarchy between the young and old.

Original text

모든 사람들은 이 말씀(삼강오륜의 말)을 들으려므나,
이 말씀이 아니면 사람이면서도 사람이 아닌 것이니,
이 말씀을 잊지 않고 배우고야 말 것입니다.

아버님이 날 낳으시고 어머님이 나를 기르시니
부모님이 아니셨더라면 이 몸이 없었을 것이다.
이 덕을 갚고자 하니 하늘같이 끝이 없구나.

종과 상전의 구별을 누가 만들어 내었던가
벌과 개미들이 이 뜻을 먼저 아는구나.
한 마음에 두 뜻을 가지는 일이 없도록 속이지나 마십시오.

남편이 밭 갈러 간 곳에 밥 담은 광주리를 이고 가서,
밥상을 들여 오되 (지아비의) 눈썹 높이까지 공손히 들어 바칩니다.

(남편은) 진시로 고마우신 분이니 (삼가고 조심해야 할) 손님을 대하는 것과 무엇이 다르겠습니까?

형님이 잡수신 젖을 내(아우)가 따라 먹습니다.
아아, 우리 아우야 너는 어머님의 사랑이야.
형제간에 화목하지 못하면 개나 돼지라 할 것입니다.

늙은이는 부모님과 같고, 어른은 형과 같으니,
이와 같은데 공손하지 않으면 (짐승과) 어디가 다른 것인가.
나로서는 (노인과 어른들을) 맞이하게 되면 절하고야 말 것입니다.

Key vocabulary

삼강오륜	Three Bonds and Five Relationships: On top of the Five Relationships outlined above, the Three Bonds refer to the bonds between king and subject, between parent and child, and between husband and wife. Together, these principles reflect the cornerstone of Confucian morality.
덕	virtue, favour
종	servant, slave
상전	master
벌	bee
개미	ant
광주리	basket
지아비	husband
진시	really, surely, verily
삼가	treat respectfully, reverently, humbly
젖	mother's breast, milk
화목	harmonious, amicable

Comprehension questions: text

1. What debt does the author owe to his parents?
2. Which animals does the author use to highlight master-servant relationships?
3. What is the correct behaviour of a wife to her husband?
4. Why must brothers get on well?
5. Why should we treat our elders with respect?

Comprehension questions: drama extract

The tvN drama *Reply 1988* (응답하라 1988, 2015) tells the story of high school student Sŏng Toksŏn and her life amongst family and friends living in northern Seoul in 1988. In the first episode, we see a wide range of different family dynamics, set within the nostalgia of the late 1980s, which both contrasts with and confirms the principles outlined in *Oryun'ga*.

1. Who smokes amongst the Sŏng family children?
2. Where has the rest of this month's salary gone?
3. Why does Toksŏn's mother feel she gets made out to be the bad guy?
4. What are Toksŏn and her sister fighting about?

6 *Family*

Additional source material

The song 'Father' (아버지, 2005), by Psy, poignantly shows how the expectations of family life load upon the father's shoulders.

Further discussion questions

1 Form two teams to debate:

   Team A: The principle of *oryun* is nothing more than a strategy by the elite to control the masses.
   Team B: *Oryun* sets up a fundamental baseline of respect necessary in order to help society function smoothly.

2 Do you think these principles are still valued today?

References

Ch'oe, Yŏng-ho. 2002. 'Private Academies and the State in Late Chosŏn Korea.' In *Culture and the State in Late Chosŏn Korea*, edited by JaHyun Kim Haboush & Martina Deuchler, pp. 15–45. Cambridge, MA; London: Harvard University Asia Center.
Deuchler, Martina. 1992. *The Confucian Transformation of Korea: A Study of Society and Ideology*. Cambridge, MA: Council on East Asian Studies, Harvard University.
Hejtmanek, Milan. 2013. 'The Elusive Path to Sagehood: Origins of the Confucian Academy System in Chosŏn Korea.' *Seoul Journal of Korean Studies* 26(2): 233–68.
Lee, Peter H. 2003. *A History of Korean Literature*. Cambridge; New York: Cambridge University Press. (Chapter 8: Early Chosŏn *Sijo*).

1.2 심청가 (*The Song of Shimch'ŏng* – Anonymous)

Introduction to the text

Shimch'ŏngga is an example of the *p'ansori* genre, a form of epic oral narrative, performed by a single performer accompanied by a drummer. Dramatic effect is heightened by alternating between song and narration, and between using slower rhythms (진양조, 중모리) and faster rhythms (중중모리, 자진모리). While *p'ansori* as a genre has suffered from a steady decrease in popularity since the beginning of the 20th century, which has been slowed by a wide variety of preservation strategies, the five *p'ansori* stories remaining today are morality tales that anyone in Korea will be familiar with. Each story exemplifies one of the Five Relationships that make up the basis of Confucianism: the relationship between king and subject, between parent and child, between husband and wife, between siblings, and between friends. *Shimch'ŏngga* tells of the filial piety of Shim Ch'ŏng, who sells herself to some sailors as a human sacrifice in order for her blind father to be able to donate 300 sacks of rice to a temple and regain his sight. When she jumps into the sea, the gods take pity on her and bring her back inside a lotus blossom, which is picked up by some sailors and brought before the emperor who, upon seeing Ch'ŏng emerge from the flower, falls in love with her and makes her his empress. Desperate to find her father again, Ch'ŏng holds a banquet for all the blind people in the kingdom, at which she is reunited with her father. At the shock of hearing his daughter's voice, his blindness is cured, and all other blind people also regain their sight at the power of Ch'ŏng's filial devotion.

Original text

Text and annotations from Ch'oe Tonghyŏn. 2008. *Shimch'ŏngga padipyŏl chŏnjip 3: Chŏng Ŭngmin padi* [A complete collection of *Shimch'ŏngga* according to different styles 3: Chŏng Ŭngmin style]. Chŏnju: Ministry of Culture, Sports, and Tourism, North Chŏlla Province.

[진양조]
눈 어두운 백발 부친 영결[1] 허고 죽을 일과
사람이 세상에 나 십오세에 죽을 일을 생각허니,
정신이 삭막허고,[2] 흉중[3]이 답답허여
하염없는[4] 설움이 간장[5]으로 솟아난다.
부친의 사시[6] 의복 빨래허여 농[7] 안에 넣어두고,
갓 망건[8] 다시 꾸며 쓰기 쉽게 걸어놓고,
행선일을 생각허니 하룻밤이 격한지라.[9]
모친 분묘[10] 찾어가서 주과포혜[11] 차려놓고,
'아이고, 어머니! 불효여식[12] 청이는,
부친 눈을 띄우랴고 삼백 석에 몸이 팔려
제수[13]로 가게 되니,
불쌍헌 아버지를 차마 어니 잊고 가며,
분묘에 돋난 풀은 뉘 손으로 벌초[14]허며,
연년이[15] 오난 기일[16] 뉘라서 받드리까?
내 손으로 부은 술을 망종[17] 흠향[18] 허옵소서.'
사배[19] 하직허고 집으로 돌아오니,
밤 적적[20] 삼경[21] 인디
부친이 잠든지라.
후원[22]에 돌아가
사당문[23]을 가만히 열고,
분향사배[24] 우는 말이,
'불효여식 청이는
선영[25] 향화[26] 를 끊게 되니
불승비통[27]허옵니다.'
방으로 들어오니
부친은 잠이 들어 아무런 줄 모르거늘,
심청이 기가막혀 크게 우든[28] 못허고,
속으로 느끼난다.[29]
'아이고, 아버지! 아버지. 아버지.
아버지를 어찌 헐꼬?
이 내 한 몸 없어지면 동리 걸인 또 될 것이니,
어찌 잊고 돌아가리?
아이고, 아버지! 날 볼 밤이 몇 밤이며, 날 볼 날이 몇 날이오?'
얼굴도 대보고, 수족[30]도 만지면서,
'아버지, 오늘 밤 오경시[31]를 함지에[32] 머무르고,
내일 아침 돋는 해는 부상[33]에다 매랑이면,[34]
불쌍허신 우리 부친 일시라도 더 뵈련만은,
인력으로 어이 허리!'
천지가 사정이 없어
벌써 닭이 '꼬끼오!'
'닭아, 우지 마라.

반야³⁵ 진관³⁶의 맹상군³⁷이 아니로고나.
네가 울면 날이 새고,
날이 새면은 나 죽는다.
나 죽기는 섧잖으나,
의지 없는 우리 부친
차마 어찌 잊고 가랴!'
[아니리]
벌써 동방³⁸이 밝아지니, 심청이 하릴없어³⁹ 정신을 다시 차려,
'내가 이래서는 못쓰겄다. 부친 진지나 망종 지으리라.'
하고 부엌으로 나오니, 벌써 문 밖에 선인들이 늘어섰거늘, 심청이 빨리 나가,
'여보시오, 선인네들. 부친 진지나 잡수시게 허고 떠나게 하옵시다.'
선인들이 허락하니, 아침밥 얼른 지어 소반⁴⁰ 우에 받쳐 들고,
'아버지, 진지 잡수시오.'
';애, 오늘 아침밥은 별로⁴¹ 일쿠나.⁴² 청아, 그런데 간밤에 내가 묘한 꿈을 꾸었다. 네가 수레를 타고 한없이 가 보이니, 꿈에 수레라 하는 것은 귀인⁴³이 타는 것인디, 내가 해몽⁴⁴을 하여 보았지. 오늘 장승상댁 부인이 너를 데려간다고 안 했느냐? 아마 가마⁴⁵가 올란가⁴⁶ 보다.'
심청이 저 죽을 꿈인 줄 짐작하고,
'아버지 진지 잡수사이다.'⁴⁷
'야, 오늘 아침밥은 별로 걸구나.'⁴⁸
진짓상을 물리고⁴⁹ 담배 붙여 올린 후에, 심청이 아무 말 못허고 우두머니⁵⁰ 앉었다가, 아무리 생각하여도 이제는 부친을 속일 수 없거늘,
[자진모리]
심청이 거동⁵¹ 봐라.
부친 앞으로 우루루루루루루.
'아이고, 아부지!'
한 번 부르더니 말 못하고 기절헌다.
심봉사 깜짝 놀래,
'아이고, 이것 웬 일이냐? 어허, 이것 웬 일이여?
이 애가 급체⁵²하였는가?
아가, 정신 차려라.
누가 봉사 딸이라고 정개⁵³하드냐?'
'아버지. 불효 여식은
아버지를 속이었소.'
'아, 이놈, 속였으면 무슨 큰일을 속였간디,⁵⁴ 이렇게 아비를 놀랜단 말이냐?
말하여라. 말해여.⁵⁵ 답답허다, 말해여.'
'공양미 삼백 석을 누가 제게 주오리까?
남경 장사 선인들께 삼백 석에 몸이 팔려,
인당수 제수로 오늘이 행선날이오.
어느 때 뵈오리까?'

Key vocabulary

영결허다	to be separated forever (永訣) – 허다 is the Chŏlla dialect variation of the verb 하다
흉중	in one's chest, one's deep-down thoughts (胸中)
삭막허다	to be desolate and forlorn
하염없다	without end

간장	restless heart, disturbed mind (肝腸)
농	a chest for holding small items of clothing (籠)
망건	a net-like item of clothing wrapped around the forehead to keep one's hair tidy when it is tied up in a topknot (網巾)
격한지라	there is this much distance, this much (time) left (隔)
분묘	tomb (墳墓)
주과포혜	alcohol, fruit, dried meat, and sweet rice punch – the four things required to hold an ancestral ritual (酒果脯醯)
불효여식	unfilial daughter – it was considered unfilial to die before one's parents (不孝女息)
제수	sacrifice for ritual, whether food or an object (祭需)
벌초허다	the act of clearing grass away from a grave (伐草)
기일	memorial day, anniversary of death (忌日)
망종	the last (亡終)
흠향	gods or spirits receiving and eating the sacrificial offerings (歆饗)
적적	extremely quiet (寂寂)
삼경	between 11pm and 1am, in the dead of the night (三更)
사당문	the door to the home shrine, where the ancestral tablets are housed (祠堂門)
분향사배	to light incense and bow four times, done to the dead (焚香四拜)
불승비통	to be unable to control one's sorrow (不勝悲痛)
우든	to cry, adaptation of 울지는
느끼난디	to weep or sob, from 흐느끼는데
오경시	between 3 and 5am, when the sun comes up (五更時)
함지에	Hamji is a legendary lake in China from which the sun is said to rise (咸池)
부상	according to Chinese legend, in the East Sea there is a tree from which the sun rises (扶桑)
맹상군	Lord Menchang of Qi, when escaping from capture by the Qin, he managed to pass a patrol point by one of his party faking a rooster call to make the soldiers think they should open the gates (孟嘗君)
수레	wagon, cart
해몽	intepret the dream (解夢)
가마	Palanquin
별로 걸구나	be especially abundant
우두머니	from 우두커니: vacantly, blankly
급체	sudden indigestion (急滯)
정개	from 정가: tease, mock
공양미	rice offered to Buddha (供養米)

Comprehension questions: text

1. Why is Shim Chŏng selling herself? For how much?
2. What preparations does she make for her departure?
3. What is the last thing Shim Chŏng does for her father?
4. What did her father dream of, and how does he interpret this dream?

Comprehension questions: drama/film extract

The 1993 film *Sopyonje* (서편제) by Im Kwŏnt'aek draws many parallels between the tragic story of Shim Chŏng's sacrifice to save her father, and the relationship between the film's protagonists, *p'ansori* singer Yubong and his adoptive daughter Songhwa, often referring to extracts from *Shimch'ŏngga* throughout the film. Yubong is desperate to get Songhwa to attain true artistry in singing *p'ansori*, and the scene where they move to a remote hut in the mountains to further her training highlights the sacrifices that Songhwa has made for her adoptive father's ambition.

1 What does Yubong think is lacking in Songhwa's voice?
2 How does Yubong respond to being beaten for stealing a chicken?
3 What did Yubong do to Songhwa?
4 How does he know she has forgiven him?

Further discussion questions

1 Form two teams to debate:

   Team A: Our parents always have our best interests at heart, and if we can help them with our sacrifice, we should.
   Team B: Appealing to filial piety is a form of emotional blackmail, and restricts our developing as individuals.

2 Traditional Confucian concepts of filial piety were focussed on ancestor worship, and hence were directed more towards men, as women were expected to shift their loyalties to their husband's family after marriage. Still, many famous stories actually hold up women (Shim Ch'ŏng, Princess Pari) as exemplaries of filial piety. What does the existence of such stories tell us about premodern Korean society?

Notes

1 永訣. 영원히 이별함.
2 잊어버려 생각이 아득하고. 황폐하여 쓸쓸하고.
3 胸中. 마음에 두고 있는 생각.
4 끝없는.
5 肝腸. 마음. 애.
6 四時. 사철.
7 籠. 자그마하게 만든 옷을 넣어두는 가구.
8 網巾. 상투를 한 사람이 머리털을 걷어 올려 가지런히 하기 위하여 이마에서 뒤통수에 눌러 쓰던, 그물처럼 생긴 물건.
9 隔한지라. 사이가 떨어진지라. 남은지라. 남았다.
10 墳墓. 무덤.
11 酒果脯醢. 술, 과일, 말린 고기, 식혜. 제삿상을 차리는 기분 음식.
12 不孝女息. 불효한 딸자식.
13 祭需. 제물. 제사를 지낼 때 쓰는 음식이나 물건.
14 伐草. 무덤의 풀을 베는 일.
15 年年이. 해마다.
16 忌日. 죽은 날. 제삿날.
17 亡終: 마지막.
18 歆饗. 신령의 제물을 받아서 먹음.
19 四拜: 네 번 절을 함.
20 寂寂. 아주 고요함.
21 三更. 밤 열한 시에서 새벽 한 시 사이. 한밤중.
22 後園. 뒤뜰.

23 祠堂門. 사당의 문. '사당'은 조상의 신주를 모셔놓은 집.
24 焚香四拜. 향을 피우고 네 번 절을 함. 죽은 사람에 대해서는 남자는 네 번 절을 함.
25 先塋. 선산(先山). 조상의 무덤, 또는 조상의 무덤이 있는 곳.
26 香火. 향불. 제사에는 언제나 향불을 피우기 때문에 제사를 가리킴.
27 不勝悲痛. 비통함을 이기지 못함.
28 울지는.
29 흐느끼는데.
30 手足. 손과 발.
31 五更時. 새벽 세 시에서 다섯 시 사이. 해가 돋는 시각.
32 咸池에. '함지'는 중국 전설에서 해가 진다는 큰 연못.
33 扶桑. 중국 전설에서, 동쪽 바다 속의 해가 뜨는 곳에 있다는 상상의 나무 이름, 또는 그곳.
34 맬 양이면. 맬 것 같으면. 맨다면.
35 半夜. 한밤중.
36 秦關. 진나라의 관. '관'은 국경이나 국내의 요지의 통로에 두어서, 외적을 경비하며, 출입하는 사람이나 화물을 조사하던 곳. 여기서는 맹산군이 닭울음소리를 잘 내는 식객의 도움으로 무사히 도망쳐 나온 함곡관을 가리킴.
37 孟嘗君. 맹산군은 전국시대 제(齊)나라 사람으로, 성은 전(田), 이름은 문(文)임. 이찌기 빈객들을 후히 대접하여 많은 사람이 그의 집에 출입하였는데, 맹상군이 진(秦)나라 소왕에게 잡혀 죽게 되었을 때, 닭울음소리를 잘내는 식객(食客)의 도움으로 함곡관을 빠져나와 무사히 도망친 일이 있었다.
38 東方. 동쪽.
39 어떻게 할 도리가 없어.
40 小盤. 자그마한 밥상.
41 別로. 특별히.
42 이르구나.
43 貴人. 귀한 사람.
44 解夢. 꿈 속에 나타난 일의 좋고 나쁨을 풀어 판단함.
45 예전에 한 사람이 안에 타고 둘이나 넷이 들거나 메던, 조그만 집 모양의 탈것. 연(輦), 덩, 초헌(軺軒), 남여(籃輿), 사인교(四人轎) 따위가 있다.
46 오려나.
47 잡수시지요.
48 차려놓은 음식의 가짓수가 많아 푸짐하구나.
49 다른 자리로 옮겨 놓고.
50 우두커니.
51 擧動. 몸을 움직이는 짓이나 태도.
52 急滯. 갑작스럽게 체함.
53 정가. 지난 허물이나 잘못을 자꾸 들춰내어 흉봄.
54 속였기에.
55 말하여! 말해!

References

Cho, Dong-il (trans. Bruce Fulton). 1994. 'The Two-Stage Transitional Period between Medieval and Modern Literature.' *Korean Studies* 18: 1–12.

Han, Seo Kyung. 2016. *Re-Claiming the Ideals of the Yŏllyŏ: Women in and with Books in Early Chosŏn Korea*. PhD Thesis, Binghamton University, New York.

Kim, Hŭnggyu. 2003. 'P'ansori.' In *A History of Korean Literature*, edited by Peter H. Lee, pp. 366–80. Cambridge; New York: Cambridge University Press.

Pettid, Michael J. 2000. 'Late-Chosŏn Society as Reflected in a Shamanistic Narrative: An Analysis of the *Pari kongju muga*.' *Korean Studies* 24: 113–41.

Pihl, Marshall R. 1994. *The Korean Singer of Tales*. Cambridge, MA: Council on East Asian Studies, Harvard University.

Walraven, Boudewijn. 1994. *Songs of the Shaman: The Ritual Chants of the Korean Mudang*. London, New York: Kegan Paul International.

12   Family

1.3 엄마를 부탁해 – 신경숙 (*Please Look After Mother* – Shin Kyŏngsuk)

Introduction to the text

Shin Kyŏngsuk was born in 1963 in a village near Jeongeup, North Jeolla Province in southern South Korea. She was the fourth child and oldest daughter of six. At 16, she moved to Seoul, where her older brother lived. She worked in an electronics plant while attending night school. She made her literary debut in 1985 with the novella, *Winter's Fable*, after graduating from the Seoul Institute of the Arts as a creative writing major. Shin is, along with Kim In-uk and Kong Chi-yŏng, one of the group of female writers from the so-called 386 Generation. She won the 2011 Man Asian Literary Prize for *Please Look After Mom*. She was the first woman to win that award.

This novel depicts the sacrificial motherhood often observed in East Asian family. So-nyo (mother) did not really choose to become a mother; it was the role she was expected to assume when she married. Once she took on that role, her self-identity was swallowed up in motherhood. She found joy in her children, but it seemed like that was the only joy she knew in her life filled with housework. Her husband and children also do not see her as a person separate from Mother, and take her for granted. So-nyo raises her children, but her job does not end when they have grown up. While they focus on their own lives and the families they make for themselves, So-nyo continues to care for her children as much as she can. They, however, neglect her without even knowing it, so self-absorbed are they. They only realise how hard she worked for them when she is gone.

Original text

엄마의 사진을 어느 걸 쓰느냐를 두고 의견이 갈라졌다. 최근 사진을 붙여야 한다는 데에는 모두 동의했지만 누구도 엄마의 최근 사진을 가지고 있지 않았다. 너는 언제부턴가 엄마가 사진 찍히는 걸 매우 싫어했다는 걸 생각해냈다. 가족사진을 찍을 때도 엄마는 어느 틈에 빠져나가, 사진에는 엄마 모습만 보이지 않았다. 아버지 칠순 때 찍은 가족사진 속의 엄마 얼굴이 사진으로 남은 가장 최근 모습이었다. 그 때의 엄마는 물빛 한복을 입고 미장원에 가 업스타일로 머리를 손질하고 입술에 붉은빛이 도는 루주를 바른, 한껏 멋을 낸 모습이었다. 사진 속 엄마는 실종되기 전의 모습과는 너무 달라 그 사진을 따로 확대해 붙여본들 사람들이 그 사람이 이 사람이라는 걸 알아보지 못하리라는 것이 네 남동생의 의견이었다. 인터넷에 그 사진을 올렸더니 어머님이 예쁘시네요. 길을 잃어버릴 분 같지 않은데요.라는 댓글이 올라온다고 했다. 너희는 각자 엄마의 다른 사진을 가지고 있는지 다시 찾아보기로 했다. 큰오빠는 너에게 문구를 더 보충해보라고 했다. 네가 큰오빠를 물끄러미 바라보자 좀 더 호소력 있는 문구를 생각해보라고 했다. 호소력 있는 문구. 어머니를 찾아주세요, 라고 쓰니 너무 평범하다고 했다. 어머니를 찾습니다,라고 쓰니 그게 그거고 어머니라는 말이 너무 정중하니 엄마,로 바꿔보라고 했다. 우리 엄마를 찾습니다,라고 쓰니 어린애스럽다고 했다. 윗분을 보면 꼭 연락바랍니다,라고 쓰자 큰오빠가 넌 대체 작가라는 사람이 그런 말밖에 쓸 수 없냐! 버럭 소리를 질렀다. 큰오빠가 원하는 호소력 잇는 문구가 무엇인지 너는 생각해낼 수가 없었다. 호소력이 따로 있어? 사례를 한다고 쓰는 것이 호소력이야, 작은오빠가 말했다. 사례를 섭섭지 않게 하겠습니다,라고 쓰자 사례를 섭섭지 않게? 이번엔 올케가 그렇게 적으면 안 된다고 했다. 분명한 액수를 적어야 사람들이 관심을 갖는다고.

그럼 얼마를 적을까요?
백만 원?
그건 너무 적어요.
삼백만원?
그것도 적은 것 같은데?
그럼 오백만원.

오백만원 앞에서는 누구도 토를 달지 않았다. 너는 오백만원의 사례금을 드리겠습니다,라고 적고 마침표를 찍었다. 작은오빠가 '사례금: 오백만원'으로 고치라고 했다. 남동생이 오백만원을 다른 글자보다 키우라고 했다. 각자 집으로 돌아가 엄마의 사진을 찾아보고 적당한 게 있으면 바로 네 이메일로 보내주기로 했다. 전단지 문안을 더 보충해서 인쇄하는 일은 네가, 그것을 각자에게 배송하는 일은 남동생이 맡기로 했다. 전단지 나눠주는 아르바이트생을 따로 구할 수도 있어, 네가 말하자, 그건 우리가 해야지, 큰오빠가 말을 받았다. 평일엔 각자 일을 하는 틈틈이 주말엔 모두 다함께, 그렇게 언제 엄마를 찾아? 네가 투덜거리자, 큰오빠는 해볼 수 있는 일은 다 하고 있어, 이건 가만있을 수 없으니까 하는 일이다. 고 했다. 해볼 수 있는 일 뭐? 신문광고, 신문광고가 해볼 수 있는 일의 다야? 그럼 어떻게 할까? 내일부터 모두 일을 그만두고 이 동네 저 동네 무조건 헤매고 다닐까? 그렇게 해서 엄말 찾을 수 있다고 보장만 되면 그리 해보겠다. 너는 큰오빠와의 실랑이를 그만두었다. 지금까지의 습성, 오빠니까 오빠가 어떻게 해봐라!고 늘 미루는 마음이던 습성이 이런 상황에도 작동하고 있음을 깨달았기 때문이다. 너의 가족들은 큰오빠 집에 아버지를 두고 서둘러 헤어졌다. 헤어지지 않으면 또 싸우게 될 것이다. 지난 일주일 동안 줄곧 그래왔다. 엄마의 실종을 어떻게 풀어나가야 할지 상의하러 모였다가 너의 가족들은 예기치 않게 지난날 서로가 엄마에게 잘못한 행동들을 들춰내었다. 순간순간 모면하듯 봉합해온 일들이 툭툭 불거지고 결국은 소리를 지르고 담배를 피우고 문을 박차고 나갔다. 너는 엄마를 잃어버렸다는 얘길 처음 듣자마자 어떻게 이렇게 많은 식구들 중에서 서울역에 마중 나간 사람이 한 사람도 없느냐고 성질을 부렸다.

그러는 너는?

나? 너는 입을 다물었다. 너는 엄마를 잃어버린 것조차 나흘 후에나 알았으니까. 너의 가족들은 서로에게 엄마를 잃어버린 책임을 물으며 스스로들 상처를 입었다.

Key vocabulary

칠순 (七旬)	70, 70th birthday
한껏 멋을 내다	be all dressed up, be all made up, be dressed up to the nines
실종(失踪)되다	go missing
확대(擴大)하다	enlarge
의견 (意見)	opinion
올리다	put up (on the internet, etc.)
보충(補充)하다	add, embellish
물끄러미 바라보다	stare
호소력	appealing, captivating, have the ability to tug on the heart strings
대체	what on earth, what the hell
버럭 소리를 지르다	shout out suddenly, bark
사례(금)	reward

14 Family

섭섭하지 않게	so that you are not disappointed; generously
올케	sister-in-law
액수 (額數)	amount, sum
토를 달다	question, complain about, comment on, put in your two cents' worth
키우다	raise, bring up, make bigger
전단지 문안 (傳單紙)	flyer
투덜거리다	grumble
가만있다	sit tight, stay still
무조건 (無條件)	unconditionally
헤매다	roam, wander
실랑이	tussle, skirmish
습성 (習性)	habit
미루다	shift (blame, responsibility, etc.)
작동(作動)하다	set going, put into action
서두르다	hurry, rush
줄곧	continuously
예기(豫期)치 않게	unexpectedly
들추다	dig up
모면(謀免)하다	avoid
봉합(縫合)하다	stitch up together
마중 나가다	go and pick up, go and meet (someone arriving an airport, station, etc.)
성질(性質)을 부리다	have a fit, have a tantrum

Comprehension questions: text

1 How did the children lose their mother?
2 What did the children decide to write on the poster, and what made them decide that?
3 What photograph did the children decide to use on the poster, and why?
4 When did the children realise they lost their mother?

Comprehension questions: music extract

g.o.d (Groove Over Dose) is one of the first generation of Korean "idol" groups. Under contract with SidusHQ, they debuted in 1999, and are still active as a group, emphasising their legendary status within the K-pop world. 'To Mother' (어머님께) is one of their most iconic songs, and is sung from the perspective of a son regretting not appreciating the sacrifices his mother made for him in the past.

1 Where did they get the money to eat *tchatchangmyŏn*?
2 Why did the boy get into a fight at school?
3 How did his mother respond?
4 What happened after the boy and his mother opened a restaurant together?

Additional source material

The 2009 film *Mother* (머더) also starkly portrays the sacrifices a mother will endure in order to take care of her son.

Further discussion questions

1 What differences do you detect between the way motherhood is portrayed in this text and in Western literature?
2 What can you learn about family relationships in Korean culture through this text?

References

Ijichi, Noriko, Kato, Atsufumi, & Sakurada, Ryoko. 2015. *Rethinking Representations of Asian Women: Changes, Continuity, and Everyday Life*. New York: Palgrave Macmillan.
Kim, Yunghee. 2002. 'Creating New Paradigms of Womanhood in Modern Korean Literature: Na Hyesok's "Kyonghui".' *Korean Studies* 26: 1–60.

1.4 흥보가 (*The Song of Hŭngbo* – Anonymous)

Introduction to the text

As the second of the five famous *p'ansori* (storytelling through song) stories, *Hŭngboga* (The Song of Hŭngbo) tells the story of two brothers. Pak Hŭngbo is a kind and gentle man, but his older brother Nolbo is vicious and greedy. One rainy day, Nolbo, tired of providing for his younger brother and his numerous offspring, summons his brother and orders him to pack his bags and leave. Destitute, Hŭngbo's family is close to starvation. Still, Hŭngbo remains kind, and saving the life of a swallow he receives a gourd seed in return. He plants the seed, and three gourds grow from it. At *Ch'usŏk* (Korean Thanksgiving, the harvest moon), Hŭngbo cuts open the gourds in order to feed his starving family. To his surprise he finds the gourds are filled with money and rice, with precious silks, and even with workmen who rebuild his house as a luxurious mansion. When Nolbo tries to emulate him by breaking a swallow's leg and then nursing it back to health, he is punished by all manner of evils. Only the intervention of his kind younger brother saves him, and the two brothers live together sharing Hŭngbo's riches, while Nolbo swears to mend his ways.

While this story is predominantly about brotherly love, and the responsibilities between siblings according to the Confucian principle of *samgang oryun* (Three Bonds and Five Relationships), it also sheds light on the economic and social environment of the mid-to-late Chosŏn dynasty. During this time, a separate class of impoverished *yangban* (aristocrats) emerged. Due to the restrictions banning one from civil service if any member of the family had ever engaged in commerce, these *yangban* felt unwilling and unable to find proper work, and were left with only three choices: stay poor, seek an influential patron, or engage in money-lending and bribery to survive. While his mooching off family members would be frowned upon in today's society, in Hŭngbo's social context there were few other options open to him.

Original text

Text and annotations from Ch'oe Tonghyŏn. 2009. *Hŭngboga padipyŏl chŏnjip 2: Pak Rokchu padi, Pak Ch'owŏl padi* [A complete collection of *Hŭngboga* according to different styles 2: Pak Rokchu style, Pak Ch'owŏl style]. Chŏnju: Ministry of Culture, Sports, and Tourism, North Chŏlla Province; Jeonju International Sori Festival Organising Committee.

[아니리]
흥보가 놀보 사랑채를 당도하여대문 안을 들어서니 어찌 겁이 났던지,

'형님 소인놈 문안이오!'
'예, 성씨가 뉘 댁이시오?'
'아이고, 형님. 흥보 동생을 모르시오?'
'나는 오대차[1] 독신[2]으로 아우가 없는 사람이오!'
흥보가 이 말을 듣더니마는,
[진양조]
두 손 합장[3] 무릎을 꿇고,
'비나이다. 비나이다. 형님전에[4] 비나이다.
살려 주오. 살려 주오. 불쌍한 동생을 살려 주오.
그저께 하루를 굶은 처자[5]가 어제 저물도록 그저 있고,
어저께 하루를 문드러니[6] 굶은 처자가 오늘 아침을 그저[7] 있사오니,
인명이 재천[8]이라 설마한들 죽사리까마는,[9]
여러 끼니를 굶사오면 하릴없이[10] 죽게가 되니,
형님 덕택에 살것내다.[11]
벼가 되거든 한 섬[12]만 주시고,
쌀이 되거든 닷 말만 주시고,
돈이 되거든 닷 냥만 주옵시고,
그도[13] 저도[14] 정 주기가 싫거든 이맥[15]이나 싸라기[16]나 양단간에[17] 주옵시면,
죽게 된 자식을 살리겠소.
과연 내가 원통하오.
분하여서 못 살겠소.
천석꾼[18] 형님을 두고 굶어죽기가 원통합니다.
제발덕분에 살려 주오.'
[아니리]
과거를 꽉꽉 대노니 뗄 수가 없지.
'오, 이제 보니 네가 흥보놈이로구나. 거 심심하던 중에 마침 잘 왔다. 애, 마당쇠야!
대문 걸고,[19] 아래 행랑[20] 동편 처마 끝에 지리산에서 건목[21] 쳐[22] 내온 박달 홍두깨[23]
있느니라. 이리 가져오너라. 이런 놈은 그저 복날[24] 개 잡듯 해야 하느니라.'
[자진모리]
놀보놈 거동[25] 봐라.
지리산 몽둥이를 눈 위에 번듯[26] 들고,
'네 이놈, 흥보놈아!
잘 살기 내 복이요,
못 살기도 네 팔자라,
굶고 먹고 내 모른다.
볏섬[27] 주자한들,
마당의 뒤주[28] 안에 다물다물이[29] 들었으니,
너 주자고 뒤주 헐며,
전곡간[30] 주자한들,
천록방[31] 금궤[32] 안에 가득가득히 관[33]을 지어 떼돈[34]이 들었으니,
너 주자고 쾌돈[35] 헐며,[36]
찌꺼기[37] 주자한들
구진방[38] 우리 안에 떼돼야지가[39] 들었으니,
너 주자고 돝[40] 굶기며,
싸라기 주자한들,
황계[41] 백계[42] 수백 마리가 턱턱하고,[43] 꼬꼬 우니,
너 주자고 닭 굶기랴?'
몽둥이를 드러메고,[44]

'네 이놈 강도놈!'
좁은 골⁴⁵ 벼락 치듯, 강짜 싸움⁴⁶에 계집 치듯, 담에 걸친 구렁이 치듯,
'후닥딱!' '철퍽!'
'아이고, 박⁴⁷ 터졌소!'
'네 이놈!'
'후닥딱!'
'아이고, 다리 부러졌소. 형님!'
흥보가 기가 막혀, 몽둥이를 피하느라고 올라갔다가 내려왔다가,
대문을 걸어노니 날도⁴⁸ 뛰도 못하고,
그저 퍽퍽 맞는데,
안으로 쫓겨 들어가며,
'아이고, 형수씨, 사람 좀 살려주오!
아이고, 형수씨! 날 좀 살려주오!'
[아니리]
이러고 들어가거든, 놀보 계집이라도 후해서 전곡간에 주었으면 좋으련마는, 놀보 계집은 놀보보다 심술보 하나가 더 있것다. 밥 푸던 주걱자루를 들고 중문⁴⁹에 딱 붙어 섰다가,
'아니, 여보! 아주뱀⁵⁰이고, 동아뱀⁵¹이고 세상에 귀찮허오. 언제 전곡을 갖다 맡겼던가? 아냐⁵² 밥! 아냐 돈! 아냐 쌀!'
하고 뺨을 때려노니, 형님한테 맞던 것은 여반장⁵³이요, 형수한테 뺨을 맞아노니 하늘이 빙빙 돌고, 땅이 툭 꺼지는 듯.
[진양조]
흥보가 기가 막혀 섰던 자리에 거꾸러지며,
'여보 형수씨! 여보, 여보, 아주머니!
형수가 시아재⁵⁴ 뺨 치는 법은 고금천지⁵⁵ 어디 가 보았소?
나를 이리 치지 말고,
살지⁵⁶·중지⁵⁷·능지⁵⁸를 하여, 아주 박살⁵⁹ 죽여 주오!
아이고 하느님! 박흥보를 벼락을 때려 주면,
염라국⁶⁰을 들어가서 부모님을 뵈옵는 날은 세세원정⁶¹을 아뢰련마는,⁶²
어이하여 못 죽는 거나?'
매운 것 먹은 사람처럼 후후 불며, 저의 집으로 건너간다.

Key vocabulary

사랑채	the men's wing of the house, sometimes a detached house
문안	inquiring after someone, sending one's regards (問安)
독신	an only child, having no siblings (獨身)
합장	to put one's hands together to indicate the unified purpose of one's mind (合掌)
문드리니	local dialect, meaning neatly/completely or intact/unscathed
인명이 재천이라	human life lies in the heavens, you can't die as you would wish (人命이 在天이라)
덕택	help, aid, support (德澤)
섬	a measurement of weight, also known as 석, roughly equivalent to 20kg
말	a special kind of bowl used to measure grain, liquids or powders, containing roughly 18 litres

냥	a unit of currency during the Chosŏn dynasty, containing roughly 37g of silver (兩)
양단간에	either one between two choices (兩端間)
싸라기	rice grains that have been broken up into fine pieces
천석꾼	an extremely rich person, owning more than a thousand *sŏk* of rice from a bottomless harvest (千石꾼)
행랑	a room attached to the main gate, where the servants lived (行廊)
홍두깨	a long club (also known as 방망이), of roughly 10cm diameter, used in washing clothes, spreading the clothes on a fulling block and beating them until they were soft
복날 개 잡듯 하다	an expression which means to beat someone very badly
천록방	lit., 'the room where the happiness and wealth of heaven descend,' a storeroom (天祿房)
금궤	chests made of gold, used to store various items (金櫃)
관	money tied together in bundles of ten *nyang* (貫), also called 쾌
떼돈	a large sum of money (떼 is usually used to describe a group of people or animals)
찌갱이	local dialect version of 재강, meaning the sediment produced while fermenting liquor
구진방	a room at the back of the house (句陳房) – 구진 refers to one of the six stars closest to North, as well as the name for a palace located towards the rear of the palace complex
돝	pig
턱턱하다	the sound of beating wings, refers to the way chickens flap their wings before squawking
강짜 싸움	a fight due to excessive jealousy, caused by unfaithfulness in a relationship
박	a disparaging term for the head
중문	gate separating the men's wing from the main part of the house (中門)
아주뱀	vulgarisation of 아주버님, someone of the same generation as the husband who is older than the husband
동아뱀	local dialect of 도마뱀, a lizard, here used as a sarcastic pairing with 아주뱀
아나	word said when giving something to someone close to you, disparaging one's interlocutor
여반장	something as easy as turning over one's palm (如反掌)
시아재	local dialect of 시아주비/시동생, the younger brother of one's husband
고금천지	since the beginnings of time, in the whole world (古今天地)
중치	beat mercilessly, from the punishment 중장(重杖), which is to beat terribly with a club
능지	to tear the body to pieces, hanging up each piece in a different location for people to see. From the punishment for high treason 능지처참(凌遲處斬)
박살	beat to death (撲殺)
염라국	afterlife (閻羅國), the country ruled by the king of the underworld, 염라대왕
세세원정	every detail of an unjust situation (細細冤情)

Comprehension questions: text

1 How does Nolbo respond to Hŭngbo's visit?
2 What does Hŭngbo ask of Nolbo?
3 Why won't Nolbo give anything to Hŭngbo?
4 How does Nolbo's wife respond to Hŭngbo's pleas?

Comprehension questions: film extract

Rather like in *The Song of Hŭngbo*, the 2016 film *My Annoying Brother* (형) tells the tale of two brothers who don't get on, where involvement with the younger brother eventually makes the older brother a better person. This contrast is particularly stark comparing the beginning of the film, when older brother Tushik cooks for his blind younger brother, Tuyŏng, only after he ends up in hospital due to malnourishment. By the end, both brothers have their own sorrows but are lying to each other over the telephone to spare each other further distress.

1 How does Tushik address Tuyŏng? Does this change over time?
2 What does Tushik claim himself to be in cooking for Tuyŏng? Does Tuyŏng accept this?
3 At the end of the film, what does Tuyŏng claim to have done for his brother who couldn't join him in Rio?
4 When Tushik says he misses Tuyŏng, what is he actually trying to say?

Additional source material

One version of the scene above, as presented at the National Gugak Centre by Sŏ Chŏngmin in 2015: https://youtu.be/oahS5K3ebtQ?t=2667 (accessed 29 January 2018).

A fun reinterpretation of the Hŭngbo story is Yukkaksu's 'Hŭngbo is stunned' (육각수 – 흥보가 기가 막혀, 1995).

Other material addressing the conflicted relationship between brothers includes:

Film, *We Are Brothers* (우리는 형제입니다, 2014).
Film, *The Bros* (부라더, 2017).
Film, *Heung-boo: The Revolutionist* (흥부, 2018).

Further discussion questions

1 Form two teams to debate.

   Team A argument: Family should take care of each other no matter what.
   Team B argument: If you are mooching off your family without making any attempt to provide for yourself, your family has no obligation to take care of you.

2 The people closest to us can be both the force that encourages us to become better people, and the source of the most pain as they know exactly how to make you hurt. Discuss how close people in your life have impacted you.

Notes

1 오대쩨.
2 獨身. 형제 없는 외아들.
3 合掌. 두 손바닥을 합하여 마음이 한결같음을 나타냄.

4 형님 앞에. 형님께.
5 妻子. 아내와 자식.
6 '멀쩡하게,' '말끔히'의 뜻으로 쓰이는 방언.
7 변함없이 이제까지.
8 人命이 在天이라. 사람의 목숨은 하늘에 있다. 곧 마음대로 죽을 수 없다는 말.
9 죽사오리까마는. 죽겠습니다마는.
10 어쩔 수 없이.
11 살겠나이다. 살겠습니다. 살고싶습니다.
12 곡식 등을 재는 부피의 단의. 석(石).
13 그것도.
14 저것도.
15 耳麥. 귀리. 보리와 비슷하며, 술, 과자의 원료, 또는 사료로 씀. 다른 사람들은 대개 '찌껭이'(술을 떠내고 남은 찌끼인 '재강'의 방언)로 부른다.
16 잘게 부스러진 쌀알.
17 兩端間에. 둘 중에서어느 것이든지 간에.
18 千石꾼. 나락 천 석을 추수하는 큰 부자.
19 자물쇠나 문고리를 채우거나 빗장을 지르고.
20 行廊. 대문간에 붙어 있는 방. 옛날 대문 안에 죽 늘어서 있어 하인들이 거처하는 방, 혹은 그 집.
21 정하게 다듬지 않고 거칠게 대강 만드는 일, 또는 그렇게 만든 물건. '건목 치다'는 정하게 만들지 않고 건목으로 대강 만들다.
22 잘라서. '치다'는 나뭇가지 등을 낫으로 잘라내다.
23 옷감을 감아서 다듬잇돌 위에 얹어놓고 방망이로 반드럽게 다듬는 기구. 지름 10cm 쯤 되는 긴 몽둥이임.
24 伏날. 초복, 중복 말복이 되는 날. '복날 개 잡듯 하다'는 말은 심하게 매를 때리는 일을 이름.
25 擧動. 일에 나서서 움직이는 태도.
26 형편이나 위세 따위가 굽히는 데 없이 당당하게.
27 몇 섬 정도의 벼.
28 '뒤지'라고도 함. 쌀 따위를 담아두는 세간. 나무로 궤짝같이 만들되, 네 기둥과 짧은 발이 있으며, 뚜껑 부분의 절반 앞쪽이 문이 된다.
29 다물다물하게. '다물다물'은 물건이 무더기로 쌓인 모양.
30 錢穀間. 돈이나 곡식이나 무엇이든지 간에.
31 天祿房. '하늘이 내린 복록이 들어찬 방'이란 뜻으로, 곳간에 붙인 이름.
32 金櫃. 금으로 만든 궤. '궤'는 물건을 넣어 두기 위하여 직육면체 꼴로 뚜껑이나 문짝이 있게 나무로 짠 그릇.
33 貫. 열 냥을 단위로 한 엽전 역 꾸러미. 쾌.
34 많은 돈.
35 열 냥을 한 꾸러미로 하여, 열 꾸러미씩 쌓아놓은 돈.
36 쌓아 놓은 물건을 뜯어내며.
37 술을 떠내고 남은 찌끼인 '재강'의 방언.
38 句陳房. '구진'은 별의 이름으로 북극에 가장 가까운 여섯 별 중의 하나, 혹은 주되는 궁전의 뒤쪽에 있는 궁전이라는 뜻이므로, '구진방'은 뒤쪽에 있는 방이라는 의미로 쓰인 듯함.
39 돼지떼.
40 돼지.
41 黃鷄. 털이 누런 닭.
42 白鷄. 털이 하얀 닭.
43 날개죽지를 턱턱 치고. 닭이 울기 전에 날개를 먼저 턱턱 치는 모양을 가리킴.
44 들어올려서 어깨에 메고.
45 골짜기.
46 간짜로 인한 싸움. '강짜'는 강새암. (부부 사이나 사랑하는 사이에서) 상대되는 이성이 다른 이성과 좋아할 경우에 지나치게 시기하는 새암.
47 '머리'를 낮잡아 일컫는 말.
48 날아가지도.
49 中門. 사랑채에서 안채로 통하는 문.
50 '아주버님'을 속되게 일컫느라고 만들어낸 말. '아주버니'는 남편과 같은 항렬에서 남편보다 나이가 많은 사람.

51 '도마뱀'의 방언. 아주뱀에 이어서 비꼬아 일컬은 말.
52 옜다. 가까이 있는 사람에게 무엇을 주면서 하는 말. 상대방을 맞추어 일컫는다.
53 如反掌. 손바닥을 뒤집는 것처럼 쉬운 일.
54 '시아주비'의 방언. 시동생. 남편의 남동생.
55 古今天地. 예부터 지금까지의 온세상.
56 殺之. 죽임. 죽이는 일.
57 '중장으로 치다'는 뜻으로 쓴 말인 듯. '중장(重杖)'은 몽둥이로 몹시 치는 형벌.
58 凌遲. 능지처참(凌遲處斬). 대역 죄인에게 과하던 최대의 형벌. 머리, 양팔, 양다리, 몸뚱이의 순으로 여섯 부분으로 찢어서 각지에 보내어 여러 사람에게 구경시키는 형벌.
59 撲殺. 때려 죽임.
60 閻羅國. '염라대왕이 다스리는 나라'라는 뜻으로, '저승'을 달리 일컫는 말.
61 細細冤情. 자세한 억울한 사정.
62 아뢸 것인데.

References

Deuchler, Martina. 1992. *The Confucian Transformation of Korea: A Study of Society and Ideology*. Cambridge, MA: Council on East Asian Studies, Harvard University. (Chapter 3: Agnation and Ancestor Worship, Chapter 5: Inheritance).

Grayson, James Huntley. 2002. 'The Hŭngbu and Nŏlbu Tale Type: A Korean Double Contrastive Narrative Structure.' *Folklore* 113(1): 51–69.

Jun, Seong Ho, Lewis, James B., & Han-Rog, Kang. 2008. 'Korean Expansion and Decline from the Seventeenth to the Nineteenth Century: A View Suggested by Adam Smith.' *The Journal of Economic History* 68(1): 244–82.

Karlsson, Anders. 2005. 'Famine, Finance, and Political Power: Crop Failure and Land-Tax Exemptions in Late Eighteenth-Century Chosŏn Korea.' *Journal of the Economic and Social History of the Orient* 48(4): 552–92.

Kim, Sun Joo. 2007. 'Taxes, the Local Elite, and the Rural Populace in the Chinju Uprising of 1862.' *The Journal of Asian Studies* 66(4): 993–1027.

Palais, James B. 2014. *Confucian Statecraft and Korean Institutions: Yu Hyŏngwŏn and the Late Chosŏn Dynasty*. Seattle; London: University of Washington Press. (Part VI: Financial Reform and the Economy, Chapter 26 and Conclusion).

Pratt, Keith, & Richard, Rutt. 1999. *Korea: A Historical and Cultural Dictionary*. Richmond, Surrey: Curzon. (Entry on Three Bonds and Five Relationships).

Yi, Ki-baek. 1984. *A New History of Korea*. Cambridge, MA: Published for the Harvard-Yenching Institute by Harvard University Press. (Chapter 12: Instability in the *Yangban* Status System and the Outbreak of Popular Uprisings).

1.5 홍길동전 – 허균 (*The Tale of Hong Kiltong* – Hŏ Kyun)

Introduction to the text

Hong Kiltongjŏn is a Robin Hood-esque story that tells the tale of the illegitimate son of minister Hong who, frustrated by his inability to put his talents to use due to his position in society, leaves home and becomes the leader of a group of bandits. After various adventures robbing corrupt officials within Korea, aided by his skills in Taoist magic, Hong Kiltong leaves Chosŏn with his loyal followers, establishing a new kingdom on an island off the coast of China with Kiltong as king. Eventually, he attains enlightenment and ascends into heaven. While this book is generally credited to Hŏ Kyun (1569–1618) as the first novel written in *han'gŭl*, both of these claims have been critiqued, so that it is difficult to ascertain its origins. The story has nevertheless remained influential, especially due to its critique of the hierarchical system of the Chosŏn period that forbade advancement to illegitimate sons, even when they were as smart and gifted as Hong Kiltong. As the various spin-offs of the original story attest, the adventure story of an unconventional hero continues to have a broad appeal even today.

Original text

길동이 점점 자라 8살이 되자, 총명하기가 보통이 넘어 하나를 들으면 백 가지를 알 정도였다. 그래서 공은 더욱 귀여워하면서도 출생이 천해, 길동이 늘 아버지니 형이니 하고 부르면, 즉시 꾸짖어 그렇게 부르지 못하게 하였다. 길동이 10살이 넘도록 감히 부형을 부르지 못하고, 종들로부터 천대받는 것을 뼈에 사무치게 한탄하면서 마음 둘 바를 몰랐다.

'대장부가 세상에 나서 공맹을 본받지 못할 바에야, 차라리 병법이라도 익혀 대장인을 허리춤에 비스듬히 차고 동정서벌하여 나라에 큰 공을 세우고 이름을 만대에 빛내는 것이 장부의 통쾌한 일이 아니겠는가. 나는 어찌하여 일신이 적막하고, 부형이 있는데도 아버지를 아버지라 부르지 못하고 형을 형이라 부르지 못하니 심장이 터질지라, 이 어찌 통탄할 일이 아니겠는가!'

하고, 말을 마치며 뜰에 내려와 검술을 익히고 있었다.

그때 마침 공이 또한 달빛을 구경하다가, 길동이 서성거리는 것을 보고 즉시 불러 물었다.

'너는 무슨 흥이 있어서 밤이 깊도록 잠을 자지 않느냐?'

길동은 공경하는 자세로 대답했다.

'소인은 마침 달빛을 즐기는 중입니다. 그런데, 만물이 생겨날 때부터 오직 사람이 귀한 존재인 줄 아옵니다만, 소인에게는 귀함이 없사오니, 어찌 사람이라 하겠습니까?'

공은 그 말의 뜻을 짐작은 했지만, 일부러 책망하는 체하며,

'네 무슨 말이냐?' 했다. 길동이 절하고 말씀드리기를,

'소인이 평생 설워하는 바는, 소인이 대감 정기를 받아 당당한 남자로 태어났고, 도낳아 길러 주신 부모님의 은혜를 입었음에도 불구하고, 아버지를 아버지라 못 하옵고, 형을 형이라 못 하오니, 어찌 사람이라 하겠습니까?'

하고, 눈물을 흘리며 적삼을 적셨다. 공이 듣고 나자 비록 불쌍하다는 생각은 들었으나, 그 마음을 위로하면 마음이 방자해질까 염려되어, 크게 꾸짖어 말했다.

'재상 집안에 천한 종의 몸에서 태어난 자식이 너뿐이 아닌데, 네가 어찌 이다지 방자하냐? 앞으로 다시 이런 말을 하면 내 눈앞에 서지도 못하게 하겠다.'

이렇게 꾸짖으니 길동은 감히 한 마디도 더 하지 못하고, 다만 당에 엎드려 눈물을 흘릴 뿐이었다. 공이 물러가라 하자, 그제서야 길동은 침소로 돌아와 슬퍼해 마지 않았다. 길동이 본래 재주가 뛰어나고 도량이 활달한지라 마음을 가라앉히지 못해 밤이면 잠을 이루지 못하곤 했다.

하루는 길동이 어미 침소에 가 울면서 아뢰었다.

'소자가 모친과 더불어 전생연분이 중하여, 금세에 모자가 되었으니, 그 은혜가 지극하옵니다. 그러나 소자의 팔자가 기박하여 천한 몸이 되었으니 품은 한이 깊사옵니다. 장부가 세상에 살면서 남의 천대를 받음이 불가한지라, 소자는 자연히 설움을 억제하지 못하여 모친 슬하를 떠나려 하오니, 엎드려 바라건대 모친께서는 소자를 염려하시고 귀체를 잘 돌보십시오.'

그 어미가 듣고 나서 크게 놀라 말했다.

'재상가의 천생이 너뿐이 아닌데, 어찌 마음을 좁게 먹어 어미 간장을 태우느냐?'

길동이 대답했다.

'옛날, 장충의 아들 길산은 천생이지만 열세 살에 그 어미와 이별하고 운봉산에 들어가 도를 닦아 아름다운 이름을 후세에 전하였습니다. 소자도 그를 본받아 세상을 벗

어나려 하오니, 모친은 안심하고 후일을 기다리십시오. 근간에 곡산댁의 눈치를 보니 상공의 사랑을 잃을까하여 우리 모자를 원수같이 알고 있습니다. 큰 화를 입을까 하오니 모친께서는 소자가 나감을 염려하지 마십시오.'

하니, 그 어머니 또한 슬퍼하더라.

원래 곡산댁은 곡산 지방의 기생으로 상공의 첩이 되었던 것인데, 이름은 초란이었다. 아주 교만하고 자기 마음에 맞지 않으면 공에게 고자질을 하기에, 집안에 폐단이 무수하였다. 자신은 아들이 없는데, 춘섬은 길동을 낳아 상공으로부터 늘 귀여움을 받게 되자, 속으로 불쾌하여 길동을 없애 버릴 마음만 먹고 있었다.

하루는 초란이 흉계를 꾸미고 무녀를 청하여 말하기를,

'내가 편안하게 살려면 길동을 없애는 방법 밖에는 없다. 만일 나의 소원을 이루어 주면 그 은혜를 후하게 갚겠다.'

고 하니, 무녀가 듣고 기뻐서 대답했다.

'지금 흥인문밖에 일류 관상녀가 있는데, 사람의 상을 한번 보면 전후 길흉을 판단합니다. 그 사람을 청하여 소원을 자세하게 말하고, 공께 소개하여 그녀로 하여금 전후사를 자신이 본 듯이 이야기하게 하면, 공이 속아 넘어가 길동을 없애고자 할 것이니, 그때를 틈타 이리이리하면 어찌 묘한 방법이 아니겠습니까?'

이에 초란이 크게 기뻐서 먼저 은돈 오십 냥을 주고 관상녀를 청해 오도록 하자, 무녀가 하직하고 갔다.

이튿날 공이 내실에 들어와 부인과 더불어 길동이 비범함을 화제로 이야기하면서 다만 신분이 천함을 안타까워하고 있던 중, 문득 한 여자가 들어와 마루 아래서 인사를 하기에, 공이 이상하게 여겨 물었다.

'그내는 어떠한 여자인데 무슨 일로 왔소?'

그 여자가 말했다.

'소인은 관상 보는 사람이온데, 우연히 상공댁에 이르렀습니다.'

공이 이 말을 듣고 길동의 장래를 알고 싶어 즉시 길동을 불러서 보이니, 관상녀가 이윽히 보다가 놀라 말하기를,

'이 공자의 상을 보니 천고 영웅이요 일대 호걸이지만, 지체가 부족하니 다른 염려는 없을 듯합니다.'

Key vocabulary

총명하다	bright, intelligent, smart
공	a respectful term of address indicating that the addressee is male and older than you
출생이 천하다	to be of low birth
천대받다	be treated with contempt or disdain
대장부	a man, a great man
공맹	Confucius and Mencius
본받다	to emulate, model oneself on
대장인	a general's seal
비스듬히	jauntily
동정서벌	conquer and subdue many countries
적막하다	deserted, forlorn, lonely
검술	fencing, swordsmanship
서성거리다	pacing up and down
소인	I, me, myself – an address term implying humbleness before a high-ranking person
책망	reproach, rebuke

정기	spirit, vital force
은혜	grace, favour, kindness
적삼	an unlined summer jacket
방자하다	rude, arrogant
재상	prime minister, high government official
침소	bedchamber
도량	broad-mindedness, generosity
소자	I, me, myself – an address term implying humbleness before one's parent
전생연분	a joined fate that was tied together in a previous life
팔자	destiny, fate (usually negative)
기박하다	unfortunate, unlucky, hapless
슬하	the care of one's parents
귀체	your esteemed body, health
도를 닦다	practice the Way, cultivate oneself morally and religiously
상공	respectful term for a high minister
교만하다	arrogant, conceited
고자질	tell on, tattle-tale
폐단	negative, harmful influence
흉계	an evil ploy
무녀	female shaman (note: most shamans in Korea are/were female)
후하게	generously, liberally
일류	first class, top-notch
관상녀	female physiognomist, face-reader
비범함	be extraordinary, gifted
천고 영웅	greatest hero that ever lived
일대 호걸	a great hero
지체	social class, status

Comprehension questions: text

1. How do the different address terms used in this text indicate the relationships between the characters?
2. What does Kiltong want to become?
3. What is the issue which causes him sorrow?
4. How does Ch'oran intend to get rid of Kiltong?

Comprehension questions: drama extract

The 2008 KBS2 fusion drama *Hong Kildong* (홍길동) combines the traditional tale of Hong Kiltong, set in an unspecified past, with modern elements. In the first episode, Hong Kiltong watches his father and older brother conduct a ritual in honour of their ancestors, which he as an illegitimate child cannot attend, and reflects on his in-between life as the slave son of a nobleman.

1. What is Hong Kiltong's first goal?
2. What is Hong Kiltong's second goal?
3. What is the law that stands in Hong Kiltong's way?

Additional source material

The SBS drama *The Heirs* (왕관을 쓰려는 자, 그 무게를 견디라 – 상속자들, 2013) is one of many dramas to feature plotlines related to illegitimate children.

Other material based on *Hong Kiltongjŏn* includes:

Film, *The Righteous Thief* (홍길동의 후예, 2009).
Film, *Phantom Detective* (탐정 홍길동: 사라진 마을, 2016).
MBC drama, *The Rebel* (역적: 백성을 훔친 도적, 2017).

Further discussion questions

1 Although he feels great affection towards Hong Kiltong, Kiltong's father always acts extremely sternly towards him in order to prevent him from getting ideas above his station. Get into teams and debate whether this behaviour was correct.

   Team A: Societal rules will not allow Hong Kiltong to develop, so any ambition should be nipped in the bud, even if this denies Kiltong from having even the slightest joy or affection.
   Team B: In such an unfair system, Hong Kiltong's father should have at least given Kiltong some affection, and perhaps room to develop within the confines of the family home, to soften the blow of an otherwise cruel world.

2 Hong Kiltong, although extremely skilled and intelligent, is held back by his social station. Think of and discuss areas in today's society where the same thing occurs (racial profiling, glass ceiling, ability grouping in schools, etc.).

References

Deuchler, Martina. 1992. *The Confucian Transformation of Korea: A Study of Society and Ideology.* Cambridge, MA: Council on East Asian Studies, Harvard University.
Kang, Minsoo (trans.). 2016. *The Story of Hong Gildong.* New York: Penguin.
Kim, Kichung. 1996. *An Introduction to Classical Korean Literature: From* Hyangga *to* P'ansori. Armonk, NY; London: M.E. Sharpe. (Chapter 7: Hŏ Kyun: *Hong Kiltong chŏn* and the Hanmun Lives).
Lee, Seung-Ah. 2014. *Conception of the Hero in Korean Popular Fiction of Late Chosŏn Period.* PhD Diss., University of California Los Angeles. (Introduction).
Peterson, Mark. 1996. *Korean Adoption and Inheritance: Case Studies in the Creation of a Classic Confucian Society.* Ithaca, NY: East Asian Program, Cornell University. (Chapters 5 and 6).

1.6 눈길 – 이청준 (*A Snowy Road* – Yi Ch'ŏngjun)

Introduction to the text

Yi Ch'ŏngjun (1939–2008) was a prominent South Korean novelist. Throughout his four decade-long career, Yi wrote more than 100 short stories, and 13 novels. He died from lung cancer at the age of 68 on 31 July 2008. Born in 1939, Yi Ch'ŏngjun graduated with a degree in German literature from Seoul National University. In 1965, he debuted with a short story titled, 'T'oewon (퇴원, lit., "Leaving the Hospital").' Two years later, he won a Dongin Literature Award for *Stupid and Fool* (병신과 머저리). Yi is one of the foremost writers of the 4.19 Generation and his literary output since has been both steady in pace and considerable in volume, and his subject matter has been varied. *Stupid and Fool* (1966) probes the spiritual malaise of the post-war Korean youth; *This Paradise of Yours* (당신들의 천국, 1976) explores the dialectics of charity and will to power, with the leper colony of Sorokdo Island as the backdrop. Yi Ch'ŏngjun's fiction encompasses a broad range of political, existential, and metaphysical concerns.

In this novel, *A Snowy Road*, the author shows how the deeply-rooted tension between the mother and son is resolved in a very subtle way. It is noticeable that most of the tension and its resolution becomes invisible in English. It is because much of the emotional craftsmanship that went into the maternal character of 'Snowy Road' is realised through the use of expressive particles. Whilst the characters' explicit words and actions are, for the most part, stilted, and unharmonious, the way in which they communicate gives the reader a great insight into their feelings about one another, even before their story is told. Therefore, before understanding the events of the story, the reader has an implicit understanding of the characters' feelings towards one another and towards their situation. This is all achieved through the use of expressive particles and verb endings expressing formality, affection, softening, and holding back. In this way, the reader feels the affection and longing of the mother figure, the reluctance of the son, and the desperation of the daughter-in-law character through the linguistic choices used in their dialogue.

Original text

'내일 아침 올라가야겠어요.'
점심상을 물러나 앉으면서 나는 마침내 입 속에서 별러 오던 소리를 내뱉어 버렸다.
노인과 아내가 동시에 밥숟가락을 멈추며 나의 얼굴을 멀거니 건너다본다.
'내일 아침 올라가다니. 이참에도 또 그렇게 쉽게?'
노인은 결국 숟가락을 상위로 내려놓으며 믿기지 않는다는 듯 되묻고 있었다.
나는 이제 내친걸음이었다. 어차피 일이 그렇게 될 바엔 말이 나온 김에 매듭을 분명히 지어 두지 않으면 안 되었다.
'예, 내일 아침에 올라가겠어요. 방학을 얻어 온 학생 팔자도 아닌데, 남들 일할 때 저라고 이렇게 한가할 수가 있나요. 급하게 맡아 놓은 일도 한두 가지가 아니고요.'
'그래도 한 며칠 쉬어 가지 않고... 난 하필 이런 더운 때를 골라 왔길래 이참에는 며칠 좀 쉬어 갈 줄 알았더니...'
'제가 무슨 더운 때 추운 때를 가려 살 여유나 있습니까.'
'그래도 그 먼 길을 이렇게 단걸음에 되돌아가기야 하겠느냐. 넌 항상 한 동자로만 왔다가 선걸음에 새벽길을 나서곤 하더라마는... 이번에는 너 혼자도 아니고... 하룻밤이나 차분히 좀 쉬어 가도록 하거라.'
'오늘 하루는 쉬었지 않아요. 하루를 쉬어도 제 일은 사흘을 버리는 걸요. 찻길이 훨씬 나아졌다곤 하지만 여기선 아직도 서울이 천리 길이라 오는 데 하루 가는 데 하루...'
'급한 일은 우선 좀 마무리를 지어 놓고 오지 않구선...'
노인 대신 이번에는 아내 쪽에서 나를 원망스럽게 건너다보았다.
그건 물론 나의 주변머리를 탓하고 있는 게 아니었다. 내게 그처럼 급한 일이 없다는 걸 그녀는 알고 있었다.
서울을 떠나올 때 급한 일들은 미리 다 처리해 둔 것을 그녀에게는 내가 말을 해 줬으니까. 그리고 이번에는 좀 홀가분한 기분으로 여름 여행을 겸해 며칠 동안이라도 노인을 찾아보자고 내 편에서 먼저 제의를 했었으니까. 그녀는 나의 참을성 없는 심경의 변화를 나무라고 있는 것이었다.
그리고 그 매정스런 결단을 원망하고 있는 것이었다. 까닭 없는 연민과 애원기 같은 것이 서려 있는 그녀의 눈길이 그것을 더욱 분명히 하고 있었다.

'그래, 일이 그리 바쁘다면 가 봐야 하기는 하겠구나. 바쁜 일을 받아 놓고 온 사람을 붙잡는다고 들을 일이겠나.'
　　한동안 입을 다물고 앉아 있던 노인이 마침내 체념을 한 듯 다시 입을 열었다.
　　'항상 그렇게 바쁜 사람인 줄은 안다마는, 에미라고 이렇게 먼길을 찾아와도 편한 잠자리 하나 못 마련해 주는 내 맘이 아쉬워 그랬던 것 같구나.'
　　말을 끝내고 무연스런 표정으로 장죽 끝에 풍년초를 꾹꾹 눌러 담기 시작한다.
　　너무도 간단한 체념이었다.
　　담배통에 풍년초를 눌러 담고 있는 그 노인의 얼굴에는 아내에게서와 같은 어떤 원망기 같은 것도 찾아볼 수 없었다. 당신 곁을 조급히 떠나고 싶어하는 그 매정스런 아들에 대한 아쉬움 같은 것도 엿볼 수가 없었다.
　　성냥불도 붙이려 하지 않고 언제까지나 그 풍년초 담배만 꾹꾹 눌러 채우고 앉아 있는 눈길은 차라리 무표정에 가까운 것이었다.
　　나는 그 너무도 간단한 노인의 체념에 오히려 불쑥 짜증이 치솟았다.
　　나는 마침내 자리를 일어섰다. 그리고는 그 노인의 무표정에 밀려나기라도 하듯 방문을 나왔다.
　　장지문 밖 마당가에 작은 치자나무 한 그루가 한낮의 땡볕을 견디고 서 있었다.
　　...
　　아직도 날이 밝기 전이었다.
　　하지만 그러고 우리는 어찌 되었던가.
　　나는 차를 타고 떠나가 버렸고, 노인은 다시 그 어둠 속의 눈길을 되돌아선 것이다.
　　내가 알고 있는 건 거기까지 뿐이었다.
　　노인이 그후 어떻게 길을 되돌아갔는지는 나로서도 아직 들은 바가 없었다. 노인을 길가에 혼자 남겨 두고 차로 올라서 버린 그 순간부터 나는 차마 그 노인을 생각하기 싫었고, 노인도 오늘까지 그 날의 뒷 얘기는 들려 준 일이 없었다. 한데 노인은 웬일로 오늘사 그날의 기억을 끝까지 돌이키고 있었다.
　　'어떻게 어떻게 장터 거리로 들어서서 차부가 저만큼 보일 만한 데까지 가니까 그때 마침 차가 미리 불을 켜고 차부를 나오는구나. 급한 김에 내가 손을 휘저어 그 차를 세웠더니, 그래 그 운전수란 사람들은 어찌 그리 길이 급하고 매정하기만 한 사람들이더냐. 차를 미처 세우지도 덜하고 덜크렁덜크렁 눈 깜짝할 사이에 저 아그를 훌쩍 실어 담고 가 버리는구나.'
　　잠잠히 입을 다문 채 듣고만 있던 아내가 모처럼 한 마디를 끼어 들고 있었다.
　　나는 갑자기 다시 노인의 이야기가 두려워지고 있었다. 자리를 차고 일어나 다음 이야기를 가로막고 싶었다. 하지만 나는 이미 그럴 수가 없었다. 사지가 말을 들어 주지 않았다. 온몸이 마치 물을 먹은 솜처럼 무겁게 가라앉아 있었다. 몸을 어떻게 움직여 볼 수가 없었다. 형언하기 어려운 어떤 달콤한 슬픔, 달콤한 피곤기 같은 것이 나를 아늑히 감싸 오고 있었다.
　　'어떻게 하기는야. 넋이 나간 사람마냥 어둠 속에 한참이나 찻길만 바라보고 서 있을 수밖에에야...그 허망한 마음을 어떻게 다 말할 수가 있을거나...'
　　노인은 여전히 옛 얘기를 하듯 하는 그 차분하고 아득한 음성으로 그날의 기억을 더듬어 나갔다.
　　'한참 그러고 서 있다 보니 찬바람에 정신이 좀 되돌아오더구나. 정신이 들어 보니 갈 길이 새삼 허망스럽지 않았겠냐. 지금까진 그래도 저하고 나하고 둘이서 함께 헤쳐 온 길인데 이참에는 그 길을 늙은 것 혼자서 되돌아서려니...거기다 아직도 날은 어둡지야...그대로는 암만해도 길을 되돌아설 수가 없어 차부를 찾아 들어갔더니라. 한 식경이나 차부 안 나무 걸상에 웅크리고 앉아 있으려니 그제사 동녘 하늘이 훤해져 오더구나...그래서 또 혼자 서두를 것도 없는 길을 서둘러 나섰는디, 그때 일만은 언제까지도 잊혀질 수가 없을 것 같구나.'
　　'길을 혼자 돌아가시던 그때 일을 말씀이세요?'

'눈길을 혼자 돌아가다 보니 그 길엔 아직도 우리 둘 말고는 아무도 지나간 사람이 없지 않았겄냐. 눈발이 그친 신작로 눈 위에 저하고 나하고 둘이 걸어온 발자국만 나란히 이어져 있구나.'

'그래서 어머님은 그 발자국 때문에 아들 생각이 더 간절하셨겄네요.'

'간절하다뿐이었겄냐. 신작로를 지나고 산길을 들어서도 굽이굽이 돌아온 그 몹쓸 발자국들에 아직도 도란도란 저 아그의 목소리나 따뜻한 온기가 남아 있는 듯만 싶었제. 산비둘기만 푸르륵 날아올라도 저 아그 넋이 새가 되어 다시 되돌아오는 듯 놀라지고, 나무들이 눈을 쓰고 서 있는 것만 보아도 뒤에서 금세 저 아그 모습이 뛰어나올 것만 싶었지야. 하다 보니 나는 굽이굽이 외지기만 한 그 산길을 저 아그 발자국만 따라 밟고 왔더니라. 내 자석아, 내 자석아, 너하고 둘이 온 길을 이제는 이 몹쓸 늙은 것 혼자서 너를 보내고 돌아가고 있구나!'

'어머님 그때 우시지 않았어요?'

'울기만 했겄냐. 오목오목 디뎌 논 그 아그 발자국마다 한도 없는 눈물을 뿌리며 돌아왔제. 내 자석아, 내 자석아, 부디 몸이나 성히 지내거라. 부디부디 너라도 좋은 운 타서 복 받고 살거라... 눈앞이 가리도록 눈물을 떨구면서 눈물로 저 아그 앞길만 빌고 왔제...'

노인의 이야기는 이제 거의 끝이 나 가고 있는 것 같았다. 아내는 이제 할 말을 잊은 듯 입을 조용히 다물고 있었다.

Key vocabulary

점심상	lunch table
밥숟가락	rice spoon
매듭	knot
팔자	fate
하필	of all things
선걸음	first steps
주변머리	surrounding area
체념	resignation
에미	mother, (self) demeaning
장죽	long pipe
원망기	hating or blaming
땡볕	scorching sunshine
장터 거리	market place street
차부	cart-drawer
덜크렁덜크렁	represents the sound of shuffling
아그	baby, child
늙은 것	referring to self as old one
동녁	East
굽이굽이	windingly

Comprehension questions: text

1 Who is 노인 referring to?
2 What are some of the different expressions used to refer to the mother and the son?
3 Who are the participants in this story setting?
4 What is the relationship between the son and the mother like?

5   What happened in the snowy road?
6   What dialectical expressions can you find in the text?

Comprehension questions: music extract

Singer-songwriter Kim Yuna has been active both as a solo artist and as the lead singer of modern rock band Jaurim (자우림). In her 2010 album *315360*, the title track 'Going Home' portrays unconditional love like that of family, with home as a place of shelter from the cruel world.

1   What is the singer doing on her way home?
2   Why does the singer feel anxious?
3   What is the singer's antidote to the cruelty of the world?
4   What are the singer's hopes for tomorrow?

Additional source material

Original K-Pop stars Seo Taeji and Boys (서태지와 아이들)'s 1995 hit song 'Come Back Home' (컴백홈) also sings of coming back home as the antidote to all the cruelties of daily life.

Further discussion questions

1   How is the mother-son relation in this text realised? Try to find out the linguistic evidence which reflects this (e.g., speech styles).
2   Try to explain how the mother-son conflict in this text, which is deep yet subtle, is resolved. Do you think this way of conflict resolution is unique to Korea, or to Asian culture in general?

References

Han'guk, Kajok Hakhoe. 2011. *Korean Families: Continuity and Change*. Seoul, ROK: Seoul National University Press.
Park, Sangyoub. 2015. 'A Silent Revolution in the Korean Family.' *Contexts* 14(2): 77.
Yi, Kwanggyu. 1997. *Korean Family and Kinship* (Korean studies series (Chimmundang (Seoul, Korea)); no. 3). Seoul: Jipmoondang Publishing.

2 Love

2.1 소나기 – 황순원 (*Rain Shower* – Hwang Sunwŏn)

Introduction to the text

황순원(黃順元, 1915〜) published his first story in 1937 and continued writing through the 1980s; during his long literary career, Hwang Sunwŏn observed firsthand the suffering of ordinary Koreans under many different forms of oppression: colonialism, ideological strife, the Korean War, industrialisation, and military dictatorships. What he sought to capture was the resilience of the Korean spirit even in times of adversity, rather than the adversity itself, and the discovery of love and goodwill in unlikeliest of circumstances.

One special trait of his writing is the organised development of each story and the elaborate writing style based on poetic sensibility. His writing style is based on fables. For that reason, the writer explains in minute detail about the natural thinking of humans, and embraces and strives to understand the extremes of reality through deep ideologies and religion.

Sonagi is a novel he published in 1959 which was published in *New Sun*. It's about the unsoiled and beautiful love between young people. The title functions as a backdrop and also shows the instantaneous uniqueness of such heartbreaking love. In this work, the author neither emphasises the purity of that love, nor does he show grief at the dramatic ending. The beautiful emotion and the weakness felt at the girl's death are all implicit, and depend solely on the reader. This novel will not be passed down as a judgment, but as a lingering image and influence.

Original text

'저기 송아지가 있다. 그리 가 보자.'
 누렁송아지였다. 아직 코뚜레도 꿰지 않았다.
 소년이 고삐를 바투 잡아 쥐고 등을 긁어 주는 체 훌쩍 올라탔다. 송아지가 껑충거리며 돌아간다.
 소녀의 흰 얼굴이, 분홍 스웨터가, 남색 스커트가, 안고 있는 꽃과 함께 범벅이 된다. 모두가 하나의 큰 꽃묶음 같다. 어지럽다. 그러나, 내리지 않으리라. 자랑스러웠다. 이것만은 소녀가 흉내 내지 못할, 자기 혼자만이 할 수 있는 일인 것이다.
 '너희, 예서 뭣들 하느냐?'
 농부(農夫)하나가 억새풀 사이로 올라왔다.
 송아지 등에서 뛰어내렸다. 어린 송아지를 타서 허리가 상하면 어쩌느냐고 꾸지람을 들을 것만 같다. 그런데, 나룻이 긴 농부는 소녀 편을 한 번 훑어보고는 그저 송아지 고삐를 풀어 내면서,
 '어서들 집으로 가거라. 소나기가 올라.'

참, 먹장구름 한 장이 머리 위에 와 있다. 갑자기 사면이 소란스러워진 것 같다. 바람이 우수수 소리를 내며 지나간다. 삽시간에 주위가 보랏빛으로 변했다.

산을 내려오는데, 떡갈나무 잎에서 빗방울 듣는 소리가 난다. 굵은 빗방울이었다. 목덜미가 선뜻선뜻했다. 그러자, 대번에 눈앞을 가로막는 빗줄기.

비안개 속에 원두막이 보였다. 그리로 가 비를 그을 수밖에.

그러나, 원두막은 기둥이 기울고 지붕도 갈래갈래 찢어져 있었다. 그런 대로 비가 덜 새는 곳을 가려 소녀를 들어서게 했다.

소녀의 입술이 파아랗게 질렸다. 어깨를 자꾸 떨었다.

무명 겹저고리를 벗어 소녀의 어깨를 싸 주었다. 소녀는 비에 젖은 눈을 들어 한 번 쳐다보았을 뿐, 소년이 하는 대로 잠자코 있었다. 그리고는, 안고 온 꽃묶음 속에서 가지가 꺾이고 꽃이 일그러진 송이를 골라 발 밑에 버린다. 소녀가 들어선 곳도 비가 새기 시작했다. 더 거기서 비를 그을 수 없었다.

밖을 내다보던 소년이 무엇을 생각했는지 수수밭 쪽으로 달려간다. 세워 놓은 수숫단 속을 비집어 보더니, 옆의 수숫단을 날라다 덧세운다. 다시 속을 비집어 본다. 그리고는 이쪽을 향해 손짓을 한다.

수숫단 속은 비는 안 새었다. 그저 어둡고 좁은 게 안 됐다. 앞에 나앉은 소년은 그냥 비를 맞아야만 했다. 그런 소년의 어깨에서 김이 올랐다.

소녀가 속삭이듯이, 이리 들어와 앉으라고 했다. 괜찮다고 했다. 소녀가 다시, 들어와 앉으라고 했다. 할 수 없이 뒷걸음질을 쳤다. 그 바람에, 소녀가 안고 있는 꽃묶음이 망그러졌다. 그러나, 소녀는 상관없다고 생각했다. 비에 젖은 소년의 몸 내음새가 확 코에 끼얹혀졌다. 그러나, 고개를 돌리지 않았다. 도리어 소년의 몸기운으로 해서 떨리던 몸이 적이 누그러지는 느낌이었다.

소란하던 수숫잎 소리가 뚝 그쳤다. 밖이 멀개졌다.

수숫단 속을 벗어 나왔다. 멀지 않은 앞쪽에 햇빛이 눈부시게 내리붓고 있었다. 도랑 있는 곳까지 와 보니, 엄청나게 물이 불어 있었다. 빛마저 제법 붉은 흙탕물이었다. 뛰어 건널 수가 없었다.

소년이 등을 돌려 댔다. 소녀가 순순히 업히었다. 걷어올린 소년의 잠방이까지 물이 올라왔다. 소녀는 '어머나' 소리를 지르며 소년의 목을 끌어안았다.

개울가에 다다르기 전에, 가을 하늘이 언제 그랬는가 싶게 구름 한 점 없이 쪽빛으로 개어있었다.

그 뒤로 소녀의 모습은 뵈지 않았다. 매일같이 개울가로 달려와 봐도 뵈지 않았다. 학교에서 쉬는 시간에 운동장을 살피기도 했다. 남 몰래 5학년 여자 반을 엿보기도 했다. 그러나, 뵈지 않았다.

그날도 소년은 주머니 속 흰 조약돌만 만지작거리며 개울가로 나왔다. 그랬더니, 이쪽 개울둑에 소녀가 앉아 있는 게 아닌가.

소년은 가슴부터 두근거렸다.

Key vocabulary

코뚜레	nose-ring for cows
고삐	bridle, reins
바투	closely
훌쩍	lightly
껑충	in a leaping way
스웨터	sweater, jumper
스커트	skirt (outfit meant to feel urban)
모두가 하나의 큰 꽃묶음 같다	it all seemed like a bunch of flowers

32 Love

농부	farmer
우수수	rustling or rushing sound of falling
삽시간	in a flash
떡갈나무	oak
선뜻선뜻	cool, refreshing
원두막	a hut on stilts, usually in a melon field
갈래갈래	torn in several places
파아랗게	pale blue
무명 겹저고리	cotton outer jacket
꽃묶음	a bunch or bouquet of flowers
수숫단	a bunch of sorghum
김	steam
속삭이듯이	in a whisper
뒷걸음질	taking steps backwards
망그러졌다	to be ruined
내음새	a smell
뚝	suddenly
흙탕물	muddy water
잠방이	farmer's breeches
쪽빛	turquoise
엿보다	to peek or peep into
조약돌	pebbles
만지작거리다	to fiddle with
개울가	the side of a stream or brook

Comprehension questions: text

1 Find examples of imagery as used by the author in this text.
2 Is it natural to translate 소년, and 소녀, as 'the boy,' and 'the girl,' respectively, throughout the text in English?
3 How are the boy's emotions reflected in the text?
4 How are the girl's emotions reflected in the text?

Comprehension questions: drama extract

The use of a rain shower as a catalyst for a deepening in the relationship between two people has become a very common trope in both dramas and films. In the tvN drama *What's Wrong With Secretary Kim* (김비서가 왜 그럴까, 2018), about a narcissistic boss, Yi Yŏngjun, and his long-suffering secretary, Kim Miso, the rain scene in episode seven evokes not just the original story of *Sonagi*, but also the film inspired by the story *The Classic* (클래식, 2003). In this scene, having just had an argument, being caught together in the rain brings them closer once more.

1 How does Yŏngjun encourage Miso to stay under his jacket together with him?
2 Is Miso worried about catching a cold? How does Yŏngjun respond?
3 How does Yŏngjun comfort Miso when she is scared by a spider?
4 What does this remind Miso of?

Additional source material

While there are countless instances of the rain shower trope being used in films and dramas, two of the most well-known films to have engaged with *Sonagi* are the above mentioned *The Classic* (클래식, 2003), and *My Sassy Girl* (엽기적인 그녀, 2001), both directed by Kwak Chaeyŏng.

Further discussion questions

1 Discuss how this novel portrays the psychological interaction between the boy and the girl.
2 How does the author show things in an implicit way rather than telling the reader how to interpret the text?

References

Garcelán, Enrique, & Domingo, López. 2007. 'Encuentros y desencuentros: El melodrama en coreano/ Encounters and Misunderstandings: The Melodrama in Korean.' *Nosferatu* 55/56.
Korea.net. 2016. 'Hwang Sun-won: One of the great Korean authors of the 21th century.' *Korea.net*, 15/03/16. Available online at: www.korea.net/NewsFocus/Culture/view?articleId=133876. Accessed 30/12/18.
Miyose, Colby Y. 2013. *Unrealistic Weeds of Love and Romance: The Korean Drama and the 'Flower Boy' Genre*. MA Thesis, University of Nevada, Las Vegas.

2.2 춘향가 (*The Song of Ch'unhyang* – Anonymous)

Introduction to the text

Ch'unhyangga (*The Song of Ch'unhyang*) is probably the most famous story of the *p'ansori* genre. It tells the tale of Ch'unhyang, the daughter of a *kisaeng* (courtesan), and Yi Mongnyong, the son of the local governor. They meet, fall in love, and marry in secret. However, soon Mongnyong has to follow his father back to Seoul and leaves Ch'unhyang behind in Namwŏn. The new governor of Namwŏn tries to force Ch'unhyang to become his concubine, but she refuses in order to stay faithful to Mongnyong. At this, the governor is angry and orders Ch'unhyang to be beaten and thrown into prison. Meanwhile, Mongnyong has passed the civil service examination with flying colours. He travels back to Namwŏn, exposes the magistrate's corruption, and sets Ch'unhyang free. Ch'unhyang is honoured by the king for her fidelity and raised to the rank of noblewoman, and she and Mongnyong live together happily every after. This story serves as a moral tale, as Ch'unhyang's faithfulness to her husband, one of the core principles of Confucianism, is rewarded. At the same time, this romance, which crosses the boundaries of social class, becomes a powerful critique of the rigid caste system that existed in the Chosŏn dynasty.

Original text

Text and annotations from Ch'oe Tonghyŏn. 2008. *Ch'unhyangga padipyŏl chŏnjip 4: Chŏng Ŭngmin padi* [*A Complete Collection of Ch'unhyangga According to Different*

Styles 4: Chŏng Ŭngmin style]. Chŏnju: Ministry of Culture, Sports, and Tourism, North Chŏlla Province.

[아니리]
'여봐라, 형리[1] 불러라!'
'예, 형리 대령[2]이오!'
'형리 들어라. 저년이 하[3] 예쁘게 생겼기로 수청 들라 하였더니, 나를 역모[4]로 모는구나. 여봐라, 춘향이 다짐[5] 받어 올려라!'
형리가 들어서 다짐장[6]을 쓴 연후에,
'춘향이 다짐 사연[7] 분부 뫼어라.[8] 살등네의등이 창가소부로, 부종관장지엄령하고 능욕존전허니 죄당만사라.'[9]
급창 불러 던져 주며,
'다짐 받어 올려라.'
춘향이 붓대를 들고 사지를 벌렁벌렁 떠는디, 죽기가 서러워 떠는 것도 아니요, 사또가 무서워 떠는 것도 아니요, 한양계신 서방님 못보고 죽을일과 칠십당년[10] 늙은노모두고 죽을 일을 생각허여, 일신수족[11]을 별별벌벌 떨더니, 한 '일' 자, 마음 '심' 자[12]로 지르르 긋고,
[진양조]
붓대를 땅에다 내던지더니
요만허고[13] 앉었구나.
[아니리]
급창[14]이 다짐 받어 올리니, 사또 보시고,
'네년의 일심[15]이 얼마나 굳은지, 어디 한번 두고 보자. 여봐라! 저년을 동틀[16] 위에 동틀 들어[17] 의법하라.'[18]
춘향의 연연약질[19]을 높은 동틀 위에다 덩그렇게 올려 매고, 왜목으로 얼른 가리고,[20] 바지 가래[21] 훨씬 추켜[22] 동틀 다리 압령[23]하여 묶은 후에,
'집장사령,[24] 분부 뫼어라.'[25]
'예이!'
'일호[26] 사정 두었다는 주장대[27]로 찌를 테니, 각별히[28] 매우 쳐라.'
'예이! 엄령지하에[29] 요망헌[30] 년을 무슨 사정 두오리까? 당장에 뼈를 빼 올리리다!'
[진양조]
집장사령 거동을 보아라.
별형장[31] 한 아름을 덤쑥[32] 안어다가 동틀 밑에다 좌르르르르르르르,
형장을 고르는구나.
이놈도 잡고 느끈능청,[33]
저놈도 잡고 느끈능청,
그 중에 손잡이 좋은 놈 골라잡고,
갓을 숙여 대상[34]을 가리고,
사또 보는 데는 엄령이 지엄허니 춘향다려[35] 속말[36]을 헌다.
'이애, 춘향아. 한두 개만 견디어라.
내 솜씨로 살려 주마.
꼼짝 꼼짝 마라. 뼈 부러지리라.'
'매우 쳐라!'
'예이!'
'딱!'
부러진 형장 가지는 공중으로 피르르르르르르르 대뜰[37] 우에 떨어 지고,
동틀 위의 춘향이는 아프단 말을 도시[38] 싫어 아프단 말을 아니허고,
고개만 빙빙 두루면서,[39]
"일' 자로 아뢰리다.
일편단심[40] 이내 마음 일부종사허랴는데,[41]

일개 형장이 웬일이오?
어서 바삐 죽여주오!'
'매우 쳐라!'
'예이!'
'딱!'
'둘이오!'
'이부불경[42] 이내 마음 이군불사[43] 다르리까?
이비사적[44] 알았거든 두 낭군을 섬기리까?
가망 없고 무가내[45]오!'
'매우 쳐라!'
'예이!'
'딱!'
'삼가히 조심하라!'
'삼생가약[46] 맺은 마음, 삼종지법[47]을 알았거든
삼월화[48]로 아지 마오.
어서 바삐 죽여주오!'
'사' 자 낱을 '딱' 붙여노니,
'사대부 사또님이 사기사[49]를 모르시오?
사지[50]를 쫙쫙 찢어 사대문에 걸쳤어도
가망 없고 무가내오!'
'오' 자 낱을 '딱' 붙여노니,
'오마로[51] 오신 사또,
오륜[52]을 밝히시오.
오매불망[53] 우리 낭군 잊을 가망이 전혀 없소!'
'육' 자 낱을 딱 붙여노니,
'육부에 맺힌 마음
육시[54]허여도 무가내오!'
'칠' 자 낱을 '딱' 붙여노니,
'칠척검[55] 높이 들어 칠 때마다 동갈라도,[56]
가망 없고 안 되지요!'
'팔' 자 낱을 '딱' 붙여 노니,
'팔방부당[57] 안 될 일을
위력공사[58] 그만허고,
어서 급히 죽여주오.'
'구' 자 낱을 '딱' 붙여 노니,
'구중분우[59] 관장[60]이 되어
궂은[61] 짓을 그만 허오.
구곡간장[62] 맺힌 마음
구사일생[63]을 헐지라도 구관자제[64]를 잊으리까?
가망 없고 무가내오!'
'십' 자를 붙여노니,
'십장가[65]로 아뢰리다.
십실[66] 적은 골[67]도 충렬[68]이 있삽거든,[69]
우리 남원 교방청[70]에 열행[71]이 없사리까?[72]
나 죽기는 섧잖으나,[73]
십맹일장[74] 날만 믿은 우리 모친이 불쌍허오.
이제라도 이 몸이 죽어 혼비중천[75] 높이 떠서,
도련님 잠든 창전[76]에 가 파몽[77]이나 하고지고.'[78]

36   Love

Key vocabulary

형리	the official in charge of the prison in the provincial government (刑吏)
대령	awaiting the orders of one's superior (待令)
역모	to plot treason (逆謀)
다짐	a letter acknowledging the crimes one has committed
일신수족	the hands and feet (一身手足)
요만하다	blankly, without a word
동틀	a special chair for interrogating and torturing criminals
연연약질	delicate and frail body (軟軟弱質)
집장사령	the person in charge of beating criminals (執杖使令)
일호	a hair's breadth, a tiny amount (一毫)
엄령지하	under a stern order (嚴令之下)
요망하다	treacherous (妖妄)
덥쑥	an onomatopoeic word indicating something being held firmly by the hands or arms
일편단심	lit., a piece of red heart, a firm heart that will not change (一片丹心)
일부종사	serving one husband (一夫從事)
무가내	there is nothing that can be done (無可奈)
삼생가약	a promise made between husband and wife to live together in the past, present, and future lives (三生佳約)
삼종지법	the three rules a woman must follow, to first obey her father, after marriage obey her husband, and as a widow obey her son (三從之法)
삼월화	spring flowers that bloom in the third month of the lunar calendar, flowers anyone can pick (三月花)
사기사	things will always end up as they were originally (事其事)
오륜	the five relationships between ruler and ministers, father, and son, elder brother and younger brother, husband, and wife, and friend and friend, which form the basis of Confucian morality (五倫)
오매불망	whether asleep or awake you cannot forget (寤寐不忘)
팔방부당	it is wrong no matter which direction you look at it from (八方不當)
위력공사	abusing one's power in a public act (威力公事)
구중분우	someone who shares the king's worries, someone who receives his orders directly from the king (九重分憂)
구곡간장	in a deep recess of the heart (九曲肝腸)
구사일생	barely surviving numerous life or death crises (九死一生)
십실	only has ten houses (十室)
충렬	loyal subject and patriot (忠烈)
열행	an act of fidelity (烈行)
십맹일장	lit., ten blind men only have one cane, something especially valuable (十盲一杖)
혼비중천	the spirit flies high in the sky (魂飛中天)
파몽	wake someone up from their dream (破夢)

Comprehension questions: text

1   What crimes is Ch'unhyang accused of?
2   What does Ch'unhyang write in her confession?
3   Does the punishment officer want to beat Ch'unhyang?
4   How does Ch'unhyang respond to the beating?

Comprehension questions: film extract

The 2000 film *Chunhyang* (춘향뎐) by Im Kwŏnt'aek blends a live *p'ansori* performance with a reenactment of the *Ch'unhyangga* story. In the scene where Ch'unhyang meets the magistrate, we see the scene from the text abstract above brought to life.

1   What statement does Ch'unhyang make regarding the governor's mother?
2   Which law does the governor cite in his accusation of Ch'unhyang?
3   Which law does Ch'unhyang use in her defence?

Additional source material

While there are plenty of other media telling of the firm desire to stay true to one's love despite all obstacles, some examples include:

- Song, 'It's You' by Super Junior (너라고 – 슈퍼주니어, 2009).
- tvN drama, *Boyfriend* (남자친구, 2018).

Further discussion questions

1   Ch'unhyang and the magistrate both employ Confucian principles to justify their arguments. Form two teams to debate from their different standpoints.

   Team A: Ch'unhyang's argument: Based on the Five Relationships (*oryun*), a core moral principle in Confucianism, a wife can only serve one husband, hence she must remain chaste even if her husband abandons her.
   Team B: The magistrate's argument: As the daughter of a concubine, Ch'unhyang is of the same social class and is required to serve him as all other concubines must; it is impossible for concubines to be chaste.

2   The meeting between Ch'unhyang and the magistrate is profoundly shaped by their gender and social status. Can we see parallels to their encounter in the present day?

Notes

1   刑吏. 지방 관천의 형반(刑房) 아전.
2   待令. 윗사람의 명령이나 지시를 기다리고 있음.
3   하도.
4   逆謀. 반역을 꾀하는 일.
5   지은 죄를 인정하는 글.
6   지은 죄를 인정하는 글.
7   지은 죄의 내용.
8   모셔라.
9   殺等汝矣等이 娼家少婦로, 不從官長之嚴令하고 凌辱尊前허니, 罪當萬死라. '말하건대 너는 창녀의 천한 몸으로 관장의 엄한 명령을 따르지 않았고, 존엄한 앞에세 그를 업시여겼으니 죄가 만 번 죽어 마땅하다.'의 뜻. '살등'은 '삶든'의 와전으로 '사뢰건대,' '아뢰건대'의 뜻. 옛날 죄인의 심문 기록은 이두로 썼다.
10 七十當年. 그 해의 나이가 일흔 살임.
11 一身手足. 소과 발.
12 한 '일(一)'이라는 글자와, 마음 '심(心)'이라는 글자. 일심 (一心), 곧 한 마음.
13 아무 말 없이 우두커니.
14 及唱. 원의 명령을 간접적으로 받아서 큰 소리로 전달하던 일을 맡아보던 사람.
15 일편단심(一片丹心). 진심에서 우러나오는 변치 않는 마음.

16 형틀. 죄인을 묶어 앉히고 심문하는 의자.
17 들어 올려.
18 依法하라. 법에 따라 다스리라.
19 軟軟弱質. 아주 여리고 약한 몸.
20 倭木으로 얼른 가리고. 왜목으로 눈을 얼른 가리고. '왜목'은 폭이 넓게 짜인 무면베인 광목을 이름.
21 가랑이.
22 모두 위로 끌어 올리고.
23 押領. 죄인 맡에 데리고 옴.
24 執杖使令. 몽둥이를 들고 죄인을 매로 치는 사령. '사령'은 각 관아에서 심부름하던 사람.
25 모셔라. 잘 듣고 시행하라.
26 一毫. 털 한 올만큼. 아주 조금.
27 朱杖대. 붉은 칠을 한 몽둥이.
28 어떤 일에 대한 마음가짐이나 자세 따위가 유달리 특별하게.
29 嚴令之下에. 엄한 명령에.
30 妖妄헌. 요사스럽고 망령된.
31 別形杖. 특별히 골라 놓은 형장. '형장'은 줄 때 사용하는 몽둥이.
32 '담쏙'의 강한 말. 손으로 탐스럽게 쥐거나 팔로 탐스럽게 인는 모양.
33 가는 막대기나 줄 따위를 탄력 있게 흔드는 모양.
34 臺上. 높은 대의 위.
35 춘향에게.
36 입속말. 남이 잘 알아듣지 못하게 입속으로 중얼거리는 말.
37 댓돌에서 집채 쪽으로 있는 좁고 긴, 벽 밖의 뜰. '댓돌'은 집채에서 빗물이 떨어지는 안 쪽으로 마당보다 높게 돌려가며 놓은 돌.
38 都是. 도무지.
39 돌리면서.
40 一片丹心. 한 조각의 붉은 마음이란 뜻으로 진심에서 우러나오는 변치 아니하는 마음을 이르는 말.
41 一夫從事하려는데. 한 남편만을 섬기려는데.
42 二夫不更. 두 지아비를 섬기지 아니함.
43 二君不事. 두 임금을 섬기지 아니함.
44 二妃史蹟. 순임금의 아내인 아황과 여영의 절행을 적은 글.
45 無可奈. 어쩔 수가 없음.
46 三生佳約. 전생과 현생과 후생의 세 삶에 걸쳐 이어질 아름다운 언약. 부부로서의 약속.
47 三從之法. 여자가 지켜야 한다는 세 가지의 법도. 어려서는 어버이를 따르고, 시집을 가서는 남편을 따르고, 남편이 죽으면 아들을 따른다는 내용.
48 三月花. 음력 삼월에 피는 봄꽃. 누구나 꺾을 수 있는 꽃.
49 事其事. 일은 원래 일대로 된다는 말.
50 四肢. 팔과 다리.
51 五馬로. 말 다섯 마리를 타고. '오마'는 태수의 수레를 말 다섯 마리가 끈 데에서 비롯된 말.
52 五倫. 사람이 살아가는 기본이 되는 다섯 가지 도리. 군산위의(君臣有義. 임금과 신하 사이에는 의리가 있어야 함), 부자유친(父子有親. 부모와 자식 사이에는 친함이 있어야 함), 부부유별(夫婦有別. 부부 사이에는 할 일이 따로 있음), 장유유서(長幼有序. 나이 많은 사람과 적은 사람 사이에는 순서가 있음), 붕우유신(朋友有信. 친구 사이에는 신의가 있어야 함)의 다섯 가지 도리.
53 寤寐不忘. 자나 깨나 잊지 못함.
54 戮屍. 찢어 죽임.
55 七尺劍. 길이가 칠 척이나 되는 큰 칼.
56 몇 덩이로 나누어도.
57 八方不當. 어느 면으로 보나 옳지 않음.
58 威力公事. 위세를 볼어 하는 공적인 일.
59 九重分憂. 임금의 근심을 나누에 받음. 임금의 분부를 받드는.
60 官長. 관가의 우두머리.
61 원래는 '언짢고 꺼림직한'의 뜻이나 여기서는 옳지 않은' 정도로 쓰였음.
62 九曲肝腸. 마음 속 깊은 곳.
63 九死一生. 여러 차례 죽을 고비에서 해매다가 겨우 살아남.
64 舊官子弟. 먼저 부임했던 사또의 아들, 즉 이도령.
65 十杖歌. 춘향이 매 맞는 관경을 그린 노래.

66 十室. 집이 열 채쯤 밖에 안 되는.
67 고을.
68 忠烈. 충신과 열사.
69 있는데, 있사온데.
70 敎坊廳. 기생들을 관리하던 곳.
71 烈行. 절개를 지키는 행동.
72 없겠슴니까.
73 싫지 않으나.
74 十盲一杖. 열명의 맹인에게 있는 하나의 지팡이. 즉 대단히 귀중함을 뜻함.
75 魂飛中天. 혼이 하늘 높이 날아감.
76 窓前에. 창문 앞에서.
77 破夢. 꿈을 깨게 함.
78 하고 싶구나.

References

Cho, Sung-Won. 2004. 'Renaissance Nun vs. Korean Gisaeng: Chastity and Female Celibacy in Measure for Measure and "Chun-hyang Jeon".' *Comparative Literature Studies* 41(4): 565–83.
Deuchler, Martina. 1992. *The Confucian Transformation of Korea: A Study of Society and Ideology*. Cambridge, MA: Council on East Asian Studies, Harvard University.
Kim, Jisoo M. 2017. 'From Jealousy to Violence: Marriage, Family and Confucian Patriarchy in Fifteenth-Century Korea.' *Acta Koreana* 20(1): 91–110.
Park, Hyun Suk. 2015. *The Government Courtesan: Status, Gender and Performance in Late Chosŏn Korea*. PhD Diss., University of Chicago.

2.3 사랑 손님과 어머니 – 주요섭 (*Mother and a Guest* – Chu Yosŏp)

Introduction to the text

Chu Yosŏp (朱耀燮, 1902–1972), the author, was born in P'yŏngyang and graduated from Hogang University in 1927. He studied abroad at Stanford University in America. He made his literary debut in 1921 when his work 'Broken Jar' was published in *Maeil Sinbo*. In his early career, he focussed on socialist-themed writing about poverty in Korea, through works such as 'Rickshaw Puller' (1925) and 'Murder' (1925). He enjoyed writing about the life of the lower class and their attitude of defiance. In the middle of his career, he presented works such as 'Mother and the Boarder,' which took a deeper tone. This was a short story published in 1935 in *Cho Kwang*, about the subtle romance of a young widow and her boarder as seen through the eyes of her six-year-old son. The story presents the friction and emotions between the mother and boarder as seen through the innocent eyes of a child. The story is successful in showing how a child approaches issues of longing and hesitation hidden deep within grown-ups' hearts as he fulfils his role as a mediator between the two characters. Thus, it can be said that this story focuses on subtly presenting hidden themes and meaning, rather than expressing them forthwith. For instance, in several scenes where the reader is likely to pick up on feelings between the mother and the boarder, the child narrator expresses confusion.

Original text

'옥희야.'
　하고 또 부르십니다.
'응?'

'옥희는 언제나, 언제나 내 곁을 안 떠나지. 옥희는 언제나, 언제나 엄마하구 같이 살지. 옥희는 엄마가 늙어서 꼬부랑 할미가 되어두, 그래두 옥희는 엄마하구 같이 살지. 옥희가 유치원 졸업하구, 또 소학교 졸업하구, 또 중학교 졸업하구, 또 대학교 졸업하구, 옥희가 조선서 제일 훌륭한 사람이 돼두, 그래두 옥희는 엄마하구 같이 살지, 응! 옥희는 엄마를 얼만큼 사랑하나?'

'이만큼.'

하고 나는 두 팔을 짝 벌리어 보였습니다.

'응? 얼만큼? 응! 그만큼! 언제나, 언제나 옥희는 엄마만 사랑하지, 그리구 공부두 잘하구, 그리고 훌륭한 사람이 되구.'

나는 어머니의 목소리가 떨리는 것으로 보아 어머니가 또 울까 봐 겁이 나서,

'엄마, 이만큼, 이만큼.'

하면서 두 팔을 짝짝 벌리었습니다.

어머니는 울지 않으셨습니다.

'응, 그래, 옥희 엄마는 옥희 하나문 그뿐이야. 세상 다른 건 다 소용없어. 우리 옥희 하나문 그만이야. 그렇지, 옥희야.'

'응!'

어머니는 나를 당기어서 꼭 껴안고 내 가슴이 막혀 들어올 때까지 자꾸만 껴안아 주었습니다.

그 날 밤, 저녁밥 먹고 나니까 어머니는 나를 불러 앉히고 머리를 새로 빗겨 주었습니다. 댕기를 새 댕기로 드려 주고, 바지, 저고리, 치마, 모두 새것을 꺼내 입혀 주었습니다.

'엄마, 어디 가?'

하고 물으니까,

'아니.'

하고 웃음을 띠면서 대답합니다. 그러더니, 풍금 옆에서 내리어 새로 다린 하얀 손수건을 내리어 내 손에 쥐어 주면서,

'이 손수건, 저 사랑 아저씨 손수건인데, 이것 아저씨 갖다 드리구 와, 응. 오래 있지 말구 손수건만 갖다 드리구 이내 와, 응.'

하고 말씀하셨습니다.

손수건을 들고 사랑으로 나가면서 나는 접어진 손수건 속에 무슨 발각발각하는 종이가 들어 있는 것처럼 생각되었습니다마는, 그것을 펴 보지 않고 그냥 갖다가 아저씨에게 주었습니다.

아저씨는 방에 누워 있다가 벌떡 일어나서 손수건을 받는데, 웬일인지 아저씨는 이전처럼 나보고 빙그레 웃지도 않고 얼굴이 몹시 파래졌습니다. 그리고는, 입술을 질근질근 깨물면서 말 한 마디 아니하고 그 손수건을 받더군요.

나는 어째 이상한 기분이 들어서 아저씨 방에 들어가 앉지도 못하고, 그냥 되돌아서 안방으로 도로 왔지요. 어머니는 풍금 앞에 앉아서 무엇을 그리 생각하는지 가만히 있더군요. 나는 풍금 옆으로 가서 가만히 옆에 앉아 있었습니다. 이윽고, 어머니는 조용조용히 풍금을 타십니다. 무슨 곡조인지는 몰라도 어째 구슬프고 고즈넉한 곡조야요.

밤이 늦도록 어머니는 풍금을 타셨습니다. 그 구슬프고 고즈넉한 곡조를 계속하고 또 계속하면서 . . .

Key vocabulary

꼬부랑 할머니	old and wrinkled lady
풍금	organ
손수건	handkerchief

얼굴이 파래지다	startled (lit., face became blue)
질근질근	the shape of tying up something tight
구슬프다	sad
고즈넉하다	gentle

Comprehension questions: text

1 Why does the mother reject the guest?
2 How does the mother reject the guest?
3 How does the guest respond?
4 How does the mother express her emotion?

Comprehension questions: drama extract

The SBS drama, *You Who Came From the Stars* (별에서 온 그대, 2013), tells the story of an alien, To Minjun, abandoned on earth for 400 years after he misses his spaceship to return home, who falls in love with a self-centred actress, Ch'ŏn Songi, who reminds him of a girl, Yihwa, that he loved in the Chosŏn dynasty. In a flashback in episode four, we see a clear portrayal of the expectation of how widows were expected to behave in the Chosŏn dynasty, which helps explain the pressures the mother faces in the story above.

1 What happened to Yihwa to cause her to return to her parents?
2 What is the relationship between To Minjun and Yihwa?
3 Why does Yihwa's mother choke her?
4 What is the last thing she does for Yihwa?

Additional source material

A film version of this story was made in 1961, *Mother and a Guest* (사랑손님과 어머니).
   Another drama which addresses a relationship going against social norms is the JTBC drama, *Secret Affair* (밀회, 2014).

Further discussion questions

1 How does the author show the relationship between the mother and guest through the child's eyes?
2 Discuss the attitude in Korea about remarriage of widows at the time the story was written. How was this different from the attitude about the remarriage of widowers?

References

Kim, Jungwon. 2014. '"You Must Avenge on My Behalf": Widow Chastity and Honour in Nineteenth-Century Korea.' *Gender & History* 26(1): 128–46.
Lee, Peter H. 2003. *A History of Korean Literature*. Cambridge: Cambridge University Press. (Chapter 23: Hyangga).
Yoo, Theodore Jun. 2005. 'The "New Woman"' and the Politics of Love, Marriage and Divorce in Colonial Korea.' *Gender & History* 17(2): 295–324.

42 Love

2.4 시조 – 황진이 (Various *shijo* – Hwang Chini)

Introduction to the text

Hwang Chini (1506–1567), also known for her artist name Myŏngwŏl (Bright Moon), was a *kisaeng*. A *kisaeng* (기생) was a professional female artist in traditional society, trained to entertain the guests at a banquet or drinking party by singing, dancing, and playing musical instruments. She was also well-versed in neo-Confucianism, and often discussed political or philosophical matters with *yangban* nobility. Her beauty and artistry, as well as her quick wits and strong-willed nature, have made her an iconic figure who has inspired numerous books, films, and dramas etc.

Shijo is a form of poetry initially exclusively of the upper class that emerged during the Koryŏ Dynasty, although it gained broader popular appeal in the later Chosŏn dynasty. Consisting of three lines averaging 14-16 syllables each, one defining characteristic of *shijo* is that they could be sung. Gatherings amongst the elite would often involve singing self-composed *shijo* in front of one's peers, and as someone expected to participate in the entertainment at such gatherings, Hwang Chini was an expert in the art form. While traditional *shijo* tended to focus on Confucian morals, Hwang's poetry highlights the opening up of new thematic material, as her poetry explores themes of love and loss, with a hefty dose of satire.

Original text

A

青山裏(청산리) 碧溪水(벽계수)야 수이 감을 자랑 마라
一到滄海(일도 창해)하면 돌아오기 어려오니
明月(명월)이 滿空山(만공산)하니 쉬어 간들 어떠리.

B

冬至 섯달 기나긴 밤을 한 허리를 잘라 내어
春風 이불 아래 서리서리 넣었다가
어론님 오신 날 밤이여든 구뷔구뷔 펴리라.

C

어져 내 일이야 그릴 줄을 모르던가.
이시랴 하더면 가랴마는 제 구태어
보내고 그리는 정은 나도 몰라 하노라.

Key vocabulary

벽계수	blue waters or 이종수(李終叔).
一到滄海 (일도 창해)	when reaching the wide sea
明月(명월)	bright moon
滿空山(만공산)	fill the empty mountain
동지	the winter solstice, also known as midwinter, occurs when one of the earth's poles has its maximum tilt away from the sun.
춘풍	spring breeze
구뷔구뷔	curvy, twisty
그리다	miss
정	heart, love, affection
구태여	intentionally
-노라	emphatic, poetic ending

Comprehension questions: text

1. What is the author rebuking the blue waters for? (A)
2. What is the author proposing? (A)
3. How does the author use natural imagery? (A)
4. What does the author want to do on the long winter night? (B)
5. What is the author regretting? (C)

Comprehension questions: drama extract

The KBS2 drama, *Hwang Jini* (황진이, 2006), tells the story of the life of Hwang Chini. At the start of episode 15, Hwang Chini uses the *shijo* above to test Pyŏk Kyesu, who is pretending to be purely devoted to his art in order to win her over.

1. What was Pyŏk Kyesu advised as the only method to make Hwang Chini fall in love with him?
2. Why does Hwang Chini feel sorry for him?
3. What else has Pyŏk Kyesu done while trying to seduce Hwang Chini?
4. Why does Pyŏk Kyesu distrust the power of sincerity?

Further discussion questions

1. Discuss *kisaeng* literature in the Chosŏn dynasty.
2. What are some key characteristics of *sijo* poems?
3. Explain the male-female relationship typical of the Chosŏn dynasty. What neo-Confucian values does this type of relationship reflect?

References

David, Bannon. 2008. 'Sijo Poetry of Korean Kisaeng.' *Hangul Herald* (Fall): 10–13.
Kevin, O'Rourke. 2003. 'Demythologizing Hwang Chini.' In *Creative Women of Korea: The Fifteenth through the Twentieth Centuries*, edited by Young-Key Kim-Renaud, pp. 96–121. London; New York: Routledge.
Lee, Younghee. 2002. *Ideology, Culture, and Han: Traditional and Early Modern Korean Women's Literature*. Edison, NJ: Jimoondang International.
Wang, Hwa, Allen, Jeffner, Angle, Stephen, Chaffee, John, & Pettid, Michael. 2018. *Confucianism and Rituals for Women in Choso˘n Korea: A Philosophical Interpretation*, ProQuest Dissertations and Theses.
Yi, Paeyong, & Chan, Ted. 2008. *Women in Korean History*. Seoul, Korea: Ewha Womans University Press.

2.5 향가 (*Hyangga* – various authors)

Introduction to the text

Hyannga introduction

Hyangga were poems written in a native writing system called Hyangchal. They were composed in the Three Kingdoms, Unified Silla, and early Goryeo periods of Korean history. The number of extant *hyangga* ranges between 25 and 27, depending on whether the *hyangga* are regarded as authentic or not. In this book, we introduce two popular *hyangga*, Sŏdongyo and Ch'ŏyongga.

Background of Sŏdongyo (from Samgukyusa)

The name of the 30th king, King Mu (580–641 (r. 600–641)), is Chang. His mother built a house on the lake bank called Namji in the capital and lived there as a widow, and she conceived him with the Dragon of the lake. His name was Sŏdong and he was extraordinarily talented and generous. He was called so because he usually made a living by farming yams. Having heard that the third daughter of the King Chinp'yŏng of Silla, Sŏnhwa, was beautiful and kind, Sŏdong cut his hair, went to the capital of Silla, and made friends with the local children by giving out yams. Then, he made a children's song and let them sing it. This children's song spread throughout the capital, and even reached the royal palace. All the officials were outraged and, as they demanded, the princess was banished to distant lands. As she was leaving, the queen gave her pure gold for travelling expenses. While the princess was on her way to the place of exile, Sŏdong suddenly came out and, bowing, said that he would escort her. Although she didn't know who he was, she was (naturally) intrigued and attracted to him, and allowed him to follow her.

Eventually she found out his name, Sŏdong, and came to believe that the children's song was correct. They came to Paekche together and she took out the gold so that they could settle down together. Sŏdong asked, 'What is this?' and she said, 'This is gold that can make us rich.' Sŏdong said, 'The place where I used to farm is covered with gold, discarded on the ground.' The Princess was greatly surprised, and said, 'This is a unique treasure which has no like. If you know where the gold is now, why don't we send the treasure to my parent's palace?' and Sŏdong said, 'Alright!' Then, they gathered the gold and piled it up mountain-high, and went to see Chimyŏngbŏpsa at the temple Saja-sa on Yonghwa-san Mountain, and asked how they might transport the gold. The Pŏpsa (the title of the monk) said, 'I can send it with spiritual power, so bring it.' The princess put the gold with a letter in front of Saja-sa, and then the Pŏpsa moved it to the royal court of Silla overnight by spiritual power. King Chinp'yŏng was amazed and sent his respects by letter. This let Sŏdong gain the people's hearts and he became the king. One day, King Mu was travelling with his wife, and they reached a big pond under Yonghwa-san Mountain. There, three Maitraya Buddhas appeared in the pond, so the King stopped the carriage and offered them a devout prayer. The King's wife told him, 'Please build a big temple here by any possible means. That is my true wish,' and the King accepted it and went to Chimyŏngbŏpsa and asked about filling in the pond. The Pŏpsa made the pond into land, tearing down the mountains and filling the pond by spiritual power. So, each of the monasteries, pagodas, and servants' quarters to enshrine the three Maitraya Buddhas were built separately, and the temple was named Mirŭksa. King Chinp'yŏng sent various master craftsmen in support, and this temple can still be seen today.

Background of Ch'ŏyongga: who is Ch'ŏyong?

Ch'ŏyong is interpreted in different ways by different people. Some regard him as a member of the Silla noble class, and some interpret him as a shaman. Some think of him as an Arabic merchant. Some, who believe in Ch'ŏyong as a shaman who is both man and god, view Ch'ŏyong as the son of the East Sea Dragon, who helped his father to run the country and overcome evil. The second view is that Ch'ŏyong came from Arabia. According to *Samguksagi*, in the time of King Hŏngang, people who looked strange and wore unfamiliar clothing appeared in Korea. Also, there was a myth that in Silla times, there was a person called Ch'ŏyong who looked very strange. It is very likely that this Ch'ŏyong was a foreigner, and, given the trade history between Silla and Arabia, when a lot of Arabian merchants came to Silla, it is very likely that Ch'ŏyong was of Arabic descent.

Sinitic text (Hyangch'al)

1　善化公主主隱
2　他密只嫁良置古
3　薯童房乙
4　夜矣卯乙抱遣去如

Modern Korean

1　선화 공주님은
2　남 몰래 시집가 두고
3　서동 서방을
4　밤에 몰래 안고 간다.

Sinitic text (Hyangch'al)

1　東京(2)明(2)期(1)月(2)良(1)
2　夜(2)入(2)伊(1)遊行(2)如(1/2)可(1)
3　入(2)良(1)沙(1)寢(2)矣(1)見(2)昆(1)
4　脚(2)烏(1)伊(1)四(2)是(1)良(1)(羅))(1)
5　二(2)兮(1)隱(1)吾(2)下(1)於(1)叱((古))(1)
6　二(2)兮(1)隱(1)誰(2)支(1)下(1)焉((古))(1)
7　本(2)矣(1)吾(2)下(1)是(1)如(1)馬(1)於((隱))(1)
8　奪(2)叱(1)良(1)乙(1)何(2)如(1)爲(2)理(1)((古))(1)

In the original text, (1) is sound borrowing and (2) is meaning borrowing.

Modern Korean

1　동경 밝은 달에
2　밤늦게 놀다가
3　집에 들어와서 다리를 보니
4　다리가 넷이어라
5　둘은 내 아내의 것이고
6　둘은 누구 것인가?
7　본래는 내 것이었지만
8　빼앗은 것을 어찌하리오

Key vocabulary

Line	Sinitic Korean	Modern Korean
1	(善化公主主隱) • 善化公主 princess. 隱 is a topic particle	• 공주 princess
2	(他)(密只)(嫁良置古) • 他 other • 密只 secretly • 嫁良置古: 嫁 means to get married and 古 is a sentence-ending particle	• 남몰래 unknown to others • 시집가 get married

3	(薯童)(房乙) • 薯童 is a name and can mean a potato/yam • 房乙: 房 is a husband and 乙 is an object/accusative particle	• 서방 one's husband
4	(夜矣)(卯乙)(抱遣去如) • 夜矣: 夜 means night and 矣 is a temporal/locative particle • 卯乙 secretly • 抱遣去如: 抱 means to embrace • 去 is to go • 如 is a sentence-ending particle	• 밤에 at night • 몰래 secretly • 안고 embrace • 가다 go

Line	Sinitic Korean	Modern Korean
1	• 東京 is the capital of Silla (신라) – that is Kyŏngju (경주) • 明期月良 明期 'bright' modifies 月 'moon' • 良 is a sentence-ending particle	• 동경 capital (lit. Eastern Capital)
2	• 夜入伊 夜 means night • 遊行如可 means to play • 如可 means whilst	• 밤늦게 late at night
3	• 入良沙 means to come back • 良沙 is an ending particle – the modern Korean translation is 와서 • 寢矣 means bed • 矣 is a locative particle • 見昆 means to see/look	• (at) home • room, space • 다 see, look
4	• 脚烏伊 means leg • 四是良羅 means four • 是良羅 in Modern Korean is 이러라 exclamative sentence ending	• 다 legs
5	• 二兮隱 means two things • 隱 is a topic particle • 吾下於叱 means mine • 古 sentence-ending particle	• 아내 wife
6	• 二兮隱 means two things • 隱 is a topic particle • 誰支下 means who • 誰支下 means whose one • 焉古 is an interrogative sentence-ending particle	
7	• 本矣 means originally • 吾下是如 means mine • 馬於隱 means however, Modern Korean equivalent word is 만은	• 본래 originally
8	• 奪叱良乙 means to steal • 乙 is an object/accusative particle • 何如爲理古 means what can I do?	• 어찌하리오 what can I do?

Discussion questions

1   Discuss the ways in which old Korean poetry was written using Chinese characters.
2   Discuss Korean history when the poem was written.
3   Who are Sŏdong and Princess Sŏnhwa referring to?
4   Discuss how the protagonist must have felt returning home to Ch'ŏyongga.

Comprehension questions: film extract

The 2008 film *A Frozen Flower* (쌍화점) is loosely based on the reign of King Kongmin of Koryŏ (1330–1374), and tells how the king, unable to impregnate the queen, asks his lover, the head of his guard, Chief Hong, to do this for him to secure an heir to the throne. Contrary to the story of Ch'ŏyong, the king begins to feel suspicious and jealous of the budding relationship between Chief Hong and the queen, despite the fact that he was the one who put them up to it in the first place. His suspicions first arise after the queen falls ill following the first consummation.

1   What does the king think is the cause of this fever? Is he right?
2   Why does the head doctor caution against drinking too much honeysuckle tea?
3   How does the king bring up the issue with Chief Hong?
4   How does the king respond to his growing suspicions?

Additional source material

One version of the Ch'ŏyong myth states that the person seducing his wife was in fact the smallpox god, and when Ch'ŏyong saw him together with his wife, rather than getting angry he danced outside in the rain. This impressed the smallpox god so greatly that he fled and swore never to enter a house with Ch'ŏyong's image on it ever again. From this legend, a court dance praying for health and prosperity was developed, called *Ch'ŏyongmu* (처용무). It is the oldest court dance still in existence today. You can see an introduction to the dance here: www.youtube.com/watch?v=iD4eoqRIJcs (accessed 07/02/19).

References

Kim, Dong-uk. 1963. 'Earliest Korean Songs and Poems.' *Korea Journal* 3(1): 8–10.
McBride, Richard D. 2010. *State and Society in Middle and Late Silla* (Early Korea Project occasional series). Cambridge, MA: Early Korea Project, Korea Institute, Harvard University.
McCann, David. 1997. 'The Story of Ch'oyong, a Parable of Literary Negotiation.' *Korean Studies* 21: 31.
Seth, Michael J. 2016. *A Concise History of Premodern Korea: From Antiquity through the Nineteenth Century* (2nd ed.). Lanham, MD: Rowman & Littlefield (Chapter 2 and Chapter 3).

2.6   구운몽 – 김만중 (*The Nine Cloud Dream* – Kim Manjung)

Introduction to the text

It is a seventeenth century Korean novel set in ninth century China. On the surface it is an entertaining tale of a young man who travels through two lifetimes accompanied by eight beautiful maidens; at its core, it is a philosophical novel about Buddhism and Confucianism. The author, Kim Manjung, wrote the novel while in exile, reputedly to console his mother.

(Gale 1922: V)

The theme of this work is that all of the world's money and fame is nothing but a passing dream. The author wanted to express the meaningless nature of mortal life to the reader. From this perspective, this work can be described as being centred on Buddhist principles, but the central elements of this novel are not limited to Buddhism, but include Confucian, Buddhist, and Taoist ideologies. The fact that the main character, who was born fatherless, has never seen his father's face and that this is a consequence of a sin from a former life is a Buddhist ideology. The descriptions of his mother's grace in raising him, and of his regret for not being more pious to her later in life, come from Confucian ideologies of filial piety. At the end of the story, the description of meaninglessness is influenced by Taoist beliefs. The character felt that his own life was meaningless and that his circumstances were futile. At this point, unable to find a place to live, he decided to return to religion by devoting himself completely to the Buddhism which he had known well earlier in life. What is the source of human life? Is there truly a paradise where eternal life and happiness can be enjoyed? Kim Manchung desired a world which was more ideal than that of dreams. When seen in this light, the text is still a Buddhist novel, but its Confucian themes of an ideal world were never far from the author's mind. In this novel, there are sections which express longing for women's liberation and equal living, but it is unique in the fact that women themselves are found professing polygamous lifestyles. This shows the extent to which polygamy at the time was defended as part of the way of life of the Confucian society's aristocrats and noble people.

Original text

태후가 말하였다. '내가 벌써 너와 의논코자 하였다. 양상서는 풍채와 문장이 세상에 으뜸일 뿐 아니라, 통소 한 곡조로 네 연분을 정하였으니 어찌 이 사람을 버리고 다른 데서 구하겠느냐. 양상서가 돌아오면 먼저 네 혼사를 지내고 정사도 여자로 첩을 삼게 하면, 양상서가 사양할 바가 없을 텐 데 네 뜻을 알지 못하여 염려스럽구나.'
　공주가 대답하여 말하였다.
'소저가 일생 투기(妬忌)를 알지 못하니 어찌 정가 여자를 꺼리겠습니까? 다만 양상서가 처음에 납폐하였다가 다시 첩을 삼으면 예가 아니요, 또 정사도는 여러 대에 걸친 재상의 집입니 다. 그 여자로 남의 첩이 되게 함이 어찌 원통치 아니하겠습니까?'
　태후가 말하였다. '네 뜻이 그러하면 어찌 하면 좋겠느냐?'
　공주가 말하였다. '들으니 제후에게는 세 부인이 가하다 합니다. 양상서가 성공하고 돌아오면 후왕(侯王)을 봉할 것이니, 두 부인 취함이 어찌 마땅치 아니하겠습니까?'
　태후가 말하였다. '안된다. 사람이 귀천이 없다면 관계치 아니하겠지마는 너는 선왕(先王)의 귀한 딸이요, 지금 임금의 사랑하는 누이다. 어찌 여염집 천한 사람과 함께 섬기겠느냐?'
　공주가 말하였다.
'선비가 어질면 만승천자(萬乘天子)도 벗한다 하니 관계치 아니하며, 또 정가 여자는 자색과 덕행이 옛 사람이라도 미치기 어렵다 하오니 그러하면 소녀에게는 다행입니다. 아무튼 그 여 자를 친히 보아 듣던 말과 같으면 몸을 굽혀 섬임이 가하고, 그렇치 아니하면 첩을 삼거나 마음대로 하십시오.'
　태후가 말하였다.
'여자의 투기는 예부터 있는데 너는 어찌 이토록 인후(仁厚)하냐? 내 명일에 정가 여자를 부르겠다.'
　공주가 말하였다.
'아무리 낭랑의 명이 있어도 아프다고 평계하면 부질없고, 더구나 재상가의 여자를 어찌 불러 들이겠습니까?'

'첩 등은 먼 지방의 천인입니다. 비록 승상의 한번 돌아보신 은혜를 입었으나 두 부인께서 한 자리 땅을 허락하지 않으실까 두려워 감히 오지 못하였습니다. 서울에 들어와 두 공주께서 관저(關雎)와 규목(樛木)의 덕이 있으심을 듣고 이제야 나아와 뵙고자 했는데, 마침 승상께서 성대히 노신다는 것을 듣고 외람되게 참예하고 돌아오니 첩 등의 영광스러운 행운인가 합니다.'

공주가 웃으며 말하였다.

'우리 궁중에 춘색(春色)이 난만한 것은 다 우리 형제의 공이니 승상은 아십니까?' 승상이 크게 웃으며 말하였다. '저 두 사람이 새로와 공주의 위풍이 두려워 아첨하는 말을 공주는 공을 삼고자 합니까?'

월왕이 말하였다.

'승상의 복은 보통 사람과 같을 바가 아닙니다. 다만 공주에게도 복이 되겠습니까? 원컨대 낭랑은 이 말씀으로 승상을 심문하십시오.'

승상이 말하였다. '월왕이 신에게 겼단 말은 이태백이 최호(崔顥)의 시를 겁내는 것과 같습니다. 공주에게 복이 되고 아니됨은 공주에게 물으십시오.'

공주가 대답하여 말하였다. '부부는 한몸이니 영욕고락(榮辱苦樂)이 어찌 다르겠습니까?'

월왕이 말하였다. '누이의 말이 비록 좋으나 자고로 부마 중에 누가 승상같이 방탕하였겠습니까? 청컨대 승상을 벌하십시오.'

Key vocabulary

태후	the Empress
연분	a close tie, connection
소저	a young lady
투기	jealousy
납폐	traditional wedding gifts (of blue and red silk)
재상	minister
부인	wife
귀천	high and low rank
선왕	His late Majesty
여염집	a commoner's house
선비	a sage or scholar (Confucian)
어질다	benevolent
만승천자	great king or emperor (son of heaven, ruler of a thousand chariots)
자색	beauty
덕행	virtuous achievement
인후	benevolence and generosity
천인	a lowly person
승상	title used by a senior to honorifically refer to a noble junior
공주	princess
관저와 규목의 덕	a phrase used to describe exceptional virtue
춘색	spring flowers or scenery
심문	to inquire or interrogate
신	a term used to refer to oneself
영욕고락	gladness and sorrow
방탕	extravagant

Comprehension questions: text

1. What problem arose in the Princess's marriage?
2. What does the Empress think about her daughter?
3. Why does the Princess say she can't command Cheung See to come to them?
4. What are the concubines' attitudes towards the two Princesses?

Comprehension questions: film extract

The 2003 film *Untold Scandal* (스캔들 – 조선남녀상열지사) is a reimagining of the 18th-century French novel, *Les Liaisons Dangereuses*, set in Chosŏn dynasty Korea. Contrary to the acceptance of multiple wives that is held up as an ideal in *Kuunmong*, in this film Lady Cho is jealous of her husband's desire for a new concubine, and formulates a plan with her cousin, the womaniser Chowŏn, to destroy this match.

1. How does Lady Cho's husband describe his new concubine?
2. Why does Lady Cho want to have the girl brought to the house earlier?
3. What is her plan for destroying the match?
4. What bet does she make with Chowŏn?

Additional source material

A recent song dealing with the issue of jealousy is Monsta X's 'Jealousy,' released in 2018.

Further discussion questions

1. What types of polygamy were considered morally acceptable in this time period, and what kinds were not?
2. What was the prevailing attitude in premodern Korea about women's jealousy?

References

Deuchler, Martina. 1992. The Confucian Transformation of Korea: A Study of Society and Ideology, Cambridge, MA: Council on East Asian Studies, Harvard University: Distributed by Harvard University Press.

Kim, Yongmin, & Pettid, Michael J. 2011. *Women and Confucianism in Chosŏn Korea: New Perspectives*. Albany: SUNY Press.

Willoughby, Heather A. 2011. 'The Performance of Virtue and the Loss of Female Individuality in Chosŏn Korea.' *Asian Women* 27(2): 51–79.

Yi, Songmi. 2002. *Fragrance, Elegance, and Virtue: Korean Women in Traditional Arts and Humanities*. Seoul, Korea: Daewonsa.

3 Friendship and loyalty

3.1 오우가 – 윤선도 (*The Song of Five Friends* – Yun Sŏndo)

Introduction to the text

This poem was written by Kosan Yun Sŏndo (1587–1671) when he was 56. It is written in the style of a *shijo*, a genre of which Yun is considered a master. This is one of his most famous poems and shows his love for nature and its virtues, as he employs characteristics of nature to describe important attributes of a true friend. The author particularly highlights *su* (수/水, water), *sŏk* (석/石, stone), *song* (송/松, pine), *chuk* (죽/竹, bamboo), and *wŏl* (월/月, moon). Water is described as clean, stone as unchanging, pine as constant, bamboo as uncompromising, and the moon as quiet and unassuming. These are the virtues of a *sŏnbi* (Confucian scholar) in the traditional sense. Kosan was persecuted by the opposition party because he didn't actively get involved in *Pyŏngjahoran* (병자호란/丙子胡亂, 1636–1637), the Qing invasion of Chosŏn, and frequently got into trouble at court due to his forthright nature. He spent most of his life in exile, and one can see how this poem emphasising proper behaviour, advocating the sort of upright and uncompromising manner that lead him into exile in the first place, is a form of defence for him having stayed true to his principles.

Original text

Middle Korean

내 버디 몃치나 하니 수석(水石)과 송죽(松竹)이라
동산(東山)의 달 오르니 긔 더옥 반갑고야
두어라 이 다삿 밧긔 또 더하야 머엇하리

구룸빗치 조타 하나 검기랄 자로 한다
바람 소래 맑다 하나 그칠 적이 하노매라
조코도 그츨 뉘 업기난 믈뿐인가 하노라

고즌 므스 일로 퓌며서 쉬이 디고
플은 어이 하야 프르난 닷 누르나니
아마도 변티 아닐산 바회뿐인가 하노라

더우면 곳 피고 치우면 닙 디거
솔아 너난 얻디 눈서리랄 모라난다
구천(九泉)의 불희 고단 줄을 글로 하야 아노라

52 *Friendship and loyalty*

나모도 아닌 거시 플도 아닌 거시
곳기난 뉘 시기며 속은 어이 뷔연난다
더러코 사시(四時)에 프르니 그를 됴하 하노라

쟈근 거시 노피 떠서 만물을 다 비취니
밤듕의 광명(光明)이 너만하니 또 잇나냐
보고도 말 아니 하니 내 벋인가 하노라

Modern Korean

나의 벗이 몇인가 헤아려 보니 水石(수석)과 松竹(송죽)이라.
東山(동산)에 달이 밝게 떠오르니 그것은 더욱 반가운 일이로다.
나머지는 그냥 두어라. 이 다섯 외에 더 있으면 무엇하겠는가?

구름의 빛깔이 깨끗하다고 하지만 자주 검어지네.
바람 소리가 맑다지만, 그칠 때가 많도다.
깨끗하고도 그칠 때가 없는 것은 물뿐인가 하노라.

꽃은 무슨 까닭에 피자마자 쉬이 져버리고,
풀은 또 어찌하여 푸른 듯하다가 이내 누런빛을 띠는가?
아마도 변하지 않는 것은 바위뿐인가 하노라.

따뜻해지면 꽃이 피고, 추워지면 잎이 떨어지는데,
소나무야, 너는 어찌하여 눈서리를 모르고 살아가는가?
깊은 땅 속(혹은저승)까지 뿌리가 곧게 뻗은 것을 그것으로 하여 알겠노라.

나무도 아니고 풀도 아닌 것이, 곧게 자라기는 누가 시켰으며,
또 속은 어찌하여 비어 있는가?
저렇게 사철 늘 푸르니, 나는 그것을 좋아하노라.

작은 것이 높이 떠서 온세상을 다 비추니
한밤중에 광명이 너보다 더한 것이 또 있겠느냐?
보고도 말을 하지 않으니 나의 벗인가 하노라

Key vocabulary

나의벗	my friends
보다	count
떠오르다	rise
반가운일	good news
~로다	indeed, it is
두어라	leave it [as is]
-느냐	rhetorical ending
구름의빛깔	the colour of the clouds
검어지다	blacken
맑다	clean, pure, sweet
그치다	ease, stop

~을 때	when
~도다	What! How! Alas!
까닭	reason, cause, grounds
피다	blossom
~자마자	as soon as
쉬이	easily
져버리다	wilt away
풀	grass
어찌하여	wherefore
푸른	green
이내	soon
누런빛	yellow colour
띠다	be tinged with
아마도	perhaps
변하다	change
바위	rock, boulder
눈서리	snow and frost
살아가다	live
저승	afterlife
뿌리	root
곧게뻗은	upright
곧게자라다	grow straight
시키다	make to do (live, grow)
비다	empty
사철	(in all) seasons
떠서	rise
온세상을	the whole world
비추다	shine
한밤중에	at midnight
광명	silver lining
더한것이	something added
보고도	even if (you) see/watch
-노라	emphatic ending

Comprehension questions: text

1 Why does Yun Sŏndo consider clouds and wind inferior to water?
2 What merit does stone have that plants do not?
3 What allows the pine tree to stay green throughout all seasons?
4 Why is the moon Yun's friend?

Comprehension questions: drama/film extract

The KBS2 drama *Sungkyunkwan Scandal* (성균관 스캔들, 2010) is a story of a woman, Kim Yunhŭi, who pretends to be her ill brother, Kim Yunshik, to provide for the family at a time when women were not allowed to work or be educated. A chance run-in with Yi Sŏnjun, the son of a high-ranking court minister, convinces him of Kim's talents, and he encourages

54 *Friendship and loyalty*

her to take the civil service exam and work in government. In episode two, the scene where the king reads Kim's exam paper highlights some of the principles that Kosan Yun Sŏndo encouraged scholars to uphold.

1   What was the exam question set by the king?
2   What did Kim Yunshik/Yunhŭi write in her exam response?
3   Why did Yi Sŏnjun hire Kim as a substitute exam taker?
4   What is the king's response to this?

Further discussion questions

1   Do you think the virtues praised by Yun Sŏndo are still highly regarded in society today?
2   From the virtues you consider most important, which aspects of nature best reflect these virtues?

References

Lee, Peter H. 2003. *A History of Korean Literature*. Cambridge; New York: Cambridge University Press. (Chapter 10: Late Chosŏn *Sijo*).
McCann, David R. 1993. 'Chinese Diction in Korean *Shijo*.' *Korean Studies* 17: 92–104.
Yun, Sŏndo (trans. Kevin O'Rourke). 2001. *The Fisherman's Calendar*. Seoul: Eastward.

3.2 지란지교를 꿈꾸며 – 유안진 (*Dreaming of a Good and Noble Friendship* – Yu Anjin)

Introduction to the text

This essay was written by the acclaimed South Korean poet, Yu Anjin (1941–). She is currently an Emeritus Professor at Seoul National University. Yu made her literary debut on the recommendation of the famous Korean poet Pak Mokwŏl (1938–1978), and eventually became well-known for her sensitive and feminine writing style as an essayist.

Kwanjung and P'osuk were historical figures who lived during the Warring States Period (475–221 BC). The two were friends from a young age. Kwanjung became a famous minister, but he always acknowledged P'osuk's help in getting to that position. Kwanjung said of his relationship with his friend:

> When I was young, we ran a business together. I took more than P'osuk, but he did not think I was greedy, and understood that it was because I was poorer than him. When I obtained my position in the government, people criticised me about my mistakes. But P'osuk did not blame me for my inabilities, but said that my time had not yet come. We went to war together. I ran away three times, and people blamed me for being a coward. P'osuk told me that it was because I had an elderly mother at home. I was also sentenced to death, but P'osuk persuaded others to spare my life. He also helped me to become a minister. I must say that it is my parents who gave birth to me, but it is P'osuk who truly understands me.

Their friendship is regarded as '*Kwanp'ojigyo*,' which literally means, 'the friendship of Kwanjung and P'osuk.' This type of close friendship is a key feature of Yu's essay.

Original text

저녁을 먹고 나면 허물없이 찾아가 차 한잔을 마시고 싶다고 말할 수 있는 친구가 있었으면 좋겠다. 입은 옷을 갈아입지 않고, 김치냄새가 좀 나더라도 흉보지 않을 친구가 우리 집 가까이에 살았으면 좋겠다.

비 오는 오후나, 눈 내리는 밤에도 고무신을 끌고 찾아가도 좋을 친구, 밤늦도록 공허한 마음도 마음놓고 열어 보일 수 있고 악의 없이 남의 얘기를 주고받고 나서도 말이 날까 걱정되지 않는 친구가 ... 사람이 자기 아내나 남편, 제 형제나 제 자식하고만 사랑을 나눈다면 어찌 행복해질 수 있을까. 영원히 없을수록 영원을 꿈꾸도록 서로 돕는 진실한 친구가 필요하리라.

그가 여성이라도 좋고 남성이라도 좋다. 나보다 나이가 많아도 좋고 동갑이거나 적어도 좋다. 다만 그의 인품은 맑은 강물처럼 조용하고 은근하며, 깊고 신선하며, 예술과 인생을 소중히 여길 만큼 성숙한 사람이면 된다.

그는 반드시 잘 생길 필요가 없고, 수수하나 멋을 알고 중후한 몸가짐을 할 수 있으면 된다.

때로 약간의 변덕과 신경질을 부려도 그것이 애교로 통할 수 있을 정도면 괜찮고, 나의 변덕과 괜한 흥분에도 적절하게 맞장구쳐 주고 나서, 얼마의 시간이 흘러 내가 평온해지거든, 부드럽고 세련된 표현으로 충고를 아끼지 않았으면 좋겠다.

나는 많은 사람을 사랑하고 싶지는 않다. 많은 사람과 사귀기도 원치 않는다. 나의 일생에 한두 사람과 끊어지지 않는 아름답고 향기로운 인연으로 죽기까지 지속되길 바란다. 나는 여러 나라 여러 곳을 여행하면서, 끼니와 잠을 아껴 될수록 많은 것을 구경하였다. 그럼에도 지금은 그 많은 구경 중에 기막힌 감회로 남은 것은 없다. 만약 내가 한두 곳 한두 가지만 제대로 감상했더라면, 두고두고 자산이 되었을걸.

우정이라 하면 사람들은 관포지교를 말한다. 그러나 나는 친구를 괴롭히고 싶지 않듯이 나 또한 끝없는 인내로 베풀기만할 재간이 없다. 나는 도 닦으며 살기를 바라지는 않고, 내 친구도 성현 같아지기를 바라지는 않는다.

나는 될수록 정직하게 살고 싶고, 내 친구도 재미나 위안을 위해서 그저 제 자리서 탄로 나는 약간의 거짓말을 하는 재치와 위트를 가졌으면 싶을 뿐이다.

나는 때때로 맛있는 것을 내가 더 먹고싶을 테고, 내가 더 예뻐 보이기를 바라겠지만, 금방 그 마음을 지울 줄도 알 것이다. 때로 나는 얼음 풀리는 냇물이나 가을 갈대숲 기러기 울음을 친구보다 더 좋아할 수 있겠으나, 결국은 우정을 제일로 여길 것이다.

우리는 흰눈 속 참대 같은 기상을 지녔으나 들꽃처럼 나약할 수 있고, 아첨 같은 양보는 싫어하지만 이따금 밑지며 사는 아량도 갖기를 바란다.

우리는 명성과 권세, 재력을 중시하지도 부러워하지도 경멸하지도 않을 것이며, 그보다는 자기답게 사는 데 더 매력을 느끼려 애쓸 것이다.

우리가 항상 지혜롭진 못하더라도, 자기의 곤란을 벗어나기 위해 비록 진실일지라도 타인을 팔진 않을 것이다. 오해를 받더라도 묵묵할 수 있는 어리석음과 배짱을 지니기를 바란다. 우리의 외모가 아름답지 않다 해도 우리의 향기 많은 아름답게 지니리라.

우리는 시기하는 마음 없이 남의 성공을 얘기하며, 경쟁하지 않고 자기하고 싶은 일을 하되, 미친 듯이 몰두하게 되기를 바란다.

우리는 우정과 애정을 소중히 여기되 목숨을 거는 만용은 피할 것이다. 그래서 우리의 우정은 애정과도 같으며, 우리의 애정 또한 우정과도 같아서 요란한 빛깔과 시끄러운 소리도 피할 것이다.

나는 반다지를 닦다가 그를 생각할 것이며, 화초에 물을 주다가, 안개 낀 아침 창문을 열다가, 가을 하늘의 흰 구름을 바라보다 까닭 없이 현기증을 느끼다가 문득 그가 보고 싶어지며, 그도 그럴 때 나를 찾을 것이다.

그는 때로 울고 싶어지기도 하겠고, 내게도 울 수 있는 눈물과 추억이 있을 것이다. 우리에겐 다시 젊어질 수 있는 추억이 있으나, 늙은 일에 초조하지 않을 웃음도 만들

Friendship and loyalty

어낼 것이다. 우리는 눈물을 사랑하되 헤프지 않게, 가지는 멋보다 풍기는 멋을 사랑하며. 냉면을 먹을 때는 농부처럼 먹을 줄 알며, 스테이크를 자를 때는 여왕보다 품위 있게, 군밤을 아이처럼 까먹고, 차를 마실 때는 백작부인보다 우아해지리라.

우리는 푼돈을 벌기 위해 하기 싫은 일을 하지 않을 것이며, 천년을 늙어도 항상 가락을 지니는 오동나무처럼, 일생을 춥게 살아도 향기를 팔지 않는 매화처럼, 자유로운 제 모습을 잃지 않고 살고자 애쓰며 서로 격려하리라.

우리는 누구도 미워하지 않으며, 특별히 한두 사람을 사랑한다 하여 많은 사람을 싫어하진 않으리라. 우리가 멋진 글을 못 쓰더라도 쓰는 일을 택한 것에 후회하지 않듯이, 남의 약점도 안쓰럽게 여기리라.

내가 길을 가다가 한 묶음 꽃을 사서 그에게 안겨줘도, 그는 날 주책이라고 나무라지 않으며, 건널목이 아닌 데로 찻길을 건너도 나의 교양을 비웃지 않을게다. 나 또한 더러 그의 눈에 눈곱이 끼더라도, 이 사이에 고춧가루가 끼었다 해도 그의 숙녀 됨이나 그의 신사다움을 의심치 않으며, 오히려 인간적인 유유함을 느끼게 될 게다.

우리의 손이 비록 작고 여리나 서로를 버티어주는 기둥이 될 것이며, 우리의 눈에 핏발이 서더라도 총기가 사라진 것은 아니며, 눈빛이 흐리고 시력이 어두워질수록 서로를 살펴주는 불빛이 되어주리라.

그러다가 어느 날이 홀연히 오더라도 축복처럼, 웨딩드레스처럼 수의를 입게 되리라. 같은 날 또는 다른 날이라도.

세월이 흐르거든 묻힌 자리에서 더 고운 품종의 지란이 돋아 피어, 맑고 높은 향기로 다시 만나지리라.

Key vocabulary

고무신	rubber slippers
밤늦도록	late into the night
공허한	empty
마음놓고	at ease
열어	open up
악의없이	harmlessly
걱정되지	worry
인품	personality
약간의	a little
괜한	unnecessary
흥분	agitation
적절하게	properly, adequately, suitably
맞장구쳐	echo
흘러	flow
사귀기도	acquainted
구경	sights
제대로	properly
두고두고	for a long time
푼돈	a few pennies/small sum
관포지교	an extremely close friendship; inseperable
가락	melody
성현	saint
나무라	scold
홀연히	all of a sudden

Comprehension questions: text

1 What are the attributes the author hopes for in a close friend?
2 What kinds of adjectives did the author use to describe an ideal friend?
3 What are some characteristics of 'close friendship' described by the author?
4 What does the author have to say about the outward appearance of an ideal friend?

Comprehension questions: drama extract

The SBS drama *A Gentleman's Dignity* (신사의 품격, 2012) follows the lives of four close friends: Kim Tojin, Im T'aesan, Ch'oe Yun and Yi Chŏngrok. Now in their 40s, they have been friends since they were 18, and have gone through all sorts of highs and lows in life together. The beginning of episode 16 is particularly poignant in showing the closeness of their relationship.

1 Where is Kim Tojin headed, and what is he planning to do there?
2 What excuse does Yi Chŏngrok give for his wedding ring being in his pocket?
3 What does Im T'aesan claim to be an expert of?
4 What does Ch'oe Yun say his friends mean to him?

Additional source material

While the above drama extract focuses on a close group of male friends, the 2011 film *Sunny* (써니) does the same for a close group of female friends.

Further discussion questions

1 What are some of the situations in this text that seem specific to Korean culture?
2 Think of the situation described about red pepper powder and other Korea-specific situations. What is a similar situation that could be seen in a Western context?

References

Cho, Namhyun, & Oh, Saeyoung. 1991. *Understanding Modern Korean Literature*. Seoul: Korean Culture and Arts Foundation.
Wu, David. (2013). 'Bao Shuya: Righteous Judge of Talent.' *The Epoch Times* B6.
Translation Tuesday: Two poems by Yoo An-Jin. Available online at: www.theguardian.com/books/translation-tuesdays-by-asymptote-journal/2017/mar/29/translation-tuesday-two-poems-by-yoo-an-jin.

3.3 달밤 – 이태준 (*Moonlit Night* – Yi T'aejun)

Introduction to the text

This novel, by Yi T'aejun (1904–1960) was first presented in 1933 in *Chung Ang*. The story links the narrator with a man named Hwang Sugŏn. Hwang Sugŏn is presented as naive and slightly dull, and the story explores the pain he experiences upon being confronted with the cruel world. He is called a failure by the people around him, and he is unsure whether he will be able to live on any longer. The narrator moves from Munan to Sŏngbukdong in

58 *Friendship and loyalty*

the countryside, where he is finally able to feel like a successful individual. This is because people who are called 'failures' are able to live happily. In Munan, successful people are everywhere and 'failures' can't even go outside – and even if they do, no one pays them any attention. But in the countryside, such people are able to live without hiding who they really are. In the countryside, there is room even for the rough and uneducated opinions of this lower class of people. The narrator eventually meets Hwang Sugŏn and enjoys conversing with him. The two people are able to connect in a way they have not connected with people before. Through these characters, the author is trying to show readers about the unfair nature of the world we live in. It is emphasised that in such a competitive world, people of less talent or less fortunate background – for example, a person whose greatest goal in life is to be a paper boy – are unable to live successfully. This emphasis allows the reader to reflect on the right these people have to a happy life, and how the world we live in makes that unattainable for them.

Original text

성북동(城北洞)으로 이사 나와서 한 대엿새 되었을까, 그날 밤 나는 보던 신문을 머리맡에 밀어 던지고 누워 새삼스럽게,
　'여기도 정말 시골이로군!'
하였다. 무어 바깥이 컴컴한 걸 처음 보고 시냇물 소리와 쏴— 하는 솔바람 소리를 처음 들어서가 아니라 황수건이라는 사람을 이날 저녁에 처음 보았기 때문이다. 그는 말 몇 마디 사귀지 않아서 곧 못난이란 것이 드러났다. 이 못난이는 성북동의 산들보다 물들보다, 조그만 지름길들보다 더 나에게 성북동이 시골이란 느낌을 풍겨 주었다. 서울이라고 못난이가 없을 리야 없겠지만 대처에서는 못난이들이 거리에 나와 행세를 하지 못하고, 시골에선 아무리 못난이라도 마음놓고 나와 다니는 때문인지, 못난이는 시골에만 있는 것처럼 흔히 시골에서 잘 눈에 뜨인다. 그리고 또 흔히 그는 태고 때 사람처럼 그 우둔하면서도 천진스런 눈을 가지고, 자기 동리에 처음 들어서는 손에게 가장 순박한 시골의 정취를 돋워 주는 것이다. 그런데 그날 밤 황수건이는 열시나 되어서 우리집을 찾아왔다. 그는 어두운 마당에서 꽥 지르는 소리로,
　'아, 이 댁이 문안서 . . .'
하면서 들어섰다. 잡담 제하고 큰일이나 난 사람처럼 건넌방문 앞으로 달려들더니,
　'저, 저 문안 서대문 거리라나요, 어디선가 나오신 댁입쇼?'
한다.
보니 합비는 안 입었으되 신문을 들고 온 것이 신문 배달부다.
　'그렇소, 신문이오?'
　'아, 그런 걸 사흘이나 저, 저 건너쪽에만 가 찾었습죠. 제기 . . .'
하더니 신문을 방에 들이뜨리며,
　'그런뎁쇼, 왜 이렇게 죄꼬만 집을 사구 와 겝쇼. 아, 내가 알었드면 이 아래 큰 개와집도 많은걸입쇼 . . .'
한다. 하 말이 황당스러워 유심히 그의 생김을 내다보니 눈에 얼른 두드러지는 것이 빡빡 깎은 머리로되 보통 크다는 정도 이상으로 골이 크다. 그런데다 옆으로 보니 장구 대가리다.
　'그렇소? 아무튼 집 찾느라고 수고했소.'
하니 그는 큰 눈과 큰 입이 일시에 히죽거리며,
　'뭘입쇼, 이게 제 업인뎁쇼.'
하고 날래 물러서지 않고 목을 길게 빼어 방 안을 살핀다. 그러더니 묻지도 않는데,
　'저는입쇼, 이 동네 사는 황수건이라 합니다 . . .'
하고 인사를 붙인다. 나도 깍듯이 내 성명을 대었다. 그는 또 싱글벙글하면서,

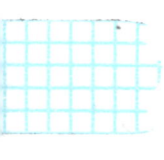

'댁엔 개가 없구면입쇼.'
한다.
'아직 없소.'
하니,
'개 그까짓 거 두지 마십쇼.'
한다.
'왜 그렇소?'
물으니, 그는 얼른 대답하는 말이,
'신문 보는 집엔입쇼, 개를 두지 말아야 합니다.'
한다. 이것 재미있는 말이다 하고 나는,
'왜 그렇소?'
하고 또 물었다.
'아, 이 뒷동네 은행소에 댕기는 집엔입쇼, 망아지만한 개가 있는뎁쇼, 아, 신문을 배달할 수가 있어얍죠.'
'왜?'
'막 깨물랴고 덤비는걸입쇼.'
한다. 말 같지 않아서 나는 웃기만 하니 그는 더욱 신을 낸다.
'그눔의 개 그저, 한번, 양떡을 멕여 대야 할 텐데...'
하면서 주먹을 부르대는데 보니, 손과 팔목은 머리에 비기어 반비례로 작고 가느다랗다.
'어서 곤할 텐데 가 자시오.'
하니 그는 마지못해 물러서며,
'선생님, 참 이선생님 편안히 주뭅쇼. 저이 집은 여기서 얼마 안 되는 걸입쇼.'
하더니 돌아갔다.
그는 이튿날 저녁, 집을 알고 오는데도 아홉시가 지나서야,
'신문 배달해 왔습니다.'
하고 소리를 치며 들어섰다.
'오늘은 왜 늦었소?'
물으니,
'자연 그럽죠.'
하고 다른 이야기를 꺼냈다.
자기는 워낙 이 아래 있는 삼산학교에서 일을 보다 어떤 선생하고 뜻이 덜 맞아 나왔다는 것, 지금은 신문 배달을 하나 원배달이 아니라 보조배달이라는 것, 저희 집엔 양친과 형님 내외와 조카 하나와 저희 내외까지 식구가 일곱이라는 것, 저희 아버지와 저희 형님의 이름은 무엇무엇이며, 자기 이름은 황가인데다가 목숨수(壽)자하고 세울건(建)자로 황수건이기 때문에, 아이들이 노랑수건이라고 놀리어서 성북동에서는 가가호호에서 노랑수건 하면, 다 자긴 줄 알리라고 자랑스럽게 이야기하다가 이날도,
'어서 그만 다른 집에도 신문을 갖다 줘야 하지 않소?'
하니까 그때서야 마지못해 나갔다.
우리집에서는 그까짓 반편과 무얼 대꾸를 해가지고 그러느냐 하되, 나는 그와 지껄이기가 좋았다. 그는 아무것도 아닌 것을 가지고 열심스럽게 이야기하는 것이 좋았고, 그와는 아무리 오래 지껄이어도 힘이 들지 않고, 또 아무리 오래 지껄이고 나도 웃음 밖에는 남는 것이 없어 기분이 거뜬해지는 것도 좋았다. 그래서 나는 무슨 일을 하는 중만 아니면 한참씩 그의 말을 받아 주었다. 어떤 날은 서로 말이 막히기도 했다. 대답이 막히는 것이 아니라 무슨 말을 해야 할까 하고 막히었다. 그러나 그는 늘 나보다 빠르게 이야깃거리를 잘 찾아냈다. 오뉴월인데도 '꿩고기를 잘 먹느냐?'고도 묻고, '양복은 저고리를 먼저 입느냐 바지를 먼저 입느냐?'고도 묻고 '소와 말과 싸움을 붙이면 어느 것이 이기겠느냐?'는 둥, 아무튼 그가 애깃거리를 취재하는 방면은 기상천외로

여간 범위가 넓지 않은 데는 도저히 당할 수가 없었다. 하루는 나는 '평생 소원이 무엇이냐?'고 그에게 물어 보았다. 그는 '그까짓 것쯤 얼른 대답하기는 누워서 떡먹기'라고 하면서 평생 소원은 자기도 원배달이 한번 되었으면 좋겠다는 것이었다.

Key vocabulary

달밤	moonlit night
대엿새	five or six years
새삼스럽게	abruptly
시골	countryside
못난이	a fool, a less-than average person
잡담	chatter, small talk
황당스러워	disoriented
마지못해	reluctantly
노랑수건	yellow towel
애깃거리	things to talk about
소원	wishes, dreams, hopes

Comprehension questions: text

1 What does the narrator say about less-than-average people?
2 How does the author show that Mr. Hwang is such a person?
3 How does the narrator's perception of Mr. Hwang seem to shift?
4 Based on this text, what contrasts seem to have existed between city and country life in Korea in this time period?

Comprehension questions: drama extract

The MBC drama, *Shopping King Louis* (쇼핑왕루이, 2016) shows the affectionate love story between Louis, a rich heir, and Ko Pokshil, a country bumpkin who comes to Seoul looking for her brother. The playing field between them is levelled when Louis loses his memory as well as all his possessions. When he first sees Pokshil in a documentary on countryside life (in episode one), he shows a similar kind of curiosity and appreciation for her simple life, much as we see the narrator having for Mr. Hwang in the text extract above. This stands in particularly stark contrast to the ostentatious but empty life Louis leads.

1 Who is Paek Mari, and why does she call Louis?
2 Why does Pokshil gather medicinal herbs to sell at the market?
3 What is the thing she most wishes to possess and why?
4 How does Louis respond to watching the documentary?

Further discussion questions

1 How does the narrator's initial prejudice about the countryside affect his interactions with Mr. Hwang?
2 Can you think of other world literature that displays a similar contrast between city and country people?
3 How does the author use language (specifically dialect) to portray this difference?
4 How do western authors do the same thing?

# References

Anna, Fifield. 2016. *Young South Koreans Call Their Country 'Hell' and Look for Ways out*, 31/01/2016. Available online at: www.washingtonpost.com/world/asia_pacific/young-south-koreans-call-their-country-hell-and-look-for-ways-out/2016/01/30/34737c06-b967-11e5-85cd-5ad59bc19432_story.html?noredirect=on&utm_term=.3674d650f33b.

Epstein, Stephen, & Jung, Sun. 2011. 'Korean Youth Netizenship and its Discontents.' *Media International Australia* 141(1): 78–86.

Kim, Mira. 2001. *Exploring Sources of Life Meaning Among Koreans*. MA Dissertation, Trinity Western University, Langley, BC.

Oh, Byungsun. 1997. 'Cultural Values and Human Rights: The Korean Perspective.' In *Human Rights in Asian Cultures, Continuity, and Change: A Regional Report in Support of the UN Decade for Human Rights Education*. Osaka: Hurights Osaka, pp. 217–49.

3.4 우리들의 일그러진 영웅 – 이문열 (*Our Twisted Hero – Yi Munyŏl*)

Introduction to the text

This work by Yi Munyŏl (b. 1948) was published in 1987 in *World Literature* and received 11 awards in the year of its publication. The narrator transfers to a small countryside school in a little place with nothing to see. The narrator is shocked and overwhelmed by the strict hierarchical system in place at the elementary school, and suffers at the hands of his classmates, the all-powerful class president, and the unhelpful teacher. His unique talents, and his parents' successful career, are of little help to him in this setting. Through the narration of a young child, and the extreme example of hierarchy among such young children, the author presents a powerful criticism of this aspect of Korean society.

In this extract, the narrator looks back and recalls the circumstances which led to his moving schools as a young boy, from a prestigious Seoul institution to a small-town backwater. He dwells on his first impressions of the new school, listing all the many points which had made him feel incredibly disappointed back then, and comparing them unfavourably with how things had been for him in Seoul. The architecture, the teachers, and the other pupils all come under his scrutiny, and invariably suffer in comparison. Throughout the extract, the narrator also hints at an 'evil fate' or destiny that was later to befall him, and which even now, almost 30 years later, causes him to look back in anger and gloom.

Original text

벌써 삼십 년이 다 돼 가지만, 그해 봄에서 가을까지의 외롭고 힘들었던 싸움을 돌이켜 보면 언제나 그때처럼 막막하고 암담해진다.

어쩌면 그런 싸움이야말로 우리 삶이[生] 흔히 빠지게 되는 어떤 상태이고, 실은 아직도 내가 거기서 벗어나지 못했기 때문에 받게 되는 느낌인지도 모르겠다.

자유당 정권이 아직은 그 마지막 기승을 부리고 있던 그해 삼 월 중순, 나는 그때껏 자랑스레 다니던 서울의 명문 국민 학교를 떠나 한 작은 읍(邑)의 별로 볼 것 없는 국민 학교로 전학을 가게 되었다.

공무원이었다가 바람을 맞아 거기까지 날려간 아버지를 따라 가족 모두가 이사를 가게 된 까닭이었을, 그때 나는 열두 살에 갓 올라간 5학년이었다.

그 전학 첫날 어머님의 손에 이끌려 들어서게 된 Y 국민학교는 여러 가지로 실망스럽기 그지없었다.

붉은 벽돌로 지은 웅장한 3층 본관을 중심으로 줄줄이 늘어섰던 새 교사(校舍)만 보아 온 내게는, 낡은 일본식 시멘트 건물 한 채와 검은 타르를 칠한 판자 가교사(假校舍) 몇 채로 이루어진 그 학교가 어찌나 초라해 보이는지
　갑자기 영락한 소공자(少公子)의 비애(悲哀)같은 턱없는 감상에 젖어들기까지 했다. 크다는 것과 좋다는 것은 무관함에도 불구하고, 한 학년이 열여섯 학급이나 되는 학교에서 공부해 온 탓인지 한 학년이 겨우 여섯 학급밖에 안 된다는 것도 그 학교를 까닭 없이 얕보게 했고, 남녀가 섞인 반에서만 공부해 온 눈에는 남학생반 여학생반이 엄격하게 나뉘어져 있는 것도 촌스럽게만 보였다.
　거기다가 그런 내 첫인상을 더욱 굳혀 준 것은 교무실이었다.
　내가 그때껏 다녔던 학교의 교무실은 서울에서도 손꼽는 학교답게 넓고 번들거렸고, 거기 있는 선생님들도 한결 같이 깔끔하고 활기에 찬 이들이었다.
　그런데 겨울 교실 하나 넓이의 그 교무실에는 시골 아저씨들처럼 후줄그레한 선생님들이 맥없이 앉아 굴뚝같이 담배 연기만 뿜어 대고 있는 것이었다.
　나를 데리고 교무실로 들어서는 어머니를 알아보고 다가오는 담임 선생님도 내 기대와는 너무도 멀었다. 아름답고 상냥한 여선생님까지는 못 돼도 부드럽고 자상한 멋쟁이 선생님쯤은 될 줄 알았는데, 막걸리 방울이 튀어 하얗게 말라붙은 양복 윗도리 소매부터가 아니었다. 머리 기름은커녕 빗질도 안해 부스스한 머리에 그날 아침 세수를 했는지가 정말로 의심스런 얼굴로 어머님의 말씀을 듣는둥 마는둥 하고 있는 그가 담임 선생이 된다는게 솔직히 그렇게 실망스러울 수가 없었다. 그 뒤 일 년에 걸친 악연(ㄷㄷ)이 그때 벌써 어떤 예감으로 와 닿았는지 모를 일이었다.
　그 악연은 잠시 뒤 나를 반 아이들에게 소개할 때부터 모습을 드러냈다.
　「새로 전학온 한병태다. 앞으로 잘 지내도록.」
　담임 선생은 그 한 마디로 소개를 끝낸 뒤 나를 뒤쪽 빈 자리에 앉게 하고 바로 수업에 들어갔다. 새로 전학온 아이에 대해 호들갑스럽게 느껴질 정도로 자랑 섞인 소개를 늘어놓던 서울 선생님들의 자상함을 상기하자 나는 야속한 느낌을 억누를 길이 없었다. 대단한 추켜세움까지는 아니더라도, 최소한 내가 가진 자랑거리는 반아이들에게 일러주어, 그게 새로 시작하는 그들과의 관계에 도움이 되기를 바랐다.
　그때 내게는 나름으로 내세울 만한 게 몇 있었다. 첫째로 공부, 일등은 그리 자주 못했지만, 그래도 나는 그 별난 서울의 일류 학교에서도 반에서 다섯 손가락 안에는 들었다. 선생님뿐만 아니라 아이들과의 관계에서도 내 이익을 지켜 주는 데 적지 않은 몫을 하던 내 은근한 자랑거리였다. 또 나는 그림에도 남다른 솜씨가 있었다. 역시 전국의 어린이 미술대회를 휩쓸었다 할 정도는 아니었어도, 서울시 규모의 대회에서 몇 번의 특선은 따낼 만했다. 내 성적과 어울러 그 점도 어머니는 몇 번이나 강조하는 듯했는데, 담임 선생은 그 모두를 무시해 버린 것이었다. 내 아버지의 직업도 경우에 따라서는 내게 힘이 될 만했다. 바람을 맞아도 호되게 맞아 서울에서 거기까지 날려가기는 했어도, 내 아버지는 그 작은 읍으로 봐서는 몇 손가락 안에 들 만큼 직급 높은 공무원이었다.
　야속스럽기는 아이들도 담임 선생님과 마찬가지다. 서울에서는 새로운 전입생이 들어오면 아이들은 쉬는 시간이 되기 바쁘게 그를 빙 둘러싸고 이것 저것 묻기 마련이었다. 공부를 잘하는가, 힘은 센가, 집은 잘 사는가, 따위로 말하자면 나중 그 아이와 맺게 될 관계의 기초가 될 자료 수집인 셈이다. 그런데 그 새로운 급우들은 새로운 담임 선생과 마찬가지로 그런 쪽으로는 별로 관심이 없었다. 쉬는 시간에는 저만치서 힐끗힐끗 훔쳐 보기만 하다가 점심 시간이 되어서야 몇 명 몰려와 묻는다는 게 고작 전차를 타봤는가, 남대문을 보았는가 따위였고, 부러워하거나 감탄한다는 것도 기껏 나만이 가진 고급한 학용품 따위였다.

Key vocabulary

막막하다　　　　unsure, unclear
암담하다　　　　dark, gloomy

Friendship and loyalty 63

자유당정권	liberal government
기승	unyieldingness
웅장하다	grand, awesome
가교사	temporary school building
초라하다	shabby, humble
영락하다	go down in life
소공자	foreign rulers
얕보다	to look down on
활기	vitality
맥없이	weakly
부스스하다	dishevelled
악연	evil fate
예감	foreboding, hunch
호들갑스럽다	frivolous, rash
추켜세움	to yell out
일류학교	top ranked school
특선	special selection
호되다	severe, harsh
야속스럽다	cold hearted
수집	collection
급우	classmate
힐끗힐끗	a glimpse
학용품	school supplies, stationery

Comprehension questions: text

1 Where was the narrator's family from?
2 What was the narrator's special talent?
3 How did the narrator describe the teacher?
4 What was the 'evil fate' the narrator kept referring to?

Comprehension questions: drama extract

As in the text extract above, in the SBS drama, *The Heirs* (왕관을 쓰려는 자, 그 무게를 견더라 – 상속자들, 2013), the threat of bullying is not far below the surface for poor protagonist Ch'a Ŭnsang in her first few days as a scholarship student at the elite Cheguk High School. She begins to realise the implications of her attending the school after talking to her love interest, Kim T'an, in their house's wine cellar in episode six.

1 What does T'an say are Ŭnsang's two options for surviving at Cheguk High School?
2 Why does the other student want Ŭnsang to move from her seat at lunch?
3 What advice does he give her?
4 Why did T'an ask Ŭnsang to have lunch together?

Further discussion questions

1 Describe the political situation of the time the novel was written.
2 What can you notice about the power structure within the classroom? What does this reflect about how the power structure works in the society as a whole?
3 Do you think the narrator's experience is relatable for students from any culture?

64 *Friendship and loyalty*

References

Chun, Sinyong. 1976. *Korean society* (Korean culture series; 6). Seoul: International Cultural Foundation.
Eaton, Joseph. 2001. 'Famous Korean Novella Breaks into U.S. Market.' *Asian Reporter*, p. 23.
Moon, Seungsook. 2002. 'Carving Out Space: Civil Society and the Women's Movement in South Korea.' *The Journal of Asian Studies* 61(2): 473–500.

3.5 안민가 – 충담사 (*Song of Peace to the People – Ch'ungdamsa*)

Introduction to the text

Unlike other *hyangga*, the contents of *Anminga* are Confucian. Other *hyangga* tend to be Buddhist in content, but *Anminga* uses Confucian principles to express the ideology of peace for all people in the country. More than a sense of personal lyricism, the song expresses a real and practical desire to rule over the people and provide them with comfort and peace. This can be seen as a combination of Confucian and Buddhist principles. It seems clear that in order to maintain the system of state, Confucian ideals of piety were more effective than Buddhist beliefs. At the time of King Kyŏngdŏk, natural disasters made farming difficult, and politically, the kingdom was threatened by the challenge of Kim Yangsang. Because of this, the people were forced to become migrants, leaving Silla for Japan. In order to deal with these issues, Confucian principles were embraced and used by the country's rulers.

Background from Samgukyusa

As the king was offered Laotzu's *Tao Te Ching*, he received it with courtesy. The king had ruled the country for 24 years, and sometimes the gods of the Five Peaks and Three Mountains appeared in the courtyard and served him.

On the third day of the third lunar month, the king came out on the Kwijŏng gate pavilion and said, 'Can anyone go out on the street and bring me a well-turned-out priest?' Just then, a priest of imposing presence wandered along, and the attendants presented him to the king. The king said, 'This man is not what I meant by a well-turned-out priest,' and sent him off.

Another priest in quilted cloth, carrying a cherry-wood basket, was coming up from the South. The king was pleased when he saw him and greeted him at the gate pavilion. The king looked into the basket and there was only a tea service.

The king asked, 'Who are you?' The priest replied, 'I am called Ch'ungdam.'

The king asked again, 'Where were you coming from?' The priest said, 'I, as a Hinayanist (Hinayana), offer tea to dear Maitreya Buddha (Sakya) on the Samhwa ridge of Namsan on the third day of the third lunar month and and the ninth day of the ninth lunar month. Today, I was just on my way back after offering tea.'

As the king said, 'Is there a preordained tie for me to take a cup of tea?' The priest immediately brewed tea and offered it to the king; the taste was rare and the odd smell almost stank. The king said, 'I heard before that your song praising Kip'arang has a very lofty meaning, is that true?' The priest answered, 'That is right.'

The king said, 'Then, compose a song of benevolent rule for me.' The priest immediately made a song and dedicated it to the king. The king praised it, and appointed him as the royal preceptor, but the priest politely bowed and declined the post.

Since the king had no son although his member was 8 ch'on long, the queen was deposed and granted instead the title of Lady Saryang. The succeeding queen was Lady Manwŏl, whose pen name is Queen Dowager Kyŏngsu, the daughter of Ŭich'ung Kakkan.

One day, the king said to the priest, P'yohun, 'I have no luck in having a child. I want you to ask the god of heaven for offspring.' P'yohun went up to heaven and told the heavenly god and returned, and said, 'God says a daughter is possible now, but not a son.'

The king said, 'I would like god to change the daughter into a son,' then P'yohun went back to heaven to ask. God said, 'I may do that, however, the country will be in danger.' As P'yohun was leaving, God called him up and said: 'The relations between heaven and earth should not be in disorder. Now, you are coming and going to heaven as if you were going around to a neighbouring village, and revealing the heavenly secret. From this day forth, never come again.'

As P'yohun came back and delivered god's word, the king said, 'Even if the country became unstable, I would still like a son to succeed to the throne.'

After that, Queen Manwŏl gave birth to the crown prince, and the king was greatly pleased. After the King's death, the crown prince acceeded to the throne at the age of 8, and he became known as the Great King Hyegong. The Queen Dowager controlled the royal court, for the king was still young, but the governance was corrupted and plunderers arose like a swarm of bees which could not be controlled anymore, just as P'yohun had warned. From the days of his first birthday and until the accession, he had always played with girls and liked to wear a silk pocket, and enjoyed playing with people like Taoist priests; all this was because the young king was divinely converted into a man from a girl. Consequently, P'yohun was killed by the King Sŏndŏk and Kim Yang-sang; it is said that after his death, there were no longer any saints from Silla.

Original text

안민가

Sinitic text (Hyangch'al)

君隱父也
臣隱愛賜尸母史也
民焉狂尸恨阿孩古
爲賜尸知民是愛尸知古如
窟理叱大肹生以支所音物生
此肹食惡支治良羅
此地肹捨遣只於冬是去於丁
爲尸知國惡支持以支知右如
後句君如臣多支民隱如
爲內尸等焉國惡太平恨音叱如

Modern Korean text

임금은 아비요
신하는 사랑하시는 어미요

66 *Friendship and loyalty*

백성은 어리석은 아이로구나
사랑하면 백성이 사랑할 것이로다
탄식하는 뭇 창생, 이를 먹도록 다스릴지어다.
이 땅을 버리고 어디로 가랴
백성이 있어야 나라가 건사할 것이다
아아 임금이 임금답고 신하가 신하답고 백성이 백성다우면
나라가 태평하도다

Key vocabulary

임금	king
신하	vessel, official, courtier
어리석다	be foolish
– 리라	to think or suppose/may, might, must, would
뭇	all, the many
창생	all the people of the world, the masses
– 도록	so that, in order that
다스리다	govern, rule over
– 을 지어다	imperative inflection: 'do as you ought,' 'do your duty'
땅	land
버리다	desert
– 랴	rhetorical question
백성	people
나라	country
건사하다	to be maintained, sustained
답다	be like
태평하다	to be at peace

Comprehension questions: text

1 What is the religious background of this text?
2 What is the relationship between king and vassal as described in this poem?
3 What is the ideal state of a nation that the author is promoting?
4 What is the relationship between the King and his subjects?

Comprehension questions: film extract

The 2012 film *Masquerade* (광해: 왕이 된 남자) tells the story of Hasŏn, a low-class entertainer, who is tasked with becoming the double of King Gwanghae following an assassination attempt. While the real king recovers, Hasŏn slowly begins to reform the palace with his more compassionate approach, acting more like a true king than the real king ever did. This becomes abundantly obvious in his final audience with the ministers before he is due to leave the court.

1 What requests are the ministers making?
2 What issue does one of the ministers raise in regard to the requests, and how is it countered by another minister?
3 What order does the King give?
4 How does he justify his order?

Additional source material

This film was remade into a drama on tvN, which first aired in January 2019.

Further discussion questions

1   Discuss the characteristics of the orthography used for the original poem.
2   How does the religious background of this text differ from most *hyangga*?

References

Cho, Dong-Il. 2005. 'Korean Literary History in the East Asian Context.' *Acta Koreana* 8(2): 97–115.
Kim, Kichung. 1996. *An Introduction to Classical Korean Literature: From Hyangga to P'ansori* (New studies in Asian culture). Armonk, NY; London: M.E. Sharpe. (Chapter 2, Chapter 3 and Chapter 4).
Lee, Peter H. 2003. *A History of Korean Literature*. Cambridge: Cambridge University Press. (Chapter 3: Hyangga).

3.6   하여가 – 이방원, 단심가 – 정몽주 (*Anyway Song* – Yi Pangwŏn; and *Steadfast Song* – Chŏng Mongju)

Introduction to the text

Yi Pangwŏn (1367–1422) was the fifth son of Yi Sŏnggye, the founder of the Chosŏn dynasty. He was also the third king of the dynasty. While the Yi family was still trying to establish their reign, he wrote the *shijo Hayŏga* (하여가) in order to test the influential scholar P'oŭn Chŏng Mongju (1337–1392), to see whether he would support their coup d'etat. However, Chŏng replied with the *shijo Tanshimga* (단심가), revealing his unshakeable loyalty to the Koryŏ dynasty. For this, Yi Bangwŏn had him assassinated, but later enshrined him as one of the epitomes of ideal Confucian sagehood and loyalty to the state.

Original text

하여가 – 이방원

Hanshi *(Classical Chinese poetry, with Korean pronunciation for the characters)*

如여此차亦역如여何하
如여彼피亦역如여何하
城성隍황堂당後후垣원
頹퇴落락亦역何하如여
吾오輩배若약此차爲위
不불死사亦역何하如여

Middle Korean

이런들 엇더하며
이런들 엇더며 져런들 엇더료.

68 *Friendship and loyalty*

萬만壽수山산 드렁츩이 얼거진들 긔 엇더료.
우리도 이치 얼거져 百백年년지 누리리라.

Modern Korean

이렇게 산들 어떠하며 저렇게 산들 어떠하리오.
만수산의 칡덩굴이 서로 얽혀진 것 처럼 살아간들 그것이 어떠하리오.
우리도 이와 같이 얽혀져 한편생을 누리리라.

단심가 – 정몽주

Hanshi

此차身신死사了료死사了료
一일百백番번更갱死사了료
白백骨골爲위塵진土토
魂혼魄백有유也야無무
向향主주一일片편丹단心심
寧영有유改개理리與여之지

Middle Korean

이몸이 죽고 죽어
일백번 고쳐 죽어
白백骨골이 塵진土토되여
넋이라도 있고 없고
임 향한 一일片편丹단心심이야
가실줄이 있으랴

Modern Korean

이 몸이 죽고 죽어 비록 일백 번이나 다시 죽어
백골(白骨)이 흙과 먼지가 되어 넋이야 있건 없건
임금님께 바치는 충성심이야 변할 리가 있으랴?

Key vocabulary

산들 – 살다+들	whether you live like this or that, it doesn't really matter
~리오	indeed!
만수산	Mansu Mountain
츩덩굴이얽히지다	become entangled in kudzu vine/arrowroot vine
한평생	one's whole life
누리다	live out, enjoy
~리라	suppose, should, may, might
비록	even though, although
일백	100
백골	the bones left over from human decay

흙	soil
먼지	dust
넋	soul
있건없건	if it is there or not
임금님	king
바치는	tribute, offerings
충성심	loyal
~이야	even, if it be, when it comes to
을 리가 [없다]	cannot be
~랴	(rhetorical question)

Comprehension questions: text

1 Does Yi Pangwŏn think our behaviour in this life is important?
2 What kind of relationship does he want to build with Chŏng Mongju?
3 Is Chŏng Mongju willing to contemplate a potential change of heart?

Comprehension questions: drama/film extract

The SBS drama *Six Flying Dragons* (육룡이 나르샤, 2015) is a vivid retelling of the establishment of the Chosŏn dynasty. In episode 36, we see the confrontation between Yi Pangwŏn and Chŏng Mongju at Sŏnjuk Bridge.

1 Why can't Chŏng Mongju give up on Koryŏ?
2 How do the people feel about the country according to Yi Pangwŏn?
3 What does Chŏng Mongju argue is the purpose of a Confucian scholar?
4 Why does Chŏng Mongju laugh at Yi Pangwŏn's threat?

Additional source material

KBS dramas *Tears of the Dragon* (용의 눈물, 1996), and *Jeong Do-jeon* (정도전, 2014), also portray the events around the establishment of the Chosŏn dynasty.

Further discussion questions

1 The drama extract portrays the two men having profound respect for each other, but each is firmly dedicated to their opposing views. Do you think it is possible to stay friends with someone who has completely different views from yourself?
2 Many coups throughout history have argued that a system is rotten and failing, and that they need to change the system in order for the people to survive. Form two teams and debate:

   Team A: System change is necessary for the survival of the common man, and any collateral damage from this change is justified for the greater good.
   Team B: When one has declared one's loyalty to a system, that bond cannot be broken, and one should attempt to fix the system from the inside rather than overthrowing it completely.

References

Clark, Donald N. 1982. 'Chosŏn's Founding Fathers: A Study of Merit Subjects in the Early Yi Dynasty.' *Korean Studies* 6: 17–40.

Duncan, John B. 1988. 'The Social Background of the Founding of the Chosŏn Dynasty: Change or Continuity?' *Journal of Korean Studies* 6(1): 39–79.

Robinson, Kenneth. 2016. 'Pak Tonji and the Vagaries of Government Service in Koryŏ and Chosŏn, 1360–1412.' *Korean Studies* 40: 78–118.

4 Satire

4.1 배비장전 (*The Tale of Aide Pae* – Anonymous)

Introduction to the text

The Tale of Aide Pae was initially one of twelve *p'ansori* stories transmitted until the mid- to late-19th century, but after the transmission of the *p'ansori*-style version was cut off, the story remained in its novelised form. It tells the tale of Aide Pae, a middle-ranking military official who is dispatched to Jeju Island, and instantly offends all his colleagues by telling them off for playing with *kisaeng* at his welcome party, instead of showing proper behaviour suitable for Confucian gentlemen. Pae's servant, Pangja, makes a bet with him that he will be seduced into losing his composure over a woman, and with the help of Jeju's most beautiful *kisaeng*, Aerang, this is exactly what happens. In the end, Pae is caught having snuck into Aerang's chambers, and mocked by everyone for his pretentiousness. This story provides a pointedly satirical view of the reality behind the façade of perfect Confucian behaviour, as well as a humorous opportunity for the lower class (servants and *kisaeng*) to humiliate the upper class and put it back in its place.

Original text

그러다가 우연히 숲 속을 바라보니, 한 미인이 어릴락 비칠락 백만 가지 교태를 다 부리면서 봄빛을 희롱하고 있는 것이었다. 그리고 상하 의복을 훨훨 벗어 던지고 물에 풍덩 뛰어드는 게 아닌가. 그러더니 물장구를 치며 온갖 장난을 다 하며 손도 씻고 발도 씻고 배, 가슴, 젖도 씻고 예도 씻고 게도 씻고 샅도 씻고 한창 이렇게 목욕을 하고 있었다. 배비장은 그 거동을 보자 어깨가 들먹거려지고 정신이 흐릿해졌다. 드디어 음남이 되어 눈을 흘끗 뜨고 도둑 나무하다가 쫓기듯이 숨을 헐떡거리며, 그 여자의 근본이 알고 싶어졌다.
　'어! 저 여자가 누군지는 모르나 사람 여럿 녹였겠다.'
　그러나 누구에게 물어 볼 수도 없으니 군침만 꿀꺽 삼키며 자탄할 뿐이었다.
　드디어 하루 해가 저무니 사또는 관으로 돌아가려고 길을 재촉하였다. 그리하여 모든 비장들과 기생들, 그리고 하인들도 일제히 길을 떠날 때였다. 배비장은 딴 마음을 먹고 꾀병으로 배를 앓는 체하였다.
　'벌써 혹했구나.'
　비장들은 그의 눈치를 채고 수군거리며 겉으로만 인사를 하였다.
　'예방께서는 침이나 한 대 맞으시오.'
　'아니오. 천만에요. 병이 아니니 조금 진정하면 나을 것이오.'
　배비장이 대답하였다.
　비장들은 웃음을 참고 방자를 불러 일렀다.

'너의 나리 병환은 대단치 않다 하니 진정되거든 잘 모시고 오도록 해라.'
그리고는 배비장에게 말하였다.
'이대로 사또께 잘 말씀을 드릴 테니 마음놓고 진정한 후에 오시오.'
'동관들께서 이처럼 염려해 주시니 감사합니다. 사또께 잘 여쭈어 주시기 바랍니다. 아이고 배야!'
그러자 동관 한 사람이 쑥 앞으로 나섰다. 이 사람은 짓궂기가 짝이 없는 사람이었다. 배비장을 놀려줄 생각으로 이렇게 말하였다.
'그건 너무 염려 마시오. 사또께서는 동관께서 이런 때없는 병이 있음을 짐작하시는 것 같습니다. 들으니 배앓이는 계집 손으로 문지르면 효력이 있다고 합니다. 기생 한 년을 두고 갈 테니 잘 문질러 달라고 하시오.'
'아니오. 내 배는 다른 이의 배와 달라서 기생은 보기만 해도 배가 더 아프니 그런 말씀을 다시 하지 마십시오.'
'참으로 그 배는 이상도 하구려. 계집 말만 들어도 더 아프다 하니 우리가 한 낙양 사람으로 천리 밖에 와서 정의가 친형제 같은데 그처럼 괴로워하는 것을 보고서야 혼자 두고 어떻게 갈 수가 있겠소? 진정된 후에 우리같이 가도록 하는 게 좋겠소이다.'
'동관께서는 내 성미를 잘 모르시는 것 같습니다. 나는 병이 나면 혼자서 진정을 해야 낫지 형제간일지라도 같이 있게 되면 낫기는커녕 더 아프니 사람을 살리려거든 어서 제발 먼저 가 주오. 애고 배야 나 죽겠소!'
'정 그러시다면 혼자 두고라도 갈 수밖에 없소이다. 우리가 간 후에 무정한 사람들이라고 하지는 마시오.'
동관들이 사또를 모시고 관으로 돌아갈 때 배비장은 그 여인을 보아야겠다는 욕심을 주체할 수가 없었다.
'애 방자야! 애고 배야!'
'예?'
'나는 여기에 온 후 눈앞이 몽롱해서 지척을 분간 못 하겠다. 애고 배야, 애고 배야.'
'소인도 나으리께서 애를 쓰시는 것을 보니 정신이 없습니다.'
'우리 사또 가시는 걸 자세히 보아라.'
'저기 내려가십니다.'
'애고 배야! 또 보아라.'
'저기 아득히 가십니다.'
'난 배가 아프기를 그만두었다.'
목욕을 하는 여자를 보려고 배비장은 골짜기 화초 사이의 좁은 길로 몸을 숨겨 가만가만 사뿐히 걸어 들어갔다. 그리고 가느다란 소리로 방자를 불렀다. 방자가 그에 대답한다. 그러나 말공대는 점점 없어지고 말았다.

Key vocabulary

교태	coquettish behaviour
봄빛	spring scenery
희롱	taunt, play with
상하의복	upper and lower garments
샅	crotch, groin area
비장	aide or secretary. During the Chosŏn period, a military position geared towards following and assisting the provincial governor, minister on rotation, cavalry or marine forces.
들먹거리다	move up and down, shake, dance
음남	a dissolute and lecherous man (음란한 남자)
흘끗	taking a glance

헐떡거리다	breathe hard, pant, gasp
자탄하다	complain/grieve to oneself
저물다	grow dark
사또	a district magistrate
재촉하다	to hurry, push, or press
일제히	all together, at the same time
꾀병	a fake illness
배를앓다	stomachache
혹하다	be charmed, madly in love, entrapped, captivated
예방	Minister of Rites – from one of the Six Ministries of Chosŏn, along with the Ministries of Personnel, Taxation, Defence, Justice, and Works
천만에요	don't mention it, not at all, you're welcome.
진정하다	calm down, relax
동관	colleagues, working together at the government office
짓궂기	to have a mischievous, impish air
때없다	unseasonal, unexpected
문지르다	rub, scour, scrub
효력	effect, efficacy
정의	affection formed from spending time together
한낙양사람	two people from Seoul meeting in a different place (동시낙양인)
성미	nature, temperament, disposition
~은/는커녕	let alone, on the contrary, anything but
정	really, truly
무정하다	heartless, cold, cruel, unfeeling
주체하다	manage, control, cope with
몽롱하다	dim, indistinct, vague, fuzzy, obscure
지척	a very short distance (one *ch'ŏk* is just over 30cm)
분간하다	to distinguish
아득히	far away, a long time ago
골짜기	valley, canyon, gorge, ravine
화초	flowers, flowering plants
사뿐히	lightly
가느다랗다	thin, faint, fine
말공대	courteous expressions, honorific language

Comprehension questions: text

1 What causes Aide Pae to lose his control?
2 How does he try to stay behind when everyone else has left?
3 How does his colleague tease him?
4 What makes Aide Pae recover?

Comprehension questions: film extract

In a reversal of the events of *The Tale of Aide Pae*, the film *Going By the Book* (바르게 살자, 2007) shows how a police officer, Chŏng Toman, who always does things 100% correctly, makes everyone else a laughing stock after he is tasked with taking the role of a bank robber in a training simulation, and outwits the rest of the police at every turn. The interview by the news team becomes a turning point, when Toman finds himself immersed in his role, and everyone else realizes that treating him lightly was a mistake.

1. How did Toman feel when he found out he was going to be the robber?
2. When pressured by the newscaster, how does he say he would feel if he was a real robber?
3. Why does he shoot the cameraman?
4. Why does his superior object to Toman's choice of gun?

Additional source material

A performance by the National Changgeuk Company of Korea of *The Tale of Aide Pae* is available on YouTube, showing the moment Aide Pae catches sight of Aerang (www.youtube.com/watch?v=d-E8k0GIEdU) and is caught in her chambers (www.youtube.com/watch?v=NUWWIC9uTfQ – accessed 5/2/2019).

Further discussion questions

1. It is better to admit to being dissolute and lecherous than to put on a pompous façade. Discuss.
2. In the end, it is the social pressure to bring Aide Pae down from his high horse which causes his downfall, as he is humiliated by those around him who think he has grown too big for his boots. Do you feel this kind of pressure in your daily life?

References

Kwon, Hyuk-Chan. 2013. 'Whose Voices Are Heard? A New Approach to Pyŏn Kangsoe-ka Interpretation.' *Acta Koreana* 16(2): 589–609.
Park, Chan E. 2008. '*Pansori* in the View of Literature.' In *Pansori*, edited by Lee Yong-Shik, pp. 128–62. Seoul: The National Centre for Korean Traditional Performing Arts.

4.2 오적 – 김지하 (*Five Bandits* – Kim Chiha)

Introduction to the text

Kim Chiha (b. 1941) is a poet widely famed for his political activism, which cause him to be arrested and tortured, and finally sentenced to death in 1974, although he was released after heavy international pressure. The poem, *Ojŏk* (Five Bandits), which was published in 1970, was partially responsible for his arrest – it is a biting critique of the corruptions and excesses Kim saw in the Pak Chŏnghŭi (Park Chung Hee, 1917–1979) government. In line with the protest trends of the Minjung movements starting in the late 1970s, Kim employs traditional Korean folk culture, in this case the style of *p'ansori*, to add depth to his political message.

Original text

셋째놈이 나온다 고급공무원 나온다.
　풍신은 고무풍선, 독사같이 모난 눈, 푸르족족 엄한 살,
　콱다문 입꼬라지 청백리(淸白吏) 분명쿠나

단 것을 갖다주니 쩔레쩔레 고개저어 우린 단것 좋아 않소,
아무렴, 그렇지, 그렇구말구
어허 저놈 뒤좀 봐라 낯짝 하나 더 붙었다
이쪽보고 히뜩히뜩 저쪽보고 헤끗헤끗, 피둥피둥 유들유들
숫기도 좋거니와 이빨꼴이 가관이다.
단것 너무 처먹어서 새까맣게 썩었구나, 썩다못해 문들어져
오리(汚吏)가 분명쿠나
산같이 높은 책상 바다같이 깊은 의자 우뚝나직 걸터앉아
공(功)은 쥐뿔도 없는 놈이 하늘같이 높이 앉아 한손으로 노땡큐요 다른 손은
땡큐땡큐
되는 것도 절대 안돼, 안될 것도 문제 없어, 책상위엔 서류뭉치, 책상밑엔 지폐뭉치
높은 놈껜 삽살개요 아랫놈껜 사냥개라, 공금은 잘라먹고 뇌물은 청(請)해먹고
내가 언제 그랬더냐 흰구름아 물어보자 요정(料亭)마담 위아래로
모두 별탈 없다더냐.

넷째놈이 나온다 장성(長猩)놈이 나온다
키크기 팔대장성, 제밑에 졸개행렬 길기가 만리장성
온몸이 털이 숭숭, 고리눈, 범아가리, 벌룸코, 탑삭수염,
짐승이 분명쿠나
금은 백동 청동 황동, 비단공단 울긋불긋, 천근만근 훈장으로 온몸을 덮고 감아
시키먼 개다리를 여기차고 저기차고
엉금엉금 기어나온다 장성(長猩)놈 재조봐라
쫄병들 줄 쌀가마니 모래가득 채워놓고 쌀은 빼다 팔아먹고
쫄병 먹일 소돼지는 털한개씩 나눠주고 살은 혼자 몽창먹고
엄동설한 막사없어 얼어죽는 쫄병들을
일만하면 땀이난다 온종일 사역시켜
막사지을 재목갖다 제집크게 지어놓고
부속 차량 피복 연탄 부식에 봉급까지, 위문품까지 떼어먹고
배고파 탈영한놈 군기잡자 주어패서 영창에 집어놓고
열중쉬엇 열중열중열중쉬엇 열중
뻥뻥들 데려다가 제마누라 화냥끼 노리개로 묶어두고
저는 따로 첩을 두어 운우서수 공방전(雲雨魚水攻防戰)에 병법(兵法)이 신출귀몰(神出鬼沒)

마지막놈 나온다
장차관이 나온다
허옇게 백태끼어 삐적삐적 술지게미 가득고여 삐져나와
추접무화(無化) 눈꼽낀눈 형형하게 부라리며 왼손은 골프채로 국방을 지휘하고
오른손은 주물럭주물럭 계집젖통 위에다가 증산 수출 건설이라 깔짝깔짝 쓰노라니
호호 아이 간지럽사와요
이런 무식한 년, 국사(國事)가 간지러워?
굶더라도 수출이닷, 안팔려도 증상이닷, 아사(餓死)한놈 뼉다귀로 현해탄에 다리
놓아 가미사마 배알하잣!
깨진 북소리 깨진 나팔소리 삐삐빼빼 불어대며 속셈은 먹을 궁리
검정세단 있는데도 벤쯔를 사다놓고 청렴결백 시위코자 코로나만 타는구나
예산에서 몽땅먹고 입찰에서 왕창먹고 행여나 냄새날라 질근질근 껌씹으며
켄트를 피워물고 외래품 철저단속 공문을 획획획획 내갈겨 쓰고나서 어히 거참
달필(達筆)이다.

76   Satire

추문듣고 뒤쫓아온 말잘하는 반벙어리 신문기자 앞에 놓고
일국(一國)의 재상더러 부정(不正)이 웬말인가 귀거래사(歸去來辭) 꿍얼꿍얼,자네 핸디 몇이더라?

오적(五賊)의 이 절륜한 솜씨를 구경하던 귀신들이
깜짝 놀라서 어마 뜨거라 저놈들한테 붙잡히면 뼉다귀도 못추리것다
똥줄빠지게 내빼 버렸으니 요즘엔 제사지내는 사람마저 드물어졌겄다.

Key vocabulary

고급공무원	high-ranking public official
고무풍선	rubber balloon
독사	venomous snake
모나다	angular
푸르족족	dull, bluish, and uneven
청백리	a clean and upright official who is not financially greedy
고개를젖다	to shake one's head
낯짝	mug, face (informal)
히뜩히뜩	describing something continually turning round
피둥피둥	describing someone fat and bloated
유들유들	describing someone extremely shameless and smooth-talking
숫기가좋다	to be unashamed, bold
~꼴	the state of something
가관	a sight to be seen, a spectacle
오리	a corrupt government official
우뚝	high, aloft
나직	low, short
걸터앉다	sit on, perch on
공	contribution, merit
쥐뿔	worthless, nothing at all
뭉치	bundle of, sheaf of
삽살개	*Sapsal* dog, a Korean breed known for its patience, friendliness, and loyalty (as well as its supposed ability to dispel ghosts)
사냥개	a hunting dog
공금	public funds, government money
뇌물	bribe
요정	high-class Korean-style restaurant (also brothel)
별탈없다	uneventful
장성	a play on words meaning long (長) monkey (猩), homophonic with general (장성將星)
졸개행렬	the lining up of his subordinates
고리눈	an eye with a white-ringed iris
범	tiger
아가리	trap, mouth
탑삭수염	short, bristly beard
훈장	medal, badge

엉금엉금	crawling, creeping on all fours
쫄병	corruption of 졸병, private
가마니	straw bag for transporting rice
엄동설한	cold and snowy winter
막사	barracks
사역	fatigue duty, labour assigned to military men not requiring the use of arms
재목	lumber, timber
위문품	care packages
탈영	desertion from the army
영창	guardhouse, confinement facility
열중쉬엇	stand at ease
빵빵들	men with bulging muscles
화냥끼	corruption of 화냥기, men that are the objects of a woman's desire, someone to have an affair with
운우서수	physical relations between a man and a woman
공방전	offensive and defensive battle
신출귀몰	to appear and disappear at will, like a ghost
장차관	vice minister
백태	a white coating on the tongue
술지게미	wine lees, dregs
눈꼽	corruption of 눈곱, gunge, sleep in the eyes
증산	increase production
수출	export
건설	construction
아사	to die of hunger
해협	sea between the straits of Korea and Fukuoka Prefecture in Japan
가미사마	from the Japanese for 'gods'
속셈	secret intention, ulterior motive
궁리	deliberation, consideration
청렴결백	Integrity
시위코자	intend to demonstrate
몽땅	all, everything
왕창	a large amount
행여나	by chance, possibly
철저단속	thoroughly crack down on
달필	a masterful piece of calligraphy, superb handwriting
추문	scandalous report
반벙어리	someone with inarticulate pronunciation, a stammer
재상	prime minister
부정	corrupt, illegal, dishonest
귀거래사	a poem by Jin dynasty poet, Tao Yuanming (365–427), titled 'Returning Home.' Giving an idealised portrayal of countryside life, it was written on occasion of Tao's withdrawal from court into voluntary exile, as he famously said he would no longer be willing to 'bow like a servant in exchange for five bushels of grain' (the salary for low-rank officials at the time).
꿍얼꿍얼	muttering, mumbling
절륜하다	peerless, matchless, unparalleled

78 *Satire*

똥줄빠지다	to be frightened out of one's wits
내빼다	take off, make off, run away (informal)
제사	ancestral rites, memorial service

Comprehension questions: text

1 What are the crimes of the third bandit?
2 What are the crimes of the fourth bandit?
3 What are the crimes of the fifth bandit?
4 Why don't people make offerings to the dead nowadays?

Comprehension questions: drama/film extract

The 2005 film *The President's Last Bang* (그때 그사람들) is a black comedy that harshly lampoons the profligate and dissolute lifestyles of the elite in the Pak Chŏnghŭi regime. The beginning of the film highlights the numerous different crimes of the regime.

1 What is the mother whose daughter caught the eye of the president trying to achieve?
2 What has Minister Jung done?
3 What recommendation does the doctor give the Director of Korean Central Intelligence?
4 How do Defence Security agents make a name for themselves?

Further discussion questions

1 Do you feel Kim Chiha's employment of vulgar expressions contributes to his political satire?
2 Does Kim's evocation of *p'ansori* work in conjunction with this piece?

References

Cumings, Bruce et al. 1977. 'Imperialism and Repression: The Case of South Korea.' *Bulletin of Concerned Asian Scholars* 9(2): 1–25.
Kang, Rosemary Se-Soon. 2009. 'Kim Chi-Ha's *Pansori* and Oe Kenzaburo: Focused on Grotesque Realism in "Ttong-Ba-Da" Exemplified by Oe Kenzaburo.' *6th Korean Studies Association of Australasia Biennial Conference Proceedings*. University of Sydney, 9–10 July.
Kim, Chiha (trans. Won-Chung Kim and James Han). 2001. *Ojŏk/Five Thieves: Selected Poems*. Seoul: Tapke. (Introduction).
Kim, Chiha (trans. Brother Anthony of Taizé). 2015. 'Five Bandits.' *Mānoa* 27(2): 94–104.
Lee, Namhee. 2009. *The Making of Minjung: Democracy and the Politics of Representation in South Korea*. Ithaca, NY: Cornell University Press.
Park, Chan E. 2008. '*Pansori* in the View of Literature.' In *Pansori*, edited by Lee Yong-Shik pp. 128–62. Seoul: The National Centre for Korean Traditional Performing Arts.
Suh, Kyung-sik. 1997. 'A Letter to Mr. Kim Chi-ha; or, the Pain of the Split Self.' *Positions* 5(1): 315–20.
Swaner, Scott Harold. 2003. *Politicizing the Aesthetic: The Dialectics of Poetic Production in Late Twentieth-Century South Korea, 1960–1987 (Kim Suyŏng, Kim Chiha, Pak Nohae, Hwang Ji-woo)*. PhD Thesis, Harvard University, Cambridge, MA.
Um, Haekyung. 2013. *Korean Musical Drama: P'ansori and the Making of Tradition in Modernity*. Farnham, Surrey: Ashgate. (Chapter 8: New *P'ansori*).

4.3 닭을 빌려타고 돌아가다 – 서거정 (*Riding Home on a Borrowed Chicken* – Sŏ Kŏjŏng)

Introduction to the text

Riding Home on a Borrowed Chicken (Sŏ Kŏjŏng) is a fable is found in 태평한화골계전(太平閑話滑稽傳, T'aep'yŏnghanhwagolgyejŏn), which was a collection of folk tales gathered and written in Chinese by the government worker Sŏ Kŏjŏng, between the end of the Koryŏ period and the beginning of the Chosŏn period (1477). It describes through satire the great importance of treating guests with grace.

Original text

김 선생은 우스갯소리를 잘 하는 사람이다. 어느 날 친구의 집을 방문했다. 주인이 술상을 차려내었는데 상 위에는 채소만 쌓여 있었다. 친구가 말했다.

  '모처럼 찾아왔는데, 집은 가난하고 시장도 멀어서 안주를 변변히 작만하지 못하였네, 그저 담박한 야채만 준비했으니 부끄럽네.' 하였다.

마침 마당에는 닭들이 몇 마리 놀고 있었다. 그 것을 본 김 선생이 말하기를

  '대장부는 벗을 위하여 천금도 아끼지 않는다 했지, 그리도 어렵다니 내가 타고 온 말을 잡아서 술안주를 하세' 하였다. 그의 말을 듣고 놀란 친구가 말했다.

  '말을 잡으면 자네는 무엇을 타고 돌아간단 말인가?' 하니, 김선생이 천연덕스럽게 말하기를

  '그야 자네 집 닭을 빌려서 타고가면 될 것이 아닌가?' 친구는 할 수 없이 닭을 잡아서 술안주로 내놓았다.

Key vocabulary

우스갯소리	joke, gag
모처럼	for the first time in a while
안주	drinking snacks
천역더스럽다	humbly and with virtue

Comprehension questions: text

1 What is the main message of this fable?
2 Why did he say that he would ride on the chicken?

Comprehension questions: film extract

The 2005 film *Welcome to Dongmakgol* (웰컴 투 동막골) tells of an isolated village during the Korean War which is unaware of the events of the outside world until an American soldier, as well as soldiers from the North and South, all meet in the village at the same time. The villagers uphold the traditional values of generosity towards guests, offering food to the soldiers even after the soldiers accidentally blow up the village's winter food storage.

1. Why does the village elder say they don't need to worry?
2. What does High Comrade Ri say the South Korean soldiers need to do if they want to see more blood?
3. Why do some of the villagers object to giving the soldiers food? Does the village elder agree?
4. Where did everyone go, leaving the South Korean soldiers behind?

Further discussion questions

1. Do you think the message of this story is still valid today?
2. Do the values of this fable apply cross-culturally or are they unique to Korean culture?

References

Hoare, James, & Pares, Susan. 1996. *The Simple Guide to Customs and Etiquette in Korea* (Simple guides. Series 1, Customs & etiquette). Folkestone: Global Books.
Kim, Taegil. 1990. *Values of Korean People Mirrored in Fiction*. Seoul, ROK: Dae Kwang Munwhasa.
Lee, Peter H. 2013. *The Story of Traditional Korean Literature*. Amherst, New York: Cambria Press.

4.4　허생전 – 박지원 (*The Tale of Mr. Hŏ* – Pak Chiwŏn)

Introduction to the text

Pak Chi-won (1737–1805) was a *Sirhak* thinker, government official and writer who lived during the late Joseon Dynasty. His main works include 열하일기 *The Chehol Diary* (Global Oriental), 양반전 *Yangbanjŏn*, 호질 *Rebuke from the Tiger*, and 허생전 *The Tale of Mr. Hŏ*. He first sat the civil service examination in 1765, but he intentionally failed the exam though he was brilliant. After that, he abandoned his ambitions in that regard and engaged in literary and philosophical pursuits. He turned his attention towards literary pursuits and the 'new culture' of the Qing Dynasty. After King Chŏngjo ascended the throne, Pak was recommended on the basis of his talent as a writer. Along with Hong Taeyong, Pak Chega, and others, he believed that Chosŏn should learn from the Qing Dynasty's remarkable industrial advancements and was an advocate of mercantilism.

The Silhak – also spelled Sirhak (Korean: 'Practical Learning') – school of thought that came into existence in the midst of the chaotic conditions of 18th-century Korea, dedicated itself to a practical approach to statecraft, instead of the blind and uncritical following of Confucian teachings. The Silhak school attacked Neo-Confucianism, particularly its formalism and concern with ritual. Members of the school originated many ideas for social reform, especially for land reform and the development of farming. Several important books on these subjects were written that give a good picture of farming practices in the 17th and 18th centuries. The greatest contribution to the Silhak school came from Yi Ik (1681–1763) and Pak Chi-won (1737–1805). Yi's concern was largely with such matters as land reform, farming, and the abolition of class barriers and slavery. Pak advocated the development of commerce and technology. With the introduction of Western culture in the late 19th century, Silhak, along with Sŏhak, or Western Learning, contributed to the development and spread of ideas that stimulated the gradual modernisation of Korea.

Three components in Sirhak are (1) kyŏngsech'iyong (경세치용, 經世致用), (2) iyonghusaeng (이용후생, 利用厚生) and (3) shilsagushi (실사구시, 實事求是). 경세치용(經世致用): in order to govern well – they argued that it is important to reform government systems, eg., land law reform. The scholars who were pursuing this idea focussed on agriculture. In contrast, 이용후생(利用厚生) scholars were interested in trade and currency reform. 실사구시(實事求是) means seeking truth through real things – empirical science.

Original text

『허생은 묵적골에 살았다. 남산 밑 골짜기로 곧장 가면 우물이 있고, 그 위로 해묵은 은행나무가 하늘을 가리고 잇다. 허생의 집 사립문은 은행나무를 향해 있고 언제나 열려 있었다. 집이라야 두어 칸 되는 초가집으로 비바람에 거의 다 쓰러져가는 오막살이였다. 허생은 집에 비바람이 새는 것은 아랑곳하지 않고 언제나 글읽기만을 좋아했으므로 가난하기 짝이 없었다. 그 아내가 삯바느질을 해서 겨우 입에 풀칠을 했다.
 어느 날, 허생의 아내는 배고픈 것을 참다못해 눈물을 흘리며 푸념을 늘어놓았다.
 '당신은 한평생 과거도 보러 가지 않으면서 어쩌자고 글만 읽는단 말입니까?'
 그러나 허생은 태연자약, 껄껄 웃었다.
 '내 아직 글이 서툴러서 그렇다네.'
 '그렇다면 공장(工匠) 노릇도 못 한단 말입니까.?'
 '공장일을 평소에 배우지 못했으니 어쩌오?'
 '그렇다면 하다못해 장사라도 해야지요.'
 '장사를 하려 해도 밑천이 없으니 어쩌오?'
 아내는 드디어 역정을 냈다.
 '당신은 밤낮없이 글을 읽더니, 그래 '어쩌오' 하는 것만 배웠수? 공장일도 못 한다, 장사도 못 한다, 그럼 도둑질은 어떻수?'
 허생은 이 말에 책장을 덮고는 벌떡 일어섰다.
 '애석한 일이로다. 내 10년을 작정하고 독서를 하려 했더니 이제 겨우 7년이로구나.'
 그 길로 허생은 문밖으로 나섰다. 그러나 장안 거리에 아는 사람이 있을 턱이 없었다. 그는 종로 거리를 오르락내리락했다. 그러면서 길가는 사람은 붙들고 물었다.
 '한양에서 제일 가는 부자가 누구요?'
 그 사람은 장안에서 제일가는 갑부라면 변씨라고 일러주었다. 허생은 그 집을 찾아갔다. 주인을 만나 길게 읍한 후에 단도직입적으로 잘라 말했다.
 '내 집이 가난하여 장사 밑천이 없소 그래. 무엇을 좀 해보고 싶으니 돈 만 냥만 빌려주시오.'
 '그렇게 합시다.'
 변씨는 대뜸 승낙하고는 만 냥을 내주었다. 허생은 고맙다는 말 한마디 없이 가지고 가 버렸다. 변씨 집에는 그 자제들과 문객이 많이 모여 있었다. 문밖을 나서는 허생의 몰골을 보아하니, 이건 영락없는 거지가 아닌가. 선비랍시고 허리끈을 매기는 했지만 술이 다 빠졌고, 가죽신이라고는 하지만 뒤꿈치가 한쪽으로 다 닳아빠졌다. 다 낡아빠진 망건이며, 땟국이 줄줄 흐르는 두루마기, 거기다가 허연 콧물까지 훌쩍거리는 품이 거지 중에도 상거지였다. 이런 자에게 만 냥을 선뜻 내주다니.
 '어른께서 아시는 분입니까?'
 '모르는 사람일세.'
 놀라 묻는 말에 대답도 태연했다.
 '하루아침에 얼굴도 모르는 사람에게 만금을 내버리시다니, 더구나 그 이름 석자도 묻지 않으시고 어쩌려고 그러십니까?'
 변씨는 정색을 하고 말했다.

'이건 그대들이 알 바가 아닐세. 무릇 돈을 빌리러 오는 사람이라면 자기의 생각을 이것저것 길게 늘어놓게 마련이야. 약속은 꼭 지킨다느니, 염려 마라느니 하고 말일세. 그러면서도 얼굴빛은 어딘가 구겨져 보이고 한말을 되뇌곤 하지. 그런데 이 사람은 옷이며 신발이 모두 떨어지긴 했지만, 우선 말이 짤막하고 사람을 대하는 눈이 아랫사람을 내려다보는 듯하며 조금도 부끄러워하는 기색이 없네. 물질 따위에는 관심이 없고 벌써 전부터 제 살림에 만족하고 있는 사람임에 틀림없어. 그러니 그가 한번 해보고 싶은 장사라는 것도 적은 일이 아닐 게고, 나 또한 그 사람을 한번 시험해보려는 거야. 게다가 주지 않았으면 모르되, 이미 만 냥을 내주었으니 구태여 그의 이름 석 자를 물어서 무엇하겠나.'

큰 장사꾼만이 할 수 있는 말이었다. 만금을 손쉽게 얻은 허생은 집에도 가지 않고 '안성은 경기와 호남의 갈림길이고 삼남의 요충이렷다'하면서 그 길로 내려가 안성에 거처를 마련했다.

다음날부터 그는 시장에 나가서 대추, 밤, 감, 배, 석류, 귤, 유자 따위 과일이란 과일을 모두 거두어 샀다. 파는 사람이 부르는 대로 값을 다 주고, 팔지 않는 사람에게는 시세의 배를 주고 샀다. 그리고 사는 대로 한정 없이 곳간에 저장해 두었다. 이렇게 되자 오래지 않아서 나라 안의 과일이란 과일은 모두 바닥이 났다. 대신들의 집에서 잔치나 제사를 지내려고 해도 과일을 구경하지 못해 제사상도 제대로 갖추지 못할 형편이었다. 과일 장수들은 이번에는 허생에게 달려와서 과일을 얻을 형편이 되었고, 저장했던 과일들은 10배 이상으로 호가하였다.

'허어, 겨우 만냥으로 이 나라를 기울게 할 수 있다니 국가의 심천(深淺)을 알만하구나!'

허생은 이렇게 탄식했다. 과일을 다 처분한 다음 그는 칼, 호미, 무명, 명주, 솜 등을 모조리 사 가지고 제주도로 건너가서 그것을 팔아 이번에는 말총이란 이름이 붙은 것은 모조리 사들였다.

'몇 해가 못 가서 나라 안 사람들은 상투도 싸매지 못하게 될 게다.'

과연 허생이 장담해 대로 얼마 가지 않아서 나라의 망건 값이 10배나 뛰어올랐다. 말총을 내다 파니 백만금이 되었다.

어느 날 허생은 늙은 뱃사공 한 사람에게 물었다.

'바다밖에 혹시 사람이 살만한 빈 섬이 있지 않던가?'

'있습지요. 옛날에 바람을 만나 곧장 서쪽으로 사흘 밤낮을 가다가 한 섬에 닿았는데, 그곳은 아마도 사문과 장기 사이라고 짐작됩니다. 꽃과 잎이 저절로 피고 과실이며 오이가 철을 따라 여물었습죠. 그뿐입니까. 고라니와 사슴이 떼를 지어 다니고 바닷고기들도 놀라지 않더이다.'

허생은 사공의 말을 듣고 크게 기뻐했다.

'사공이 만일 나를 그곳으로 인도해준다면 평생 동안 함께 부귀를 누리도록 해주겠네.'

사공은 허생의 말을 좇았다. 이리하여 바람이 알맞게 부는 날을 기다려 동남쪽으로 곧장 배를 몰아 사공이 말한 섬에 이르렀다. 허생은 섬에 상륙하여 높은 바위 꼭대기로 올라가 사방을 바라보고 나서 썩 마음에 들지는 않는 듯 이렇게 말했다.

'땅이 1000리가 채 못 되니 무엇에 쓴단 말이냐. 다만 땅이 기름지고 샘물이 맛이 있으니 한갓 부잣집 늙은이 노릇이나 할 수 있겠다.'

사공이 말했다.

'섬이 텅텅 비고 사람 하나 구경할 수 없으니 누구와 더불어 산단 말입니까?'

'덕이 있는 사람에게는 사람들이 저절로 찾아오게 마련이지. 덕이 없는 것이 걱정이지, 어찌 사람이 없는 것을 근심하겠는가.'

이때 변산 지방에 수천 명의 도둑이 나타나 노략질을 하고 있었다. 여러 고을에서는 나졸들까지 풀어서 도둑을 잡으려 하였으나 도둑의 무리를 쉽사리 소탕하지 못했다. 그러나 도둑의 무리 역시 각 고을에서 대대적으로 막고 나서니 쉽게 나아가 도둑질하기가 어려워져 마침내 깊은 곳에 몸을 숨기고, 급기야는 굶어 죽을 판국에 이르렀다. 허생은 이 소문을 듣고 도둑의 소굴을 찾아 들어갔다. 그리고 도둑의 괴수를 만나 설득하기 시작했다.

'너희들 1000명이 천금을 노략질해서 나누어 가진다면 한 사람 앞에 얼마씩 돌아가느냐?'

'그야 한 사람에 한 냥이지.'

'그럼 너희들에게 처는 있는가?'

'없소.'

'그럼 논밭은?'

'흥, 밭이 있고 처가 있으면 왜 도둑질을 해?'

'정말 그렇다면 왜 장가를 들어 집을 짓고 소를 사서 농사를 짓지 않나? 그렇게 하면 도둑이란 더러운 이름도 듣지 않을 테고, 살림살이하는 부부의 재미도 있을 것이고, 아무리 밖으로 나가서 쏘다닌다고 해도 아무도 잡아가지 않을 테니 얼마나 좋은가? 길이길이 의식이 풍족할 것이다.'

'허허, 누가 그걸 몰라서 그래? 돈이 없으니까 그렇지.'

허생은 웃으며 말했다.

'너희들이 도둑질을 하면서 어찌 돈이 없는 것을 근심한단 말이냐? 정 그렇다면 내가 마련해주지. 내일 바다에 나가면 붉은 기를 단 배들이 보일 게다. 그것은 다 돈을 가득 실은 배야. 갖고 싶은 대로 가져가거라.'

이렇게 말하고는 어디론가 가버렸다. 도둑들은 하도 말 같지 않아서 모두 미친놈이라고 웃어댔다. 그러나 다음날 혹시나 해서 바다로 나가 보니, 허생은 이미 30만냥이나 되는 돈을 배에 싣고 기다리고 있지 않은가. 도둑들은 크게 놀라, 이건 보통 사람이 아니라고 생각했다. 모두 줄을 지어 절했다.

'그저 장군님의 분부대로 따르겠습니다.'

'그렇다면 어디 너희들이 질 수 있는 대로 가지고 가 보아라!'

Key vocabulary

묵적골	Mukchŏk village
해묵은	very old, many years old
사립문	gate made of twigs
오막살이	thatched house
아랑곳	care, attention
삯바느질	needlework
풀칠	day-to-day survival, lit. to smear rice around the mouth
과거	high civil service examination
껄껄	sound of loud laughter
공장	factory
밑천	founding money
벌떡	swiftly
한양	Seoul
단도직입적	straightforward
자제	children
영락	glory and comfort
뒤꿈치	heel
두루마기	overcoat

태연	calm as if nothing has happened
냥	unit of money
뱃사공	boatman
노릇	status
노략질	theft
소탕	completely win over
소굴	thieve's den, hideout
처	wife
분부	command

Comprehension questions: text

1 What was the wife's complaint to her husband?
2 How did the protagonist become rich?
3 Who lent him his money?
4 What did he plan after becoming rich?

Comprehension questions: drama extract

The KBS2 drama, *The Merchant: Gaekju 2015* (장사의 신 – 객주 2015, 2015), tells the story of Ch'un Pongsam, who from humble beginnings works his way up to becoming a powerful merchant who influences the market and business strategies. In episode six, we see him getting his first big break, as he creates a new system for selling cows. Like Heosaeng, he continues to keep the common good in mind as he multiplies his businesses.

1 What were Pongsam's father's last words?
2 Why is the cattle from Songpa Stables so popular?
3 Why is the detailed cattle report such a clever business strategy?
4 How can a village can buy a cow on credit?

Further discussion questions

1 What does the text reveal about the social problems related to the *yangban* class?
2 How do these social problems relate to our society today?
3 How does this text relate to Neo-Confucian ideology?

References

Kang, Chae-on, & Lee, Suzanne. 2006. *The Land of Scholars: Two Thousand Years of Korean Confucianism*. Paramus, NJ: Homa & Sekey Books (Chapter 18).

Li, Yingshun. 2011. 'A Comparative Study of Practical Learning in China and Korea During the Seventeenth and the Mid-Nineteenth Centuries.' *Chinese Studies in History* 44(4): 64–78.

Pastreich, Emanuel. 2011. *The Novels of Park Jiwon: Translation of Overlooked Worlds* (1st ed.). Seoul: Seoul National University Press.

Yun, Sasun, & Son, Yutaek. 2015. *Korean Philosophy: Sources and Interpretations*. Seoul: Korea University Press (Part 5).

4.5 대하 – 김남천 (Scenes from the Enlightenment – Kim Namch'ŏn)

Introduction to the text

Kim Namch'ŏn (1911–1953) is a North Korean writer, born in P'yŏngan province. Inspired by his involvement with the Korean Artists Proletarian Federation, his works tend to demonstrate a socialist realist style. It is assumed that his death was due to execution in a cultural purge. His novel *Scenes from the Enlightenment*, first published in 1939, shows how modernity slowly began to be integrated into traditional Korean life around the turn of the century. Gently comedic in tone, it both demonstrates the often incongruous mixtures of tradition and modernity that characterised this period, and raises deeper questions on the meaning of progress or staying faithful to the old ways. It should be noted that this text contains many non-standard spellings, as well as North Korean dialect versions of words.

Original text

얼마 아니 해서 오정이 되리라는 때에, 형선이는 많은 사람이 둘러선 가운데서 받뜰어 주는 사람도 없이 말안장 우에 닝큼 올러앉었다.

박 참봉네 행길 건너집은 이 칠성(李七星)이네 집이고, 웃집은 나까니시 상점 (中西商店)이고, 아렛집은 조그만 사탕장수라고, 깨엿도 놓고 호두엿도 놓았는데 진소위 사탕이라 명칭이 붙는 것으론 채다리과자와 얼음과자가 적은 나무통에 들어 있는, 김용구(金容九)네 집이다. 사나히라고 생긴 건 아이까지 나서고, 늙은 여편네들도 부엌챙 바자 옆에 나섰다. 바자틈으로 힐끗힐끗 흰 그림자가 보이는 것은, 행길가에 나설 수 없는 젊은 안악네와 나차른 처녀들이 숨어서 행길 쪽을 엿보는 탓이다. 나까니시네 집에서는 본시 나까니시가 혼자 호래비 생활을 하고 있으니, 다른 누구가 나설 이도 없다. 처음에 체부(遞夫)를 단니면서 처음에 이곳에 온, 이 나까니시는, 그 뒤에 진위대(鎭衛隊)가 없어지면서 수비대가 얼마간 주둔해 있을 때에, 용달을 맡아서 일년 안짝에 적지않은 이를 보아 지금은 제법 큼직한 잡화상이 되었다.

아래 웃거리에서도, 부잣집이고 행세하는 집들간의 혼삿날이니만큼, 많은 사람들이 쓸어 모이였다. 이 집과 친히 내왕하는 사람은 박 참봉 옆에 서 있고, 거래가 그리 많지 않은 사람은 저이끼리 두세 사람식 패를 지어 수군거리며 말 있는 행길 가운데를 구경하고 있다.

신랑이 타고 있는 돌채번 흰 말이나, 후행이 탈 갈색으로 팡파짐하니 다부지게 생긴 노새나, 안부(雁夫)가 탄 맨 앞에 자그막한 당나귀나, 모두 박 참봉 제 집에서 친히 길르는 즘생들이다. 흰 말과 당나귀는 먼 길을 갈 때나, 추수할 때 타작하려 가노라고 가끔 타고, 노새는 연자질을 시키노라고 손수 맥역 길른다. 길 가운데 서서 수많은 눈이 저이들을 보고 있는 걸 아는지 모르는지, 발굽을 올리며 커다란 눈을 꺼벅거리고 탈 사람들을 기대리고 있다.

마바리꾼에게 줄 것으로 흰 무명 세 필을 한 끝식 풀어서, 안장과 즘생의 코숭이와 꼬리 있는 데까지 회게 줄을 느린 것이, 풍족해 보여 볼품이 좋았다. 말꾼들은 말초리가 끝에 붙은 챗딕을 등곺에 쫓고, 말꿉지를 단단히 밭게 부뜰고서, 그중의 한 사람은 말의 머리를 가만가만히 쓸어 주고 서 있다. 기러기를 안은 구 훈장이 탄 당나귀 앞에 저만치 앞서, 권마상꾼 둘이 서서 박 참봉 쪽을 눈이 찌그뚱해서 바라보고 있다. 이들의 고함소리가 청높은 염불처럼 거리를 뒤흔들 때엔, 말방울이 울고, 말꾼의 챗딕이 보기 좋게 말궁둥이를 후려갈기는 때이다.

모든 준비가 되었는데 박 참봉과 후행갈 최 관술이가 대문 안에서 무슨 일인가 수군거리고 있다. 사람들의 시선은 모다 그쪽으로 쏠려 있다. 말탄 채 벌서 적지않은 동안을 기대리고 서 있는 구 훈장과 신랑도, 궁금해선지, 하나는 기러기를 안고, 또 하나는 뻔히 사선을 든 채 그쪽을 바라보고 있다.

　이야기는 최 관술이가 쓰고 있는 국자보시를 벗고, 갓을 대신으로 쓰라는 교섭이다. 그러나 최 관술이는 좀처럼 박 참봉의 말을 듣지 않는다.

　지금까지 이 고을서 쓰는 개화된 신식 모자는 두 가지밖에 없었다. 학도들이 쓰는 삽포 – 다시 말하면 학생모자가 그의 하나요, 학도 아닌 사람이 쓰는 국자보시가 다른 또 하나다. 국자보시라는 건 한팅 비슷한 건데, 이곳서는 그것을 도리우찌라고도 않 하고 국자보시라 한다. 물론 그것을 쓰는 사람도 별로 없다. 최 관술이가 금테로 맨든 개화경을 코허리에 걸고 검정 명주 두루막이에 발목덜미까지 높이 엮어올린 구두를 신고, 반반히 깎은 머리 우에 댕그렁하니 올려놓은 것이 이 국자보시란 게다. 그는 다시 울통불퉁한 황양목을 껍질을 벗겨서, 옹지 있는 곳을 약간 불에 태워 그것을 개화장이라고 집고 댄닌다.

　다른 것 다 말고, 저 덥부룩하니 깎은 머리 우에 홀랑하니 방정막게 올라앉은 꼭지 있는 바리깨 같은, 국자보신가 저까락보신가 한 것만 벗어 버리고, 그 대신 구 훈장처럼 점잖은 감투와 갓만 써준다면, 그까짓 코허리가 시근시근한 개화경이니, 개박정 들이나 들고 다닐 개화정이니 한 것 같은 건, 그런대로 모른 척도 할 수 있을 것 같다.

　처음 박 참봉은 이왕 신식 사람을 보내는 바엔, 그가 어떠한 모양을 하건 눈감어 둘 라 했었는데, 정각 말이 나서고 사람들이 모인 가운데서 처남이 하고 있는 품을 바라보니, 아모래도 마음 한 모퉁이가 께름하고 믿음성이 가지 않아 참을 수가 없는 것이다.

　그러나 당자가 옥여대는 판국이니, 지금 이 자리에서 아옹다옹 다투고 있을 수도 없는 형편이다. 소견대로 하라고 내맡기니, 최 관술이는 자개수염을 한 번 부비고, 성 큼성큼 개화장을 둘러가며 노새 있는 쪽으로 걸어간다. 말을 타고 개화장을 둘을 수도 없는 터이라, 말 옆에 우뚝 서서 몽둥이를 횡횡 객적게 둘러본 뒤에, 그 놈을 난뜨럭 말안장 옆에다 가루 찔러 끼운다. 획하니 말 우에 올라타드니 한 번 개화경을 햇빛에 번적 하니 빛내이고,

　'자, 가자구.' 하면서 말뒤굼치로 노새 뱃통머리를 가만히 두어 번 찌른다. 이 말이 떠러지기가 무섭게 잔뜩 대기하고 있는 권마성꾼이, '아 – 아으아 – ' 하고 앞에서 목청을 도두 세워서 소래기를 지른다. 당나귀가 아장거리고, 신랑탄 흰 말이 꼬리를 두어 번 치다가 떼꾹떼꾹 걸어간다. 새서방은 사선으로 얼굴을 가리우고 눈앞에 우쭐거리는 먼 앞 길을 황홀하게 빛이여 본다. 손우수가 탄 노새도 냉금냉금 발굽을 두어 번 굴르듯 하드니, 방정맞게 외해항 소리를 치며 앞말을 따라간다. 말이 강선루를 바라보며 앞으로 움직이는 대로, 권마성과 말방울소리에 맞후어 구 훈장의 갓과 신랑의 사모와 손우수의 국자보시가 후물후물 춤추듯 한다.

Key vocabulary

오정	noon, midday
말안장	saddle
닁큼	from 넝큼: without hesitation
채다리과자	ice pops (North Korean dialect, lit., sieve-frame leg sweet)
얼음과자	ice cream (North Korean dialect)
사나히	from 사나이: a man, men
바자	bamboo or reeds linked together to make a fence
호래비	dialect version of 홀아비: widower
체부	postman
진위대	regional army post
수비대	defensive garrison

퉁파짐하다	stocky, well-rounded, pudgy
노새	mule
안부	the person who goes in front of the groom carrying the wild goose to be presented to the bride's parents
즘생	dialect version of 짐승: beast, animal
추수	harvest
연자질	turning the millstone
마바리꾼	packhorse driver
볼품	appearance, look
말초리	dialect version of 말총: horsehair
챗딕	archaic version of 채찍: whip
등곬	corruption of 등골: the furrow down the middle of the back
말꼽지	dialect version of 고삐: reins
권마상꾼	herald
후행	escort the bridegroom
국자보시	flat cap, lit., ladle + hat (*bōshi* in Japanese), also called 도리우찌
교섭	negotiation
개화경	lit., 'enlightened glasses,' glasses in the modern style
명주	silk
두루막	dialect version of 두루마기: traditional style overcoat
황양목	corruption of 회양목: boxwood tree
신식	new style, modern style
께름하다	same as 꺼림하다: to feel uneasy
판국	situation, state of affairs
자개수염	North Korean dialect: Moustache that sticks out firmly on either side
뒤굼치	뒤꿈치: heel
소래기	coarse way to say 소리: sound
사선	a piece of gauze supported between two sticks that the groom holds in front of his face as he travels to the bride's house
방정맞게	frivolously, flippantly

Comprehension questions: text

1   Who is Nakanishi?
2   In what order is the procession laid out?
3   What are Assistant Curator Pak and Ch'oe Kwansul arguing about?
4   How is Ch'oe Kwansul dressed?

Comprehension questions: drama extract

The SBS drama, *Rooftop Prince* (옥탑방 왕세자, 2012), tells of a Chosŏn dynasty prince, Yi Kak, who travels into the present day after his wife dies under mysterious circumstances, landing in the rooftop home of Pak Ha. In contrast to the text above, where modern elements caused a stir as they began to intrude into traditional lifestyles, here we see how people are intrigued seeing elements of traditional life intruding into the modern everyday.

1   What is Pak Ha's predicament regarding the strawberries?
2   What does she threaten Yi Kak with if he doesn't help pick the strawberries?

3   How does Yi Kak adjust his speech in an attempt to fit in?
4   How does he get people to come help with the strawberry picking?

Additional source materials

One film that portrays the clash between traditional and modern lifestyles is the 2016 film *Love, Lies* (해어화).
  Further source material involving a time travel element include:

Film, *Jeon Woo Chi: The Taoist Wizard* (전우치, 2009).
tvN drama, *Queen In-hyun's Man* (인현왕후의 남자, 2012).
MBC drama, *Dr. Jin* (닥터 진, 2012).
SBS drama, *Faith* (신의, 2012).
MBC drama, *Splash Splash Love* (너에게 풍당, 2015).
SBS drama, *Moon Lovers: Scarlet Heart Ryeo* (달의 연인 – 보보경심 려, 2016).

Further discussion questions

1   What do you think is the role of humour in smoothing over the awkwardness of the meeting between tradition and modernity?
2   Do you think we should always follow new trends, or are there times when it is important to hold onto tradition?

References

Chandra, Vipan. 1988. *Imperialism, Resistance, and Reform in Late Nineteenth-Century Korea: Enlightenment and the Independence Club* (Korea research monograph; 13). Berkeley: Center for Korean Studies, Institute of East Asian Studies, University of California.
Kang, Junggeun, & Morgan, Michael. 1988. 'Culture Clash: Impact of US Television in Korea.' *Journalism Quarterly* 65(2): 431–38.
Kim, Sonja M. 2016. 'Women, Gender, and Social Change in Colonial Korea.' In *Routledge Handbook of Modern Korean History*, edited by Michael Seth, p. 141. London: Routledge.
La Shure, Charles. 2016. 'The Clash of Culture in Kim Namchon's Scenes from the Enlightenment.' *Acta Koreana* 19(2): 87–108.
Lee, Yeaann. 2018. 'The Appropriation of "Enlightenment" in Modern Korea and Japan: Competing Ideas of the Enlightenment and the Loss of the Individual Subject. *Educational Philosophy and Theory* 1–12.

4.6 맹진사댁경사 – 오영진 (*The Happy Day of Maeng Chinsa –* O Yŏngjin)

Introduction to the text

This was written by Oh Yŏngjin (1916–1974). The text is a criticism of the greed and foolishness of humans. It is based on the traditional Korean belief that good people will be rewarded and bad people will be punished (kwŏnsŏnjing'ak 권선징악(勸善懲惡)). The text sharply displays the foolishness and vanity of humans, and shows a special Korean style through its satirical and humorous expressions.

Section 1: Maeng Chinsa, who wants to wield authority by connecting powerful families with his in-laws, brags after promising to marry his only daughter, Kappuni, to the son of Judge Kim's family [Opening]. However, one day Kim Myŏngjŏng comes by in the clothing of a customer and hints that the groom is a cripple, and Meng Chinsa's family is turned upside-down [Development].

Section 2: Kappuni, now knowing this fact, whines that she won't be married. Maeng Chinsa has the excellent idea to dress a servant girl, Ippuni, as Kappuni, and to go forward with the marriage. Later, the son of the Minister confesses that he was the one who actually spread the rumour about his leg in order to be married to the servant girl Ippuni.

Original text

맹진사: 예! 아무도 없느냐 아무도 없어? 헛 내가 어떤 길을 다녀왔다구 쥐새끼 한마리 얼씬 않느냐 (사람들이 안에서 나온다)
삼돌 : 에그 나리마님 어느새 당겨 오셨군 입쇼
맹진사 : 에끼 이놈 그래 . . . 마님 계시냐?
삼돌 : 네. 가셨던 일 어찌나 되셨나 그렇찮아두 지금 안절부절 . . .
맹진사 : 안절부절은 왜? 그런 걱정말구 냉큼 나오시라고 그래
삼돌 : (안으로 들어간다. 그와 스쳐 사랑에서 길보 뛰어 나온다)
길보 : 에그 나으리 어느새 당겨 오셨어유?
맹진사 : 꼭두새벽에 도라지골을 떠났다.
길보 : 그렇찮아두 가셨던 일이 어찌나 되셨나 큰나리마님허구 운산골 나리꺼정 오셔서 . . .
맹진사 : 운산골 나리? 오 숙부님께서도 오셨단 말이겠지? 그러면 그럴테지
길보 : 네 가셨던 일 하회가 어찌나 되셨나 하구
맹진사 : 계서두 안절부절들이냐?
길보 : 아 그야 . . .
맹진사 : 에이 걱정들두 . . . 나가 여쮜라 곧 나아가 뵙겠다구
길보 : 그럼 거지반 성사가 됐군입쇼.
맹진사 : 헛! 누가 나선 일인데
길보 : 암으렴입쇼. 네가 뭐랬습니까.
맹진사 : 예 갑분아씬 어딨느냐
길보 : 갑분아가씬 이뿐이 거나리구 이웃 색씨들허구 뒷산에 도라지 캐러 가셨나 봅니다.
맹진사 : 뭣이? 도라지 캐러? 에이 조심성 없는것 냉큼 쫓어가 모셔 오너라.
길보 : 네에 (발씻을 물을 떠다놓고 사랑으로 나간다)
맹진사 : 저때문에 이 애비 이 고초도 몰르고 . . . 그나마 지체높은 김판서댁 며누리가 되느냐 못되느냐 하는 판국에 에이 조심성 없는 계집애 같으니라구 (한씨와 유모 안에서 나온다)
(. . .)
효원 : 네가 처음 도라지골에 갔을 때 정녕 아무말도 한배가 없었겠다?
맹진사 : 네?
효원 : (패물상자를 가리키며) 선치네 대해서 말이다
맹진사 : 네 네 아 아무말두
효원 : 적실이? 그렇다면 더욱이나 고이허지가 않느냐 그럼 이 물건을 받을 때 도대체 어떤 생각으로 받았느냐 응

맹진사 : 전 . . . 선치라군 생각지 않았습니다
효원 : 뭣이 어째? 그럼 딸자식 팔아먹은 응당 받아야 할 값이란 말이냐
맹진사 : 작은아버지
효원 : 따져 말할 지경이면 이건 일종의 매매혼이야 패물로서 딸자식을 파는것
이나 다를게 뭐냐말야?
맹진사 : 작은 아버지 그건 좀 너무하신 . . .
효원 : 아냐 명문집안을 생각하거들랑 잔말말고 퇴해버려
맹진사 : 작은 아버지 말씀은 지당하시나 그렇다구 이제와서 이걸 퇴해 보낸다든
가 하면 저편에서 어찌 알겠습니까 되레 세도권 문가 예의범절에 거슬려서 모
처럼 이룩해논 혼사에 세삼스레 긁어 부스럼이나 되지않을까 전 두렵습니다
효원 : 대관절 넌 말끝마다 예의범절 예의범절 하면서 어째 너의 집 예의는 찾
을줄 모르느냐 응
맹진사 : 작은 아버지 그럼 저두 한마디 똑똑히 여쭙겠습니다 (공세를 취한다)
효원 : 말해봐
맹진사 : 전 그댁허구 사둔관계를 맺음으로서 우리집 문벌을 높일겸 또한편으
론 저이가 살아가는데도 그 덕으로 어떤힘도 얻어 보려는 긍량으로 . . .
효원 : 무슨 소리냐 그럼 너도 세도가 탐이 난단 말이냐?
맹진사 : 세도가 나쁠건 또 뭡니까? 가문을 한칭 더 빛나게 하려는게 나쁠건 뭡
니까 작은아버지
효원 : 듣기싫여 (벌떡 일어나며) 선치를 받어 모욕을 당하구 이집안 세도가 올
라가? 천치같은것 되레 당신인줄은 왜 모르구 . . . 좋을대로 해라 그대신 어
물전 망신은 꼴뚜기가 시키드라 그세상 웃길 짓만 해봐라 용서치 않을테다
. . . 에이 난간다
맹진사 : 작은아버지
효원 : 더 얘기하구 싶지두 않구 구구한 변명을 듣고 싶지도 않어 일이 있거들
랑 운산골루 오너라 (사랑으로 퇴장)
맹진사 : 제기랄 고집두 내참 어쨌단 말이유 어 내딸가지구 내맘대로 하는데 작
은아버지면 제일이야 왜 이러시우 이러시길 내참 (한씨 등장)

Key vocabulary

숙부	uncle
나으리	Lord
마님	Lady
계집애	derogatory word for young, unmarried lady
아씨	honorific title for woman
매매혼	contractual marriage
지체	nobility
선치	dowry
문벌	pedigree
어물전 망신은 꼴뚜기가 시킨다.	one bad apple spoils the bunch

Comprehension questions: text

1 What can you tell about Maeng Chinsa's attitude towards his daughter's marriage?
2 What are the conflicts between Maeng Chinsa and his uncle and how are they resolved?

3   How is the attitude of the uncle towards Maeng Chinsa realised through language?
4   What kind of language does Maeng Chinsa use to his servants?

Comprehension questions: film extract

As in the tale of Maeng Chinsa, the popular JTBC drama *Sky Castle* (SKY캐슬, 2018) starkly shows the price to be paid for boundless ambition. In episode 16, Ch'a Minhyŏk's attempts to encourage his sons, Sŏjun and Kijun, to take advantage of their rivals' moment of weakness also meets an undignified end.

1   How does Ch'a Minhyŏk understand the situation at school?
2   How do his sons respond to his suggestion?
3   What is Ch'a Minhyŏk's life philosophy?
4   How does Kijun react to this?

Additional source material

Two film versions of the tale of Maeng Chinsa were made: *A Happy Day of Jinsa Maeng* (맹진사댁 경사, 1962), and *The Wedding Day* (시집 가는 날, 1956).

Further discussion questions

1   Discuss marriage as practiced in the Joseon dynasty.
2   Was cross-class marriage possible in the Joseon dynasty?
3   How is the ethos of kwŏnsŏnjing'ak realised in this work?

References

Han, Seo. 2016. *Re-Claiming the Ideals of the Yŏllyŏ˘: Women in and with Books in Early Chosŏn Korea*, ProQuest Dissertations and Theses.
Ho, Swee Lin. 2012. 'Fuel for South Korea's "Global Dreams Factory": The Desires of Parents Whose Children Dream of Becoming K-Pop Stars.' *Korea Observer* 43(3): 471–502.
Kendall, Laurel. 1996. *Getting Married in Korea: Of Gender, Morality, and Modernity*. Berkeley: University of California Press.
Kim, Jungwon. 2007. *Negotiating Virtue and the Lives of Women in Late Chosŏn Korea*, ProQuest Dissertations and Theses.

5   *Han*

5.1   제망매가 – 월명사 (*Song for a Departed Sister – Wŏlmyŏngsa*)

Introduction to text

Song for a Departed Sister is a text based on Wŏlmyŏngsa's song for his deceased sister. This song is a ten-line *hyangga*, and its contents can be divided into three sections. The last section is headed by an expression of emotion. These attributes are typical of other *hyangga* as well.

In the first section, the song describes the current situation of the sister's death. In the second section, the relationship of the sister and the rest of society is described. In the last section the song describes a future which includes another meeting in paradise. The song is based on the Buddhist ideology of three generation reincarnation. Accordingly, Wŏlmyŏngsa doesn't stop showing his devoted affection to his sister, and uses this to sing of faith in Buddhism – specifically in Amita Buddha. The song describes the Buddhist belief that all meetings must end in parting, and promises another meeting in the future. Similarly to Han Yongun's 'Silence,' the approach here is to overcome human sadness through religion.

Background from Samgukyusa

Wŏlmyŏng had held a funeral for his younger sister who had died early. When he made a *hyangga* and held a ceremony, a sudden wind blew the paper money away and it disappeared to the south.

Wŏlmyŏng had always lived in the Sach'ŏnwangsa temple (Temple of the Four Deva Kings) and played the traditional flute well. On a moonlight night, he was walking down the street by the big gate, playing his flute, and the moon stopped moving because of his music. So the street is called Wŏlmyŏng-ri, and he became well-known. The priest was Nŭngjundaesa's follower. Sillan people have long admired *hyangga*, which is normally similar to a poem or hymn. Moving heaven and earth and gods was not done just once or twice: the praising song reads as follows:

Original text

Sinitic text (Hyangch'al)

1   生死路隱
2   此矣有阿米次﹁伊遣
3   吾隱去內如辭叱

4 都毛如云遣去內尼叱古
5 於內秋察早隱風未
6 此矣彼矣浮良落尸葉如
7 一等隱枝良出古
8 去奴隱處毛冬乎丁
9 阿也彌陀刹良逢乎吾
10 道修良待是古如

Modern Korean

삶과 죽음의 길은
여기서 갈라지거늘
나는 간다 말도
못 이르고 갑니까
어찌 가을 이른 바람에
이에 저에 떠다니다 질 잎처럼
한 가지에 나고
가는 곳 모르랴
아아 미타찰에서 만날 나
도 닦으며 기다려 다오

Key vocabulary for Sinitic text

Line 1

生死 means life or death
路 means road
隱 means grammatical morpheme, sound borrowing. This is a topic particle, and can be translated as 'talking about, to my opinion on X'

Line 2

此矣 means here
有阿米 means existing, however

Line 3

吾 means I, me
隱 is a grammatical morpheme, sound borrowing. This is a topic particle, and can be translated as 'talking about, to my opinion on X'
去 means to go; here means to die

Line 4

毛如云 means without saying
去內尼叱古 means going, expressing the speaker's frustration.

Line 5

秋察早隱風未 means through the autumn breeze

Line 6

落尸葉如 means fallen leaves

Line 7

一等隱枝 means one same branch

Line 8

出古 means being born
去奴隱處 means place where we are going
隱 is used as a genitive, modifying particle.
毛冬乎丁 means don't know (how frustrating it is)

Line 9

阿 means oh, ah!
彌陀刹 means a Buddhist paradise

Line 10

道修良 means the pursuit of virtue

Key vocabulary for modern Korean

삶	life
죽음	death
갈라지다	to be devided
이르다	to say
어찌	how dare
잎	leaves
모르랴	don't know (and how is it that we don't know)
도 닦다	pursuing virtues
기다려 다오	please wait for me.

Comprehension questions: text

1. How does Wŏlmyŏng respond to the death of his sister?
2. How did he resolve to overcome his sadness?
3. What did he compare to life and death?
4. How are the religious views of the author reflected in this text?

Comprehension questions: drama extract

The KBS2 drama, *Good Doctor* (굿 닥터, 2013), tells the story of an autistic savant, Pak Shion, who works in paediatric surgery at the hospital, and how he convinces the people around him that he is qualified for his job. Having lost his brother as a child, Pak continues to have difficulty processing this loss – this comes to a head in episode 11, when, having had a dream, he goes to his saviour, the hospital director Ch'oe Usŏk, to talk about it.

1. What has Shion been dreaming about?
2. Why does he think his brother should have been saved?
3. Why does he think he was saved?
4. Why did Ch'oe Usŏk save him?

Additional source material

The 2018 film *Be With You* (지금 만나러 갑니다) also poignantly shows how a family deals with the loss of a wife and mother.

Further discussion question

1   What is the historical background of the genre of this text?
2   What is the view of death in Buddhism?

References

Cheolwon, Seo. 2014. 'Afterlife Ideas of Silla People in Hyangga and Samgookyoosa.' *Korean Classical Poetry Studies* 37: 109–38.
Ko, Changsu. 2015. 'The Narrative Attitude of <Jemangmaega, Lyric for a Dead Sister>.' *Korean Cultural Studies* (66): 253–70.
Park, Jin-Ho. 2008. 'The Interpretation of Hyangga and Historical Grammar of Korean.' *Journal of Korean Linguistics* (51): 313–38.

5.2 향수 – 정지용 (*Thoughts of Home* – Chŏng Chiyong)

Introduction to the text

Chŏng Chiyong (1902–1950) is considered among the most important poets to emerge from the modernist movement in Korea. In fact, he has been described as 'the first modern Korean poet.' He uses a rich command of the Korean language to present a variety of sensual images which describe his longing for his hometown.

The poem, 'Hyangsu,' was included in *Chosŏn Chigwang* (1927.3). The poem includes beautifully phrased, wistful images of the author's hometown and childhood. Such visual images are important to this poem. Most of these images are simple and earthy, and the sensual information portrayed is sharp and original. The poem depicts the very human characteristic of longing for home. It also has a retrospective and reflective feeling, which finds its place in the intersection of poetry and story writing displayed in the rhythm of the piece. The chorus brings the main themes of the poem into sharp relief.

Original text

넓은 벌 동쪽 끝으로
옛이야기 지줄대는 실개천이 휘돌아 나가고,
얼룩백이 황소가
해설피 금빛 게으른 울음을 우는 곳,
                              – 그 곳이 참하 꿈엔들 잊힐리야.

질화로에 재가 식어지면
뷔인 밭에 밤바람 소리 말을 달리고
엷은 졸음에 겨운 늙으신 아버지가
짚벼개를 돋아 고이시는 곳
                              – 그 곳이 참하 꿈엔들 잊힐리야.

흙에서 자란 내 마음
파아란 하늘 빛이 그리워
함부로 쏜 화살을 찾으려
풀섶 이슬에 함추름 휘적시던 곳,
　　　　　　　　　　　　　－ 그 곳이 참하 꿈엔들 잊힐리야.

전설 바다에 춤추는 밤물결 같은
검은 귀밑머리 날리는 어린 누의와
아무렇지도 않고 예쁠 것도 없는
사철 발 벗은 안해가
따가운 햇살을 등에 지고 이삭 줏던 곳,
　　　　　　　　　　　　　－ 그 곳이 참하 꿈엔들 잊힐리야.

하늘에는 성근 별
알 수도 없는 모래성으로 발을 옮기고,
서리 까마귀 우지짖고 지나가는 초라한 집웅,
흐릿한 불빛에 돌아 앉어 도란 도란거리는 곳,
　　　　　　　　　　　　　－ 그 곳이 참하 꿈엔들 잊힐리야.

Key vocabulary

넓은벌	wide field
지줄대다	to chatter
휘돌아	to turn around, back
얼룩백이	striped
해설피금빛	golden sunlight
참하꿈엔들	even in dreams
질화로	the furnace, oven
뷔인	empty
엷은졸음	light sleep
짚벼개	straw pillow
파아란	very blue
이슬	dew
함추름휘적시다	get soaking wet
밤물결	night-time waves
귀밑머리	pigtails
누의	sister
사철	four seasons
이삭	ear, grain
집웅	roof
도란도란	round

Comprehension questions: text

1 Find the poetic expressions in this poem and explain the poetic nature of those words and phrases.
2 How does the author use personification to describe the setting of the poem?

Comprehension questions: film extract

The 2014 film *Ode to my Father* (국제시장) shows many of the events in modern Korean history through the eyes of a refugee from North Korea during the Korean War. Yun Tŏksu is one of the men who travel to Germany in the 1960s to work in the mines, and it is there that he meets Yŏngja, a trainee nurse. They bond over missing their home, especially Korean food.

1. Why is Yŏngja surprised that Tŏksu remembered her saying she wanted to have Korean food?
2. Why was Yŏngja singing a sad song the day they first met?
3. What does Tŏksu tell her to do when she next feels sad?
4. What does Yŏngja call Tŏksu, and what would he prefer to be called?

Further discussion questions

1. How do Korean values as shown through images of sobakham (honestly, simplicity, rusticity) differ from Western values?
2. How does the author describe his wife, and how do you interpret his feelings?

References

Chŏng, Chiyong, & Kister, Daniel A. 1994. *Distant Valleys: Poems of Chŏng Chi-Yong*. Berkeley, Calif: Asian Humanities Press.
Grinker, Roy Richard. 1995. 'Mourning the Nation: Ruins of the North in Seoul.' *Positions: East Asia Cultures Critique* 3(1): 192–223.
Lee, Peter H. 2003. *A History of Korean Literature*. Cambridge: Cambridge University Press. (Chapter 18).
Sym, Myungho. 1985. *The Making of Modern Korean Poetry: Foreign Influences and Native Creativity* (2nd printing ed.). Seoul: Seoul National University Press.

5.3 은세계 – 이인직 (*Silver World* – Yi Injik)

Introduction to the text

Yi Injik (1862–1916) is credited as one of the first writers of Korean New Fiction (신소설). However, he is not without controversy, as he was active as a pro-Japanese collaborator during the colonial period in Korea, and his works alternate between art and didacticism as he tries to advocate learning and education as means to raise society up from the squalor and suffering that he perceived premodern Korea to be. The novel, *Ŭnsegye*, is a clear example of this: the beginning of the story, telling of the sufferings of self-made man Ch'oe Pyŏngdo at the hands of the local governor who wants to get his hands on Ch'oe's riches, is written in a lyrical style borrowing heavily from *p'ansori* for inspiration, even to the extent of inserting songs into the text. In contrast, the second half, when Ch'oe's children go to America to study and come back to find their mother and help educate the masses, reads more like a philosophical treatise than a novel.

Original text

'최변도가 죄 없는 사람이라.'
 '애매히 잡혀 온 사람이라.'

'그 정경이 참 불쌍한 사람이라.'

하며 수군거리는 소리는 사람마다 있는 측은한 마음에서 나오는 말이라. 그러나 그중에 측은한 마음이 조금도 없는 사람은 감사 하나뿐이라. 부끄러운 생각이 있던지 얼굴이 벌게지며 두 볼이 축 처지도록 율기(律己)를 잔뜩 뽐고 앉아서 불호령을 하는데, 최병도의 죄목은 새 제목이라.

무슨 죄가 삽시간에 생겼는고? 최 씨는 순리로 말을 하였으나 감사는 그 말을 듣고 관정발악(官庭發惡)한다 하면서, 형틀을 들어라, 별형장을 들어라, 집장 사령을 골라 세라 하는 영이 떨어지며, 물 끓듯 하는 사령들이 이리 몰려가고 저리 몰려가고 갈팡질팡하더니, 일반 형틀을 들여놓으며 일변 산장을 끼없더니, 최병도를 형틀 위에 동그랗게 올려 매고 형문을 친다. 형방 영리는 목청을 돋워서 첫 매부터 피를 묻혀 올리라 하는 영을 전하는데 형문 맞는 사람은 고사하고 집장 사령이 죽을 지경이라. 사령은 젖 먹던 힘을 다 들여 치건마는 감사는 헐장한다고 벼락령이 내린다. 집장 사령의 죽지를 떼어라, 오금을 끊어라 하는 서슬에 집장 사령이 매질을 어떻게 몹시 하였던지 형문 한치에 최병도가 정신이 있을락 없을락 할 지경인데, 그러한 최병도를 큰칼을 씌워서 옥중에 내려 가두니 그 옥은 사람을 하나씩 가두는 별옥이라. 별옥이라 하면 최 씨를 대접하여 특별히 편히 있을 곳에 가둔 것이 아니라 부자를 잡아 오면 가두는 곳이 따로 있는 터이라.

무슨 까닭으로 별옥을 지었으며 무슨 까닭으로 부자를 잡아 오면 따로 가두는고? 대체 그 감사가 백성의 돈 뺏어 먹는 일에는 썩 솜씨 있는 사람이라. 별옥이 몇 간이나 되는 옥인지 부민을 잡아 오면 한 간에 사람 하나씩 따로따로 가두고 뒤로 사람을 보내서 으르고 달래고 꾀이고 별 농락을 다하여 돈을 우려낼대로 우려내는 터이라.

최병도가 그런 옥중에 여러 달 동안을 갇혀 있는데 장처가 아물 만하면 잡혀 들어가서 형문 한 치씩 맞기 간히나, 그러나 최 씨는 종시 감사에게 돈을 바치고 놓여 나갈 생각이 없고 밤낮으로 장독이 나서 앓는 소리와 감사가 미워서 이 가는 소리뿐이라. 옥중에서 그렇게 세월을 보내는데 엄동설한에 잡혀갔던 사람이 그 이듬해가 되었더라.

하지 머리에 비가 뚝뚝 떨어지며 시골 농가에서는 논코 뜰 새 없이 바쁜 터이라. 밀보리 타작을 못다 하고 모심기가 시작되었는데, 강릉 대관령 밑 경금 동네 앞 논에서 농부가가 높았더라. 보리곱삶이 댓 되 밥을 먹은 후에 곁두리로 보리 탁주를 사발로 퍼먹은 농부들이 북통 같은 배를 질질 끌고 기억 자로 꾸부리고 서서 왼손에 모춤을 들고 오른손으로 모포기를 찢어 심으며 뒷걸음을 슬슬 하여 나가는데 힘들고 괴로운 줄은 조금도 모르고 흥이 나서 소리를 한다. 그 소리는 선소리꾼이 당장 지어 하는 소리인데 워낙 입심이 좋은 사람이라, 서슴지 아니하고 소리를 먹이는데 썩 듣기 좋게 잘하는 소리라.
(...)
여허여허 어여라 상사디야.
염려되네 염려되네 박 첨지 집이 염려되네.
지붕 처마 두둑하고 볏섬이나 쌓였다고 앞뒤 동네 소문났네,
관가 영문 들어가면 없는 죄에 걸려 톡톡 털고 거지 되리.
여허 여허 이여라 상사디야.
우리 동네 최 서방님 굳기는 하지마는 그를 일은 없더니라,
벼 천이나 하는 죄로 영문에 잡혀가서 형문 맞고 큰칼 쓰고
옥중에 갇혀 있어 반년을 못 나오네.
여허 여허 어여라 상사디야.
삼대록자 최 서방님 조실부모하였으니
불효, 부제 죄목 듣기 그 아니 원통한가?
순사도 그 양반이 정 씨 성을 가지고
돈 소리에만 귀가 길고, 원망 소리에는 귀먹었데,

여허 여허 어여라 상사디야.
우리 동무 내 말 듣게.
이 농사를 지어서 먹고 입고 남거든 돈 모을 생각 말고
술 먹고 노름하고 놀대로 놀아 보세.
마구 뺏는 이 세상에 부자 되면 경치느니.
여허 여허 어여라 상사디야.

Key vocabulary

애매히	unfairly, unjustly
측은하다	compassionate, pitiful
감사	governor, ruler of a province
율기	to bring oneself under control
뿜다	gush, belch, spout, fume
불호령	impetuous order, strict command, howl of rage
죄목	charges
제목	title, name
관정발악	contempt of court, when someone curses a government official during questioning
형틀	the rack, a special seat for torturing prisoners during interrogation
형장	clubs used during interrogation in the Chosŏn period
집장사령	person in charge of carrying out punishment such as flogging
갈팡질팡	flustered, confused, wavering, incoherent
산장	interrogation technique, where the various torture instruments are spread out in front of the prisoner
형문	punishment by striking the shins of the prisoner with clubs
영리	clerk, secretary
목청을돋우다	to raise one's voice
고사하다	to refuse, decline
죽을지경이다	to be in a tight spot, in a tough position
헐장	to make a punishment beating as light and painless as possible
죽지를떼다	to let out your anger on your subordinates
큰칼	cangue, a large flat board with a hole for the prisoner's head, preventing the prisoner from sitting or lying comfortably, and sometimes even preventing them from feeding themselves
씌우다	cover, wrap around
별옥	solitary confinement, single-person cell
솜씨	skill, ability
부민	wealthy people
으르다	threaten, intimidate
달래다	comfort, soothe
꾀이다	lure, entice, tempt
농락	cajoling, seduction, persuasion
돈을우려내다	extort money out of
장처	wounds from torture or punishment

아물	heal
종시	to the last, to the very end
바치다	offer, present, give
장독	poison/infection emerging from wounds through severe beating
이갈다	gnashing/grinding teeth
이듬해	next year, the following year
하지	summer solstice
눈코뜰새없이바쁘다	be extremely busy
타작	threshing
모심기	rice transplanting season
보리곱샄이	double-boiled barley
댓	around five
되	unit of measure, roughly 1.8 litres
곁두리	snacks for farmhands at work
탁주	raw unrefined wine
사발	(porcelain) bowl
모춤	bundle of rice seedlings
입심	eloquence
상사소리	the songs sung while planting
여허여허어여라상사디야	this is a vocalisation that functions as a chorus in planting songs
첨지	derogative/informal way of describing an elderly person
처마	eaves of the roof
두둑하다	plentiful, ample – here, most likely referring to fruits/fish etc. hung from the eaves of the roof to dry
그른일	an evil deed
삼대독자	the only son for three generations
조실부모	to lose one's parents at a young age
불효	to be unfilial
부제	to not act properly towards one's older siblings
귀먹었다	to be deaf
경치	to be severely punished

Comprehension questions: text

1 What crime is Ch'oe accused of?
2 Does the governor think Ch'oe's beating is sufficient?
3 Why does the prison have separate solitary confinement cells?
4 Why are the farmers worried for Old Man Pak?

Comprehension questions: film extract

The 2014 film *Kundo: Age of the Rampant* (군도: 민란의 시대) which broke box-office records at the time of its release, tells the story of a group of bandits in mid-19th-century Chosŏn Korea, who steal from the noblemen who take advantage of and torment the poor. In the scene where Tolmuch'i, the butcher protagonist of the story, has been taken to prison after storming into the *sŏja* (noble son of a concubine) Cho Yun's home wanting to exact revenge for Cho's henchmen killing his family, we see just how easy it is for the rich and powerful to flaunt the laws of society.

1. What is Cho Yun asking the magistrate to do to Tolmuch'i? Does the magistrate agree to this request?
2. What is the reason Cho Yun gives for Tolmuch'i going on a rampage at his brother's funeral?
3. What does the magistrate find suspicious about the recent events?
4. How does Cho Yun overcome the magistrate's misgivings?

Additional source material

The 2019 SBS drama series *Nokdu Flower* (녹두꽃) addresses the Donghak Rebellion (1894–1895), when the peasants rose up against the kind of oppression described in Yi Injik's novel.

Further discussion questions

1. Does Yi Injik's status as a pro-Japanese collaborator negate the value of his writing?
2. How does his *p'ansori*-inspired style differ from other *p'ansori*-style texts in this textbook?

References

Allen, Chizuko T. 2005. 'Ch'oe Namsŏn at the Height of Japanese Imperialism.' *Sungkyun Journal of East Asian Studies* 5(1): 27–49.
Killick, Andrew P. 2010. *In Search of Korean Traditional Opera: Discourses of Ch'anggŭk*. Honolulu: University of Hawai'i Press. (Chapter 2: Origins and Origin Myths).
Kim, Kichung. 1981. '*Ŭnsegye*: Art versus Ideology.' *Korean Studies* 5: 63–77.
Pettid, Michael J. (ed.). 2018. *Silvery World and Other Stories*. New York: Cornell University East Asia Program.
Robinson, Michael E. 1989. *Cultural Nationalism in Colonial Korea, 1920–1925*. Seattle: University of Washington Press.
Shin, Michael D. 2012. 'Yi Kwang-su: The Collaborator as Modernist against Modernity.' *The Journal of Asian Studies* 71(1): 115–20.
Yang, Yoon Sun. 2009. *Nation in the Backyard: Yi Injik and the Rise of Korea New Fiction, 1906–1913*. PhD Thesis, University of Chicago.
Yi, Ki-baek. 1984. *A New History of Korea*. Cambridge, MA: Published for the Harvard-Yenching institute by Harvard University Press. (Chapter 15: Development of the Nationalist Movement).

5.4 한중록 -혜경궁 홍씨 (*The Memoirs of Lady Hyegyŏng* – Lady Hyegyŏng)

Introduction to the text

Lady Hyegyŏng (1735–1816) was the wife of Crown Prince Sado (1735–1762), who was killed by his father, King Yŏngjo (1694–1776, r. 1724–1776), by being nailed inside a rice chest and left to starve. Very little information of this event remains in the official palace records. However, the memoirs of Lady Hyegyŏng provide a detailed personal account of this event. Separated into four separate memoirs, written in vernacular Korean in 1795, 1801, 1802, and 1805, these memoirs tell the life of Lady Hyegyŏng upon her entry into the palace as the Crown Prince's wife, including the death of her husband and the aftermath of the event. The memoirs are written in the style of testimonial narratives, often composed as petitions presented to the throne to testify to the innocence of someone accused of wrongdoing. In her memorial, Lady Hyegyŏng defends the conduct of herself and her family with regards to their involvement in the Crown Prince's death. She portrays the Crown Prince as having suffered from mental illness brought on by harsh treatment at the hands of his father, which manifested in increasing violence, killing palace staff, and threatening his family's life. In doing so, Lady Hyegyŏng breaks the mould of official history, which tended to portray the royal family as noble and beyond reproach, instead portraying a key historical event as an intensely personal family conflict.

Original text

대조께서 거동을 지체하시더니 오후 1시가 지나서야 대조께서 휘령전으로 오신다는 말이 있었다. 그럴 때에 소조께서 나를 덕성합으로 오라 하시기에 가 뵈오니, 그 장하신 기운도 없으시고 좋지 않은 말씀도 않으셨다. 소조께서는 고개를 숙이고 깊이 생각하시며 힘 없이 벽에 기대어 앉아 계셨다. 소조의 안색은 놀라서 핏기가 없었다. 나를 보시고 응당 화를 내실 것이 분명 분명했다.

'소조의 화증이 오죽 심하지 않을까?'

싶어 내 목숨이 그날 마칠 줄 알고 스스로 염려하였다. 그래서 세손에게 경계를 부탁하고 왔던 것이다. 그런데 소조의 모습은 내가 생각했던 것과는 달랐다. 소조가 나를 보시더니 힘없이 말씀하셨다.

'아무래도 괴이하니 자네는 잘 살게 하겠네. 그 뜻들이 무서우이.'

나는 눈물을 머금고 말없이 있다가 황당하여 손을 비비고 앉았다. 대조께서는 휘령전으로 오셔서 소조를 부르신다고 하였다. 이상한 마음이 들었지만, 그렇다고 어찌하겠는가. 소조께서는 피하자는 말도, 달아나자는 말도 않으셨다. 좌우를 치우지도 않고 조금도 화를 내신 기색이 없었다.

'빨리 용포를 달라.'

하여 용포를 입으셨다. 그러더니,

'내가 학질을 앓는다고 말씀드리려 하니 세손의 휘항을 가져오라.'

내가 생각하기에 세손의 휘항은 작은 것이었기에 당신 휘항을 쓰시는 것이 좋을 듯하였다. 그래서 내인에게 소조의 휘항을 가져오라고 하였다. 그랬더니 소조가 천만 뜻밖에 말씀하셨다.

'자네는 무섭고 흉한 사람으로세. 자네는 세손을 데리고 오래도록 함께 살려 하는군. 내가 오늘 내가 죽을 터이니 그를 꺼리어 세손의 휘항을 쓰지 못하게 하려는 심술을 내 잘 알겠네.'

내 마음은 당신이 그날 그 지경에 이르실 줄을 어찌 알았으리오.

'이 끝이 대체 어찌될꼬? 사람이 다 죽을 일이요, 우리 모자의 목숨이 어떠할런고?'

내가 어찌한다 말씀을 하지 않았는데 천만 뜻밖의 말씀을 하시니 내가 더더욱 서러워 다시 세손의 휘항을 가져다 드렸다.

'그 말씀은 너무 마음에 없는 말이시니 세손의 휘항을 쓰소서.'

'싫다. 꺼려하는 것을 써서 내 무엇할꼬?'

이런 말씀을 하실 때면 병환이 있으신 분 같지 않았다. 그런데 어이 공손히 나가려 하셨던 것일까. 모든 것이 다 하늘의 뜻이니 원통하고도 원통하구나. 그러할 때에 날이 이미 늦었다. 재촉하여 나가시니 대조께서 휘령전에 앉아 계셨다. 칼을 안고 두드리시더니, 처분을 하시었다. 차마 망극하고도 망극하니 이 모습을 내가 어찌 기록하겠는가. 서럽고도 서러울 뿐이다.

소조께서 나가시자 대조의 노한 목소리가 쩌렁쩌렁 들려왔다. 휘령전과 덕성합이 멀지 않았으므로 담 밑에 사람을 보냈다.

'벌써 세자께서 용포를 벗고 엎디어 계십니다.'

대처분인 줄 알고 천지가 망극하여 내 마음이 무너지고 깨지는 듯하였다. 하늘도 땅도 무너지고 이제 어찌해야 하는 것인지 가슴이 먹먹하여 아무 것도 할 수가 없었다. 거기 있는 것이 부질없어 세손이 있는 곳에 와서 서로를 붙들고 있을 뿐이었다. 오후 3시가 넘어서자 내관이 다급히 들어와 말했다.

'밧소주방의 쌀 담는 궤를 내라 하십니다.'

대체 이것이 어쩐 말인고! 저들도 어찌할 줄 몰라 궤를 내지 못하고 있는 가운데, 세손궁이 망극한 일이 있는 줄을 알고 대문 안에 들어가 아뢰었다.

'마마! 아비를 살려 주소서! 마마! 아비를 살려 주소서!' '썩 나가라!'

대조께서 엄히 말씀하셨다. 할 수 없이 세손은 왕자 재실로 돌아가 앉아 있었다. 그때의 정경이야, 고금천지간에 없었다. 세손이 나가자, 하늘과 땅이 맞붙는 듯, 해와 달이 깜깜한 듯하니, 내가 어찌 잠시나마 세상에 머물 마음이 있었겠는가. 칼을 들어 목숨을 끊으려 하자 옆에 있던 사람이 빼앗아 뜻대로 못하였다. 다시 죽고자 하였지만 촌철이 없어 못하였다. 숭문당을 지나 휘령전으로 나아가는 전복문 밑으로 갔다. 아무 것도 보이지 않고 다만 대조께서 칼을 두드리는 소리와 소조가 말씀하시는 소리만 들렸다. 이것이 꿈인지 현실인지, 내가 죽었는지 살았는지, 도무지 알 수가 없는 지경이었다.

'아버님! 아버님! 잘못하였습니다. 이제는 아버님께서 하라고 하시는 대로 다 하겠습니다. 글도 읽고, 말씀도 다 들을 것이니 이리 마소서. 용서하소서! 제발 살려주소서!'

내 간장은 마디마디 끊어지고 눈앞이 캄캄하였다. 가슴을 두드린들 대체 이 일을 어찌하겠는가. 당신의 용맹스러운 힘과 건장한 기운으로 어찌 궤에 들어가셨는고. 아무리 생각하고 또 생각하여도 하늘이 원망스러울 뿐이다.

'궤에 들어가라!'

아무리 엄히 명하신들 아무쪼록 들어가시지 말 것인지 어찌 들어가셨는가. 처음에는 뛰어나오려 하다가 이기지 못하여 그 지경에 이르니, 하늘이 어찌 이렇게 하셨는지. 만고에 없는 설움뿐이다. 하늘아, 하늘아, 어찌 이리 만드시는고. 내가 문 밑에서 목 놓아 슬피 울었지만 소용없는 일이었다. 소조는 벌써 폐위되었으니 처자인 내가 어찌 편안히 대궐에 있겠는가. 세손을 밖에 그저 두어서 될지 어떨지 차마 두렵고 조마조마하여, 그 문에 앉아 대조께 상소하였다.

'마마, 처분이 이러하시니 죄인의 처자인 제가 편안히 대궐에 있기 황송합니다. 또 세손을 저리 오래 밖에 두면 죄가 더 무거워질까 두렵습니다. 이제 친정집으로 나가겠습니다. 천은으로 세손을 보존하여 주소서.'

Key vocabulary

대조	title given to the king during the crown prince's regency (大朝)
소조	title given to the crown prince when he becomes prince regent (小朝)

장하다	be deranged, mentally ill
응당	naturally, of course (應當)
화증	symptoms of anger, fury (火症)
세손	the grandson of the king and heir to the throne (世孫)
괴이하다	strange, weird, peculiar, fearful (怪異하다)
용포	royal robes (龍袍)
학질	malaria (瘧疾)
휘항	a hat worn in cold weather (揮項)
꺼리다	avoid, shun, be reluctant or unwilling
모자	the relationship between mother and son, mother and son (母子)
병환	disease, illness (病患)
원통하다	bitter, resentful, sorrowful (冤痛하다)
망극하다	immeasurable, great, extreme, terrible (罔極하다)
세자	the crown prince
대처분	carrying out the great deed, in this case the execution
밧소주방	the royal kitchens (밧燒廚房) outside the King's residence
왕자재실	the waiting room at the Crown Prince's residence
고금천지간에	from the distant past until now, all over the world (古今天地間에)
마마	Your Majesty
거동	movement, behaviour, conduct (擧動)
당신	in this context, an honorific reflexive third-person pronoun
궤	a special rice cabinet (櫃)
만고	in all time, ever (萬古)
폐위되다	to be dethroned (廢位되다)
처자	wife and child (妻子)
대궐	royal palace (大闕)
황송하다	to be indebted or grateful. In this case, the implication is that the debt is too much (惶悚하다)
천은	heavenly grace, bestowed by God or kings (天恩)

Comprehension questions: text

1 What was the order given by the King Yŏngjo?
2 Did Prince Sado follow the order immediately?
3 How did Lady Hyegyŏng feel about the situation?
4 How did the heir (Prince Sado's son) respond to the situation?

Comprehension questions: drama extract

Contrary to Lady Hyegyŏng's account, the 2014 SBS drama, *Secret Door* (비밀의 문), portrays Crown Prince Sado as an idealist attempting to create a society free of social hierarchy, whose relationship with his father is strained by factional tensions. In the final episode, we see King Yŏngjo being confronted by his ministers, followed by Lady Hyegyŏng, then the Noron faction, then King Yŏngjo and Hong Ponghan, Lady

Hyegyŏng's father, all of whom voice their opinions on the conflict that has emerged around the Crown Prince.

1 What is King Yŏngjo's plan to deal with Crown Prince Sado?
2 Why does the Noron faction object to this plan?
3 What does the Noron faction want to do with the Crown Prince and his family?
4 Why does Hong Ponghan tell the King he must kill the Crown Prince?

Additional source material

Other material addressing the death of Prince Sado include:

- MBC drama, *Lee San, Wind of the Palace* (이산, 2007).
- Channel CGV drama, *Eight Days, Assassination Attempts against King Jeongjo* (정조암살 미스터리 8일, 2007).
- Film, *The Throne* (사도, 2015).
- KBS Drama, *KBS Drama Special: Red Moon* (붉은 달, 2015).

Further discussion questions

1 History vs. herstory: Form two teams to debate.

   Team A argument: Lady Hyegyŏng's memoirs are not a legitimate historical source due to her personal motivation to clear her family's name and her bias in telling the story in defence of her husband.
   Team B argument: Lady Hyegyŏng's memoirs lend a private voice usually suppressed by official, male-centred history. Her account is particularly valuable in light of the lack of 'official' records.

2 One cannot be a ruler and a parent at the same time. Discuss.

References

Hyegyŏnggung, Hong Ssi. 2013[1996]. *The Memoirs of Lady Hyegyŏng: The Autobiographical Writings of a Crown Princess of Eighteenth-Century Korea* (trans. JaHyun Kim Haboush). Berkley; Los Angeles; London: University of California Press.
———. 1987[1985]. *Memoirs of a Korean Queen* (trans. Yang-hi Choe-Wall). London: Kegan Paul International.
Kim Haboush, JaHyun. 2004. 'Private Memory and Public History: The Memoirs of Lady Hyegyŏng and Testimonial Literature.' In *Creative Women of Korea: The Fifteenth Through the Twentieth Centuries*, edited by Young-Key Kim-Renaud, pp. 122–41. Armonk, NY; London: M.E. Sharpe.
Lee, Ji-Eun. 2014. 'Literacy, Sosŏl, and Women in Book Culture in Late Chosŏn Korea.' *East Asian Publishing and Society* 4: 36–64.
Lee, Younghee. 2002. *Ideology, Culture and Han: Traditional and Early Modern Korean Women's Literature*. Edison, NJ: Jimoondang International.
Lee, Young-Oak. 2007. 'An Interview with Margaret Drabble.' *Contemporary Literature* 48(4): 477–98.

5.5 풀 – 김금숙 (*Grass* – Keum Suk Gendry-Kim)

Introduction to the text

Comfort women were women who were taken during World War II to serve in brothels – euphemistically called 'comfort stations' – for the Japanese army. Most of these women came from Korea, then China, although there were also women from other regions, mostly Japanese colonies, and even around 300 Dutch women. Particularly in East Asian countries, many comfort women returning after the war found themselves ostracised by their families, as premarital chastity was traditionally considered more important even than one's life – choosing to survive the ordeal and come home was considered to be bringing shame on one's family. It hence took a long time for former comfort women to come forward to address the issue: Kim Haksun (1924–1997) was the first to come forward in 1991. This issue continues to remain contentious in Japan-Korea relations. Although an official agreement was made between the Japanese and Korean governments in 2015, supposedly settling the issue for good, campaigners continue to argue that the Japanese government's apology is insufficient. The comic book, *Grass* (풀), by Keum-Suk Gendry-Kim is an effort by the author to present comfort women not just as victims, but as human beings, whose tenacity to not just survive, but live, is like grass, which stands up again no matter how many times you step on it.

Original text

피는 또 얼마나 나오던지.

결혼도 안 했는데 더럽혀졌으니.

그러니까 다들 자살하는 거야.

나도 더 이상 살고 싶지 않았어.

근데 죽을 수도 없었어.

아무리 죽고 싶어도 어떻게 죽을 방법이 없어.

하긴, 살아도 이젠 더 이상
산 목숨이 아니었으니까.

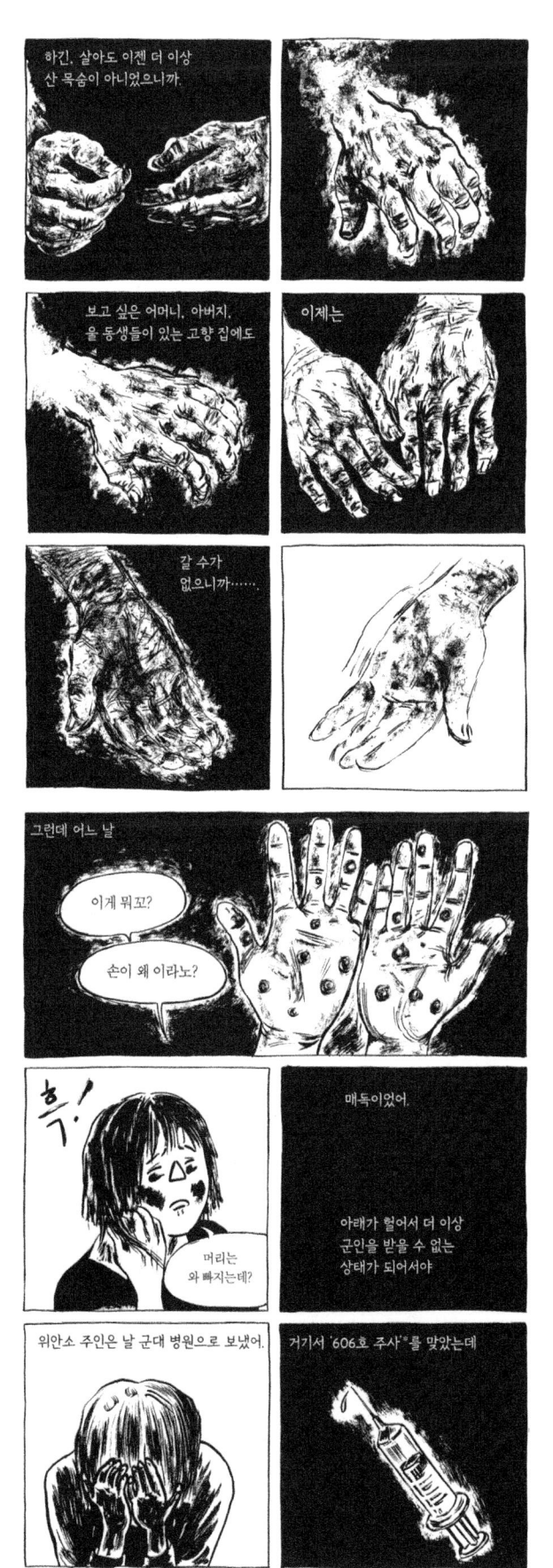

보고 싶은 어머니, 아버지,
울 동생들이 있는 고향 집에도

이제는

갈 수가
없으니까······

그런데 어느 날

이게 뭐꼬?

손이 왜 이라노?

흑!

머리는
와 빠지는데?

매독이었어.

아래가 헐어서 더 이상
군인을 받을 수 없는
상태가 되어서야

위안소 주인은 날 군대 병원으로 보냈어.

거기서 '606호 주사'를 맞았는데

* 606호 주사 : 정식 명칭은 살바르산으로 매독과 성병 치유제로 쓰였다.

두어 달이 지나도 낫질 않는 거야.

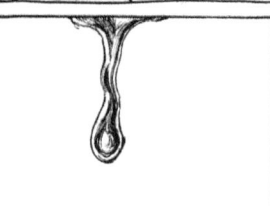

돈을 못 벌고 그러고 있으니까 위안소 주인이 다급했는지

어디선가 수은을 구해 왔어.

군의관한테 받아 왔다는데 그걸 작은 종지에 부어 놓고 불로 끓여서 그 김을 쬐라고 하더군.

얼굴을 가리고 아래 옷을 벗은 뒤 수은 액체가 끓는 종지 위에 쪼그리고 앉아서 그 김을 쬐게 했어.

결국 병은 나았지만 그 때문에 평생 아이를 갖지 못하게 되었지.

Source: These pictures are all taken from Gendry-Kim, Keum Suk. 2017. *P'ul* [Grass]. P'aju: Boribooks, pp. 206–7, 262–5, 436–7, who retains copyright for this work. Used with permission.

Key vocabulary

늦둥이	a child with older parents, a child born of an old couple
뜨개질	knitting, crotcheting
매독	syphilis
헐다	get sores, be inflamed
위안소	'comfort station,' the brothels where the comfort women were held
다급하다	urgent, pressured
수은	mercury
군위관	army surgeon
종지	bowl
쬐다	heat, warm (yourself)
액체	liquid, fluid
여태껏	thus far, until now

Comprehension questions: text

1 How does Grandma Oksŏn tease the writer?
2 Why couldn't she return home anymore?
3 How was she treated for syphilis?
4 Why was she disappointed about her life after returning to Korea?

Comprehension questions: film extract

The 2017 film *I Can Speak* (아이 캔 스피크) tells the story of an old lady, Na Okpun, who is considered a nuisance by everyone around her as she keeps submitting complaints to the local government office and pestering one of the young officials there to teach her English. However, we come to learn how her meddling is based on caring for the people around her, and due to her loneliness from living life alone. At the turning point of the film, it is revealed that she used to be a comfort woman, but kept this a secret for decades. The scene where she finally decides to go public demonstrates the indomitable spirit shown by these women who stood up for their rights and dignity.

1 What has happened to Okpun's friend, Chŏngshim?
2 What is the purpose of the HR 121 coalition?
3 How did Okpun's family respond to her being a comfort woman?
4 Why doesn't Okpun want to forget her past?

Additional source material

Films dealing with the comfort women issue, as well as dealing with sexual trauma, include:

Silenced (도가니, 2011).
Han Gong-ju (한공주, 2013).
Spirit's Homecoming (귀향, 2016).
A Snowy Road (눈길, 2017).
Herstory (허스토리, 2018).

Further discussion questions

1 In her comic, author Gendry-Kim purposefully avoided drawing explicit scenes of the comfort women being raped, as she felt that laying everything bare was insensitive to their experience. Separate into two teams and discuss:

   Team A: Insofar as many still negate the experience of comfort women, it is essential to make the violence perpetrated against them explicit in popular culture, in order to help people realise the extent of their suffering.

   Team B: Showing these scenes only serves to reopen their wounds, and portrays a masculinist bias that does not acknowledge the legitimacy of the women's accounts in their own right, without additional mediation or explanation from others.

2 Has the Japanese government made a suitable apology for these events? Discuss.

References

Hicks, George L. 1995. *The Comfort Women: Japan's Brutal Regime of Enforced Prostitution in the Second World War*. New York: W. W. Norton.

Pilzer, Joshua D. 2012. *Hearts of Pine: Songs in the Lives of Three Korean Survivors of the Japanese 'Comfort Women.'* Oxford: Oxford University Press.

Rich, Motoko. 2018. 'Japan Balks at Calls for New Apology to South Korea Over "Comfort Women".' *The New York Times*, 12/01/18. Available online at: www.nytimes.com/2018/01/12/world/asia/japan-south-korea-comfort-women.html. Accessed 10/02/19.

Tolbert, David. 2016. 'Japan's Apology to South Korea Shows What Public Apologies Should (Not) Do.' *Huffington Post*, 29/01/16. Available online at: www.huffingtonpost.com/david-tolbert/japans-apology-to-south-k_b_9111566.html?guccounter=1. Accessed 10/02/19.

Yoshimi, Yoshiaki (trans. Suzanne O'Brien). 2000. *Comfort Women: Sexual Slavery in the Japanese Military during World War II*. New York: Columbia University Press.

5.6 민요 아리랑, 가시리 (Folk songs *Arirang, Will You Go* – Anonymous)

Introduction to the text

This section includes popular folk songs. In terms of contents, the themes of these songs vary, including love between men and women or parents and children, agricultural life, and satire. The vocabulary used in the songs was typically used in daily life, reflecting the commoners' simple lives. *Will You Go* (가시리) is one of the most well known Koryŏ kayo. This genre includes poems and songs that were sung in the Koryŏ period. They were often sung by the general public. It is common for them to include interjections, repetition, and nonsensical phrases that provoke emotion and have only melodic function. This text includes similar elements. A three foot structure is popular. Arirang (아리랑) is the most popular folksong in Korea (both North and South), with each region having their own version. The version shown here is from Kyŏnggi Province, around Seoul.

Original text

Middle Korean

A

1 가시리 가시리잇고 나는
2 버리고 가시리잇고 나는
3 위 증즐가 大平成代(대평성대)
4 날러는 엇디 살라 하고
5 버리고 가시리잇고 나는
6 위 증즐가 大平成代(대평성대)
7 잡사와 두어리마는
8 선하면 아니 올세라
9 위 증즐가 大平成代(대평성대)
10 설온 님 보내옵나니 나는
11 가시는 듯 돌아오소서 나는
12 위 증즐가 대평성대(大平成代)

The refrain of the song 위 증즐가 大平成代(대평성대) is onomatopoeia for a musical instrument, and passed down to future generations, it became an accepted part of music at the Royal Court, without special meaning, as a way to put in reverberation to match the music's rhythm.

Modern Korean

가시겠습니까
버리고 가시겠습니까?
나더러는 어찌 살라 하고
버리고 가시렵니까?
붙잡아 둘 일이지마는
서운하면 아니 올까 두렵습니다.
임을 보내옵나니,
가자마자 곧 가시는 것처럼 돌아서서 오십시오.

B

아리랑, 아리랑, 아라리요
아리랑 고개로 넘어간다
아리랑, 아리랑, 아라리요
아리랑 고개로 넘어간다
나를 버리고 가시는 님은
십리도 못가서 발병난다
아리랑, 아리랑, 아라리요
아리랑 고개로 넘어간다
아리랑, 아리랑, 아라리요
아리랑 고개로 넘어간다
청천하늘엔 찬별도 많고
우리네 가슴엔 희망도 많다

Key vocabulary (A)

Line	Middle Korean	Modern Korean
1	• 가시리 will you go • 잇고 formal, polite question	• ~시~ honorific, -니까 formal ending
2	• 나는 sounds used to fit the rhythmic structure	• 버리고 leave
3	• 버리고 leave	• 더러 for me
4	• 엇디 how	• 어찌 how
7	• 잡사와 to grasp, hold	• 붙잡아 hold • 임 one's lover
8	• 선하면 if upset, sad	• 두렵다 be afraid of
9	• 올세라 afraid that you will not be coming • -ㄹ세라 ending implies concern and fear	• -자마자 as soon as

Key vocabulary (B)

아리랑   while there are numerous theories as to the origin of this word, it is also a melodic phrase widely used in folk songs
발병나다   foot will be diseased
청천하늘   clear sky

Comprehension questions

1. Can you think of any English words that are used as sounds without meaning to express a specific emotion?
2. What are the expressions which show the author's emotion towards his/her lover who is going to leave him/her?
3. What are the author's attitudes towards his/her lover? Are they different between A and B?

Comprehension questions: film extract

The 2016 film *Spirit's Homecoming* (귀향) tells the story of a comfort woman survivor remembering her experiences through the help of a shamanic medium. In the past, we see the story of 14-year-old Chŏngmin and 16-year-old Yŏnghŭi, who help each other to stay sane throughout their ordeal, and make a promise to return home together. Halfway through the film, the girls gain a brief moment of respite from their ordeal, and we see how the song, *Will You Go*, acts as a bittersweet moment, giving full voice to their sorrow while also providing a small moment of healing before they return to their torturous existence.

1. How does Punsuk manage to get some women-only time for the other girls?
2. What happened to Suni?

3 Why is one girl's comment about the good weather mocked by the other girls?
4 Why does Punsuk know how to sing?

Discussion

1 Try to translate either Poem A or B suitable for an English speaker.
2 Discuss the prosodic or melodic nature of these poems.

References

Atkins, E Taylor. 2007. 'The Dual Career of "Arirang": The Korean Resistance Anthem That Became a Japanese Pop Hit.' *The Journal of Asian Studies* 66(3): 645–87.
Choi, Ann. 2000. *Overcoming the Purity of Purpose: Korean Poetry of the 1920s*, ProQuest Dissertations and Theses.
Seen, Daechol (ed.). 2013. *Arirang in Korean Culture and Beyond: Arirang from Diverse Perspectives*. Kyonggi-do: The Academy of Korean Studies Press.
Yi, Chongmyon. 2013. *Arirang of Korea: Han, Sorrows and Hope*. Seoul: Easy Publishing Co.

6   Social change

6.1   무정 – 이광수 (*Heartless* – Yi Kwangsu)

Introduction to the text

Yi Kwangsu (1892–1950) was one of the pioneers of modern Korean fiction, as well as an independence activist and nationalist, although he was later accused of collaborating with the Japanese. *Mujŏng* (The Heartless), arguably the most famous of his works, was first published in 1917, and has gained particular interest for its advocacy of free love. As with his other three major novels, *Chaesaeng* (Rebirth), *Hŭk* (Soil), and *Sarang* (Love), it follows a parallel structure, telling a story both of love between a man and a woman, as well as love for one's nation. In *Mujŏng*, the protagonists Hyŏng-sik and Yŏng-ch'ae a promised to each other as children, but are separated, and only meet again eight years later, when Hyŏng-sik is working as a teacher and Yŏng-ch'ae has had to sell herself as a *kisaeng*, although she has kept herself chaste in the hope of still being able to marry Hyŏng-sik. When she is raped by a patron, she intends to commit suicide, but on the train she encounters Pyŏng-uk, who encourages her to abandon her Confucian obligations and live as a modern woman. Meanwhile Hyŏng-sik, thinking Yŏng-ch'ae is dead, marries Sŏn-hyŏng, the daughter of a rich Elder in the Presbyterian church. They meet again on the train, as they all travel towards the port in order to go study abroad. Encountering a terrible flood which hinders their journey, they form the motivation to return after their studies to improve their country.

Original text

이러하는 동안에 집 잃은 사람들은 여전히 어찌할 줄을 모르고 땅바닥에 앉아 있었다. 차차 시장증이 나고 몸이 떨리기 시작하였으나 그네에게는 아무 방책도 없었다. 그네는 다만 되어 가는 대로 되기를 바랄 뿐이다.

  그네는 과연 아무 힘이 없다. 자연(自然)의 폭력(暴力)에 대하여서야 누구라서 능히 저항(抵抗)하리요마는 그네는 너무도 힘이 없다. 일생에 뼈가 휘도록 애써서 쌓아 놓은 생활의 근거를 하룻밤 비에 다 씻겨 내려 보내고 말리만큼 그네는 힘이 없다. 그네의 생활의 근거는 마치 모래로 쌓아 놓은 것 같다. 이제 비가 그치고 물이 나가면 그네는 흩어진 모래를 긁어 모아서 새 생활의 근거를 쌓는다. 마치 개미가 그 가늘고 연약한 발로 땅을 파서 둥지를 만드는 것과 같다. 하룻밤 비에 모든 것을 잃어버리고 발발 떠는 그네들이 어찌 보면 가련하기도 하지마는 또 어찌 보면 너무 약하고 어리석어 보인다.

  그네의 얼굴을 보건대 무슨 지혜가 있을 것 같지 아니하다. 모두 다 미련해 보이고 무감각(無感覺)해 보인다. 그네는 몇 푼 어치 아니 되는 농사한 지식을 가지고 그저 땅을 팔 뿐이다. 이리하여서 몇 해 동안 하느님이 가만히 두면 썩은 볏섬이나 모아 두었다가는 한번 물이 나면 다 씻겨 보내고 만다. 그래서 그네는 영원히 더 부(富)하여짐 없이 점점 더 가난하여진다. 그래서 (몸은 점점 더 약하여지고 머리는 점점 더) 미련하여진다. 저대로 내어버려 두면 마침내 북해도의 '아이누'나 다름없는 종자가 되고 말 것 같다.

저들에게 힘을 주어야 하겠다. 지식을 주어야 하겠다. 그리해서 생활의 근거를 안전하게 하여 주어야 하겠다.

'과학(科學)! 과학!' 하고 형식은 여관에 돌아와 앉아서 혼자 부르짖었다. 세 처녀는 형식을 본다.

'조선 사람에게 무엇보다 먼저 과학(科學)을 주어야겠어요. 지식을 주어야겠어요' 하고 주먹을 불끈 쥐며 자리에서 일어나 방 안으로 거닌다. '여러분은 오늘 그 광경을 보고 어떻게 생각하십니까.'

이 말에 세 사람은 어떻게 대답할 줄을 몰랐다. 한참 있다가 병욱이가,

'불쌍하게 생각했지요' 하고 웃으며, '그렇지 않아요?' 한다. 오늘 같이 활동하는 동안에 훨씬 친하여졌다.

'그렇지요, 불쌍하지요! 그러면 그 원인이 어디 있을까요?'

'무론 문명이 없는 데 있겠지요--- 생활하여 갈 힘이 없는 데 있겠지요.'

'그러면 어떻게 해야 저들을 . . . 저들이 아니라 우리들이외다 . . . 저들을 구제할까요?' 하고 형식은 병욱을 본다. 영채와 선형은 형식과 병욱의 얼굴을 번갈아 본다. 병욱은 자신 있는 듯이,

'힘을 주어야지요? 문명을 주어야지요?'

'그리하려면?'

'가르쳐야지요? 인도해야지요!'

'어떻게요?'

'교육으로, 실행으로.'

영채와 선형은 이 문답의 뜻을 자세히는 모른다. 무론 자기네(가) 아는 줄 믿지마는 형식이와 병욱이가 아는 이만큼 절실(切實)하게, 단단하게 알지는 못한다. 그러나 방금 눈에 보는 사실이 그네에게 산 교육을 주었다. 그것은 학교에서도 배우지 못할 것이요, 대웅변에서도 배우지 못할 것이었다.

일동의 정신은 긴장하였다. 더구나 영채는 아직도 이러한 큰 문제를 논란하는 것을 듣지 못하였다. '어떻게 하면 저들을 구제하나?' 함은 참 큰 문제였다. 이러한 큰 문제를 논란하는 형식과 병욱은 매우 큰 사람같이 보였다. 영채는 두자미며, 소동파의 세상을 근심하는 시구를 생각하고, 또 오 년 전 월화와 함께 대성학교장의 연설을 듣던 것을 생각하였다. 그때에는 아직 나이 어려서 찌찌(분명히) 알아듣지는 못하였거니와 '여러분의 조상은 결코 여러분과 같이 못생기지는 아니하였습니다' 할 때에 과연 지금 날마다 만나는 사람은 못생긴 사람들이다 하던 생각이 난다. 영채는 그 말과 형식의 말에 공통한 점이 있는 듯이 생각하였다. 그러고 한번 더 형식을 보았다. 형식은, '옳습니다. 교육으로, 실행으로 저들을 가르쳐야지요, 인도해야지요! 그러나 그것은 누가 하나요?' 하고 형식은 입을 꼭 다문다. 세 처녀는 몸에 소름이 끼친다. 형식은 한번 더 힘있게,

'그것을 누가 하나요?' 하고 세 처녀를 골고루 본다. 세 처녀는 아직도 경험하여 보지 못한 듯한 말할 수 없는 정신의 감동을 깨달았다. 그러고 일시에 소름이 쪽 끼쳤다. 형식은 한번 더,

'그것을 누가 하나요?' 하였다.

'우리가 하지요!' 하는 대답이 기약하지 아니하고 세 처녀의 입에서 떨어진다. 네 사람의 눈앞에는 불길이 번쩍하는 듯하였다. 마치 큰 지진이 있어서 온 땅이 떨리는 듯하였다. 형식은 한참 고개를 숙이고 앉았더니,

'옳습니다. 우리가 해야지요! 우리가 공부하러 가는 뜻이 여기 있습니다. 우리가 지금 차를 타고 가는 돈이며 가서 공부할 학비를 누가 주나요? 조선이 주는 것입니다. 왜? 가서 힘을 얻어 오라고, 지식을 얻어 오라고, 문명을 얻어 오라고 . . . 그리해서 새로운 문명 위에 튼튼한 생활의 기초를 세워 달라고 . . . 이러한 뜻이 아닙니까' 하고 조끼 호주머니에서 돈지갑을 내어 푸른 차표를 내어 들면서,

'이 차표 속에는 저기서 들들 떠는 저 사람들 . . . 아까 그 젊은 사람의 땀도 몇 방울 들었어요! 부대 다시는 이러한 불쌍한 경우를 당하지 말게 하여 달라고요?' 하고 형식은 새로 결심하는 듯이 한번 몸과 고개를 흔든다. 세 처녀도 그와 같이 몸을 흔들었다.

이때에 네 사람의 가슴속에는 꼭 같은 '나 할 일'이 번개같이 지나간다. 너와 나라는 차별이 없이 온통 한몸, 한마음이 된 듯하였다.

Key vocabulary

시장증	hunger
방책	way, plan
저항하다	resist
둥지	nest
가련하다	pitiful, pathetic
어리석다	foolish, stupid, absurd
미련하다	stupid, foolish, silly
무감각	insensible, numb, senseless
볏섬	a sack of rice
부하다	rich, fat
북해도	Hokkaido
종자	derogative way of saying blood, descent, pedigree
처녀	unmarried woman, virgin, young woman
광경	sight, scene, spectacle
무론	of course
문명	civilisation
실행	practice, action, put into practice
문답	question and answer
절실	acute, urgent, desperate, pressing
웅변	oratory, speeches
논란	controversy (논란하다: to attack through debate)
두자미	Tang dynasty poet, Du Fu (712–770)
소동파	Northern Song dynasty poet, Su Shi (1037–1101)
근심하다	worry, be concerned for
시구	line of a poem or text
연설	speech, address
인도하다	guide, lead, shepherd
골고루	evenly, equally, one after the other
기약	promise, arrangement
불길	flame, blaze
조끼호주머니	waistcoat pocket

118 *Social change*

Comprehension questions: text

1. How do the protagonists perceive the victims of the flood?
2. What is the solution for their plight?
3. How does Yŏng-ch'ae feel listening to the discussion?
4. How do the three women respond to Hyŏng-sik's ideas?

Comprehension questions: film extract

The 2016 film *Love, Lies* (해어화) tells the story of the complicated relationship between three young people in 1940s Japanese-controlled Korea. Chŏng Soyul and Sŏ Yŏnhŭi are *kisaeng* trained in classical singing, while Kim Yunu, Soyul's lover, is a pop song composer. In the scene where Soyul meets up with Yunu after being forced to perform for the Japanese police commissioner, we see Yunu proclaiming similar ideals to those presented by the protagonists of *Mujŏng* above.

1. Why does Yunu say being successful is a sin?
2. How does Yunu critique Soyul's unconditional love for traditional songs?
3. What does Yunu think the people need?
4. What does Soyul want to become?

Additional source material

The SBS drama, *Hymn of Death* (사의 찬미, 2018), also portrays the activities of the Cultural Nationalist movement.

Further discussion questions

1. Separate into two teams and discuss:

    Team A: Yi Kwangsu and the Cultural Nationalists were elitists who pandered to the Japanese colonial powers on the pretext of helping the country to modernise.
    Team B: The Cultural Nationalists realised that they were too weak to achieve development independently, and they accepted that until they could stand on their own two feet, learning from the model of Japan was the lesser of two evils.

2. How does gender play out in the modernising ideology portrayed in this section?

References

Choi, Ellie. 2018. 'Memories of Korean Modernity: Yi Kwangsu's *the Heartless* and New Perspectives in Colonial Alterity.' *The Journal of Asian Studies* 77(3): 659–91.
Kim, Kichung. 1982. '"Mujong": An Introduction to Yi Kwangsu's Fiction.' *Korean Studies* 6: 125–39.
Lee, Ann Sung-hi. 2005. *Yi Kwangsu and Modern Korean Literature:* Mujŏng. Ithaca, NY: Cornell University East Asia Program.
Treat, John Whittier. 2012. 'Choosing to Collaborate: Yi Kwang-su and the Moral Subject in Colonial Korea.' *The Journal of Asian Studies* 71(1): 81–102.

Social change   119

6.2 삼포 가는 길 – 황석영 (*The Road Going to Sampo –* Hwang Sŏkyŏng)

Introduction to the text

This novel draws a picture of the warmth and love shared between three people who have been displaced because of industrialisation as they walk down a 'snowy road.' It was published in 1973 in *Sindonga*.

The three characters have each been involved in difficult physical labour and relate to each other in that they have been driven out of work because of industrialisation. They are described as being especially warm and loving individuals, and as such they are affectionately empathetic to each other's situation.

However, this text is not merely unique for the way it portrays its characters. As a prime example of literary realism, the story explores the many unfortunate circumstances brought about because of industrialisation. The story is set in the time when South Korea was solidifying its place as a leading industrial nation. Though this modernisation and industrialisation brought many positive results, it is a fact that it had detrimental effects as well. A representative example of this is the harm it brought to agriculture and those who earned their living through it. Many other problems also came along with it. In the final scene of the book, we learn that the Samp'o which the characters have been planning to return to is no longer the place it once was – it has been connected to the mainland and now there is no difference between the two. The story emphasises the pain and difficulty brought about by this period of Korean history, and stands in contrast to other literature which tends to focus on the benefits of this time of change.

Original text

'얼마나 있었소?'
   사내가 물었다. 가까이 얼굴을 맞대고 보니 그리 흉악한 몰골도 아니었고, 우선 그 시원시원한 태도가 은근히 밉질 않다고 영달이는 생각했다. 그가 자기보다는 댓살쯤 더 나이 들어 보였다. 그리고 이 바람 부는 겨울 들판에 척 걸터앉아서도 만사 태평인 꼴이었다. 영달이는 처음보다는 경계하 지 않고 대답했다.
   '넉 달 있었소. 그런데 노형은 어디루 가쇼?'
   '삼포에 갈까 하오.'
   사내는 눈을 가늘게 뜨고 조용히 말했다. 영달이가 고개를 흔들었다.
   '방향 잘못 잡았수. 거긴 벽지나 다름없잖소. 이런 겨울철에.'
   '내 고향이오.'
   사내가 목장갑 낀 손으로 코 밑을 쓱 훔쳐냈다. 그는 벌써 들판 저 끝을 바라보고 있었다.
   영달이와는 전혀 사정이 달라진 것이다. 그는 집으로 가 는 중이었고 영달이는 또 다른 곳으로 달아나는 길 위에 서 있었기 때문이었다. '참 . . . 집에 가는군요.' 사내가 일어나 맹꽁이 배낭을 한쪽 어깨에다 걸쳐 매면서 영달이에게 물었다. '어디 무슨 일 자리 찾아가쇼?' '댁은 오라는 데가 있어서 여기 왔었소? 언제나 마찬가지죠.' '자, 난 이제 가 봐야겠는걸.' 그는 뒤도 돌아보지 않고 질척이는 둑길을 향해 올라갔다. 그가 둑 위로 올라서더니 배낭을 다른 편 어깨 위로 바꾸어 매고는 다시 하반신부터 차 례로 개털 모자 끝까지 둑 너머로 사라졌다. 영달이는 어디로 향하겠다는 별 뾰족한 생각도 나지 않았고, 동행도 없이 길을 갈 일이 아득했다. 가다 가 도중에 헤어지게 되더라도 우선은 말동무라도 있었으면 싶었다.

Social change

그는 멍청히 섰다가 잰걸음으로 사내의 뒤를 따랐다. 영달이는 둑 위로 뛰어올라 갔다. 사내의 걸음이 무척 빨라서 벌써 차도로 나가는 샛길에 접어들어 있었다. 차도 양쪽에 대빗자루를 거꾸로 박아 놓은 듯한 앙상한 포플라들이 줄을 지어 섰는 게 보였다. 그는 둑 아래로 달려 내려가며 사내를 불렀다. '여보쇼, 노형!' 그가 멈춰 서더니 뒤를 돌아보고 나서 다시 천천히 걸어갔다. 영달이는 달려가서 그 뒤편에 따라붙어 헐떡이면서 '같이 갑시다, 나두 월출리까진 같은 방향인데...' '했는데도 그는 대답이 없었다. 영달이는 그의 뒤통수에다 대고 말했다. '젠장, 이런 겨울은 처음이오. 작년 이맘 때는 좋았지요. 월 삼천 원짜리 방에서 살림을 시작했으니까. 엄동설한에 정말 갈 데 없이 빳빳하게 됐는데요.'

'우린 습관이 되어 놔서.' 사내가 말했다. '삼포가 여기서 몇 린 줄 아쇼? 좌우간 바닷가까지만도 몇 백리 길이요. 거기서 또 배를 타야 해요.' '몇 년 만입니까?'

'십 년이 넘었지. 가 봤자... 아는 이두 없을 거요.' '그럼 뭣하러 가쇼?' '그냥... 나이 드니까, 가보구 싶어서.'

그들은 차도로 들어섰다. 자갈과 진흙으로 다져진 길이 그런 대로 걷기에 편했다. 영달이는 시린 손을 잠바 호주머니에 처박고 연방 꼼지락거렸다.

'어이 육실허게는 춥네. 바람만 안 불면 좀 낫겠는데.'

사내는 별로 추위를 타지 않았는데, 털모자와 야전 잠바로 단단히 무장한 탓도 있겠지만 원체가 혈색이 건강해 보였다. 사내가 처음으로 다정하게 영달이에게 물었다.

'어떻게 아침은 자셨소?' '웬걸요.'

영달이가 열적게 웃었다.

'새벽에 몸만 간신히 빠져나온 셈인데...'

'나두 못 먹었소. 찬샘까진 가야 밥술이라두 먹게 될 거요. 진작에 떴을 걸. 이젠 겨울에 움직일 생각이 안 납디다.'

'인사 늦었네요. 나 노영달이라구 합니다.' '나는 정가요.' '우리두 기술이 좀 있어 놔서 일자리만 잡으면 별 걱정 없지요.' 영달이가 정씨에게 빌붙지 않을 뜻을 비쳤다.

'알고 있소, 착암기 잡지 않았소? 우리넨, 목공에 용접에 구두까지 수선할 줄 압니다.' '야 되게 많네. 정말 든든하시겠구만.' '십 년이 넘었다니까.' '그래도 어디서 그런 걸 배웁니까?' '다 좋은 데서 가르치고 내보내는 집이 있지.' '나두 그런데나 들어갔으면 좋겠네.' 정씨가 쓴웃음을 지으며 고개를 저었다. '지금이라두 쉽지. 하지만 집이 워낙에 커서 말요.' '큰집...' 하다 말고 영달이는 정씨의 얼굴을 쳐다봤다. 정씨는 고개를 밑으로 숙인 채 묵묵히 걷고 있었다. 언덕을 넘어섰다. 길이 내리막이 되면서 강변을 따라서 먼 산을 돌아 나간 모양이 아득하게 보였다. 인가가 좀처럼 보이지 않는 황량한 들판이었다. 마른 갈대밭이 헝클어진 채 휘청대고 있었고 강 건너 곳곳에 모래바람이 일어나는 게 보였다.

정씨가 말했다. '저 산을 넘어야 찬샘골인데. 강을 질러가는 게 빠르겠군.' '단단히 얼었을까.' 강물은 꽁꽁 얼어붙어 있었다. 얼음이 녹았다가 다시 얼곤 해서 우툴두툴한 표면이 그리 미끄럽지는 않았다. 바람이 불어, 깨어진 살얼음 조각들을 날려 그들의 얼굴을 따갑게 때렸다. '차라리, 저쪽 다릿목에서 버스나 기다릴 걸 잘못했나 봐요.' 숨을 헉헉 들이키던 영달이가 투덜대자 정씨가 말했다.

Key vocabulary

시원시원하다	without hesitation
만사태평	everything is alright
노형	slightly polite way to address older man
여보쇼	hey, hello

엄동설한	frigid winter
꼼지락거리다	wiggle around
다정하다	kind, warm
자시다	a respectful way of saying eat
꽁꽁	frozen solid
우툴두툴	bumpy
헉헉	breathlessly

Comprehension questions: text

1   Why was the protagonist heading towards Sampo?
2   What skills did Youngdal have?
3   What sort of place is Sampo? How is it described?
4   What did the two main characters call each other?
5   How can you tell if Youngdal or the older man is speaking?

Comprehension questions: film extract

The 2010 film *He's on Duty* (방가? 방가!) tells the story of Pang T'aeshik, who can't hold down a job because of his impatient character and appearance. It is only when he pretends to be a migrant worker from Bhutan that he finally gets a job, but this also becomes a learning opportunity as he begins to understand the experiences of migrant workers in Korea. Like the two characters in the text extract, he has had to work a variety of jobs and acquired various different skills, as he brags to his mother at the start of the film.

1   Which jobs does Pang T'aeshik say he has done so far? What was he actually doing?
2   How did he end up in his current job?
3   How does he describe his work to his mother?
4   How does he really feel about his job?

Further discussion questions

1   Discuss the effects of industrialisation in 1960s–1970s Korea.
2   What happened in those times? Where did young people go and why?

References

Cho, Hein. 1989. *Secularization of Neo-Confucianism and Industrialization of Korea: A Study of Counter-Secularization*, ProQuest Dissertations and Theses.

Conde-Costas, L. 1996. 'A Sociological Inquiry Into the Historical Bases for the Industrialization of Korea.' *Korea Observer* XXVII(1): 115–34.

Kim, Hyung-a. 2004. *Korea's Development Under Park Chung-Hee: Rapid Industrialization, 1961–1979* (RoutledgeCurzon/Asian Studies Association of Australia East Asia series). London: RoutledgeCurzon.

6.3 1964 년 서울 – 김승옥 (*Seoul: 1964, Winter* – Kim Sŭngok)

Introduction to the text

This sharp criticism of modernisation and industrialisation in Korea begins with the meeting of the narrator and An, a friend of the same age. By a chance meeting, they end up having a conversation, but neither of them shares the truth with the other. Neither of them proposes to talk about real personal issues of substance, and instead they discuss meaningless things of little value. Their conversation reveals that each of them are extremely individualistic people.

When a man in his thirties seems eager to share and discuss everything about himself without hesitation, including his difficulties and concerns, the narrator and An find him very uncomfortable to be around. They act as if they are listening to him, but they really just want to leave as quickly as possible. The man shares with them extremely difficult aspects of his life, but they continue to merely act uncomfortable. When they find lodging, the three men sleep in separate rooms, and despite finding out that the man in his thirties is planning to commit suicide, An does nothing to stop him. Through the three characters, the author tries to show how in a modernising society, individualism causes failure in communication and a lack of connection or ability to care for others.

Original text

1964 년 겨울을 서울에서 지냈던 사람이라면 누구나 알고 있겠지만, 밤이 되면 거리에 나타나는 선술집 오뎅과 군참새와 세 가지 종류의 술등을 팔고 있고, 얼어붙은 거리를 휩쓸며 부는 차가운 바람이 펄럭거리게 하는 포장을 들치고 안으로 들어서게 되어 있고, 그 안에 들어 서면 카바이드 불의 길쭉한 불꽃이 바람에 흔들리고 있고, 염색한 군용(軍用) 잠바를 입고 있는 중년 사내가 술을 따르고 안주를 구워 주고 있는 그러한 선술집에서, 그날밤, 우리 세 사람은 우연히 만났다. 우리 세 사람이란 나와 도 수 높은 안경을 쓴 안(安)이라는 대학원 학생과 정체를 알 수 없었지만 요컨대 가난뱅이라는 것만은 분명하여 그의 정체를 꼭 알고 싶다는 생각은 조금도 나지 않는 서른 대 여섯 살짜리 사내를 말한다. 먼저 말을 주고받게 된 것은 나와 대학원생이었는데, 뭐 그렇고 그런 자기 소개가 끝났 을 때는 나는 그가 안씨라는 성을 가진 스물다섯 살짜리 대한민국 청년, 대학 구경을 해보지 못한 나로서는 상상이 되지 않는 전공(專攻)을 가진 대학원생, 부잣집 장남이라는 걸 알았고, 그는 내가 스물다섯 살짜리 시골 출신, 고등학교는 나오고 육군사관학교를 지원했다가 실패하고 나서 군대에 갔다가 임질에 한 번 걸려 본 적이 있고, 지금은 구청 병사계(兵事係)에서 일하고 있다는 것을 아마 알았을 것이다. 자기 소개는 끝났지만, 그러고 나서는 서로 할 애기가 없었다. 잠시 동안은 조용히 술만 마셨는데, 나는 새카맣게 구워진 참새를 집을 때 할말이 생겼기 때문에 마음속으로 군참새에게 감사하고 나서 애기를 시작했다. '안 형, 파리를 사랑하십니까?' '아니오. 아직까진 . . .' 그가 말했다. '김 형은 파리를 사랑하세요?' '예.'라고 나는 대답했다. '날 수 있으니까요. 아닙니다. 날 수 있는 것으로서 동시에 내 손에 붙잡힐 수 있는 것이니까요. 날 수 있는 것으로서 손안에 잡아본 것이 있으세 요?' '가만 계셔 보세요.' 그는 안경 속에서 나를 멀거니 바라 보며 잠시 동안 표정을 꼼지락거리고 있었다. 그리고 말했 다. '없어요. 나도 파리밖에는 . . .' 낮엔 이상스럽게도 날씨가 따뜻했기 때문에 길은 얼음이 녹아서 흙물로 가득했었는데 밤이 되면서부터 다시 기온이 내려가고 흙물은 우리의 발밑에서 다시 얼어붙기 시작 했다. 쇠가죽으로 지어진 내 검정 구두는 얼고 있는 땅바 닥에서 올라오고 있는 찬 기운을 충분히 막아내지 못하고 있었다. 사실 이런 술집이란, 집으로 돌아가는 길에 잠깐 한잔하고 싶은 생각

이 든 사람이나 들어올 테지, 마시면서 곁에 선 사람과 무슨 얘기를 주고받을 데는 되지 못하는 곳이다. 그런 생각이 문득 들었지만 그 안경쟁이가 때마침 나에게 기특한 질문을 했기 때문에 나는 '이 놈 그럴듯하다'고 생각되어 추위 때문에 저려 드는 내 발바닥에 조금 만 참으라고 부탁했다. '김 형, 꿈틀거리는 것을 사랑하십니까?' 하고 그가 내게 물었던 것이다. '사랑하구 말구요..' 나는 갑자기 의기 양양해져서 대답했 다. 추억이란 그것이 슬픈 것이든지 기쁜 것이든지 그것을 생각하는 사람을 의기 양양하게 한다. 슬픈 추억일 때는 고즈넉이 의기 양양해지고 기쁜 추억일 때는 소란스럽게 의기 양양해진다...

  '지금 몇 시쯤 되었습니까?' 하고 힘없는 아저씨가 안에게 물었다. '아홉 시 십 분 전입니다.'라고 잠시 후에 안이 대답했다. '저녁들은 하셨습니까? 난 아직 저녁을 안 했는데, 제가 살 테니까 같이 가시겠어요?' 하고 힘없는 아저씨가 이번 엔 나와 안을 번갈아 보며 말했다. '먹었습니다' 하고 나와 안은 동시에 대답했다. '혼자서 하시죠'라고 내가 말했다. '그만 두겠습니다.' 힘없는 아저씨가 대답했다. '하세요. 따라가 드릴 테니까요.' 안이 말했다. '감사합니다. 그럼...' 우리는 근처의 중국 요릿집으로 들어갔다. 방으로 들어가 서 앉았을 때, 아저씨는 또 한 번 간곡하게 우리가 뭘 좀 들 것을 권했다. 우리는 또 한 번 사양했다. 그는 또 권했 다. '아주 비싼 걸 시켜도 괜찮겠습니까?'라고 나는 그의 권유 를 철회시키기 위해서 말했다. '네, 사양 마시고.' 그가 처음으로 힘있는 목소리로 말했 다. '돈을 써 버리기로 결심했으니까요.' 나는 그 사내에게 어떤 꿍꿍이속이 있는 것만 같은 느낌 이 들어서 좀 불안했지만, 통닭과 술을 시켜 달라고 했다. 그는 자기가 주문한 것 외에 내가 말한 것도 사환에게 청 했다. 안은 어처구니없는 얼굴로 나를 보았다. 나는 그때 마침 옆방에서 들려 오고 있는 여자의 불그레한 신음 소리를 듣고만 있었다. '이 형도 뭘 좀 드시죠?'라고 아저씨가 안에게 말했다. '아니 전...' 안은 술이 다 깬다는 듯이 펄쩍 뛰고 사양 했다. 우리는 조용히 옆방의 다급해져 가는 신음 소리에 귀를 기울이고 있었다. 전차의 끽끽거리는 소리와 홍수 난 강물 소리 같은 자동차들의 달리는 소리도 희미하게 들려 오고 있었고 가까운 곳에선 이따금 초인종 울리는 소리도 들렸 다. 우리의 방은 어색한 침묵에 싸여 있었다. '말씀드리고 싶은 게 있는데요.' 마음씨 좋은 아저씨가 말 하기 시작했다. '들어 주시면 고맙겠습니다... 오늘 낮에 제 아내가 죽었습니다. 세브란스 병원에 입원하고 있었는데...' 그는 이젠 슬프지도 않다는 얼굴로 우리를 빤히 쳐다보며 말하고 있었다. '네에에.' '그거 안되셨군요.'라고 안과 나는 각각 조의를 표했다. '아내와 나는 참 재미있게 살았습니다. 아내가 어린애를 낳지 못하기 때문에 시간은 몽땅 우리 두 사람의 것이었습니다. 돈은 넉넉하지 못했습 니다만 그래도 돈이 생기면 우리는 어디든지 같이 다니면 서 재미있게 지냈습니다. 딸기철엔 수원에도 가고, 포도철에 안양에도 가고, 여름이면 대천에도 가고, 가을엔 경주에도 가보고, 밤엔 영화 구경, 쇼구경하러 열심히 극장에 쫓아다니기도 했습니다...' '무슨 병환이셨던가요?' 하고 안이 조심스럽게 물었다. '급성 뇌막염이라고 의사가 그랬습니다. 아내는 옛날에 급성 맹장염 수술을 받은 적도 있고, 급성 폐렴을 앓은 적도 있다고 했습니다만 모두 괜찮았는데 이번의 급성엔 결국 죽고 말았습니다... 죽고 말았습니다.'

Key vocabulary

선술집	pub
오뎅	fish cake
군참새	roasted sparrow
펄럭거리게	flutter
군용(軍用) 잠바	army coat
사내	a guy

124　*Social change*

대학원학생	graduate student
정체	status
새까맣게	pitch black
형	an address term used to refer to a person older than oneself
파리	fly (or flies): there is no singular/plural distinction in Korean.
안경쟁이	a person who wore glasses. 쟁이 means a person with particular attributes or jobs, used in a derogatory manner
의기양양	confidently
소란스럽게	noisy
요릿집	restaurant
간곡하게	earnestly
꿍꿍이속	have a plot in mind
술이깨다	become sober
신음소리	groaning sound
딸기철	season for strawberry
포도철	season for grapes
병환	illness in honorific form
급성뇌막염	acute aseptic meningitis
급성폐렴	acute pneumonia
죽고말다	eventually died

Comprehension questions: text

1　Find the descriptions which reflect the winter of Seoul in 1964.
2　How did the author portray the relationship between the people in the story?
3　In what way did the older man describe his wife's death?
4　What is the difference between the social backgrounds of the two men in the text?

Comprehension questions: film extract

The 1999 film *Peppermint Candy* (박하사탕, 1999) traces how one man, Kim Yŏngho, caught up in the events of contemporary Korean history, finds himself increasingly isolated and depressed, beginning with his suicide and working back towards when it all began. The beginning of the film, when Yŏngho commits suicide, reveals the same individualism and lack of connection that is critiqued in the text extract above.

1　What excuse does their student group president give for not having contacted Yŏngho about the class reunion?
2　How do his old classmates respond to seeing Yŏngho up on the train bridge?
3　What statistic does one old classmate cite for why they don't need to worry about Yŏngho?
4　Why do the other classmates suddenly want to dance?

Further discussion questions

1　Discuss the problems of modernisation and industrialisation in Seoul in the 1960s.
2　Discuss the problem of feeling lonely in a highly populated area such as Seoul.

References

Kim, Hyung-A, & Sorensen, Clark W. 2011. *Reassessing the Park Chung Hee Era, 1961–1979: Development, Political Thought, Democracy & Cultural Influence* (Center for Korea Studies Publication Series). Seattle: University of Washington Press.

Kim, S.-ok, & Phil, Marshall, 2008. *Seoul-1964-Winter Sŏul*. Elizabeth, NJ: Hollym International Corp.

Ku, Ponho. 1992. *Sociocultural Factors in the Industrialization of Korea* (Occasional papers (International Center for Economic Growth); no. 32). San Francisco, Calif: ICS Press.

Mason, Edward S. 1980. *The Economic and Social Modernization of the Republic of Korea* (Studies in the modernization of the Republic of Korea, 1945–1975). Cambridge, MA: Council on East Asian Studies, Harvard University: distributed by Harvard University Press.

Seth, Michael J. 2016. *A Concise History of Modern Korea: From the Late Nineteenth Century to the Present* (2nd ed.). Lanham: Rowman & Littlefield.

6.4   소년이 온다 – 한강 (*Human Acts* – Han Kang)

Introduction to the text

This is the sixth novella by Han Kang (1970–). It has been translated by Deborah Smith and is based on the story of the Kwangju Uprising of the 18th of May, 1980. In this novel, the author tells what happened for the ten days of the uprising. A boy, Tongho, who was 16 years old, was recruited to help dispose of the corpses of the people who had died during the fighting. His suffering was compounded when he witnessed the death of his own friend. This novel shows the tragic events which occurred as innocent people died during the devastating attack on Kwangju by the new military government. The author was born in Kwangju and moved to Seoul four months before the Kwangju Uprising happened. She heard about the terrible events from her relatives who lived through them, and she found a photo album which contained pictures of what happened during the time. She was led to write this book based on those personal experiences. This novel shows the value of human goodness, which should not be overlooked.

Original text

더 이상 내가 열여섯살이라는 느낌이 들지 않았어. 서른여섯, 마흔여섯 같은 나이들고 여리고 조그맣게 느껴졌어. 예순여섯, 아니 일흔여섯살이라고 해도 이상할 것 같지 않았어. 더이상 나는 학년에서 제일 작은 정대가 아니었어. 세상에서 누나를 제일 좋아하고 무서워하는 박정대가 아니었어. 이상하고 격렬한 힘이 생겨나 있었는데, 그건 죽음 때문이 아니라 오직 멈추지 않는 생각들 때문에 생겨난 거였어. 누가 나를 죽였을까, 누가 누나를 죽였을까, 왜 죽였을까.

생각할수록 그 낯선 힘은 단단해졌어. 눈도 뺨도 없는 곳에서 끊임없이 흐르는 피를 진하고 끈적끈적하게 만들었어. 어디선가 누나의 혼도 어른거리고 있을 텐데, 그곳이 어딜까. 이제 우리한텐 몸이 없으니 만나기 위해서 몸을 움직일 필요는 없을텐데. 하지만 몸 없이 누나를 어떻게 만날까. 몸 없는 누나를 어떻게 알아볼까.

진수 오빠가 어떻게 여자들을 설득했는지 그녀는 후에 정확히 기억할 수 없었다. 기억하고 싶지 않아서 잊은 건지도 몰랐다. 여자들을 도청에 남겨서 함께 죽게 하면 시민군의 명예가 다칠 거라던 그의 말이 어렴풋이 떠올랐지만, 그 말이 정직하게 그녀를 설득했는지 자신할 수 없었다. 죽어도 좋다고 생각했지만, 동시에 죽음을 피하고 싶었다. 죽은 사람들의 모습을 많이 봤기 때문에 둔감해졌다고 생각했지만, 그래서 더 두려웠다. 입을 벌리고 몸에 구멍이 뚫린 채, 반투명한 창자를 쏟아내며 숨이 끊어지고 싶지 않았다.

　그녀에게 영혼이 있었다면 그때 부서졌다. 땀에 젖은 셔츠에 카빈 소총을 멘 진수 오빠가 여자들에게 인사하기 위해 웃어 보였을 때. 어두운 길을 되밟아 도청으로 돌아가는 그들의 뒷모습을 얼어붙은 듯 지켜보았을 때. 아니, 도청을 나오기 전 너를 봤을 때 이미 부서졌다. 하늘색 체육복 위에 교련 점퍼를 걸친, 아직 어린애 같은 좁은 어깨에 소총을 메고서 고개를 끄덕이고 있는 너를 발견하고 그녀는 놀라며 불렀다. 동호야, 왜 집에 안 갔어? 장전하는 법을 설명하고 있던 청년 앞으로 그녀는 끼어들었다. 이 애는 중학생이에요. 집에 보내야 돼요. 청년은 놀라는 기색이었다. 고등학교 2학년이라고 해서 그런 줄 알았는데... 아까 고등학교 1학년까지 내보낼 때 이 애는 안 갔어요.

　선생은 압니까, 자신이 완전하게 깨끗하고 선한 존재가 되었다는 느낌이 얼마나 강렬한 것인지. 양심이라는 눈부시게 깨끗한 보석이 내 이마에 들어와 박힌 것 같은 순간의 광휘를.

　그날 도청에 남은 어린 친구들도 아마 비슷한 경험을 했을 겁니다. 그 양심의 보석을 죽음과 맞바꿔도 좋다고 판단했을 겁니다. 하지만 이제는 아무것도 확신할 수 없습니다. 총을 메고 창 아래 웅크려앉아 배가 고프다고 말하던 아이들, 소회의실에 남은 카스텔라와 환타를 얼른 가져와 먹어도 되느냐고 묻던 아이들이, 죽음에 대해서 뭘 알고 그런 선택을 했겠습니까?

　어떤 기억은 아물지 않습니다. 시간이 흘러 기억이 흐릿해지는 게 아니라, 오히려 그 기억만 남기고 다른 모든 것이 서서히 마모됩니다. 색 전구가 하나씩 나가듯 세계가 어두워집니다. 나 역시 안전한 사람이 아니란 걸 알고 싶습니다. 이제는 내가 선생에게 묻고 싶습니다.

　그러니까 인간은, 근본적으로 잔인한 존재인 것입니까? 우리들은 단지 보편적인 경험을 한 것뿐입니까? 우리는 존엄하다는 착각 속에 살고 있을 뿐, 언제든 아무것도 아닌 것, 벌레, 짐승, 고름과 진물의 덩어리로 변할 수 있는 겁니까? 굴욕당하고 훼손되고 살해되는 것, 그것이 역사 속에서 증명된 인간의 본질입니까?

　부마항쟁에 공수부대로 투입됐던 사람을 우연히 만난 적이 있습니다. 내 이력을 듣고 자신의 이력을 고백하더군요. 가능한 한 과격하게 진압하라는 명령이 있었다고 그가 말했습니다. 특별히 잔인하게 행동한 군인들에게는 상부에서 몇십만원씩 포상금이 내려왔다고 했습니다. 동료 중 하나가 그에게 말했다고 했습니다. 뭐가 문제냐? 맷값을 주면서 사람을 패라는데, 안 팰 이유가 없지 않아?

　베트남전에 파견됐던 어느 한국군 소대에 대한 이야기도 들었습니다. 그들은 시골 마을회관에 여자들과 아이들, 노인들을 모아 놓고 모두 불태워 죽였다지요. 그런 일들을 전시에 행한 뒤 포상을 받은 사람들이 있었고, 그들 중 일부가 그 기억을 지니고 우리들을 죽이러 온 겁니다. 제주도에서, 관동과 난징에서, 보스니아에서, 모든 신대륙에서 그렇게 했던 것처럼, 유전자에 새겨진 듯 동일한 잔인성으로.

　잊지 않고 있습니다. 내가 날마다 만나는 모든 이들이 인간이란 것을. 이 이야기를 듣고 있는 선생도 인간입니다. 그리고 나 역시 인간입니다.

Key vocabulary

열여섯살	lit., 16 years old (Korean traditional age is calculated with everyone becoming a year older on New Year's day; hence, it is about one to two years greater than age as calculated elsewhere in the world)
서른여섯	lit., 36
마흔여섯	lit., 46
학년	year in school

도청	provincial government building
시민군	people's militia
동호야	동호 is a given name. 야 is added by intimates of the same age or older.
선생	literally teacher, but the dropped honorific particle 님 makes this title rough and impolite
부마항쟁	the Pusan and Masan uprising
공수부대	special forces
베트남전	the Vietnam War
마을회관	the Village Hall
전시	wartime
잔인성	cruelty

Comprehension questions: text

1   How does the boy feel about what is happening around him?
2   How does the author use the boy's perspective to show readers more about the calamity?
3   What is the author's view about traumatic memories?
4   What points does the author make about the nature of human beings?

Comprehension questions: film extract

The 2017 film *A Taxi Driver* (택시운전사) shows the events of the Kwangju Uprising from the perspective of a taxi driver, Kim Mansŏp, who drove from Seoul with Jürgen Hinzpeter, the German ARD reporter who would go on to spread the news of the event around the world. On their arrival in Kwangju, they come across a group of young protesters, demonstrating the same pairing of dedication and naïvité regarding the violence that was to come as we see in the text above.

1   Where are the protesters going?
2   Why does the taxi driver run away?
3   Why does the old lady need to get to hospital?
4   Why does the Kwangju taxi driver refuse to take the reporter?

Further discussion questions

1   Discuss the significance of the Kwangju Uprising in Korean history.
2   Discuss the human rights movement and democratic movements in the 1980s in Korea.

References

Ch'oe, Chong-un, & Yu, Yongnan. 2006. *The Gwangju Uprising: The Pivotal Democratic Movement That Changed the History of Modern Korea*(1st ed.). Paramus, NJ: Homa & Sekey Books.
Han, Kang, & Deborah Smith. 2016. *Human Acts*. London: Portobello Books.
Kim, Hang. 2011. 'The Commemoration of the Gwangju Uprising: Of the Remnants in the Nation States' Historical Memory.' *Inter-Asia Cultural Studies* 12(4): 611–21.
Lee, Hyunji, & Schwartz, Thomas A. 2012. *The Gwangju Uprising: A Movement, a Memory, a Myth of Modern South Korea*, Dissertation, Vanderbilt University.

6.5 바리데기 – 황석영 (*Princess Pari* – Hwang Sŏkyŏng)

Introduction to the text

In a North Korean city, a seventh daughter is born to a couple longing for a son. She is abandoned hours after her birth, but is eventually rescued by her grandmother. The grandmother names the child Pari, after a legend telling of a forsaken princess who undertakes a quest for an elixir that will bring peace to the souls of the dead. As a young girl, Pari escapes North Korea and takes refuge in China before embarking on a journey across the ocean. She lands in London, where she finds work as a masseuse. Pari makes her home amongst other immigrants living in London. Hwang Sŏkyŏng (b. 1943) is one of Asia's most renowned authors and a human rights activist. He served seven years in a South Korean prison for breach of national security after an unauthorised visit to North Korea.

Background from shamanist story, **Princess Pari**

The Dragon Queen had another baby, who turned out to be another daughter. She cried, and the king was disappointed as well. He said, 'I have sinned so much, so I've only had seven daughters. I'm going to send my seventh daughter as a present to the Dragon King in the west sea.' He made a beautiful box and labelled it 'Princess.'

  The queen cried, 'You are so harsh! How can you throw away your own daughter? What about giving her to one of your vassals who doesn't have children?' But the king did not listen to his wife, so the queen suggested, 'Even if we do throw her away, let us at least give her a name.'

  The name they chose was 'Princess Pari,' which means 'the deserted princess.'

The original text

우리 식구는 할머니, 아버지, 어머니, 그리고 내 위로 언니들이 여섯이나 있었다.

  그러니까 우리 엄마는 거의 십오년 동안이나 배가 불러 있었고 몸을 풀자마자 곧이어 다시 아기를 가졌다는 뜻이다. 우리 자매들은 거의가 한두살 터울로 태어났는데, 큰언니와 둘째언니는 엄마가 애를 낳던 날의 두려움을 차례로 기억하고 있었다.

  그래도 엄마가 애를 낳을 적마다 곁에서 산파 노릇을 해줄 할머니가 있어서 다행이었다.

  셋째까지는 아버지도 방문 앞이나 마당에서 줄담배를 붙여물고 서성댔지만 그다음부터는 엄마 아기를 낳을 기미가 보이면 그날은 사무실에서 퇴근하지 않고 아예 숙직을 자청했다고 한다. 아버지가 참고 참던 화통을 터뜨린 것은 다섯째 숙이 언니를 낳을 때부터였다.

  안방에서 할머니와 엄마가 물을 데워다 방금 낳은 아기를 함지 안에 잠그고 씻겨주고 있는데

  아침에 아버지가 숙직실에서 돌아왔단다. 아버지는 방문을 열고 들어서자마자

  '이 까짓거는 또 낳아 멀 하니?' 하면서 숙이 언니를 채뜨려서는 물에다 푹 담갔다.

  할머니가 질겁을 하여 아기를 얼른 물속에서 건져올렸는데 갓난쟁이가 물을 들이키고 한동안 숨이 막혔는지 울지도 못하고 캑캑거렸다. 여섯째 현이 언니 때는 화풀이로 아침밥상을 마당으로 집어던지는 바람에 뒷간에 다녀오던 큰언니가 김치를 뒤집어썼다는 것이다. 그러니 내가 태어 났을 때는 어땠을까? '우린 모두 뒤켠 아이들 방에 몰려서 숨을 죽이고 있댔다.' 라고 첫째인 진이 언니가 말했다.

  ...

아버지는 홀어머니 밑에서 자랐다. 할아버지는 내가 태어나기 훨씬 전에 일어난 전쟁에서 죽었다.

할머니 말에 의하면 당신의 남편은 전쟁영웅이었다고 하는데 중앙방송 라디오에까지 나온 얘기라고 한다. 저 아득한 남쪽 어느 바닷가 도시에서 할아버지는 탱크를 앞세우고 진격해오던 코쟁이 부대를 그것도 혼자서 격퇴했다고 한다. 할머니가 밥상을 물린 저녁때다 여름밤에 앞마당에 멍석을 깔고 앉아 별하늘을 바라볼 적이면 그 얘기를 꺼내곤 했는데, 아버지가 듣다 못해 말참견을 하는 바람에 할아버지의 영웅담은 빛이 바래고 말았다.

허허 꾸미지 맙세. 기건 쏘련 영화 얘기하구 같단 말입니다.

머가 같네?

지하구 오마니하구 시내 나가서리 본 영화요. 인민반에서 단체루 구경가지 않았음둥. 기걸 아부지 얘기루 혼동하시는 거외다....

하여튼 아버지 말에 따르면 할아버지가 동부전선에서 전사한 것은 사실인 모양이었다. 할머니는 인민위원회에 불려나가 전사통고와 함께 위로품을 받아왔고, 아버지도 학교에 갔더니 담임 선생이 교단에 세워 두고 학생들에게 묵념을 시켰다고 한다. 그런데 할머니는 할아버지가 돌아가신 날을 정확하게 알고는 제삿날을 정했다. 언제나 그랬지만 우리 할머니는 꿈을 통해서 미리 다가올 일을 알아챘다....

하루는 칠성이가 온데간데 없이 사라져서 해가 저물고 어두워질 때까지 돌아오지 않았다. 내가 돌담 밖에까지 나아가 서성거리니까 할머니가 따라나와 말했다.

일없다, 죽진 않아서. 좀 있으믄 돌아오갔지비. 너 아버지한테는 이르지 말구 담부턴 풀어놓지 말구서리.

나는 담 모퉁이에 쪼구려 앉았다. 그리고 눈을 꼭 감고 칠성이를 생각했다. 어둠 속에 부연 빛이 조금씩 열리더니 길과 들판이 보이고 바람에 쓰러지고 넘어진 옥수수밭 고랑이 나타났고 그 안에 하얀 짐승이 보였다. 우리 칠성이가 네 발을 모로 뻗고 누워 있다. 나는 눈을 번쩍 뜨고 어둠속을 보면서 말했다. 할마니, 나 칠성이 어딨는 줄 알아. 저어 강냉이밭 속이야. 나는 무서운 줄도 모르고 뛰기 시작했다. 할머니도 나를 따라서 종종걸음을 치며 뛰다가 걷다가 했다. 들판에는 안개가 부옇게 깔리고 있었다. 야야, 좀 천천히 가두 돼. 칠성인 일 없대는데두. 나는 기차역 지나 철도 건널목을 건너 나지막한 언덕으로 뛰어 올라갔다. 옥수수밭이 보였다. 바람 속에 옥수숫대와 너푼한 잎들이 흔들리는 소리가 들려왔다. 나는 두 손을 입가에 모으고 어둠 속을 향하여 외쳤다. 칠성아, 칠성아! 할머니가 숨을 헐떡이며 둔덕을 올라왔다.

알리와 나는 아래층의 나이지리아 부부가 살던 방에 들어가 살림을 시작했지만 취사는 언제든지 위층의 할아버지 부엌을 사용하기로 했다. 그래야 한가족으로 매일 식사를 함께할 수 있었기 때문이다. 저녁에 직장에서 돌아오자마자 오후에 할아버지가 우리의 메모대로 장을 보아온 것들을 추려서 요리를 했는데 보통은 할아버지와 단둘이서 식사를 할 때가 많았다.

일이 많은 주말을 피하여 주중에는 이틀 정도 알리가 저녁을 함께 먹고 늦게 밤일을 나가는 날도 있었다.

Key vocabulary

배가부르다	pregnancy
몸을풀다	recovering from delivery
터울	age difference – important in heavily age-influenced Korean society
산파	midwife
숙직	night shift
화통	anger

130 *Social change*

뒷간	toilet
숨을죽이다	to hold one's breath
오마니	mother (North Korean dialect)
아부지	father (North Korean dialect)
지	self (colloquial dialect)
인민반	labour community (communist term)
일없다	don't worry (North Korean dialect)
살림	life, living
취사	cooking

Comprehension questions: text

1 Describe what happened at Pari's birth.
2 How did Pari survive?
3 Describe Pari's marriage. Who did she marry and where did they live?
4 Describe Pari's father's life.

Comprehension questions: film extract

The 2018 film *Beautiful Days* (뷰티풀 데이즈) tells of a North Korean refugee who abandons her husband and young child for a better life. Several years later, when her now-adult son comes to look for her in Seoul, the truth about her departure finally comes to the light. A particularly poignant scene is when the father goes to seek out the trafficker who brought his wife out of North Korea after she has left him.

1 Why did the husband report the trafficker to the police?
2 How does the trafficker defend his actions?
3 What work has the wife been doing?
4 Why does the wife think the husband shouldn't complain about this?

Further discussion questions

1 What does the text suggest about the life of North Korean defectors?
2 How did Pari's life echo the legend of Princess Pari?
3 What can you tell about the perspective on sons and daughters in premodern Korea? How is it different or similar to contemporary views?

References

Edlund, Lena, & Lee, Chulhee. 2013. *Son Preference, Sex Selection and Economic Development [Electronic Resource]: The Case of South Korea* (Working paper series (National Bureau of Economic Research: Online); working paper no. 18679). Cambridge, MA: National Bureau of Economic Research.

Kim, Jisoo M. 2016. *The Emotions of Justice: Gender, Status, and Legal Performance in Choson Korea* (Korean studies of the Henry M. Jackson School of International Studies). Seattle; London: University of Washington Press.

Wong, Wai-Ching, Dennis Elton Walters, & Siumi Maria Tam (eds.). 2014. *Gender and Family in East Asia* (Routledge research on gender in Asia series; no. 5). Abingdon; New York: Routledge.

6.6 완득이 – 김려령 (*Wandŭgi-Punch* – Kim Ryŏryŏng)

Introduction to the text

Wandŭgi – Punch (완득이) by Kim Ryŏryŏng (b. 1971) is a young adult novel that tells of rebellious high school student To Wandŭk, who is inspired to get his act together by his meddling homeroom teacher, Yi Tongju. Contrary to many other texts on multiculturalism in Korea, which often dehumanise and objectify immigrant workers, this novel shows how poverty, disability, and multiculturalism intersect and portrays its characters from a sympathetic, humanised perspective.

Original text

머리가 희끗한 할아버지가 휠체어에 앉아 똥주 옆에 있었다. 나는 다시 나가려고 문을 열었다.
　'와놓고 어디 가?'
　똥주가 나를 불렀다.
　'손님이 계셔서요.'
　'옆에 앉아 있어.'
　똥주는 옆에 빈 침대를 턱으로 가리켰다. 나는 침대 뒤에 섰다. 동네 의원 이인용 병실이라 방도 좁았고, 냉랭한 분위기도 영 갑갑했다.
　'하나밖에 없는 아들이라는 게 . . .'
　'하나밖에 없는 아들이니까 그러는 거에요.'
　'그래서 제 아비 공장을 신고했냐?'
　'힘든 사람들을 험하게 대하셨잖아요.'
　'나는 그 사람들, 합법적으로 대했다.'
　'합법적으로 법을 피해서 대했겠죠.'
　'. . .'
　'곰팡이 잔뜩 핀 숙소, 매번 퉁퉁 분 라면, 허술한 안전장치 . . .'
　'그것마저 제공하지 않는 곳도 많다.'
　'그것보다 나은 걸 제공하는 곳도 많아요. 당연히 그래야 하고요.'
　'이노오옴 . . .'
　할아버지는 휠체어 바퀴를 꽉 잡았다.
　'베트남에서 온 티로 누나 기억하시죠? 가족이나 마찬가지라고 집안일까지 시켰던 누나요. 아 왜, 필통 판금하다가 절단기에 손가락 잘려서 귀국시켰던. 저요, 그때부터 철로 된 필통 안 썼어요.'
　'자원봉사도 아니고, 노동이 안 되는 사람을 계속 데리고 있을 수 없었다.'
　'하하하. 치료는 하고 보내셨어야죠. 안 그래요? 잘린 손가락 세 개가 손등까지 썩을 때까지 부려먹다 보냈잖아요! 제가 모를 줄 아세요? 저 고등학교 때 일이에요. 근데 월급은 왜 안 줘서 보낸 거예요? 알아보니까 아버지는 아직도 그러던데, 도대체 왜 외국인 노동자한테만 그러세요? 아! 맞다. 아버지는 원래 약자한테만 무지 강한 분이셨죠. 그걸 자꾸 잊네, 내가.'
　'정 기사, 정 기사!'
　할아버지는 뒤도 돌아보지 않고 소리쳤다.
　밖에서 양복을 말끔하게 차려입은 남자가 들어왔다.
　'천하의 못된 놈!'
　남자는 할아버지가 탄 휠체어를 끌고 문 쪽으로 왔다. 할아버지와 눈이 마주쳤다. 나는 얼른 고개를 돌렸다. 할아버지와 남자다 병실을 나갔다.
　'아이고 나 죽네. 너 이 새끼, 퇴원하면 디졌어.'

똥주가 갑자기 신음 소리를 냈다.
'물어보니까, 아주 살짝 금 갔대요. 아주 살짝.'
나는 똥주 옆 빈 침대에 앉았다.
'누가 그래? 나 죽을지도 몰라, 새끼야.'
'그러게 왜 남의 집에 계세요. 열쇠는 어디서 나셨어요?'
'니 아버님이 너한테 일 생기면 봐달라고 열쇠를 하나 줬다, 새끼야.'
'나한테 무슨 일이 있다고 왔어요, 그럼?'
'니가 아니라 나한테 있어서 갔지.'
'무슨 일이요?'
'아까 그 영감이 밤에 갑자기 들어닥쳤잖아.'
'선생님 아버지 같던데.'
'맞어.'
'몸이 많이 안 좋은가 봐요.'
'하하하. 노인네가 궁주에 몰릴 때마다 휠체어를 애용해.'
똥주 웃는 얼굴이 쓸쓸해 보였다.
'기사까지 있는 거 보면, 부잔가 봐요.'
'꽤 부자지. 할아버지 재산을 듬뿍 물려받았거든.'
'선생님도 부자겠네요.'
'왜, 부자라 싫으냐?'
'저 원래 선생님 싫어해요.'
'알아.'
'근데 왜 가난한 척하고 다녔어요?'
'새끼야, 척이 아니라 진짜야. 옥탑방에 사는 거 보면 몰라?'
'나도 아버지가 부자면 옥탑방이 아니라 지하도에서도 살 수 있어요. 사고 쳐도 다 해결해주는 아버지가 있는데 뭐다 걱정이에요? 선생님이 아무리 아니라고 해도, 아닌 건 아닌 거예요! 하도 가난해서 다른 나라로 시집온 어머니 있어 봤어요? 쪽팔려 죽겠는데 안 가져가면 배고프니까, 할 수 없이 수급품 받아가 본 적 있어요?'
'새끼가 주둥이로 킥복싱을 배웠나. 말 잘하네.'
'선생님은 그냥 가난을 체험해보고 있는 것뿐이에요. 든든하게 돌아갈 곳을 저기에 두고, 가난 체험을 하고 있는 거라고요! 갈 곳 없는 가난을 선생님이 알아요?'
'그럼 일개 교사가 벤츠 타고 출근하리? 보안장치 빵빵한 타워팰리스에 살면서 주말마다 골프 치러 다니면, 욕 안 할래? 이래저래 욕할 새끼가 뭔 말이 이렇게 많아.'
'가난한 사람이 부자인 척하면 재수 없다고 하죠? 부자가 가난한 척해도 재수 없어요.'
'너처럼 멋도 없는 새끼가 멋있는 척해도 재수 없어. 솔직히 너도 진짜 가난이 뭔지 모르잖아. 아버님이 너한테 금칠은 못해줘도, 먹고 자는 데 문제없게 해주셨잖아. 너, 나 욕할 자격 없어, 새끼야. 쪽팔린 줄 아는 가난이 가난이냐? 햇반 하나라도 더 챙겨 가는 걸 기뻐해야 하는 게 진짜 가난이야. 햇반 하나 푹 끓여서 서너 명이 저녁으로 먹는 집도 있어! 문병 오면서 복숭아 하나 안 사 오는 싸가지 없는 새끼. 아이고, 나 죽네.'
'부자 아버지 계시잖아요. 왜 나한테 사 오라고 해요!'

Key vocabulary

희끗하다	touched with grey
턱	chin

냉랭하다	cold, chilly, frigid
영	really, very
신고하다	report, declare, notify
험하게	roughly, dangerously
합법적	legal, legitimate, lawful
허술하다	lax, slack
안전장치	safety equipment
판금	thin and wide pieces of metal
절단기	cutting machine
자원봉사	volunteer work, charity
부려먹다	keep someone hard at work
무지	really, extremely
말끔하다	neat and tidy, looking sharp
병실	ward, hospital room
디지다	Kangwŏndo dialect for 뒈지다: to be dead, die, croak (informal)
심음	groan, moan
금가다	have a hairline fracture
들어닥치다	corruption of 들이닥차다: to come in suddenly
궁지	corner, predicament, fix
듬뿍	generously, up to the brim
지하도	underpass
쪽팔리다	ashamed, embarrassed
수급품	food bank, extra supplies for disadvantaged households
주둥이	trap, gob, hole, mouth (informal)
일개	only, mere
보안장치	security system
재수없다	unlucky, unfortunate
금칠	guilt
문병	going to visit an ill person
싸가지없다	rude
허구한	all the time, doing nothing but
부릅뜨다	glare

Comprehension questions: text

1 Why is Yi Tongju (Ttongju)'s father angry with him?
2 What happened to Tilo from Vietnam?
3 Why is Wandŭk angry upon finding out that Yi Tongju is rich?
4 What does Yi Tongju think is real poverty?

Comprehension questions: TV show extract

The KBS reality show, *My Neighbour Charles* (이웃집 찰스, since 2015), shows the experiences of foreigners living in Korea. In episode ten, we follow the lives of Sum, the only African working at Noryangjin fish market, and Zachary, the head of a foreign food delivery

134 *Social change*

company who speaks no Korean. This episode in particular highlights how the experiences of migrants in Korea can vary widely.

1   Why does Sum cry on the way home from work?
2   Why has Sum's wife Flora refused to integrate into Korean society?
3   How did Zachary come up with the idea for his business?
4   Why has Zachary not learned Korean?

Additional source material

Further sources addressing the experience of migrants in Korea include:

> Film, *Failan* (파이란, 2001).
> Film, *He's on Duty* (방가? 방가!, 2010).
> Talk show, *Global Talk Show* (미녀들의 수다, 2006–2010).
> Talk show, *Abnormal Summit* (비정상회담, 2014–2017).

Further discussion questions

1   How do you think Korea can become a more multicultural society?
2   Do you think Yi Tongju's decision to cut himself off from his father's wealth is a noble statement of principles, or just hypocritical?

References

Ahn, Ji-hyun. 2012. 'Transforming Korea Into a Multicultural Society: Reception of Multiculturalism Discourse and Its Discursive Disposition in Korea.' *Asian ethnicity* 13(1): 97–109.
Cheng, Sealing. 2011. 'Sexual Protection, Citizenship and Nationhood: Prostituted Women and Migrant Wives in South Korea.' *Journal of Ethnic and Migration Studies* 37(10): 1627–48.
Choi Sung-jin. 2018. 'In Love with Korea: More Korean than Most Koreans.' *Koreana* 32(2). Available online at: https://koreana.or.kr/user/0010/nd3037.do?View&boardNo=00001682&zineInfoNo=0010&pubYear=2018&pubMonth=SUMMER&pubLang=English. Accessed 27/12/18.
———. 2018. 'In Love with Korea: "Immigrant Wives Want Equal, Self-Reliant Lives."' *Koreana* 32(3). Available online at: https://koreana.or.kr/user/0011/nd39573.do?View&boardNo=00001854&zineInfoNo=0011&pubYear=2018&pubMonth=AUTUMN&pubLang=English. Accessed 21/12/18.

7 Women in Korean society

7.1 내훈 – 소혜왕후 (*Instructions for Women* – Queen Sohye)

Introduction to the text

Admonishment for Women (*Naehun*), was written by the mother of King Sŏngchong (1457–1494), Queen Sohye, who is also called Queen Mother Insu. This was the first book written directly to women in *han'gŭl*. It was written in 1475. The Queen Mother lived as a widow after her husband, the Crown Prince, died, and she subsequently had to leave the royal palace. However, because the Crown Prince had been the eldest son, her sons were in line to become king. Her second son became the king. Even though she couldn't live at the palace, she enabled her second son to become King Sŏngjong. The Queen Mother was a very active woman, even though she lived as a widow, and she was very actively involved in royal affairs. She was very much an intellectual person, and we can see that clearly because of her publication of *Naehun*. She published this book because there were many great works of literature at the time, but they were difficult for women, who had less education than men, to digest. The Queen, therefore, thoroughly studied those books, tried to find the main messages of these books, and condensed them into seven chapters for the women of the Chosŏn dynasty. The main reason she wrote this book was that she realised that the women of the dynasty were accustomed to Buddhism, which she also promoted, but that Neo-Confucianism was likely to become the most influential ideology of the time, and she wanted women to be equipped with it. In the preface, she said that she was troubled by the lack of Confucian knowledge of the women of the time and wanted to equip them with this new ideology. In this way, she was very forward thinking, and wanted women to take a major role in the changing society.

Original text

부녀에게 네 행적이 있나니 하나는 부녀의 덕이요, 둘은 부녀의 말이요, 셋은 부녀의 모습이요, 넷은 부녀의 공이다.

부녀의 덕은 구태여 재주와 총명이 가장 남다름이 아니요, 부녀의 말을 구태여 입이 특출하며(달변이고) 말씀이 날카로움(시비를 분명히 가리는 것)이 아니고, 부녀의 모습은 구태여 얼굴이 좋으며 고움이 아니요, 부녀의 공은 구태여 공교함이(남보다 뛰어남이)아니다. 깨끗하며 조용하며 바르며 안정하여 절개를 잡아 가다듬고, 몸을 행함에 부끄러움을 두며, 움직임과 가만히 있음에 법 있음이(법도에 맞게 함이) 이른바 부녀의 덕이다. 말씀을 분별하여 일러 모진 말은 이르지 아니하며, 시절인 후에야(한동안 신중히 생각한 후에야) 일러 사람에게 싫지 않게 함이 이른바 부녀의 말이다. 더러운 것을 씻어 옷과 꾸밈이 깨끗하며 목욕을 때때로 하여(자주 하여) 몸을 더럽게 아니함이 이른바 부녀의 모습이다. 길쌈에 마음을 오로지 하여(전심하여) 놀이와 웃음을 즐기지 아니하며 술과 밥을 깨끗이 하여 손님을 대접함이 이른바 부녀의 공이다.

3. 이 넷의 부녀의 큰 덕으로 없을 수 없으리니, 그러나 행함이 심히 쉬우니 오직 마음가짐에 있을 따름이다. 옛 사람이 이르되 '인(仁)이 먼가? 인을 행하고자 하면 이르리라' 하니 이를 말한 것이다.

...

공자께서 말씀하시기를, 부인은 혼자 생각에 따라 멋대로 일을 처리하지 않으며, 세 가지 따라야 하는 도리[삼종지도, 三從之道]가 있다고 했다.

출가 전 친정에 있을 때에는 친정아버지의 뜻을 따르고(종부, 從父), 시집을 가서는 남편의 뜻을 따르고(종부, 從夫), 남편이 죽으면 자식의 뜻을 따르며(종자, 從子), 감히 자기 스스로 일을 처리하는 일이 없어야 한다.

가장의 명을 안방 밖으로 나가게 하지 말아야 하며, 일은 밥 먹을 때에나 멈출 뿐이다. 그러므로 여자는 가정 안에서 날이 저물고, 일을 자기 멋대로 하지 않으며, 혼자 독단으로 행동하지 않는다.

무슨 일이든 모두 자세히 알고 난 뒤에 움직이며, 자신이 직접 겪어본 뒤에야 말을 하고, 대낮에 집 뜰에서 놀지 않으며, 밤에 다닐 때에는 불을 켜 가지고 다닐 일이니 이것은 여자가 갖추어야 할 부덕(婦德)을 바르게 하기 위함이다.

부부간에도 그 성(性)이 다르니, 양(陽)인 남자는 굳셈을 덕으로 삼고, 음(陰)인 여자는 부드러움을 그 힘으로 삼아 아름답게 여기니, 세속에 이르기를 '아들을 이리처럼 낳아도 오히려 나약할까봐 두려워하고, 쥐같은 딸을 낳아도 오히려 호랑이 같이 될까봐 두려워한다'고 했다.

Key vocabulary

부녀	wife, woman
덕	virtue, good action
공	action
구태	purposefulness
재주	ability
총명	intellect
공교함	elaborateness
가다듬다	straighten
인	virtue, good action
공자	Confucius
도리	one's duty, doing what is right
출가	leaving for marriage
대낮	the middle of the day

Comprehension questions: text

1. What do you think the saying about wolves and mice means in terms of sons and daughters?
2. What does the author think about women's work?
3. What are the four achievements described for women?
4. Whose will does Confucius say a woman should follow throughout her life?

Comprehension questions: drama extract

The KBS2 drama, *The Virtual Bride* (별난 며느리, 2015), tells the story of an idol singer, O Inyŏng, who takes part in a reality TV show where she has to pretend to be daughter-in-law to a very traditionally minded matriarch, Yang Ch'unja. In episode two, the scene where another of Yang's (real) daughters-in-law, Kim Semi, returns to work after having stayed at home caring for her son, highlights the expectations and demands towards women within the family in Korea today.

1   What was Kim's nickname when she used to teach?
2   What are the challenges her boss acknowledges she will need to overcome?
3   What is Yang asking of Kim, and why?
4   How does Kim's husband think she should respond?

Additional source material

The Channel A talk shows, *Welcome to Si-World* (웰켐 투 시월드), and *Queen of Housewives* (내조의 여왕), feature panels discussing various aspects of married life for women in Korea today.

The MBC drama, *Queen of Housewives* (내조의 여왕, 2009), and the KBS2 drama *Confession Couple* (고백부부, 2017) are also some of the many dramas revolving around the frustrations and difficulties of the role of a married woman.

Further discussion questions

1   Discuss the status of women as portrayed by the female author of the text.
2   Find examples from Korean drama or films which suggest that these ideals are still present in Korean society today.

References

Duncan, John. 2003. 'The *Naehun* and the Politics of Gender in Fifteenth-Century Korea.' In *Creative Women of Korea: The Fifteenth Through the Twentieth Centuries*, edited by Young-Key Kim-Renaud, pp. 26–57. London; New York: Routledge.
Kim, Jungwon. 2007. *Negotiating Virtue and the Lives of Women in Late Chosŏn Korea*, ProQuest Dissertations and Theses.
Koh, Eunkang. 2008. Gender Issues and Confucian Scriptures: Is Confucianism Incompatible with Gender Equality in South Korea? *Bulletin of the School of Oriental and African Studies 71*(2): 345–62.

7.2 규원가 – 허난설헌 (*Lament of the Inner Chamber – Hŏ Nansŏrhŏn*)

Introduction to the text

Hŏ Ch'ohŭi (1563–1589, pen-name Hŏ Nansŏrhŏn) was a tragic figure, whose artistic life was cut short when she died in sorrow at the age of 27. She grew up in an environment in which it was frowned upon for women to receive anything more than the most basic education, unless they were *kisaeng*. While Hŏ lived at the family home, she was free to pursue her literary gifts in a supportive environment, as one brother, Hŏ Kyun (1569–1618), was a celebrated writer, and another, Hŏ Pong (1551–1588), even brought a friend of his to teach poetry to his sister alongside his brother. But after moving to her husband's house some years after marriage (in *Chosŏn* Korea, it was common for a married couple to live in the wife's home until the birth of the first child), her duties as a wife, as well as the disapproval of her in-laws, would have put a significant damper on her literary activities. This was especially true given that both her children died young, hence making Hŏ fail in the single most important task of a married woman (this being to produce an heir). The atmosphere towards her must have been very cold. Dealing with these and other sorrows, Hŏ's work expresses these emotions in a way that resonates for many.

Her main medium in poetry was *hanshi*, poems with strict structure in Classical Chinese. However, the poem translated here is a form of *kasa*, narrative song, and can be placed in the category of *kyubang kasa*, songs written by anonymous women, often for other women, on 'a variety of matters, such as family etiquette, the instruction of children, and the loves and sorrows of family life' (Chong, Kwon and Lee 2001). There is in fact some controversy on whether or not this *kasa* can be attributed to Hŏ (see, for example, Hŏ (trans. Choe-Wall) 2003), but due to the poem's beauty and importance as a document of women's experiences, we have chosen to include it in this textbook. Hŏ's experiences, so eloquently set down, shed light on the life of noblewomen in *Chosŏn* Korea, and the struggles and pressures they faced despite their life of privilege.

Original text

엊그제까지 젊었는데 어찌 벌써 이렇게 다 늙어 버렸는가?
어릴 적 즐겁게 지내던 일을 생각하니 말을 해도 소용이 없구나.
이렇게 늙음 위에다가 서러운 사연을 말하자니 목이 메이는구나.
부모님이 나를 낳으시고 기르시며 몹시 고생하여 이 내 몸 길러낼 때는
높은 벼슬아치의 배필은 바라지 못할지라도, 군자의 좋은 짝이 되기를 원하셨더니
전생에 지은 원망스러운 업보요, 하늘이 준 부부의 인연으로
장안의 호탕하면서도 경박한 사람을 꿈과 같이 만나서
시집 간 뒤에 남편을 시중하면서 조심하기를 마치 살얼음 디디는 듯하였다.
열다섯, 열여섯 살을 겨우 지나면서 타고난 아름다운 모습이 저절로 나타나니
이 얼굴과 이 태도로 평생을 살 것을 약속하였더니
세월이 빨리 지나고 조물주마저 시샘이 많아서
봄바람과 가을 물, 곧 세월이 베틀의 올이 감기는 북이 지나가듯 빨리 지나가
꽃같이 아름다운 얼굴은 어디 두고 모습이 얄밉게도 되었구나.
내 얼굴을 내가 보고 알거니와 어느 임이 나를 사랑할 것인가?
스스로 부끄러워 하니 누구를 원망할 것인가?
삼삼오오 여러 사람이 떼를 지어 다니는 술집에 새로운 기생이 나타났다는 말인가?
꽃 피고 날이 저물 때면 정처없이 나가서
흰 말과 금 채찍(호사스런 행장)으로 어디어디에서 머물러 노는가?
(집안에만 있어서) 가깝고 먼 지리를 모르는데 임의 소식이야 더욱 알 수 있겠는가?
인연을 끊었지마는 생각이야 없을 것인가?
임의 얼굴을 보지 못하니 그립기나 말았으면 좋으련만,
하루가 길기도 길구나, 한 달이 지루하기만 하구나.
규방 앞에 심은 매화는 몇 번이나 피고 졌는가?
겨울 밤 차고 찰 때는 진눈깨비 섞어 내리고
여름 날 길고 긴 때에 궂은비는 무슨 일인가?

봄날 온갖 꽃이 피고 버들잎이 돋아나는 좋은 시절에 아름다운 경치를 보아도 아무 생각이 없구나.
가을 달빛이 방 안을 비추어 들어오고 귀뚜라미가 침상에서 울 때,
긴 한숨으로 흘리는 눈물 헛되이 생각만 많도다.
아마도 모진 목숨이 죽기도 어려운가 보구나.

돌이켜 여러 가지 일을 하나하나 생각하니 이렇게 살아서 어찌할 것인가?
등불을 돌려놓고 푸른 거문고를 비스듬이 안고서
벽련화 한 곡조를 시름으로 함께 섞어서 연주하니
소상강 밤비에 댓잎 소리가 섞여 들리는 듯
망주석에 천 년만에 찾아온 이별한 학이 울고 있는 듯
아름다운 여자의 손으로 타는 솜씨는 옛날 가락이 그대로 있다마는
연꽃 무늬의 휘장이 드리워진 방 안이 텅 비었으니, 누구의 귀에 들리겠는가?
간장이 구곡되어 굽이굽이 끊어질 듯 애통하구나.
차라리 잠이 들어 꿈에나 임을 보려고 하였더니
바람에 지는 잎과 풀 속에서 우는 벌레는
무슨 일로 원수가 되어 잠마저 깨우는가?
하늘의 견우와 직녀는 은하수가 막혔을지라도
칠월칠석 일년에 한 번씩 때를 어기지 않고 만나는데
우리 임 가신 후는 무슨 장애물이 가려 있길래
온다간다는 소식마저 그쳤을까?
난간에 기대어 서서 임 가신 곳을 바라보니
이슬은 풀에 맺혀 있고, 저녁 구름이 지나가는 때이구나.
대숲 우거진 푸른 곳에 새소리가 더욱 서럽구나.
세상에 서러운 사람이 많다고 하겠지만
운명이 기구한 젊은 여자야 나 같은 이가 또 있을까?
아마도 임의 탓으로 살 듯 말 듯하구나.

Key vocabulary

엊그제까지	from yesterday, a few days before yesterday
젊다	be young
늙다	be old
~아/어 버리다	of an action, the implication that it is irreversible
어릴적	childhood
지내던일	thing done (how [I] passed the time)
소용이없다	no use
~구나	informal exclamative ending
말을해도	even saying that
늙음	old age
서러운	sad, sorrowful
사연	story
목이메이다	choke with emotion
낳다	give birth to
~시~	honorific verb marker
기르다	raise, bring up
몹시	heavily, awfully

고생하다	suffer, have a hard time of it
길러내다	bring up, raise
벼슬아치	government official
배필	spouse, become close with
군자	nobleman, virtuous gentleman
좋은짝	good match, good pair
전생	past life, previous life
지은	built
원망스러운	resentful
업보	karma
하늘	heavens, sky
부부	married couple
인연	relationship
장안의	of the town
호탕	magnanimous, warm-hearted
경박한	flippant, frivolous
시집	husband's home
시중하다	wait on [someone]
마치	like, akin to
살얼음	thin ice
디디다	step on
겨우	barely
타고난	innate
모습	visage
저절로	naturally, by itself
얼굴	face
태도	attitude
약속	promise
세월	time
조물주마저	even the creator
시샘	envy
베틀이올	thread of the loom
감기다	thread, entwine, weave
북	shuttle
꽃같이	like flowers
두고	leave, put down
얄밉다	impudent, odious, hateful
임이	one's beloved
스스로부끄러워하다	be embarrassed, ashamed of oneself
원망하다	blame, resent
삼삼오오	groups of two and three, small groups
술집	bar, pub
기생	*kisaeng*, Korean geisha
날이저물때면	at the close of day
흰	white
금채찍	gold/metal/silver whip
호사스런	the fat of the land, opulent

행장	behaviour
머물다	stay
집안	household, home
끊다	sever, cut
그립다	miss, yearn for
한달이지루하다	bored for a month
규방	women's quarters
심은	planted
매화는	plum
진눈깨비	sleet
궂은비	inclement rain
온갖	all kinds of
버들잎	willow leaves
돋아나는	appearing, budding
경치	view, landscape, scenery
달빛이	moonlight, moonlit
비추어	in the light
귀뚜라미	crickets
침상	couch, bed
한숨	sigh, breath
흘리는눈물	tears falling
헛되이	in vain, for nothing
모진목숨	cruel life
돌이켜	on second thoughts, in retrospect
어찌하다	what to do, have no idea
등불	lantern
돌려놓고	put back
푸른거문고	blue kŏmun'go, six-stringed Korean zither
비스듬	obliquely, diagonally
벽련화	deep blue flower of the lotus
곡조	tune
시름	worries
연주하다	to play
밤비	night rain
댓잎	bamboo blade
망주석	a pair of stone posts in front of a tomb
이별한	separated
학	crane
가락	rhythm
연꽃	lotus
무늬	pattern, design
휘장	insignia, curtain
드리워진	fall, hanging
간장	soy sauce
구곡	last year's grain
굽이굽이	winding, meandering
끊어지다	snap, cut

142 Women in Korean society

애통하다	be mournful, grief-stricken
차라리	rather
잎과풀	leaves and grass
벌레	insect, worm
원수	enemy
~마저	even
견우와직녀	the Altair and the Vega (the two love stars)
은하수	Milky Way
칠월칠석	Tanabata, seventh day of the seventh month of the lunar calendar, day when two love stars are allowed to meet because the Milky Way parts to let them through
장애물	obstacle
가려	screen, eclipse
그치다	cease
난간에	on the railings
기대어	leaning
이슬	dew
대숲	bamboo grove
우거진	lush, forested, lined
새소리	birdsong
서럽다/서러운	sad
운명	fate, destiny
기구한	strange
이	person
탓으로	because of

Comprehension questions: text

1 Why is the protagonist of the poem sad?
2 How does the poet use flower imagery to help transmit the emotion of the poem?
3 What images does the poet use to portray the passing of time?

Comprehension questions to film extract

Rather like the poetic voice in *Kyuwŏn'ga*, the titular character of the 2001 film *Failan* (파이란), spends all her time waiting for her husband, while writing him letters she doesn't send. In this case, the wife is a Chinese immigrant, who enters into a fake marriage with Kangjae, a Korean gangster, in order to be able to stay in Korea to live and work. She goes straight to another town to work, so the couple never meet, but after Failan succumbs to illness and dies, Kangjae has to go to sort out her affairs. In the scene where he reads the letter she left for him after her death, he is confronted with the lack of responsibility he showed towards her while she was still alive.

1 How did Failan come to fall in love with Kangjae?
2 Why did that make things harder for her?
3 Why does Failan think Kangjae is the kindest of them all?
4 What is the favour Failan asks of Kangjae?

Further discussion questions

1 How does the act of waiting for the husbands to come home epitomise the role of the wife in pre-modern (and also modern) Korea?
2 How long are you willing to wait for someone before you would give up on them?

References

Kim, Kichung. 1996. *An Introduction to Classical Korean Literature: From Hyangga to P'ansori*. Armonk, NY; London: M.E. Sharpe.
Kim-Renaud, Young-Key (ed.). 2004. *Creative Women of Korea: The Fifteenth Through the Twentieth Centuries*. Armonk, NY; London: M.E. Sharpe.
Lee, Younghee. 2002. *Ideology, Culture and Han: Traditional and Early Modern Korean Women's Literature*. Edison, NJ: Jimoondang International.

7.3 음식디미방 – 장계향, 규합총서 – 이빙허각 (*Recipes for Tasty Foods* – Chang Kyehyang; and *Encyclopaedia of the Inner Chambers* – Yi Pinghŏgak)

Introduction to the text

These two texts provide rare instances of women passing on practical knowledge in written form in premodern Korea. *Ŭmshiktimibang* (음식디미방, *Recipes for Tasty Foods*), by Chang Kyehyang (1598–1680), was intended as an instruction booklet for her female descendants, and was never intended to be circulated beyond the close family circle. Having been discovered in the house of a descendant in 1960, it has been widely credited as being the first cookbook written in *han'gŭl* in Korea, and the first cookbook to be written by a woman in East Asia. *Kyuhap ch'ongsŏ* (규합총서, *Encyclopedia of the Inner Chambers*), by Yi Pinghŏgak (1759–1824), was also initially only circulated within the family circle, but then went on to be published after her death in 1869, making her one of only very few women to have been published in Chosŏn dynasty Korea. Her text deals not only with food, but also with various other aspects of home management, as well as some discussion on the philosophy behind these actions. While most previous writings on food by men focussed on the medicinal qualities of food, these two texts stand out due to their practical instructions, allowing the recipes to be reconstructed by anyone with access to the texts. Although they both remained firmly in what was considered socially acceptable activities for women, in writing down these recipes, these two women broadened the boundaries of what knowledge was considered suitable to be recorded for prosperity.

Original text

From *Ŭmshiktimibang*

> **Modified quote from Tang dynasty poetry collection *Chŏndangshi* (全糖時)**
>
> 三日入廚下
> 洗水作羹湯

未諳姑食性
先遣少婦嘗

시집온 지 삼일만에 부엌에 들어,
손을 씻고 국을 끓이지만,
시어머니의 식성을 몰라서,
어린 소녀 (젊은 아낙)를 보내어 먼저 맛보게 하네.

Commentary on concluding page of book

이 책을 이렇게 눈이 어두운데 간산히 썼으니, 이 뜻을 알아 이대로 시행하고, 딸자식들은 각각 베껴 가되, 이 책을 가져 갈 생각일랑 절대로 내지 말며, 부디 상하지 않게 간수하여 빨리 떨어져 버리게 하지 말아라.

Extracts from recipes

연계찜 – 영계찜
연계를 전날 저녁에 잡아 거꾸로 매달아 두었다가 이튿날 아침에 잔 깃털이 없게 뜯어 안의 내장을 꺼내고 핏기 없이 많이 씻는다. 아주 단 건장을 체에 걸러 기름을 흥건히 넣고 자소잎, 파, 염교를 잘게 썰어 생강, 후추, 천초가루로 양념을 하고, 밀가루를 한데 개면 즙이 되거든 여기에 간장을 조금 넣고 갠다. 닭 뱃속에 넣어 밥보자기로 싸매어 사기그릇에 담아 솥에 물을 붓고 중탕하여 찐다. 아주 무르게 뼈가 빠질 수 있을 만큼 익거든 꺼내어 식으면 쓴다. 눅게 하는 즙도 걸쭉한 된장을 걸러서 갖은 양념을 넣고 밀가루즙을 눅게 하여 찌면 아주 좋다. 즙이 눅으면 닭이 즙 속에 들어 쪄진다.

From Kyuhap ch'ongsŏ

규합총서 서
  기사 가을에 내가 동호 행정에 집을 삼아, 집안에서 밥짓고 반찬 만드는 틈틈이 우연히 사랑에 나가 옛글이 인생일용에 절실한 것과 산야에 묻힌 모든 글을 구하여 보고 손길 닿는대로 펼쳐 보아 오직 문견을 넓히고 심심풀이를 할 뿐이었다. 문득 생각하니 옛사람이 말하기를 총명이 무딘 글만 못하다 하니 그러므로 적어 두지 않으며 어찌 잊을 때를 대비하여 일에 도움이 되리오. 그래서 모든 글을 보고 그 가장 요긴한 말을 가려 적고, 혹 따로 자기의 소견을 덧붙여 유취 다섯 편을 만드니, 첫째는 주사의니 무릇 장 담그며 술 빚는 법과 밥, 떡, 과줄, 온갖 밥반찬이 갖추지 않은 것이 없다. 둘째는 봉임칙이니 심의, 조복을 손으로 마르고 짓는 척수 겨냥 및 물들이기, 길쌈하기, 수 놓기, 누에치는 법하며 그릇 때우고 등잔 켜는 모른 잡방을 덧붙였다. 셋째는 산가락이니 무릇 밭일을 다스리고 꽃과 때를 심는 일로부터 그 아래로 말이나 소를 치며 닭 기르는데 이르기까지 시골 살림살이의 대강을 가추었다. 넷째는 청낭결이니 태교, 아기 기르는 요령과 삼 가르기와 구급하는 방문이며 아울러 태살의 소재와 약물금기를 덧붙였다. 다섯째는 술수략이니 집을 진압하고 있는 곳을 정히 하는 법과 음양구기하는 술을 달아 부적과 귀신 쫓는 일체의 속방에 미쳤으니, 이로써 뜻밖의 환을 막고 무당, 박수 따위에 빠짐을 멀리한 것이다. 무릇 각각 조항을 열어 적기에 힘써 밝고 자세하고 분명케 하고자 하였으므로, 한 번 책을 열면 가히 알아 보아 행하게 하고, 그 인용한 책이름을 각각 작은 글씨로 모든 조항 아래 나타내고, 혹시 자기 소견이 있으면 신증이라 썼다. 이미 글이 이루어짐에 한데

통틀어 이름 짓기를 규합총서라 하니 무릇 부인의 하는 일이 안채밖을 나지 아니하므로, 비록 예와 이젯 일을 통하는 식견과 남보다 나은 재주가 있더라도, 혹 문자로 펴현하여 남에게 보고 듣게 하려 함은, 아름다움을 속에 품어 간직하는 이의 도리가 아니다. 하물며 나의 어둡고 어리석음으로 어찌 스스로 감히 글로 표현하는 방법을 생각하리오마는 이 책이 비록 많으나, 그 귀결점을 구한 즉 이것들이 다 건강에 간직하는 첫일이요, 집안을 다스리는 중요한 법이라 진실로 일용에 없지 못할 것이요, 부녀의 마땅히 연구할 바다. 그러므로 마침내 이로써 서를 삼아 집안의 딸과 며늘아기들에게 준다.

지뢰내복하는 동짓날에 서하다.

송편

가루를 곱게 하여 흰떡을 골무떡보다 눅게 하여 쪄서 꽤 쳐 굵은 수단처럼 가루 묻히지 말고 비벼 그릇에 서려 담고 떼어 얇게얇게 소가 비치게 파고, 거피팥 꿀 달게 섞고, 계피, 후추, 건강가루 넣어 빚는다. 너무 잘고 동글면 야하니 크기를 맞추어 버들잎같이 빚어 솔잎 격지 놓아 찌면 맛이 유난히 좋다.

Key vocabulary

식성	taste, preference, palate
간산히	with great difficulty
연계	a young chicken, slightly older than a chick
찜	steaming or broiling
건장	usually called 된장, a form of bean paste used for seasoning food
체	sieve, strainer
거르다	filter, sift
자소	차조기, beefsteak plant
염교	shallot
썰다	chop, dice, julienne, shred
천초	Sichuan pepper
개다	mix something with water
보자기	wrapping cloth
솥	Korean traditional cauldron made of cast iron
중탕하다	heat in boiling water, cook in a double boiler
무르다	soft, runny
눅다	thin, soft
걸쭉하다	thick
서	prologue, introduction
기사	1869, although this is presumed to be a spelling mistake, and she is actually referring to 1809
인생일용	everyday use in human life
절실하다	urgent, needed
요긴하다	be of vital importance
주사의	a discussion on alcohol and food
과줄	sweet prepared by frying sweetened dough
봉임칙	methods of weaving and sewing
심의	scholarly robes
조복	robes worn at court
척수	measurement, size

길쌈하기	weaving
누에치다	raise silkworms
때우다	fill, patch, solder
산가락	the joy of living in the countryside
청낭결	medical know-how, refers to a pocket in which medicine was kept or a medical book
태교	prenatal education
삼가르기	cutting the umbilical cord
태살	lit. 'child evil force,' places with bad energy that affect particular people, in this case pregnant women
술수략	a list of books on tricks and charms compiled by Liu Xin of the Han Dynasty on order of the emperor
진압하다	repress, suppress, subdue
부적	charm, amulet, talisman
속방	folk methods
무당	shaman (female)
박수	male shaman
신증	new discovery
안채	main building of house, inner chambers
식견	intelligence, discernment
귀결	conclusion, consequence, result
지뢰내복	stormy
동짓날	winter solstice, the day when daughters-in-law present their parents-in-law with new socks to step in the first sunlight of the year
송편	half-moon rice cakes, eaten on Ch'usŏk, the Korean harvest festival
곱게	finely
골무떡	thimble-shaped rice cake
서리다	coil up
소	stuffing
거피팥	red beans whose skin has been removed
계피	cinnamon
건강가루	dried ginger powder
빚다	make
잘다	small, fine
야하다	erotic, vulgar, racy
버들잎	willow leaves
솔잎	pine leaves
격지	layers

Comprehension questions: text

1 Why did Chang Kyehyang ask a servant girl to taste her stew first?
2 What does Chang Kyehyang want her descendants to do with the recipe book?
3 How does Yi Pinghŏgak defend herself against potential critiques that she is putting herself forward too much in compiling such an extensive piece of work?
4 What do you need to be careful of when shaping rice cakes?

Comprehension questions: drama extract

The MBC drama, *Jewel in the Palace* (대장금, 2003), was one of the first dramas to gain huge success abroad, providing the impetus for what would become the Korean Wave. It tells the tale of the orphan, Changgŭm, who goes through many trials and tribulations before becoming the king's first female doctor. At the beginning of the drama, however, she works in the palace kitchens. In episode four, we see how Changgŭm begins to be taught about the philosophy behind food preparation by her mentor, Lady Han.

1 What task does Lady Han give Changgŭm?
2 What was the solution to the task?
3 Why is this important in relation to preparing food?
4 Who taught Changgŭm this attitude?

Additional source material

The 2018 film *Little Forest* (리틀 포레스트) also includes numerous scenes showing both the care that goes into making food, as well as the emotional healing power that can come from it.

The tvN drama *Let's Eat* (식샤를 합시다, 2013) which was renewed for a second and third season in 2015 and 2018 respectively, is also based on the premise of how food can bring people together.

Further discussion questions

1 What makes the existence of these records (recipes, home encyclopaedia) important?
2 Separate into two teams to debate:

   Team A: The fact that these clearly educated women decided to focus their mental energies on the home shows that they were complicit in their own victimhood as part of an extremely patriarchal system.
   Team B: Declaring their expertise within a socially acceptable zone of influence demonstrates the pragmatic strategies employed by highly educated and intelligent women in carving out power for themselves within a system in which the odds were overwhelmingly stacked against them.

References

Deuchler, Martina. 2003. 'Female Virtues in Chosŏn Korea.' In *Women and Confucian Cultures in Premodern China, Korea, and Japan*, edited by Dorothy Ko, JaHyun Kim Haboush & Joan R. Piggott, pp. 142–69. Berkeley: University of California Press.

Lee, Janet Yoon-sun. 2017. 'The Matrix of Gender, Knowledge and Writing in the *Kyuhap Ch'ongsŏ*.' *Sungkyun Journal of East Asian Studies* 17(2): 211–32.

Lee, SoonGu. 2011. 'The Exemplar Wife: The Life of Lady Chang of Andong in Historical Context.' In *Women and Confucianism in Chosŏn Korea: New Perspectives*, edited by Youngmin Kim & Michael J. Pettid, pp. 29–48. Albany: State University of New York Press.

Ro, Sang-ho. 2016. 'Cookbooks and Female Writers in Late Chosŏn Korea.' *Seoul Journal of Korean Studies* 29(1): 133–57.

Yeongyang-Gun District Office. 2015. 'Eumsik Dimibang.' *Google Arts & Culture*. https://artsandculture.google.com/exhibit/AQXUFTc6. Accessed 4/06/18.

7.4 이춘풍전 (*The Tale of Yi Ch'unp'ung* – Anonymous)

Introduction to the text

Yi Ch'unp'ung was written by an anonymous author in the time of King Yŏngjo and Chŏngjo (1724–1800). The setting of this novel is Pyongyang. It depicts the ineptitude of men – particularly nobility – and the corruption of society. It is the story of a family which has been destroyed by the husband's squandering lifestyle, and is restored by the wisdom and abilities of the wife. The story aims to criticise male dominated society and tries portray the abilities of women. This is different from the normal image of women depicted in the Joseon dynasty.

Original text

이춘풍은 본래 부자였으나, 그의 부모가 죽은 후 주색잡기로 재산을 탕진한다. 이춘풍의 처가 5년간 갖은 고생을 하여 먹고사는 데 지장이 없어지자, 이춘풍은 호조에서 돈을 빌려 장사를 하겠다며 평양으로 떠난다. 하지만 기생 추월을 만나 그녀에게 홀려 돈을 다 뺏기고 한다.

추월의 거동 보소. 춘풍의 재물을 빼앗고 팔세하여 내친다. 슬픈 거동 가련하다. 만나 보면, '내 눈에 보기 싫다.'

석경 면경 헷던지며 생증내어 구박할 제, 성외 성내 한량에게 의론하되 들경막의 장작인가. 전당 집의 은촛댄가, 썩은 나무 박힌 뿌리런가. 이러할 줄 몰랐던가.

'어디로 갈랴시오. 노자가 부족하면 한 대나 보태시오.'

돈 한 돈 내어 주며 바삐 나가라 재촉하니, 춘풍의 거동 보소, 분한 마음 폭발하여 추월에게 하는 말이,

'우리 둘이 갓 만나서 원앙금침 마주 누워 불원상리 굳던 언약 태산같이 언약하여 대동강이 마르도록 떠나가지 말래더니, 이렇듯 깊은 맹세 농담인가 진정인가. 이제 이 말 웬 말인가.' / 추월이 이 말 듣고 변색하여 하는 말이,

'이 사람아, 내 말을 들어 보소. 청루 물정 몰랐던가. 장 낭부 이 낭청도 동가식 서가숙하고 노류장화는 인개가절이라. 평양 기생 추월 성식 몰랐던가. 자네가 가져온 돈냥 혼자 먹던가.'

춘풍은 추월의 사환이 되기로 한다. 그 사실을 알게 된 춘풍의 처가 평양 감사로 가는 참판댁에 부탁하여 비장 벼슬을 얻게 되고 남장을 하여 평양에 내려온다.

이때 평양 비장으로 회계 비장을 겸하고, 분부하여 추월을 잡아들여 돈 5천 냥 바치라 하시니, 뉘 영이라 거역할까. 성화같이 재촉하여 불일 내에 받아 가니, 춘풍이 비장 덕에 돈 받아 실어 놓고, 갓 망건 의복치레 하여 은안준마 높이 타고 경성을 올라 와서 제 집을 찾아가니, 이대 춘풍의 처 문밖에 썩 나서서 춘풍의 소매 잡고 깜짝 놀라며 하는 말이,

'어이 그리 더디던고. 장사에 소망 얻어 평안히 오시니까?'

춘풍이 반기면서, '그새 잘 있던가.'

춘풍이 20아리 돈을 여기저기 벌여 놓고 장사에 남긴 듯이 의기양양하니, 춘풍 아내 거동 보소, 주찬을 소담히 차려 놓고.

'자시오.' 하니 저 잡놈 거동 보소. 없던 교태 지어 내어 제 아내 꾸짖으되,

'안주도 좋지 않고 술 맛도 무미하다. 평양서는 좋은 안주로 매일 장취하여 입맛이 높았으니, 평양으로 다시 가고 싶다. 아무래도 못 있겠다.'

젓가락도 그릇 박고 고기도 씹어 버리며 하는 말이,

'평양 일색 추월이와 좋은 안주 호강으로 지내더니, 집에 오니 온갖 것이 다 어설프다. 호조 돈이나 다 셈하고 약간 전량 수쇄하여 전 주인에게 환전 부치고 평양으로 내려가서 작은집과 한가지로 음식을 먹으리라.'

그 거동은 차마 못 볼러라. 춘풍 아내 거동 보소. 춘풍을 속이려고 상을 물려 놓고 황혼시에 밖에 나가 비장 복색 다시 하고 오동수복 화간죽을 한 발이나 빼쳐 물고 대문 안에 들어서서 기침하고. '춘풍 왔느냐?'

춘풍 자세히 보니 평양서 돈 받아 주던 회계 비장이라. 춘풍이 황겁하여 버선발로 뛰어 내 달아 하여 여쭈오되,

'소인이 오늘 와서 날이 저물어 명일에 댁 문하에 문안코자 하옵더니, 나으리 먼저 행차 하옵시니 황공 만만하여이다.'

'내 마침 이리 지나가다가 너 왔단 말 듣고 네 집에 잠깐 들렀노라.'

방 안에 들어가니, 춘풍이 아무리 제 안방인들 어찌 들어갈싸. 문밖에 섰노라니,

'춘풍아, 들어와서 말이나 하여가.'

'나으리 죄정하신데 감히 들어가오리까.'

'잔말 말고 들어오라.'

춘풍이 어쩌지 못하여 들어오니 비장이 가로되,

'그때 추월에게 돈을 진작 받았느냐?'

'나으리 덕택에 즉시 받았나이다. 못 받을 돈 5천 냥을 일조에 다 받았나오니, 그 덕택이 태산 같사이다.'

'그때 맞던 매가 아프더냐.'

'소인에게 그런 매는 상이로소이다. 어찌 아프다 하리이까.'

비장이 왈, '네 집에 술이 있느냐?'

춘풍이 일어서서 주안을 드리거늘, 비장이 꾸짖어 왈,

'네 계집은 어디 가고 내게 내외시키느냐. 네 계집 빨리 불러 술 준비 못 시킬소냐.'

춘풍이 황겁하여 아무리 찾은들 있을소냐.

Key vocabulary

주색잡기	an expression referring to alcohol, women, and gambling
호조	department of finance
내친다	to throw away from oneself
거동	movement
석경	mirror
헷던지며	throw away
생증내어	expressing irritation, being annoyed
성외성내	outside the city, inside the city
한량	often refers to nobility squandering away their lives without a job
원앙금침	a special duvet and a pillow sewn with the image of a Mandarin duck, which symbolises a happy marriage
노류장화인개가절	the flowers on the road; used symbolically to refer to gisaeng or prostitutes
사환	servant
비장	a government officer in the Joseon period
잡놈	bastard
교태	arrogant attitude
작은집	literally 'small house,' this refers to a second wife or mistress
황혼시	sunset
오동수복	a kind of vessel which is said to contain blessings
버선발	wearing traditional socks without shoes (in a hurry)
복지	a low bow
계집	derogatory term for women

Comprehension questions: text

1. What is the narrator's opinion of Ch'unp'ung and how does this appear in the text?
2. What are some words that reflect the class differences in the text?
3. What are some words that are used to reflect the relationship between husbands and wives in premodern Korea?

Comprehension questions: drama extract

The JTBC drama, *Strong Woman Do Bong-Soon* (힘쎈여자 도봉순, 2017), tells the story of a young woman, To Pongsun, who has inherited superhuman strength from the women in her family. An Minhyŏk, a game company CEO, hires her as his bodyguard after witnessing her strength, and various hijinks ensue as the drama plays with the expectation that women are always frail and in need of protecting. Mirroring the efforts of Ch'unp'ung's wife in the text above, in episode six Pongsun is left to pick up the pieces after Minhyŏk and Kukdu, a childhood friend of Pongsun's, get into a drinking competition.

1. How is the way Pongsun behaves towards Kukdu and Minhyŏk different?
2. What excuse are the men making while they pick Kukdu and Minhyŏk's pockets?
3. What does one of the pickpockets suggest to Pongsun?
4. What do the gangsters watching Pongsun beat up the two men think she is?

Further discussion questions

1. What can you tell about class differences and male and female equality in this time period?
2. Discuss the female role model portrayed in this text. Can you find an equivalent figure in other world literature?

References

Kim, Jisoo. 2010. *Voices Heard: Women's Right to Petition in Late Chosŏn Korea*, ProQuest Dissertations and Theses.

Kim, Jungwon. 2007. *Negotiating Virtue and the Lives of Women in Late Chosŏn Korea*, ProQuest Dissertations and Theses.

Kim, Kyungran. 2018. 'Female Heads of Households Registered in Korea's Census Registers Between the Seventeenth and Nineteenth Centuries and Their Historical Significance.' *International Journal of Korean History* 23(2): 167–94.

7.5 탁류 – 채만식 (*Turbid Rivers – Ch'ae Manshik*)

Introduction to the text

The father of Chobong's family, Mr. Jeong, squandered their wealth through gambling and their debts continued to increase. Chobong fell in love with Seungjae, who was also very poor, but Taesu, who was a corrupt banker, negotiated with Chobong's father that if he gave him his daughter, he would pay the debt and open a new, small shop. Mr. Jeong agreed with Taesu's offer, and married Taesu and his daughter, Chobong. But Taesu's adultery was exposed within ten days, and he was killed. Hyeongbo, who was Taesu's friend, raped Chobong.

Chobong ran away from her hometown, Gunsan, and met the pharmacist, Jaeho. Jaeho made Chobong his concubine. Chobong had a daughter, Songhee, and they lived together. Hyeongbo visited Jaeho and Chobong, and gave Chobong a really difficult time. Hyeongbo also continued to harass Songhee, Chobong's daughter, so Chobong killed him. Chobong tried to commit suicide after killing Hyeongbo, but right at that moment she met her sister Kyebong along with Seungjae. She decided to turn herself in. Ch'ae Manshik (1902–1950) is a Korean novelist known for his satirical style. He wrote many works critical of the Japanese government before being captured, after which time he wrote pro-Japanese pieces until the end of colonialism. After that time, he then returned to writing pieces criticising pro-Japanese writings by intellectuals, including his own.

Original text

치료를 받고 난 태수는 그 길로 개복동 행화(杏花)의 집을 들렀다.
　언제나 마찬가지로 오늘도 형보가 먼저 와서, 아랫목 보료 위에 가 사방침을 베고 드러누웠고, 행화는 가야금을 심심삼아 누르고 있다.
　'자네, 집 장만했다면서 방이 몇인가? 남을 게 있나?'
　태수가 마루로 올라서노라니까, 방에서 형보가 이런 소리를 먼저 묻는다. 형보는 태수가 결혼을 하고 살림을 차리면 비벼 뚫고 들어갈 요량을 대고 있는 참이다.
　'염려 말게. 그러잖아두, 다아 . . .'
　태수는 방으로 들어서면서 우선 양복 저고리를 훌러덩 벗어 들고 휘휘 둘러보다가 행화가 차고 앉은 가야금 위에다 휙 내던지고 모자는 벗어서 행화의 머리에다 푹 눌러 씌운다.
　'와 이리 수선을 피우노? . . . 남 안 가는 여학생 장가나 가길래 이라제?'
　행화는 익살맞게 그대로 까딱 않고 앉아서 태수한테 눈을 흘긴다.
　'하하하하, 그래그래, 내가 요새 대단히 유쾌해!'
　'참 볼 수 없다! . . . 그 잘난 재미할 여학생 장가로 못 갈까 봐서 코가 쉰댓 자나 빠져 갖고 댕길 때는 언제고, 저리 좋아서 야단스레 굴 때는 언제꼬!'
　'하 이 사람, 그러잖겠나? 평생 소원을 이뤘으니. . . . 그렇지만 염려 말게 . . . 신정이 좋기루 구정이야 잊을 리가 있겠나?'
　'아이갸! 내 차 타고 서울로 가서 한강 철교에 자살로 할라 캤더니, 그럼 그 말만 꼬옥 믿고 그만두오, 예?'
　'아무렴, 그렇구말구 . . . 다아 염려 말래두 그래!'
　시방 행화는 농담으로 농담을 하고 있지만, 태수는 진정을 농담으로 하고 있다. 그는 초봉이와 약혼을 한 그날부터는 근심과 불안을 요새 하늘처럼 말갛게 싹싹 씻어 버렸다.
　그새까지는 근심이 되고 답답하고 할 적마다, 염불이나 기도를 하는 것과 일반으로, 뭘! 약차하거든 죽어 버리면 고만이지, 하고 그 임시 그 임시의 번뇌를 회피하기는 했지만, 그러면서도 한편으로는 어떻게 일을 좀 모면하고 싶은 마음이 간절하여, 늘 불안과 더불어 그것이 가슴에 서리고 있었다.
　영 그를 모피하지는 못할 형편인데 일변 한 걸음 두 걸음 몸 바투 다가는 오고 그러자 마침 초봉이와 뜻대로 약혼까지 되고 나니, 그제는 아주 예라! 이놈의 것 . . . 하고, 정말로 죽어 버릴 결심을 하고 말았던 것이다.
　해서, 그 무겁던 불안과 노심으로부터 완전히 해방을 받은 것이다.
　제일 큰 소원이던 초봉이한테 여학생 장가를 들어 마지막 원을 푼 다음에야 단 하루라도 좋고 이 생에 아무 미련도 없다. 그리고 (그래서 장차 어느 날일지는 몰라도 그날에 임하여 종용자약하게 죽음을 자취할 테나) 그러나 그날의 최후의 일순간까지라도 이 세상을 깊이 있고 폭 넓게, 단연코 즐거운 생활을 해야만 한다.

152 Women in Korean society

그리하자면 첫째 초봉이로 더불어 맺은 꿈을 최대한으로 호화롭게 꾸며야 한다. 그러나 그러면서도 한편으로는 많이 많이 뚱땅거리고 술을 마시면서 놀아야 한다. 계집도 할 수 있는 껏 여럿을 두고 지내야 한다. 하니까 행화도 그대로 데리고 지낼 테다.

돈도 도적질도 좋고 빚도 좋고 사기 횡령 다 좋다. 재주껏 끌어 대면 그만이다.

즐겁고 유쾌하자면 그러므로 몸에 고통이 없어야 한다. 이렇듯 태수는, 마치 무슨 의식을 거행하는 데 순서를 작정해 논 것처럼, 앞일을 가뜬하고 분명하게 짜놓았다.

해서 그는 진정으로 유쾌하고 명랑했던 것이지 조금도 억지로 그러는 것이 아니던 것이었다.

태수와 행화가 주거니 받거니 한참 지껄이는 동안, 형보는 제 생각에 골몰해 있다가 이윽고 끙 하면서 일어나 앉더니 태수 앞에 놓인 해태 곽을 집어다가 한 대 피워 물고는, 저도 말에 한몫 끼자고,

'행화가 말루는 아무렇지도 않은 체해두 다아, 속은 단단히 꽁한 모양이지?'

'와?'

'아, 저렇게 이쁜 서방님을 뺏기니깐 . . .'

'하! 고주사가 이쁘문 거저 이뻤나? 돈을 주니 이뻤제 . . .'

'조건 농담을 해두 꼭 저따우루 한단 말야!'

'와 농담고? 진정인데 . . .'

'그래그래, 말이야 말루 바른말이다 . . . 그런데, 아무튼 고주사가 장가를 든다니깐 섭섭하긴 섭섭하지?'

Key vocabulary

훌러덩	whipping motion
요량	estimation, intention
가야금	traditional Korean string instrument
장가	refers to the marriage of a man
코가빠지다	describing a long wait
신정	new love
구정	old love
싹싹	the sound of washing or wringing hands constantly. Can also refer to repeated movement.
염불	Buddhist chant or prayer
번뇌	worldly worries
회피하다	to avoid or evade
미련	a sense of leaving something undone, similar to regret
사기횡령	fraud, embezzlement
지껄이다	jabbering away
해태곽	해태 is the cigarette brand name, and 곽 is the packet
주사	a man's title

Comprehension questions: text

1 Find interjections used by the author throughout the text.
2 Try to determine who is speaking to whom throughout the text.
3 What is Henghwa's attitude towards Taesu?
4 Why did Taesu decide to commit suicide?

Comprehension questions: film extract

The tvN drama series *Misaeng: Incomplete Life* (미생 – 아직 살아 있지 못한 자, 2014) documents the everyday struggles people go through as they try to survive in the workplace. Episode five in particular highlights the issues faced by women employees – this comes to a head during the team meeting.

1 How does Manager Ma respond to Deputy Director Sŏn defending Chief Oh against his accusations of embezzlement?
2 Why does Chief Oh think Manager Ma is being harsh on him?
3 How does Manager Ma defend himself?
4 Does Yŏngi agree with Manager Ma?

Additional source material

The 2013 film *Norigae* (노리개) deals with the real-life suicide of actress Chang Chayŏn, who was taken advantage of as she tried to develop her career, and the efforts made to reveal the truth of what happened to her.

Further discussion questions

1 How is the expression of male power linked to the possession of women in the text and film extract?
2 Has the situation for women in Korea improved since premodern times?

References

Cho, Erin. 1998. 'Caught in Confucius's Shadow: The Struggle for Women's Legal Equality in South Korea.' *Columbia Journal of Asian Law* 12(2): 125–89.
France-Presse, Agence. 2018. 'South Korea: #MeToo Anger as Politician Found not Guilty of Rape.' *The Guardian*, 15/08/18. Available online at: www.theguardian.com/world/2018/aug/15/south-korea-metoo-anger-as-politician-found-not-guilty-of. Accessed 06/02/19.
Haynes, Suyin & Aria Hangyu Chen. 2018. 'How #MeToo Is Taking on a Life of Its Own in Asia.' *TIME*, 09/10/18. Available online at: http://time.com/longform/me-too-asia-china-south-korea/. Accessed 06/02/19.
Kim, Jinsook. 2017. '#iamafeminist as the "Mother Tag": Feminist Identification and Activism against Misogyny on Twitter in South Korea.' *Feminist Media Studies* 17(5): 804–20.
Kim, Kyong-dong & *The Korea Herald*. 2008. *Social Change in Korea*. Paju-si: Jimoondang. (Chapter 5: Marriage, Family and Women in Society)
Maresca, Thomas. 2018. 'South Korea's Me Too Movement Topples High-Profile Politicians and Entertainment Icons.' *USA Today*, 03/04/18. Available online at: https://eu.usatoday.com/story/news/world/2018/04/03/south-koreas-me-too-movement-topples-politicians-entertainment-icons/476895002/. Accessed 06/02/19.
Park, Cheong et al. 2013. 'Sexual Harassment in Korean College Classrooms: How Self-Construal and Gender Affect Students' Reporting Behaviours.' *Gender, Place and Culture* 20(4): 432–50.

154 *Women in Korean society*

7.6 채식주의자 – 한강 (*The Vegetarian* – Han Kang)

Introduction to the text

The Vegetarian by Han Kang (b. 1970) was the winner of the Man Booker International Prize for its translation by Deborah Smith, although along with the great popularity of this novel, there was significant debate on the appropriateness of Smith's translation (see below). It tells the story of Yŏnghye, a 'completely unremarkable' woman who one day suddenly decides to stop eating meat, and the conflicts that emerge from this choice. Having been deeply influenced by a nightmare about human cruelty, Yŏnghye gradually attempts to purge meat and other human influences from her life in order to turn into a plant. After a suicide attempt, Yŏnghye is placed in a mental institution, where only her sister Inhye still cares for her, transferring her to another hospital after the institution force feeds Yŏnghye who refuses to eat.

Han Kang is the daughter of novelist Han Sŭngwŏn and sister to writer Han Dong Rim. She has won numerous prizes, both national and international, for her work, and currently teaches creative writing at the Seoul Institute of the Arts.

Original text

'가만있어봐라. 영혜 너, 애비가 그만큼 알아듣게 말했는데 . . .'
 장인의 호통에 이어, 처형이 야무지게 아내를 나무랐다.
 '너 정말 어쩌려구 그러니? 사람한테 필요한 영양소가 있는 건데 . . . 채식을 하려면 제대로 식단을 잘 쪄서 하든가. 얼굴이 그게 뭐야.'
 처남댁도 거들었다.
 '저는 딴사람인 줄 알았어요. 얘기는 들었지만, 그렇게 몸 상해가면서 채식하는 줄은 몰랐지 뭐예요.'
 '지금부터 그 채식인지 뭔지 끝이다. 이거, 이거, 이거, 다 먹으라 얼른. 없어 못 먹는 세상도 아니고 무슨 꼴이냐.'
 장모는 쇠고기볶음과 탕수육, 닭찜, 낙지소면 접시들을 들어 아내 앞에 펼쳐놓으며 말했다.
 '뭐 하고 있는 거냐? 어서 먹어.'
 장인이 기차 화통 같은 목소리로 채근했다.
 '영혜야, 먹어. 먹으면 힘이 날 거야. 사람이 사는 날까진 힘차게 살아야지. 절에 들어간 스님들은 그만큼 수도를 하고 독신생활을 하니까 살 수 있는 거야.'
 처형이 조곤조곤 타일렀다. 눈을 동그랗게 뜬 아이들이 아내의 모습을 지켜보고 있었다. 아내는 이게 무슨 갑작스런 소란인지 영문을 모르겠다는 듯 멍한 시선으로 가족들의 얼굴을 건너다보았다.
 긴장된 침묵이 흘렀다. 나는 새카맣게 그을린 장인의 얼굴을, 한때 젊은 여인이었으리라는 것을 믿을 수 없을 만큼 쪼글쪼글한 장모의 얼굴을, 그 눈에 어린 염려를, 처형의 근심어린, 치켜올라간 눈썹을, 동서의 방관자적인 태도를, 막내처남 내외의 소극적이지만 못마땅한 듯한 표정을 차례로 둘러보았다. 아내가 무슨 말이든 꺼내놓을 것이라고 나는 기대했다. 그러나 그녀는 들고 있던 젓가락을 상에 내려놓는 것으로, 그 모든 얼굴들이 쏘아보내는 무언의, 하나의 메시지에 대한 대답을 대신했다.
 작은 술렁임이 지나갔다. 장모는 이번에는 젓가락으로 탕수육을 들었다. 안애의 입 바로 앞까지 내밀며 말했다.
 '자. 어서 아, 해라. 먹어.'
 아내는 입을 다문한 채, 예의 영문을 모르겠다는 듯한 눈으로 자신의 어머니를 바라보았다.
 '어서 입 벌려. 이거 싫으냐? 그럼 이거.'

장모는 이번에는 쇠고기볶음을 들었다. 아내가 여전히 입을 다물고 있자 장모는 다시 그것을 내려놓고 굴무침을 집었다.
'너 어릴 때부터 이거 좋아했잖냐. 이거 실컷 먹어보고 싶다고 한 적도 있었는데...'
'예, 저도 기억나요. 그래서 어디 가서 굴을 보면 영혜 생각이 나는데.'
처형은 아내가 굴무침을 먹지 않는 것이 무엇보다 큰일이라는 듯 장모를 거들었다. 굴무침이 집힌 젓가락이 입을 향해 점점 가까이 다가오자, 아내는 몸을 뒤로 힘껏 젖혔다.
'얼른 먹어. 팔 아프다...'
장모의 팔이 실제로 떨렸다. 아내는 마침내 자리에서 일어섰다.
'저, 안 먹어요.'
처음으로 아내의 입에서 또렷한 음성이 흘러나왔다.
'뭐야!'
고함을 지른 것은, 비슷한 다혈질인 장인과 처남이 함께였다. 처남댁이 얼른 처남의 팔을 잡았다.
'보고 있으려니 내 가슴이 터진다. 이 애비 말이 말 같지 않아? 먹으라면 먹어!'
나는 아내가 '죄송해요, 아버지. 하지만 못 먹겠어요'라고 대답하리라고 예상했다. 그러나 그녀는 조금도 죄송하지 않은 듯한 말투로 담담히 말했다.
'저는, 고기를 안 먹어요.'
절망한 장모의 젓가락이 거두어졌다. 늙은 그녀의 얼굴은 금방이라도 울음을 터뜨릴 것 같았다. 곧 폭발할 듯한 정적이 흘렀다. 장인이 젓가락을 집어들었다. 탕수육 한점을 집어들고 상을 돌아 아내 앞에 우뚝 섰다.
평생의 노동으로 단련된, 단단한, 그러나 어쩔 수 없이 허리가 구부정하게 굽은 뒷모습으로 장인은 탕수육을 아내의 얼굴에 들이밀었다.
'먹어라. 애비 말 듣고 먹어. 다 널 위해서 하는 말이다. 그러다 병이라도 나면 어쩌려고 그러는 거냐.'
가슴 뭉클한 부정(父情)이 느껴져, 나도 모르게 눈시울이 뜨거워졌다. 아마 그 자리에 모인 모든 사람들이 그랬을 것이다. 허공에서 조용히 떨고 있는 장인의 젓가락을 아내는 한손으로 밀어냈다.
'아버지, 저는 고기를 안 먹어요.'
순간, 장인의 억센 손바닥이 허공을 갈랐다. 아내가 뺨을 감싸쥐었다.
'아버지!'
처형이 외치며 장인의 팔을 잡았다. 장인은 아직 흥분이 가시지 않은 듯 입술을 실룩거리고 있었다. 한때 성깔이 대단했다는 것은 알고 있었지만, 장인이 누군가에게 손찌검하는 광경을 직접 본 것은 처음이었다.
'정서방, 영호, 둘이 이쪽으로 와라.'
나는 머뭇거리며 아내에게 다가갔다. 뺨에서 피가 비칠 만큼 아내는 세게 맞았다. 그녀는 그제야 평정이 깨진 듯 숨을 몰아쉬고 있었다.
'두 사람이 영혜 팔을 잡아라.'
'예?'
'한번만 먹기 시작하면 다시 먹을 거다. 세상천지에, 요즘 고기 안 먹고 사는 사람이 어디 있어!'
불만스러운 얼굴로 처남이 자리에서 일어섰다.
'누나, 웬만하면 먹어. 예, 하고 먹는 시늉만 하면 간단하잖아. 아버지 앞에서 이렇게까지 해야겠어?'
장인이 고함쳤다.
'무슨 얘길 하기 있어. 어서 팔 잡아라. 정서방도.'
'아버지, 왜 이러세요.'
처형이 장인을 잡은 팔힘보다 처남이 아내를 잡은 팔힘이 셌으므로, 장인은 처형을 뿌리치고 탕수육을 아내의 입에 갖다댔다.

156 *Women in Korean society*

Key vocabulary

장인	wife's father, father-in-law
호통	roar, angry scolding
처형	wife's elder sister
나무라다	scold, rebuke
영양소	nutrients
식단	diet plan, menu
처남댁	brother-in-law's wife
꼴	look, state, sight
장모	wife's mother, mother-in-law
쇠고기볶음	stir-fried beef
탕수육	sweet and sour pork
닭찜	steamed/stewed chicken
낙지소면	octopus with thin noodles
화통	smokestack, funnel
수도	ascetic practice
독신생활	celibacy
조곤조곤	quietly
타이르다	reason with, persuade
영문을 모르다	to not know the reason
그을리다	blacken
쪼글쪼글하다	wrinkled, withered, crumpled
근심	worry, anxiety, apprehension
방관자적	on the sidelines
내외	husband and wife
못마땅하다	displeased, dissatisfied, unhappy
무언	silent, mute, taciturn
술렁임	change in the atmosphere, moment of tension
굴무침	seasoned oysters
또렷하다	clear, distinct, evident
고함	shout, yell, roar
다혈질	hot-tempered
정적	silence, stillness, hush
우뚝	high, aloft, towering
구부정하다	slightly bent, curved, stooped
뭉클하다	touching, moving
실룩거리다	twitch
성깔	fierce temper
손찌검	beat, strike, slap
서방	son-in-law, husband
평정	composure, calmness
시늉	pretense, fake

Comprehension questions: text

1 What is the family's main argument against Yŏnghye's refusing to eat meat?
2 Why are Inhye and their mother so shocked that she won't eat oysters?

3　How does Yŏnghye's father try to persuade her to eat?
4　Why does he want to force her to eat a piece of meat?

Comprehension questions: drama/film extract

The 2006 film *I'm a Cyborg but That's OK* (싸이보그지만 괜찮아) tells the story of Yŏnggun, a young woman who believes she is a cyborg, and can't eat in case it breaks her machinery. At the mental institution into which she is admitted, she meets the antisocial kleptomaniac Ilsun, who forms a bond with her. Ilsun builds a 'rice megatron' to help Yŏnggun get over her fear of eating food.

1　What is the function of a 'rice megatron'?
2　Why can't Yŏnggun thank Ilsun?
3　What are the steps to eating rice?
4　Why does Yŏnggun not need to worry about the rice megatron breaking down?

Additional source material

The posthumously released album *Poet | Artist*, by Shinee's Jonghyun, provides a wealth of material for analysis in terms of mental health pressures on Korean celebrities, as it lays bare some of the pressures he faced before his suicide.

Further discussion questions

1　Is the portrayal of mental health issues in *The Vegetarian* and *I'm a Cyborg but That's OK* helpful in creating awareness and understanding, or does it cause more harm than good?
2　Comparing Deborah Smith's translation to the Korean original text, do you feel her adaptation for English readers goes too far, or is it justified?

References

Armitstead, Claire. 2018. 'Lost in (mis)translation? English take on Korean novel has critics up in arms.' *The Guardian,* 15/01/18. Available online at: https://www.theguardian.com/books/booksblog/2018/jan/15/lost-in-mistranslation-english-take-on-korean-novel-has-critics-up-in-arms. Accessed 06/02/19.
Fan, Jiayang. 2018. 'Han Kang and the Complexity of Translation.' *The New Yorker,* 15/01/18. Available online at: https://www.newyorker.com/magazine/2018/01/15/han-kang-and-the-complexity-of-translation. Accessed 06/02/19.
Im, Jeong Soo, B.C. Ben Park and Kathryn Strother Ratcliff. 2018. 'Cultural Stigma Manifested in Official Suicide Death in South Korea.' *OMEGA – Journal of Death and Dying* 77(4): 486–403.
Roh, Sungwon et al. 2016. 'Mental health services and R&D in South Korea.' *International Journal of Mental Health Systems* 10:45.
Saeji, CedarBough et al. 2018. 'Regulating the Idol: The Life and Death of a South Korean Popular Music Star.' *Asia Pacific Journal: Japan Focus* 16(13:3): 1–32.
Stobie, Caitlin E. 'The Good Wife? Sibling Species in Han Kang's *The Vegetarian.*' *ISLE: Interdisciplinary Studies in Literature and Environment* 24(4): 787–802.
Yun, Charse. 2017. 'You Say Melon, I Say Lemon. Deborah Smith's Flawed Yet Remarkable Translation of "The Vegetarian."' *Korea Exposé*, 02/07/17. Available online at: https://www.koreaexpose.com/deborah-smith-translation-han-kang-novel-vegetarian/. Accessed 06/02/19.

8 Nature, beauty, and aesthetics

8.1 멋설 – 조지훈 (*On Beauty* – Cho Chihun)

Introduction to the text

The term Ch'ŏngnokp'a 청록파(青鹿派) describes three poets – Cho Chihun (1920–1968), Pak Tuchin, and Pak Mokwŏl – who debuted through *Munjang* <문장> in 1940. These three poets, who all entered the poetry scene around the same time through *Munjang* 《문장》, happened to have similarities in poetic style. They each used nature as the main background for their poems, which were written in a traditionally prosodic style. For this reason, they are known as Ch'ŏngnokp'a, or Chayŏnp'a.

Original text

하늘이 드높아 가니 벌써 가을인가 보다. 가을이 무엇인지 내 모르되 잎이 진 지 오래고 뜰 앞에 두어 송이 황국(黃菊)이 웃는지라. 찾아오는 이마다 가을이라 이르니 나도 가을이라 믿을 수밖에 없다. 촛불을 끄고 창 앞에 턱을 괴었으나 무엇을 생각해야 할지 생각이 나질 않는다.

    다시 왜 사는가. 문득 한 줄기 바람에 마른 잎이 날아간다. 유위전변(有爲轉變) – 바로 그것을 위해서 모든 것이 사나 보다.

    우주의 원리 유일의 실재에다 '멋'이란 이름을 붙여 놓고 엊저녁 마시다 남은 머루술을 들이키고 나니 새삼스레 고개 끄덕여지는 밤이다. 산골 물소리가 어떻게 높아 가는지 열어젖힌 창문에서는 달빛이 쏟아져 들고, 달빛 아래는 산란한 책과 술병과 방우자(放牛子)가 네 활개를 펴고 잠들어 있는 것이다.

    '멋,' 그것을 가져다 어떤 이는 '도(道)'라 하고 '일물(一物)'이라 하고 '일심(一心)'이라 하고 대중이 없는데, 하여간 도고 일물이고 일심이고 간에 오늘 밤엔 '멋'이다. 태초에 말씀이 있는 것이 바로 무상(無常)인가 하면 무상을 무상하게 하는 것이 또한 '멋'이다. 변함이 없는 세상이라면 무슨 멋이 있겠는가. 이 커다란 멋을 세상 사람은 번뇌(煩惱)라 이르더라. 가장 큰 괴로움이라 하더라.

    우주를 자적(自適)하면 우주는 멋이었다. 우주에 회의(懷疑)하면 우주는 슬픈 속(俗)이었다. 나와 우주 사이에 주종의 관계있어 이를 향락하고 향락 당하겠는가. 우주를 내가 향락하는가 하면 우주가 나를 향락하는 것이다. 나의 멋이 한 곳에서 슬픔이 되고 속(俗)이 되고 하는가 하면 바로 그 자리에서 즐거움이 되고 아(雅)가 되는구나. 죽지 못해 살 바에는 없는 재미도 짐짓 있다 하라.

    한 바리 밥과 산나물로 족히 목숨을 이으로 일상(一床)의 서(書)가 있으니 이로써 살아 있는 복이 족하지 않은가. 시를 읊을 동쪽 두던이 있고 발을 씻을 맑은 물이 있으니 어지러운 세상에 허물할 이가 누군가. 어찌 세상이 괴롭다 하느뇨. 이는 구태여 복을 찾으려 함이니, 슬프다, 복을 찾는 사람이여. 행복이란 찾을수록 멀어가는 것이 아닌가.

마음의 흐름대로 따르는 것이 곧 행복이라, 다만 알려고 함으로써 멋을 삼노라.

Key vocabulary

황국(黃菊)	a yellow chrysanthemum
유위전변(有爲轉變)	the world is prone to constant change
방우자(放牛子)	the pen name of the author
도(道)	the road; the way
일물(一物)	one thing/object/existence
(一心)	one heart
무상(無常)	a realisation given from Buddha; the ever changing-ness of the world
번뇌(煩惱)	intense personal suffering
자적(自適)	self-satisfaction
회의(懷疑)	scepticism
속(俗)	the things of the world or of a specific time period
아(雅)	clear; bright; clean
일상(一床)	one set
서(書)	writings

Comprehension questions: text

1 How does the author define autumn?
2 How do people think of the word 멋?
3 What is the blessing/happiness of life according to the author?

Comprehension questions: drama extract

The MBC drama *Goddess of Fire* (불의 여신 정이, 2013) is based loosely on the real-life Paek P'asŏn (1560–1656), who was the first female potter in the Chosŏn dynasty. In episode four, the main character Chŏngi is tasked with making the most beautiful thing in the world in order to save her father from execution. When she is stumped for how to achieve this, a dream visitation by her father's teacher, Teacher Mun, helps give her some inspiration.

1 What is the most beautiful thing in the world for Teacher Mun?
2 How does he describe the most beautiful thing that Chŏngi must find?
3 Why does Chŏngi say she would not be able to make what the king would find most beautiful?
4 What did Chŏngi make and why?

Further discussion questions

1 What do you think is the best way to translate the word 멋? Discuss this with your Korean friend.
2 Is Korean aesthetics different from Western aesthetics? Discuss how.

160 Nature, beauty, and aesthetics

3   Discuss the genre of this work. Can it be a poem or not?
4   Think of Buddhist philosophy embedded in this text.

References

Chung, Chongwha. 1995. *Modern Korean Literature: An anthology, 1908–1965* (Korean culture series (London, England)). London: Kegan Paul International.

Lee, Peter H. 2003. *A history of Korean Literature*. Cambridge: Cambridge University Press. (Chapter 18).

8.2 강호사시가 – 맹사성 (*Song of Four Seasons by Rivers and Lakes – Maeng Sasŏng*)

Introduction to the text

Maeng Sasŏng (孟思誠; 1360–1438) was a writer, politician, and representative intellectual and Confucian scholar in King Sejong's time. This work is included in Ch'ŏnggu Yŏngŏn.

There was one song for every season, and each song began with '江湖' and ended with '亦君恩이샷다.' Themes such as comfortable and peaceful life in nature and gratitude for the King's grace were included.

This is counted as one of the great stanza poems of Korea, and is seen as a major influence for later nature poets, including Yi Hwang and Yi Yi. The work follows the poetic pattern typical of the time, which stirred up feelings of praise of and loyalty to the political stability of the Chosŏn dynasty. The repetition in each section of the poem is one of its uniquely notable features.

Original text

1 江湖(강호)에 봄이 드니 미친 興(흥)이 절로 난다.
2 濁醪溪邊(탁료계변)에 錦鱗魚(금린어)ㅣ 안주로라.
3 이 몸이 閒暇(한가)옴도 亦君恩(역군은)이샷다.
4 江湖(강호)에 녀름이 드니 草堂(초당)에 일이 업다.
5 有信(유신)한 江波(강파)는 보내느니 바람이다.
6 이 몸이 서늘음도 亦君恩(역군은)이샷다.
7 江湖(강호)에 가을이 드니 고기마다 살져 잇다.
8 小艇(소정)에 그물 시러 흘리 여 더뎌 두고,
9 이 몸이 消日(소일)음도 亦君恩(역군은)이샷다.
10 江湖(강호)에 겨월이 드니 눈 기픠 자히 남다.
11 삿갓 빗기 쓰고 누역으로 오슬 삼아
12 이 몸이 칩지 아니음도 亦君恩(역군은)이샷다.

Modern Korean text

강호(자연)에 봄이 찾아오니 깊은 흥이 절로 일어난다.
막걸리를 마시며 노는 시냇가에 싱싱한 물고기가 안주로다.
이 몸이 이렇듯 한가하게 노니는 것도 역시 임금님의 은덕이시도다.

강호에 여름이 찾아오니 초당에 있는 이 몸은 할 일이 없다.
신의가 있는 강물결은 보내는 것이 시원한 바람이로다.
이 몸이 이렇듯 시원하게 지내는 것도 역시 임금님의 은덕이시도다.
강호에 가을이 찾아오니 물고기마다 살이 올라 있다.
작은배에 그물을 싣고 가 물결 따라 흐르게 던져 놓고
이 몸이 이렇듯 소일하며 지내는 것도 임금님의 은덕이시도다.
강호에 겨울이 찾아오니 쌓인 눈의 깊이가 한 자가 넘는다.
삿갓 을 비스듬히 쓰고 도롱이 를 둘러 덧옷 을 삼으니
이 몸이 이렇듯 춥지 않게 지내는 것도 임금님의 은덕이시도다.

Key vocabulary

강호	nature
흥	pleasure
싱싱한	fresh
임금님	the king
신의	loyalty
강물결	waves in the river
소일하다	idle away one's time
은덕	benefit, favour
삿갓	traditional hat made of bamboo
비스듬히	askew
도롱이	rain cape, coat
덧옷	over-clothing

Comprehension questions: text

1 Which phrase is repeated throughout the text?
2 What is the theme of this poem?
3 What is the joy of summer to the author as described in this text?
4 Find expressions the author uses to describe his feelings towards the King.

Comprehension questions: film extract

Just as *Kanghosashiga* describes the simple pleasures of countryside living, so too does the 2018 film *Little Forest* (리틀 포레스트). It shows failed student Hyewŏn coming back to her home village in order to find peace and the answers to her life's purpose. While *Kanghosashiga* focuses on leisure activities, *Little Forest* shows the same kind of ideals being demonstrated in farm work, for example when Hyewŏn visits her friend Chaeha at his apple orchard after it has been damaged in a storm.

1 Why does Chaeha enjoy farming so much?
2 What's wrong with Hyewŏn?
3 Why does Chaeha give Hyewŏn a healthy apple?
4 How does the process of drying persimmons reflect the ideals of country life?

Additional source material

The turn of the seasons remains a popular theme in Korean popular culture, as can be seen in the multitude of season-themed K-pop songs, usually to do with how the season corresponds to a relationship, or how the season makes one think of a past relationship. A selection of season-themed songs:

Spring-themed songs

HIGH4, IU – Not Spring, Love, or Cherry Blossoms (봄, 사랑, 벚꽃 말고)
Busker Busker – Cherry Blossom Ending
BTS – Spring Day (봄날)
Eric Nam and Red Velvet's Wendy – Spring Love (봄인가봐)
GFRIEND's Yuju, Loco – Spring is gone by chance (우연히 봄)
aPink's Chŏng Ŭnji – The Spring (너란 봄)
Sŏ Inguk – Bomtanaba (봄타나봐)

Summer-themed songs

F(x) – Hot Summer
Infinite – That Summer (그해여름)
aPink – Remember (리맴버)
San E, Raina – A Midsummer Night's Sweetness (한여름밤의 꿀)

Autumn-themed songs

Crush – Fall (어떻게 지내)
IU – Autumn Morning (가을 아침)
AKMU – Time and Fallen Leaves (시간과 낙엽)
Davichi – Autumn Night (가을의 밤)
BTS – Autumn Leaves (고엽)
Kyuhun – *Fall, Once Again* album
Crucial Star featuring Kim Na Yŏng – Fall (가을엔)
ZIA featuring Hong Taekwang – Nostalgic Autumn (가을타나 봐)
K.Will – Hello Autumn (안녕 가을)

Winter-themed songs (excluding explicitly Christmas-themed songs)

EXO – Miracles in December (12월의 기억)
BTOB – The Winter's Tale (울면 안 돼)
Teen Top – Snow Kiss (눈 사탕)
Zion T. featuring Yi Munsae – Snow (눈)
Shinee's Jonghyun – Our Season (따뜻한 겨울)

In addition, the film *Spring, Summer, Fall, Winter . . . and Spring* (봄여름가을겨울 . . . 그리고봄, 2003) showcases the beauty of the four seasons in Korea.

Further discussion questions

1   Discuss the birth of *sasŏlsijo*.
2   Discuss the poet's attitude toward nature and life in *kanghosashiga*.

References

Margo, Joshua. 1993. *Elements of Taoism in Chosŏn Dynasty Korea*. MA Thesis, University of Souther California, Los Angeles.

O'Rourke, Kevin. 2014. *The Book of Korean Poetry: Chosŏn Dynasty*. Singapore: Stallion Press.

8.3 실록예찬 – 이양하 (*In Praise of Fresh Green* – Yi Yangha)

Yi Yangha (1904–1963) was an essayist and scholar of English literature. This work was published in the Korean newspaper *Chosŏn Ilbo* in 1937. It praises nature, focussing on the greenness of May. In a calm and speculative writing style, the author shows a meditative and positive attitude about life whilst observing humanity and nature, and in a romantic style the author uses parables and comparisons to give life to the details of the piece. Through the intimate way in which nature is described, an attitude of respect and appreciation is preserved.

Original text

봄, 여름, 가을, 겨울 두루 사시(四時)를 두고 자연이 우리에게 내리는 혜택에는 제한이 없다. 그러나 그 중에도 그 혜택을 풍성히 아낌없이 내리는 시절은 봄과 여름이요, 그 중에도 그 혜택을 가장 아름답게 나타내는 것은 봄, 봄 가운데도 만산(萬山)에 녹엽(綠葉)이 싹트는 이 때일 것이다. 눈을 들어 하늘을 우러러보고 먼 산을 바라보라. 어린애의 웃음같이 깨끗하고 명랑한 5월의 하늘, 나날이 푸르러 가는 이 산 저 산, 나날이 새로운 경이를 가져오는 이 언덕 저 언덕, 그리고 하늘을 달리고 녹음을 스쳐 오는 맑고 향기로운 바람— 우리가 비록 빈한하여 가진 것이 없다 할지라도, 우리는 이러한 때 모든 것을 가진 듯하고, 우리의 마음이 비록 가난하여 바라는 바, 기대하는 바가 없다 할지라도, 하늘을 달리어 녹음을 스쳐 오는 바람은 다음 순간에라도 곧 모든 것을 가져올 듯하지 아니한가?

오늘도 하늘은 더할 나위 없이 맑고, 우리 연전(延專) 일대를 덮은 신록은 어제보다도 한층 더 깨끗하고 신선하고 생기 있는 듯하다. 나는 오늘도 나의 문법 시간이 끝나자, 큰 무거운 짐이나 벗어 놓은 듯이 옷을 훨훨 떨며, 본관 서쪽 숲 사이에 있는 나의 자리를 찾아 올라간다. 나의 자리래야 솔밭 사이에 있는, 겨우 걸터앉을 만한 조그마한 소나무 그루터기에 지나지 못하지마는, 오고 가는 여러 동료가 나의 자리라고 명명(命名)하여 주고, 또 나 자신도 하룻동안에 가장 기쁜 시간을 이 자리에서 가질 수 있으므로, 시간의 여유가 있을 때마다 나는 한 특권이나 차지하는 듯이, 이 자리를 찾아 올라와 앉아 있기를 좋아한다.

물론, 나에게 멀리 군속(群俗)을 떠나 고고(孤高)한 가운데 처하기를 원하는 선골(仙骨)이 있다거나, 또는 나의 성미가 남달리 괴곽하여 사람을 싫어한다거나 하는 것은 아니다. 나는 역시 사람 사이에 처하기를 즐거워하고, 사람을 그리워하는 갑남을녀(甲男乙女)의 하나요, 또 사람이란 모든 결점이 있음에도 불구하고, 역시 가장 아름다운 존재의 하나라고 생각한다. 그리고 또, 사람으로서도 아름다운 사람이 되려면 반드시 사람 사이에 살고, 사람 사이에서 울고 웃고 부대껴야 한다고 생각한다.

그러나 이러한 때— 푸른 하늘과 찬란한 태양이 있고, 황홀(恍惚)한 신록이 모든 산, 모든 언덕을 덮는 이 때, 기쁨의 속삭임이 하늘과 땅, 나무와 나무, 풀잎과 풀잎 사이에 은밀히 수수(授受)되고, 그들의 기쁨의 노래가 금시라도 우렁차게 터져 나와, 산과 들을 흔들 듯한 이러한 때를 당하면, 나는 곁에 비록 친한 동무가 있고, 그의 재미있는 이야기가 있다 할지라도, 이러한 자연에 곁눈을 팔지 않을 수 없으며, 그의 기쁨의 노래에 귀를 기울이지 아니할 수 없게 된다.

그리고 또, 어떻게 생각하면, 우리 사람이란— 세속에 얽매여, 머리 위에 푸른 하늘이 있는 것을 알지 못하고, 주머니의 돈을 세고, 지위를 생각하고, 명예를 생각하는 데 여념이 없거나, 또는 오욕 칠정(汚辱七情)에 사로잡혀, 서로 미워하고 시기하고 질투하고 싸우는 데 마음에 영일(寧日)을 가지지 못하는 우리 사람이란, 어떻게 비소(卑小)하고 어떻게 저속한 것인지, 결국은 이 대자연의 거룩하고 아름답고 영광스러운 조화를 깨뜨리는 한 오점(汚點) 또는 한 잡음(雜音)밖에 되어 보이지 아니하여, 될 수 있으면 이러한 때를 타서, 잠깐 동안이나마 사람을 떠나, 사람의 일을 잊고, 풀과 나무와 하늘과 바람과 한가지로 숨쉬고 느끼고 노래하고 싶은 마음을 억제할 수가 없다.

그리고 또, 사실 이즈음의 신록에는, 우리의 마음에 참다운 기쁨과 위안을 주는 이상한 힘이 있는 듯하다. 신록을 대하고 있으면, 신록은 먼저 나의 눈을 씻고, 나의 머리를 씻고, 나의 가슴을 씨고, 다음에 나의 마음의 구석구석을 하나하나 씻어낸다. 그리고 나의 마음의 모든 티끌— 나의 모든 욕망(欲望)과 굴욕(屈辱)과 고통(苦痛)과 곤란(困難)이 하나하나 사라지는 다음 순간, 별과 바람과 하늘과 풀이 그의 기쁨과 노래를 가지고 나의 빈 머리에, 가슴에, 마음에 고이고이 들어앉는다. 말하자면, 나의 흉중(胸中)에도 신록이요, 나의 안전(眼前)에도 신록이다. 주객 일체(主客一體), 물심 일여(物心一如)라 할까, 현요(眩耀)하다 할까, 무념무상(無念無想), 무장무애(無障無礙)), 이러한 때 나는 모든 것을 잊고, 모든 것을 가진 듯이 행복스럽고, 또 이러한 때 나에게는 아무런 감각의 혼란(混亂)도 없고, 심정의 고갈(枯渴)도 없고, 다만 무한한 풍부의 유열(愉悅)과 평화가 있을 따름이다. 그리고 또, 이러한 때에 비로소 나는 모든 오욕(汚辱)과 모든 우울(憂鬱)에서 완전히 자유로울 수 있고, 나의 마음의 상극(相剋)과 갈등(葛藤)을 극복하고 고양(高揚)하여, 조화 있고 질서 있는 세계에까지 높인 듯한 느낌을 가질 수 있다.

그러기에, 초록(草綠)에 한하여 나에게는 청탁(淸濁)이 없다. 가장 연한 것에서 가장 짙은 것에 이르기까지 나는 모든 초록을 사랑한다. 그러나 초록에도 짧으나마 일생이 있다. 봄바람을 타고 새 움과 어린 잎이 돋아 나올 때를 신록의 유년이라 한다면, 삼복 염천(三伏炎天) 아래 울창한 잎으로 그늘을 짓는 때를 그의 장년 내지 노년이라 하겠다. 유년에는 유년의 아름다움이 있고, 장년에는 장년의 아름다움이 있어 취사(取捨)하고 선택할 여지가 없지마는, 신록에 있어서도 가장 아름다운 것은 역시 이즈음과 같은 그의 청춘 시대— 움 가운데 숨어 있던 잎의 하나하나가 모두 형태를 갖추어 완전한 잎이 되는 동시에, 처음 태양의 세례를 받아 청신하고 발랄한 담록(淡綠)을 띠는 시절이라 하겠다. 이 시대는 신록에 있어서 불행히 짧다. 어떤 나무에 있어서는 혹 2, 3주일을 셀 수 있으나, 어떤 나무에 있어서는 불과 3, 4일이 되지 못하여, 그의 가장 아름다운 시절은 지나가 버린다. 그러나 이 짧은 동안의 신록의 아름다움이야말로 참으로 비할 데가 없다. 초록이 비록 소박(素朴)하고 겸허(謙虛)한 빛이라 할지라도, 이러한 때의 초록은 그의 아름다움에 있어, 어떤 색채에도 뒤서지 아니할 것이다. 예컨대, 이러한 고귀한 순간의 단풍(丹楓) 또는 낙엽송(落葉松)을 보라. 그것이 드물다 하면, 이즈음의 도토리, 버들, 또는 임간(林間)에 있는 이름 없는 이 풀 저 풀을 보라 그의 청신한 자색(姿色), 그의 보드라운 감촉, 그리고 그의 그윽하고 아담(雅淡)한 향훈(香薰), 참으로 놀랄 만한 자연의 극치(極致)의 하나가 아니며, 또 우리가 충심으로 찬미하고 감사를 드릴 만한 자연의 아름다운 혜택의 하나가 아닌가?

Key vocabulary

사시	four seasons
녹음	shade of trees
더할나위	without any limit
일대	surroundings

신록	greenness
그루터기	a tree stump
군속	the people (of the world)
갑남을녀	any regular person
황홀하다	ecstasy
수수	acceptance, accepting
오요칠정	five passions, seven emotions
비소	small and insignificant
오점	a blemish
잡음	static
욕망	desire, greed
무념무상	freedom from thoughts/ideas
무장무애	without obstacle
초록	green
유년	childhood
장년	the prime of life
노년	old age
청춘	youth
삼복염천	the hottest point of summer
세례	baptism
소박	humble, homey feeling
겸허	modesty, humility

Comprehension questions: text

1   What are the things that the author is praising?
2   What are the things that the author says that *sillok* can bring us?
3   What expressions about colour does the author use in the text?
4   Why does the author visit his special 'spot?'

Comprehension questions: music extract

Contrary to the exultation Yi Yangha feels at the onset of spring, the song 'What the Spring??' (봄이좋냐??, 2016) by singer-songwriter duo 10cm instead grumbles about the arrival of yet another season in which couples can show off about their relationship.

1   What do couples do in winter and in summer?
2   How does the singer think the boyfriend feels about his girlfriend?
3   What is the common trait of flowers and relationships?
4   How does the singer respond to the different seasons?

Further discussion questions

1   Discuss the Korean view of nature as described in this text.
2   How might this view differ from a Western outlook on nature?
3   How does this text relate to premodern Korean poetry praising nature?
4   What implications does this text have for us today?

References

Hughes, Theodore. 2011. 'Korean Literature Across Colonial Modernity and Cold War.' *PMLA* 126(3): 672–7.

Lee, Yumi., & Son, Yeon-A. 2014. 'The Study of Koreans' View of Nature.' In *International Conference on Science Education 2012 Proceedings*, edited by Zhang B., Fulmer G., Liu X., Hu W., Peng S. & Wei B. Berlin; Heidelberg: Springer.

Park, Sunyoung. 2018. 'Anarchism and Culture in Colonial Korea: Minjung Revolution, Mutual Aid, and the Appeal of Nature.' *Cross-Currents: East Asian History and Culture Review* 7(2): 504–32.

8.4 무소유 – 법정 (*Non-possession – Pŏpchŏng*)

Introduction to the text

Pak Chaech'ŏl (법정(法頂, 박재철(朴在喆), 1932–2010) was a Buddhist priest and essayist. He is well-known for his concept of 'non-possession,' and he has spread his philosophies far and wide through works like the 'Ideology of non-possession,' and 'Exercises for living in a clear and natural way.' This work claims that true freedom and liberation is found when we free ourselves from greed and obsession.

Original text

"나는 가난한 탁발승이오. 내가 가진 거라고는 물레와 교도소에서 쓰던 밥그릇과 염소젖 한 깡통, 허름한 담요 여섯 장, 수건 그리고 대단치도 않은 평판, 이것 뿐이오." 마하트마 간디가 1931년 9월 런던에서 열린 제2차 원탁회의(圓卓會議)에 참석하기 위해 가던 도중 마르세유 세관원에게 소지품을 펼쳐 보이면서 한 말이다. K.크리팔라니가 엮은 <간디 어록(語錄)>을 읽다가 이 구절을 보고 나는 몹시 부끄러웠다. 내가 가진 것이 너무나 많다고 생각되었기 때문이다. 적어도 지금의 내 분수로는.

사실, 이 세상에 처음 태어날 때 나는 아무것도 갖고 오지 않았었다. 살 만큼 살다가 이 지상(地上)의 적(籍)에서 사라져 갈 때에도 빈손으로 갈 것이다. 그런데 살다보니 이것저것 내 몫이 생기게 된 것이다. 물론 일상에 소요되는 물건들이라고 할 수도 있다. 그러나 없어서는 안 될 정도로 꼭 요긴한 것들만일까? 살펴볼수록 없어도 좋을 만한 것들이 적지 않다.

우리들이 필요에 의해서 물건을 갖게 되지만, 때로는 그 물건 때문에 적잖이 마음이 쓰이게 된다. 그러니까 무엇인가를 갖는다는 것은 다른 한편 무엇인가에 얽매인다는 뜻이다. 필요에 따라 가졌던 것이 도리어 우리를 부자유하게 얽어맨다고 할 때 주객(主客)이 전도되어 우리는 가짐을 당하게 된다. 그러므로 많이 갖고 있다는 것은 흔히 자랑거리로 되어 있지만, 그만큼 많이 얽히어 있다는 측면도 동시에 지니고 있다.

나는 지난해 여름까지 이름 있는 난초(蘭草) 두 분(盆)을 정성스레, 정말 정성을 다해 길렀었다. 3년 전 거처를 지금의 다래헌(茶來軒)으로 옮겨 왔을 때 아는 스님이 우리 방으로 보내준 것이다. 혼자 사는 거처라 살아 있는 생물이라고는 나하고 그 애들 뿐이었다. 그 애들을 위해 관계 서적을 구해다 읽었고, 그 애들의 건강을 위해 하이포넥이라는 비료를 바다 건너 가는 친지들에게 부탁하여 구해 오기도 했었다. 여름철이면 서늘한 그늘을 찾아 자리를 옮겨주어야 했고, 겨울에는 나는 떨면서도 실내 온도를 높이지 않았다.

이런 정성을 일찍이 부모에게 바쳤더라면 아마 효자 소리를 듣고도 남았을 것이다. 이렇듯 애지중지 가꾼 보람으로 이른 봄이면 은은한 향기와 함께 연둣빛 꽃을 피워 나를 설레게 했고, 잎은 초승달처럼 항시 청청했었다. 우리 다래헌을 찾아온 사람마다 싱싱한 난을 보고 한결같이 좋아라 했다.

지난해 여름 장마가 개인 어느 날 봉선사로 운허 노사(耘虛老師)를 뵈러 간 일이 있었다. 한낮이 되자 장마에 갇혔던 햇볕이 눈부시게 쏟아져 내리고 앞 개울물 소리에 어울려 숲 속에서는 매미들이 있는 대로 목청을 돋구었다.

아차! 이때에야 문득 생각이 난 것이다. 난초를 뜰에 내놓은 채 온 것이다. 모처럼 보인 찬란한 햇볕이 돌연 원망스러워졌다. 뜨거운 햇볕에 늘어져 있을 난초잎이 눈에 아른거려 더 지체할 수가 없었다. 허둥지둥 그 길로 돌아왔다. 아니나다를까, 잎은 축 늘어져 있었다. 안타까워 안타까워하며 샘물을 길어다 축여주고 했더니 겨우 고개를 들었다. 하지만 어딘지 생생한 기운이 빠져버린 것 같았다.

나는 이 때 온몸으로, 그리고 마음속으로 절절히 느끼게 되었다. 집착(執着)이 괴로움인 것을. 그렇다, 나는 난초에게 너무 집착해버린 것이다. 이 집착에서 벗어나야겠다고 결심했다. 난을 가꾸면서는 산철[僧家의 遊行期]에도 나그네길을 떠나지 못한 채 꼼짝 못 하고 말았다. 밖에 볼일이 있어 잠시 방을 비울 때면 환기가 되도록 들창문을 조금 열어놓아야 했고, 분을 내놓은 채 나가다가 뒤미처 생각하고는 되돌아와 들여놓고 나간 적도 한두 번이 아니었다. 그것은 정말 지독한 집착이었다.

며칠 후, 난초처럼 말이 없는 친구가 놀러왔기에 선뜻 그의 품에 분을 안겨주었다. 비로소 나는 얽매임에서 벗어난 것이다. 날을 듯 홀가분한 해방감. 3년 가까이 함께 지낸 유정(有情)을 떠나 보냈는데도 서운하고 허전함보다 홀가분한 마음이 앞섰다. 이때부터 나는 하루 한 가지씩 버려야겠다고 스스로 다짐을 했다. 난초를 통해 무소유(無所有)의 의미 같은 걸 터득하게 됐다고나 할까.

인간의 역사는 어떻게 보면 소유사(所有史)처럼 느껴진다. 보다 많은 자기네 몫을 위해 끊임없이 싸우고 있는 것 같다. 소유욕(所有慾)에는 한정도 없고 휴일도 없다. 그저 하나라도 더 많이 갖고자 하는 일념으로 출렁거리고 있을 뿐이다. 물건만으로는 성에 차질 않아 사람까지 소유하려고 든다. 그 사람이 제 뜻대로 되지 않을 경우는 끔찍한 비극도 불사(不辭)하면서. 제 정신도 갖지 못한 처지에 남을 가지려 하는 것이다.

소유욕은 이해(利害)와 정비례한다. 그것은 개인뿐 아니라 국가간의 관계도 마찬가지다. 어제의 맹방(盟邦)들이 오늘에는 맞서게 되는가 하면, 서로 으르렁대던 나라끼리 친선사절을 교환하는 사례(事例)를 우리는 얼마든지 보고 있다. 그것은 오로지 소유에 바탕을 둔 이해 관계 때문이다. 만약 인간의 역사가 소유사에서 무소유사(無所有史)로 그 틀을 바꾼다면 어떻게 될까. 아마 싸우는 일은 거의 없을 것이다. 주지 못해 싸운다는 말은 듣지 못했으니까.

간디는 또 이런 말도 하고 있다.

'내게는 소유가 범죄처럼 생각된다…'

그가 무엇인가를 갖는다면 같은 물건을 갖고자 하는 사람들이 똑같이 가질 수 있을 때 한한다는 것. 그러나 그것은 거의 불가능한 일이므로 자기 소유에 대해서 범죄처럼 자책하지 않을 수 없다는 것이다. 우리들의 소유 관념이 때로는 우리들의 눈을 멀게 한다. 그래서 자기의 분수까지도 돌볼 새 없이 들뜨게 된다. 그러나 우리는 언젠가 한 번은 빈손으로 돌아갈 것이다. 내 이 육신마저 버리고 홀홀히 떠나갈 것이다. 하고 많은 물량(物量)일지라도 우리를 어떻게 하지 못할 것이다.

크게 버리는 사람만이 크게 얻을 수 있다는 말이 있다. 물건으로 인해 마음을 상하고 있는 사람들에게는 한 번쯤 생각해 볼 교훈이다. 아무것도 갖지 않을 때 비로소 온 세상을 차지하게 된다는 것은 무소유의 역리(逆理)이니까.

Key vocabulary

원탁회의	round-table conference
세관원	customs officer
소지품	belongings

168 *Nature, beauty, and aesthetics*

브끄럽다	to be embarrassed
분수	from one's perspective, position
지상	Earth
적	the time of
소요	cost
요긴하다	to be vital, essentially important
측면	side
난초	orchid
다래헌	the name of the place
생물	living things
하이포넥	a kind of fertiliser
실내온도	room temperature
효자	a filial son
연둣빛	hunter green
애지중지	to treasure or cherish
초승달	crescent moon
한결같이	unchangingly
장마	rainy season, monsoon
봉선사	Pongsŏn temple
운허노사	temple name
목청	one's voice
찬란하다	brilliant, radiant
지체	hesitate
아니나다를까	sure enough
샘물	fountain water, stream water
축여주고	to quench thirst
집착	obsession
산철	mountain stream
들창문	window to the outside
해방감	sense of liberation
유정	oil well
무소유	non-possession
불사	to not decline, act unreserved
정미례	a normal ratio
맹방	allied powers, a confederation
사례	example
무소유사	A History of Non-possession
관념	ideology
육신	physical body
물량	objects
교훈	teaching
역리	opposing principle

Comprehension questions: text

1   How did the author first come to realise the importance of 무소유?
2   What is the author's view on 'obsession'?

3 How does the author understand the relationship between human history and possession?
4 What was Mahatma Gandhi's view on possession?

Comprehension questions: drama extract

The classic KBS2 drama, *Boys Over Flowers* (꽃보다 남자, 2009), tells the story of poor girl Kŭm Chandi and her involvement with F4, four young, handsome, and rich students at Shinhwa High School, where Chandi enters as a scholarship student. Through her relationship with F4's leader Ku Chunp'yo, we see how the extremely rich are also tied down and limited by their possessions and responsibilities. In episode five, we see this hit home for Chunp'yo, while he is on a beach date with Chandi, when he realises there may be things he cannot achieve with money alone.

1 What does Chandi worry are Chunp'yo's intentions in bringing her to a deserted island?
2 How does Chunp'yo respond to Chandi saying he is like a genie?
3 What are the three things genies can't do?
4 Why does Chandi's phone call with her family make her sad?

Additional source material

Many dramas show the problems of being too rich. Two examples are the SBS drama, *The Heirs* (왕관을 쓰려는 자, 그 무게를 견뎌라 – 상속자들, 2013), and the MBC drama *Shopping King Louis* (쇼핑왕 루이, 2016), which also show to what extent being rich and having a lot of possessions can leave you tied up with more burdens than only having a little or nothing at all.

Further discussion questions

1 Share your opinion about the philosophy of non-possession.
2 Discuss possible differences in application of this principle between western and eastern cultures.

References

Gimello, Robert M., Koh, Seung-hak, McBride, Richard D., Buswell, Robert E., Kim, Hwansoo Ilmee, & Kim, Yong-t'ae. 2014. *The State, Religion, and Thinkers in Korean Buddhism* (Humanities Korea Buddhism series; no. 2). Seoul, Korea: Institute for Buddhist Culture, Dongguk University.
Kim, Sanghyon. 2007. *Korean Buddhism in East Asian Perspectives* (Korean studies series; no. 35). Seoul: Jimoondang.
Muller, A. Charles. 2012. *Collected Works of Korean Buddhism*. Seoul, Korea: Jogye Order of Korean Buddhism.
Sim, Jaeryong. 1999. *Korean Buddhism: Tradition and Transformation* (Korean studies series (Chimundang (Seoul, Korea)) no. 8). Seoul, Korea: Jimoondang Pub.

8.5 죽은 왕녀를 위한 파바느 – 박민규 (*Pavane for a Dead Princess – Pak Minkyu*)

Introduction to the text

Pak Minkyu (Park Min-Gyu, b. 1968) is an acclaimed novelist, whose writing is defined by its pervasive humour and critique of the commodification of human existence. In this novel, he critiques the fetishisation of beauty in popular culture, describing the love story between a good-looking boy and 'the ugliest woman of the century.' Having met at the department store where they both work, they gradually become closer as the boy gradually overcomes the defences the girl (neither character is ever named) has built up to cope with the harshness of appearance-focused Korean society. They end up separating, but Pak ends the novel with multiple alternate endings, letting readers think for themselves how the story will actually end.

Original text

누구보다 열심히 일했다, 자부하고 있었지만 이 세상은 학교와 다른 곳이었습니다. 억울하다는 기억보다는 일상에서 툭툭 던지던 그들의 신념이 떠오릅니다. 여직원은 사무실의 꽃이야! 확실히, 맞는 말이라고 저도 생각합니다. 열심히 일하는 아름다운 여직원들은 누구에게라도 기분 좋은 대상이 아닐 수 없을 것입니다. 사무실의 꽃은 아니라 해도, 반드시 필요한 사무실의 '인간'일 거라 생각했습니다. 하지만 현실은 그렇지 않았습니다. 시간이 흐를수록 저는 밀려나고, 또 밀려난다는 느낌을 지울 수 없었던 것입니다.

역시나 대인관계가 중요한 업종이라 생각했습니다. 활달한 표정을 짓고, 대화에 동참하고 . . . 무엇보다 성실히 책임을 다하는 모습을 보이려 노력도 많이 했습니다. 하지만 . . . 힘들었습니다. 무엇보다 상사나 남자직원들이 저와 대화를 원하지 않는다 – 라는 느낌을 강하게 받았기 때문입니다. 웃지 마, 웃으면 더 이상해. 면전에서 그런 말을 듣기도 했습니다. 그런 말을 듣고 나면 누구라도 웃을 수 없을 거라 저는 생각합니다. 도대체 어떻게 . . . 웃을 수 있겠어요? 밥을 같이 먹으러 가자거나, 힘들지 않냐는 말조차 들은 적이 없습니다. 외근을 하거나, 더러 저와 단둘이 업무를 진행해야 할 경우엔 이것 참 난감하다는 그들의 표정을 읽을 수 있었습니다. 저는 점점 묵묵히 일만 하는 직원이 되어야 했고, 곧 사라진 사실조차 눈에 띄지 않을 그런 직원이 되어야 했습니다.

매장을 돌면서는 더 힘든 일들이 많았습니다. 직접 고객을 상대해야 했으므로 누구나 저를 꺼리는 분위기였습니다. 노골적인 말투와 표정에서 매출에 지장이 있어! 라는 느낌을 받은 적도 많습니다. 가서 짐이나 가져와 – 그런 느낌으로 저는 점점 주차장과 창고를 들락거리는 직원이 되어갔습니다. 그렇습니다. 그것이 저라는 여자의 위치였습니다. 아름다움에는 . . . 대접을 받아야 할 충분한 가치가 있다고 저도 생각합니다. 인간이 누구나 같을 수 없다는 사실도 잘 알고 있습니다. 다만 억울한 점이 있다면 . . . 그런 것입니다. 왜 균등한 조건이 주어진 듯, 가르치고 노력을 요구했냐는 것입니다. 더불어 누군가에게 잣대를 들이댄다면 . . . 그것은 분명 노력으로 극복이 가능한 부분이어야 한다는 생각입니다. 저는 한 번도 스스로의 인생을 평가받지 못했습니다. 저는 오로지 스스로의 태생만을 평가받아온 인간입니다. 당신을 만나던 무렵 부터도 저는 줄곧 다른 직장을 알아보고 있었습니다. 여러 모로, 특히나 백화점은 제게 견디기 힘든 곳이었습니다. 그리고 그곳을 떠나왔습니다. 겨우 . . . 떠나올 수 있었던 것입니다.

달이 보입니다.

서울의 방에서는 보이지 않던 . . . 오랜만의 달입니다. 돌이켜보면 저는 늘 이곳, 이 책상에 앉아 저 달을 바라보던 소녀였습니다. 고단한 새 학기를 보내고 있는지 동생은 이미 잠이 든 지 오래입니다. 조금씩 저도 졸음이 몰려오고 있습니다. 조금씩, 매일 밤 쓰고 있는 이 편지가 그래서 문득 저 달을 닮았다는 생각이 듭니다. 말하자면 조금씩 졸음이 몰려온다는 어제의 문장에 이어, 문득 이 편지가 달을 닮았다는 오늘의 문장을 쓰는 것입니다. 잠을 자고 출근을 하고 . . . 그런 일상의 모습을 건너뛰어, 저는 다시 이 편지를 쓰고 있습니다. 즉 편지를 쓰는 한 면만을 끝끝내 당신에게 보여주고 있는 것입니다. 어쩔 수 없긴 해도 . . . 인간은, 특히 여자는 저 달과 비슷한 존재라 저는 믿고 있습니다. 언제나 보여주고 싶은 면과, 끝끝내 감추고 싶은 면이 있는 것입니다.

보이는 면과 감춰진 면 . . .

처음 화장을 했던 때가 떠오릅니다. 취업시즌이 시작되고 . . . 곧 사회로 나가야 할 아이들은 위해 학교에선 메이크업 강좌를 열어 주었습니다. '언니'에 가까운 선생님 한 분이 교실을 도는 게 고작인 강좌였지만, 또래의 아이들이 그렇듯 한껏 들떠 있는 분위기였습니다. 조금은 . . . 저도 그랬습니다. 그런 건 나와 어울리지 않아, 나와는 먼 세계야 . . . 라 믿었던 화장을, 수업이란 이름을 빌미로 시도해 볼 수 있었기 때문입니다. 두근거리는 마음으로, 또 떨리는 손으로 그려가던 아이라인이며 루즈의 감촉이 떠오릅니다. 서로의 화장을 고쳐주기도, 또 와아 하며 서로를 칭찬하던 아이들의 목소리도 여전히 귓가를 맴도는 느낌입니다. 그리고 거울 속의 . . . 역시나 이상해 보이던 제 얼굴을 잊을 수 없습니다. 어쩔 수 없구나, 거울 속의 얼굴을 보며 마음은 다시 고개를 숙였습니다.

하지만 무척 이상한 기분이었습니다. 뭐랄까, 그럼에도 불구하고 화장을 하는 여자의 마음 . . . 을 너무나 쉽게 이해할 수 있었기 때문입니다. 비록 아름답진 않다 해도 그것은 새로운 얼굴이었습니다. 화장을 시작한 여자에겐 두 개의 얼굴이 생긴다는 것을 . . . 그리고 여자에겐 두 개의 자아가 있다는 사실을 저는 느낄 수 있었습니다. 꺄~ 선생님이 직접 완성한 아이의 변화 앞에서 모두가 탄성을 질렀던 순간도 머릿속에 남아 있습니다. 그것은 누구를 위하거나 누구에게 보이려는 것이 아니라, 자신을 위한 일이었습니다. 난 오늘 씻지 않고 잘 거야. 서투른 화장을 지우지도 않은 채 매점과 복도를 몰려다니던 아이들과 . . . 그런 아이들을 부러워하던 후배들의 모습도 눈앞에 떠오릅니다. 그렇습니다. 실은 여자는 남자를 위해 화장을 하는 것이 아닙니다. 스스로를 위해 . . . 자기, 자신을 위해 화장을 하는 것입니다.

그리고 언제고 . . . 그 모습으로 세상을 살아가고 싶은 것입니다. 저 달처럼, 오로지 한 면만을 모두에게 보여주면서 말이죠. 그래, 이 정도면 나 . . . 추하다고는 생각지 않아. 아무리 형편없는 얼굴이라 해도 화장을 마치고 집을 나서는 여자의 마음은 그런 것입니다. 그리고 끝끝내 . . . 자신의 '어쩔 수 없는' 모든 부분을 달의 뒷면 같은 곳에 묻어두는 것입니다. 늦은 밤 화장을 지우는 여자의 마음은 . . . 그래서 달처럼 먼 곳에 머무르다 지상으로 돌아온 우주인과 같은 것입니다. 저 역시 그랬습니다. 그래도 조금은 나아진 게 아닐까, 부질없는 생각도 했지만 그것은 교실의 . . . 게다가 강좌라는 빌미가 있어 가능한 일이었습니다. 웃지마, 웃으면 더 이상해와 하나 다를 바 없는 . . . 하지마, 화장하면 더 이상해 – 의 시선을 저는 느낄 수 있었습니다. 스스로의 열등감이 아닐까 생각도 해봤습니다. 어쩔 수없이(유니폼이었으니까요) 백화점에서 짧은 원피스를 입었을 때도 마찬가지였습니다. 세상에서 가장 큰 비웃음을 사는 일이 무엇인지 아세요? 아름다워지겠다고 발버둥치는 못생긴 여자의 '노력'입니다. 다 쓰러져가는 철거민의 단칸방을 허물고 불태우듯 . . . 세상은 못생긴 여자의 발버둥을 결코 용서하지 않습니다.

Key vocabulary

자부하다	be confident, have confidence
신념	belief, principle, conviction
대인관계	interpersonal relations, face-to-face contact
업종	type of business
동참하다	participate, join in
성실히	faithfully, sincerely, earnestly
상사	one's superiors, boss
면전	in one's presence, to one's face
묵묵히	mute, in stony silence
꺼리다	avoid, shun, be reluctant or unwilling
노골적이다	blatant, in-your-face
지장이있다	hindering, impeding
들락거리다	be going in and out of somewhere
균등하다	to be equal or even
잣대	standard, measure, criterion
들이대다	resist, challenge, defy, protest
무렵	about the time when . . .
줄곧	all the time, constantly
고단하다	tired, exhausted, weary
고작	only, barely, no more than
들뜨다	excited, cheery, aflutter
빌미	excuse, reason, pretext
감촉	touch, feeling
자아	self, ego, identity
추하다	ugly, hideous
형편없다	terrible, dreadful, awful
열등감	complex, sense of inferiority
발버둥치다	squirm and struggle
철거민	residents being evicted or relocated from buildings due to be demolished
단칸방	single room, bedsit
허물다	tear down, demolish

Comprehension questions: text

1 Why does the girl object to being pushed aside for not being beautiful?
2 Why does she think people are like the moon?
3 Why does the girl think women put on makeup?
4 What does she find the most pitiful thing in the world?

Comprehension questions: drama/film extract

The 2006 film *200 Pounds Beauty* (미녀는 괴로워) tells the story of someone who has been shunned and ridiculed by society for being ugly, or in this case fat, who chooses to undergo full body plastic surgery in her pursuit of happiness. While mostly a light-hearted comedy which seems to argue that, in the end, things will go well for you once you become

Nature, beauty, and aesthetics 173

beautiful, there is one scene in which the conversation between protagonist Kang Hanna and her love interest Han Sangjun questions the double standards regarding plastic surgery.

1   What argument against plastic surgery, first made by Hanna, does Sangjun repeat here?
2   Who does Hanna blame for women's desire to do plastic surgery?
3   What does Hanna compare plastic surgery to? Does Sangjun agree?
4   Does Sangjun come to understand and accept plastic surgery?

Additional source material

Zion.T (자이언티)'s song, 'No Make Up' (노메이크업, 2015), sings of a man who perceives his lover as being most beautiful when she is not wearing makeup. This contrasts with the image 'that girl' gives of makeup being a kind of shield for women, highlighting the often stark differences in the discourse on makeup between men and women.

2ne1's song, 'Ugly' (2011), also perfectly encapsulates the emotions of the girl that we see in the letter.

Also, the music videos by girl group SixBomb, 'Getting Pretty Before' (예뻐지는 중입니다before), and 'Getting Pretty After' (예뻐지는 중입니다 after), chart the members' journey as they undergo plastic surgery in the hopes of becoming a more popular band. This became a huge issue in Korea at the time.

Further discussion questions

1   How do you feel about this male author's portrayal of a female voice?
2   One should be judged by one's ability alone vs. Appearance is a form of ability. Discuss.

References

Baricz, Carla. 2015. 'Book Reviews: Park Min-gyu's "Pavane for a Dead Princess."' *Words Without Borders*, 02/15. Available online at: www.wordswithoutborders.org/book-review/park-min-gyus-pavane-for-a-dead-princess. Accessed 15/01/19.
BBC Newsbeat. 2017. 'K-pop Band Six Bomb "Celebrate" Plastic Surgery with before and after videos.' *BBC Newsbeat*, 17/03/17. Available online at: www.bbc.co.uk/newsbeat/article/39302637/k-pop-band-six-bomb-celebrate-plastic-surgery-with-before-and-after-videos. Accessed 20/09/18.
Marx, Patricia. 2015. 'About Face: Why Is South Korea the World's Plastic-Surgery Capital?' *The New Yorker*, 23/03/15. Available online at: www.newyorker.com/magazine/2015/03/23/about-face. Accessed 20/09/18.

8.6 마네킹 – 최윤 (*Mannequin* – Ch'oe Yun)

Introduction to the text

Ch'oe Yun (born Ch'oe Hyŏnmu in 1953) is not only a writer, but also works as a professor of French literature. Having only started writing age 40, she has nevertheless become established as a key figure in modern Korean literature. While much of her work addresses political and historical themes, the novel, *Mannequin*, is less tied to a specific event, and more an almost dreamlike reflection on the nature of true beauty. The novel tells the story of the disappearance of teenage supermodel Jini from multiple different perspectives, including those of Jini herself, her family, her agent, and a man who saw her modelling once and is searching the country desperate to see her again. Within the novel, the sea takes on a particularly symbolic role, as can also be seen in the fact that most characters are known by their sea-themed nicknames. In its pursuit of true beauty, this novel also asks some difficult questions on the commodification of beauty.

Original text

오늘은 지니에 관한 소식이 조금이라도 들려올까? 그러나 솔직히 내 생각을 말하라면, 소식이 있는 것도 소식이 없는 것만큼 불안하기는 마찬가지라는 거야. 대체 무슨 소식이 있을 수 있을까. 어딘가에 무사하게 있다는 소식과 가장 극단적인 불행한 소식을 들을 수 있는 확률은 똑같애. 그래서, 매일 아침 이 시간쯤 식구들은 이런 종류의 해결책을 택하게 되는 거야. 지니에 대한 아무런 단서도 소식도 없어 모두 습관적으로 절망하지만, 그러나 아직 사체가 발견되지 않았다는 데, 아무런 단서도 소식도 없다는 사실에 절망의 양과 동일한 양의 희망을 갖는 거지. 늘 같은 시간대에 방영되는 홈 드라마처럼 이 집안의 드라마는 매일 조금씩 다른 분위기를 싣고 아침마다 재연되는 거야. 그래야 각자 자기 방으로 흩어질 수 있는 거지. 식구 한 명이 없어졌는데 그런 정도의 성의는 보여야지, 그렇지?

상어는 풀이 많이 죽었지. 그렇지만 오래 가지 않을 거야. 나는 우리 몸 속을 돌고 있는 싫증과 분노와 증오의 혈구들을 믿어. 그게 우리를 다시 살게 할 거야. 할 일을 잊은 건 소라도 마찬가지지. 지니가 없는 지금, 상어도 소라도 무슨 일을 해야 할지 몰라 안절부절못해. 그건 실직이나 마찬가지니까. 그래서 상어는 화가 나는 거야. 화가 나면 때리는 거야. 사람도 물건도 가리지 않고 상어는 때리지. 상어가 그렇게 한바탕 난리를 치고 나면 나까지 시원해지는 걸 느껴. 나, 나는 달라. 지니가 집을 나가자마자 나는 할 일을 찾았어.

지니에 관계된 일 아니면 상어는 흥미도 없고 할 줄도 몰라. 상어는 '나는 아무것도 배우고 싶지 않아,' 라고 말하곤 하지. '나는 지니 전문가야,' 라는 농담까지 곁들여서. 분 단위로 계산되는 지니의 출연료나 촬영료, 지니의 전신 촬영, 지니의 목덜미와, 광고 제안의 건수로 따지면 단연 일위를 차지하는 지니의 발과 팔꿈치, 손, 하다 못해 귓바퀴 … 지니 몸의 세부의 가격을 꿰뚫고 있는 사람은 상어밖에 없어. 벌써 수년을 이 일만 했으니까.

사실, 상어는 어류도감에서 보는 상어처럼 날카로운 이빨도 무장한 근육도 가지고 있지 않아. 창백하다 싶을 정도의 흰 얼굴에 가냘픈 몸매, 생긴 것이 꼭 계집처럼 여려 보이지. 그래도 키가 크고 속근육을 피나게 단련한 데다 잘생긴 편이야. 그게 우리 식구의 무기이자 미끼이고 재산이야. 격세유전이라나 봐. 할아버지 때 형제들이 모두 잘생겼었다고 하더군. 좋은 건 좋은 거야. 한 번은 나와 상어가 시장에서 물건을 훔친 일이 있지. 그저 연습 삼아 해본 거였어. 들킨 것을 알고 우리는 훔친 물건을 옆 가게에 슬쩍 던져놓았지. 그런데 상점 주인은, 순진무구한 표정을 지어 빤히 올려다보는 우리 형제를 보고 고개를 갸웃하고 가버리더군. 상어가 여덟 살 내가 여섯 살 때의 일이지. 우리는 어떻게 사람을 속이는지 잘 알고 있지. 그건 실은 죽 먹기야. 우리는 지금도 길거리를 걷다가 서로 눈을 찡긋하고 물건을 훔치지. 늘 그렇지는 않지만 때때로 스릴 있어서 좋아. 우리는 절대 잡히지 않아.

상어는 화가 나면 무서워. 상어는 마치 약 기운이 떨어진 환자처럼 포악스럽게 식구에게 대드는 거야. 식구라서가 아니야. 그는 인간이라는 영장류에 대해서 대드는 거래. 그래도 며칠 전 상어는 말했어.

'지니는 엄마 생일날에는 돌아올 거다. 생일상 잘 차려놔!'

몇 년 만인가 엄마는 엉뚱하게 생일상을 다 받아보게 된 거지. 상어는 자기가 들어오기 전에는 저녁식사를 시작하면 안 된다고 으름장을 놓고 나가더니 다 늦은 밤에야 돌아왔어. 모두들 배가 고파 기절할 것 같았지만 참았지. 지니가 오기는커녕 연락 하나 없었어. 열두 시가 되자 마침내 상어는 생일상 차려놓은 것을 발로 차 뒤집어엎었지. 오랜만에 받아본 생일상에 엄마가 손을 대보지도 못한 채 말이지. 사실 지니가 엄마 생일을 모르고 지나친다는 것은 상상이 안 돼. 나는 지니가 엄마 때문에 우는 걸 여러 번 보았지. 그애는 말을 할 수 없었기 때문에 마치 상처받은 동물이 신음하는 것처럼 울어. 지니가 울 때마다, 우는 것도 아름답구나, 하는 생각이 들어. 그래서 참아주지. 그런 거지 뭐, 인생이라는 게 별거야. 사은품으로 주는 패키지 선물 같은 거야. 거기에는 마음에 드는 물건도 있지만, 도저히 참아줄 수 없는 것들이 한둘은 꼭 끼여 있게 마련이지.

상어와 나는 말하지 않아도 통하는 게 있어. 우리는 가끔 시내에서 만나 호텔에 들어가. 그리고 세상의 껍질을 벗고 가만히 누워서 살을 대고 부비며 서로를 위로해줘. 우리는 불쌍하니까. 상어 말대로 진화를 그친 영장류니까. 우리는 비싼 음식을 룸서비스로 시켜먹고 그런 즐거움을 허락하게 해준 지니에게 건배해. 우리가 형제사이라는 걸 아는 사람들이 봤다면 지레짐작하고 분명 손가락질했겠지. 그렇지만 그런 유들이 상상하는 일 같은 거 우리는 흥미 없어. 우리가 원하는 것은 단순한 살의 위로야. 보드랍고 탄력성 있는 우리 자신의 살을 확인하면서 지루한 세상사를 잠시 잊는 거지. 상어가 부드러울 때는 이때뿐이야. 우리는 깊게, 오래 잠들어.

그렇게 만나서 우리는 사업을 해. 나는 잊지 않고 우리 둘 사이의 무언의 계약서를 수정하지. 상어는 그것을 작은 수첩에 적어놔. 그렇게 해서 나는 여러 번에 걸쳐, 지니의 손과 목덜미, 머리카락… 으로 나의 지분을 넓혔지. 지니 몸의 그 분위에 대한 수입은 내 것이 되는 거야. 이렇게 해서 모인 돈이 꽤 되지. 아무런 목적 없이 돈을 모으는 거, 그게 내 취미야. 아무에게도 쓰지 않고 나도 쓰지 않고. 상어는 내가 돈 수집광 중의 하나일 뿐이라는군. 사방에 널린.

물론 상어는 지니의 전신과 발과 얼굴, 팔목 등 광고주들이 가장 선호하는 몸 부위를 독점하고 있지. 어떻건 지니의 계약들을 주선하고, 계약금을 챙기고, 부수입을 늘리고, 촬영과 인터뷰에 대동하고 일을 상어가 맡아 하니까. 생활비와 소라 월급도 상어가 관리하니 당연하잖아. 우리는 투명하고 정확한 거래를 좋아해. 잠에서 깨어났을 때, 상어는 늘 어디론가 가버리고 없어. 그런 거지 뭐. 우리는 통하지만 딱히 할 말은 없어.

Key vocabulary

극단적	extreme, radical
해결책	solution
단서	clue, lead
사체	dead body, corpse
양	quantity, amount, volume
동일하다	same, equivalent
방영되다	be broadcast, aired, televised
싣다	load up, take in
성의	sincerity
풀이죽다	wilted, dejected
싫증	dislike, aversion, be tired of

176 *Nature, beauty, and aesthetics*

증오	hatred, loathing, abhorrence
혈구	blood cells
실직	unemployment
분단위로	(calculated) in minutes
목덜미	nape of the neck, back of the neck
단연	decidedly, by far and away
차지하다	to win, take possession of
팔꿈치	elbow
귓바퀴	ear flap, auricle
세부	details, particulars
꿰뚫다	pierce, penetrate, see through
어류도감	illustrated book about fish
무장하다	armed, powerful
창백하다	pale, ashen, pallid, wan
가냘프다	thin, slight, faint, feeble
속근육	core muscles
미끼	bait, decoy, lure
격세유전	atavistic
순진무구	innocent and naïve
갸웃하다	incline, tilt, put to one side
죽먹기	lit., eating porridge: easy as pie, a piece of cake
포악	atrocity, violence, tyranny, savagery
대들다	defy, oppose, put oneself against one's superior
영장류	primates
엉뚱하다	extraordinary, extravagant, fantastic
으름장	threat, menace, intimidation
신음	groan, moan
별거	separation
사은품	free gift, freebie
부비다	touch, rub together
진화	evolution
지레짐작	presume, jump to conclusions
유들	shameless, brazen
보드랍고	smooth, soft
무언	unspoken, tacit
수정하다	modify, amend, revise
수첩	pocket notebook
걸치다	spread over, extend
지분	stake, share in something
광고주	advertiser
독점하다	monopolise
주선하다	arrange, organise, set up
부수입	extra income, perks, side income
늘리다	increase, expand, add to
대동하다	accompany, take along with

Comprehension questions: text

1. How did Shark and Starfish get out of trouble when they were caught stealing?
2. What happened on Mom's birthday?
3. What do Shark and Starfish do when they meet up?
4. Which parts of Jini belong to Starfish, and which parts belong to Shark? Why?

Comprehension questions: drama/film extract

The 2015 film *The Beauty Inside* (뷰티 인사이드) tells the story of Kim Ujin, who changes into a different person, even of a different age, gender or nationality, every time he goes to sleep. The scene in which Ujin meets his lover Hong Isu, and finally asks her out on a date, really highlights the question of whether it is internal or external beauty which attracts one to the person one loves.

1. What attracts Ujin to Isu?
2. Why does Ujin struggle to decide to ask Isu out?
3. What does Ujin wait for before he finally asks Isu out? Why?
4. How does Ujin ask Isu out?

Material for further discussion

Contrary to the genuine, almost spiritual experience of beauty which permeates most of Ch'oe Yun's novel, Primary (프라이머리)'s song, 'Mannequin' (마네퀸) (featuring Beenzino and Suran (수란)) focuses on the superficial experience of beauty, especially how it is linked to monetary value, as seen in the text extract above.

Further discussion questions

1. Can beauty be assigned monetary value?
2. The focus on beauty of the Korean idol industry objectifies bodies and turns people into commodities for sale. Discuss.

References

Fedorenko, Olga. 2017. 'Korean-Wave Celebrities between Global Capital and Regional Nationalisms.' *Inter-Asia Cultural Studies* 18(4): 498–517.
Kang, Inkyu. 2015. 'The Political Economy of Idols: South Korea's Neoliberal Restructuring and Its Impact on the Entertainment Labour Force.' In *K-pop: The International Rise of the Korean Music Industry*, edited by JungBong Choi & Roald Maliangkay, pp. 51–65. Abingdon; New York: Routledge.
Kim, Yeran. 2011. 'Idol Republic: The Global Emergence of Girl Industries and the Commercialization of Girl Bodies.' *Journal of Gender Studies* 20(4): 333–45.
Leem, So Yeon. 2017. 'Gangnam-Style Plastic Surgery: The Science of Westernized Beauty in South Korea.' *Medical Anthropology* 36(7): 657–71.

Appendix
English translations

1.1 오륜가 – 주세붕 (*The Song of Five Relationships* – Chu Sebung)

Translation by Jieun Kiaer

> The Song of Five Relationships
>
> All people everywhere, hear these words and live by them.
> If not living by these words, one is not truly a person.
> Forget not these words, and learn them well.
>
> My father gave me life, and my mother raised me.
> If not for my parents, my body would not be here.
> Never will I be able to repay this debt.
>
> Who created the difference between master and servant?
> Even bees and ants have always known this truth.
> Lie not that one heart can follow the will of two.
>
> The wife goes to the place in the fields where her husband works, bringing him a tray of food.
> Though they eat together, she looks not into his eyes.
> As a friend to be appreciated, should the husband be venerated less than an honored guest?
>
> I drank the same milk as my elder brother
> Oh, younger brother, you are our mother's love.
> If brothers cannot be at peace with each other, they are just like dogs or pigs.
>
> The aged are like our parents, and our elders are like our older brothers.
> If they are truly the same, but we honor them not, how are we different from the beasts?
> As for myself, when I meet such people, I will bow to them in respect.

1.2 심청가 (*The Song of Shimch'ŏng* – Anonymous)

Translation by Pak Sŭngbae in Ch'oe Tonghyŏn. 2008. *Shimch'ŏngga padipyŏl chŏnjip 3: Chŏng Ŭngmin padi* [*A Complete Collection of Shimch'ŏngga According to Different Styles 3: Chŏng Ŭngmin Style*]. Chŏnju: Ministry of Culture, Sports and Tourism, North Chŏlla Province, pp. 91–7.

birthday party. Mom was dressed up to the nines in a pale-blue hanbok, having had her hair put up at a salon, and she was even wearing red lipstick. Your younger brother thinks your mom looks so different in this picture from the way she did right before she went missing that people would not identify her as the same person, even if her image is enlarged. He reports that when he posted this picture of her, people responded by saying, 'Your mother is pretty, and she doesn't seem like the kind of person who would get lost.' You all decide to see if anyone has another picture of Mom. Hyong-chol tells you to add some more words to the flyer. When you stare at him, he tells you to think of some words that would tug on the reader's heartstrings. Words that would tug on the reader's heartstrings? When you write, Please help us find our mother, he says it's too plain. When you write, Our mother is missing, he says that 'mother' is too formal, and tells you to write 'mom.' When you write, Our mom is missing, he decides it's too childish. When you write, Please contact us if you see this person, he barks, 'You're a writer and you can't write anything except for that?' You can't think what Hyong-chol could want as words that tug on the readers' heartstrings. Is there really such a thing as tugging on heartstrings? Your second-eldest brother says, 'You'd tug on people's heartstrings if you write that there will be a reward.' When you write, We will reward you generously, your sister-in-law questions this. You can't write like that. People take notice only if you write a specific amount, she says.

'So how much should I say?'

'One million won?'

'That's not enough.'

'Three million won?'

'I think that's too little, too.'

'Then five million won.'

Nobody complains about five million won. You write, We will give you a reward of million won, and add a period. Your second-eldest brother says you should change it to, Reward: five million won. Your younger brother tells you to put five million won in bigger letters. Everyone agrees to go home and look for more pictures of Mom and e-mail you one if they find something suitable. You're in charge of adding more to the flyer and printing copies, and your younger brother volunteers to distribute them to everyone. When you suggest, 'We can hire a student to give out flyers,' older brother says, 'We're the ones who need to do that. We'll give them out on our own if we have some free time during the week, and all together over the weekend.' You grumble, 'How will we ever find Mom at that rate?' 'We're trying everything we can, because we can't just sit tight,' says Hyong-chol. 'What do you mean, we're trying everything we can?' 'We put ads in the newspaper.'

'So doing everything we can is putting ads in newspapers?' 'Then what do you want to do? Should we all quit work tomorrow and just roam around from one neighborhood to another aimlessly? If there was a guarantee we could find Mom like that, I'd do it.' You stop this scuffle with older brother. This is because you realise that you're putting into action your normal habit of pushing him to take care of everything just because he is your older brother. Leaving Father at older brother's house, you all head home. If you don't leave then, you will continue to argue. You've been doing that continuously for the past week. You'd meet to discuss how solve the problem of Mom's disappearance, and one of you would unexpectedly dig up the different ways someone else had wronged her in the past. Things that had been built up as if they had been avoided moment by moment, got blown up and finally you all yelled and smoked and slammed the door in rage. When you first heard Mom had gone missing, you angrily asked why nobody from your large family went to pick her up at Seoul Station.

'And where were you?'

182   *Appendix*

Me? You clammed up. You didn't even find out that Mom had been lost until four days later. You all blamed each other for Mom's going missing, and you all got hurt.

1.4   흥보가 (*The Song of Hŭngbo* – Anonymous)

Translation by Anna Yates-Lu

[Narration]

Hŭngbo arrives in front of the men's wing of the house. Going through the main gate, how scared he is!

'My esteemed brother, this lowly individual has come to give his regards!'
'Yes, what family are you from?'
'Oh my dear brother, do you not recognize your younger brother Hŭngbo?'
'As the only son for five generations in a row, I am a person without younger siblings.'
When Hŭngbo hears Nolbo's words,

[Slow rhythm]

he places his hands together and kneels down.
'I beg you. I beg you. I beg in front of you, brother.
Please save me. Please save me. Please save your pitiful younger brother.
My wife and children went hungry all day the day before yesterday, without change until late at night.
Yesterday, my wife and children starved completely, without change even until this morning.
It is said that a human life lies in the heavens, so surely we won't die easily.
But having starved so many meals, they may have no choice but to die.
With your help, I would hope to save them.
If you can give unhulled rice, then please just give me one sack.
If you can give hulled rice, then please give me just five bowlfuls.
If you can give money, then please just give me five *nyang*.
If you truly do not wish to give any of those things, please give me at least either oats or crushed rice,
Then I can save my dying children.
Indeed, I feel bitter.
I'm so angry I can't live like this.
It feels bitter to die when my brother is rich beyond measure.
Please, in your mercy, save me.'

[Narration]

Since Hŭngbo so firmly brings up the talk of the past, there is no way Nolbo can push him away.
'Oh, looking at you now, you are that fellow Hŭngbo. I was bored, so you came at a good time. Hey there servant! Lock the main gate. Below the eaves on the eastern side of the lower gatehouse there is a roughly hewn laundry club made of birch from Jiri Mountain. Bring it over here. Such a villain should be beaten like a dog being caught in the hot days of spring.'

[Fast rhythm]

Behold Nolbo.
He raises the club from Jiri Mountain high above his eyes.
'You villain, Hŭngbo, you villain!
It is my luck to be rich,
It is your fate to be poor.
I don't care if you starve or eat.
I could give you some unhulled rice.
It is piled up in a great mound in the rice chest in the yard.
How could I pull down that pile for you?
I could give you some money or grain.
The storeroom is filled with bundles of money stored in golden chests.
How could I untie a bundle for you?
I could give you the dregs of my rice wine.
But I have a herd of pigs round the back of the house.
How could I give you those dregs and let my pigs go hungry?
I could give you some crushed rice.
But hundreds of yellow hens and white hens are flapping their wings and crying 'cock-a-doodle-doo.'
How could I give you the crushed rice and let my hens go hungry?'
Nolbo carries the club on his shoulder.
'You villain, you robbing villain!'
Like lighting striking a narrow valley, like beating a wife in a jealous rage, like beating a snake draped over the fence:
'Thud, thwack!' 'Splat!'
'Ouch! My head has burst open.'
'You villain!'
'Thud, thwack!'
'Ouch! You've broken my legs, brother!'
Hŭngbo is shocked, running here and there trying to avoid the club.
With the gate locked, he can't fly or run.
He just takes the beating, 'thunk, thunk.'
He is chased into the house.
'Oh, my sister-in-law, please save me.
Oh, my sister-in-law, save me please!'

[Narration]

Saying this, Hŭngbo goes in. It would have been nice if at least Nolbo's wife were generous and gave Hŭngbo some money or rice, but Nolbo's wife is even more ill-tempered than Nolbo. She stands braced firmly against the entrance to the main building, holding the handle of a rice paddle.
'Well, look here. Whether you're my brother-in-law or a lizard, you're so troublesome. Did you ever leave money or rice to us? Here is your rice! Here is your money! Here is your unhulled rice!'
She hits him on the cheek. Being beaten by his brother was as easy as turning over his palm. Being hit on the cheek by his sister-in-law, he feels as though the sky is turning in circles and the ground collapses with a thud.

[Slow rhythm]

> Astonished, Hŭngbo falls down on the spot.
> 'Look here, sister-in-law! Look here, look here, madam!
> Have you ever seen a sister-in-law hit her brother on the cheek anywhere on this earth, since the beginnings of time?
> Don't hit me like this.
> Kill me, beat me mercilessly, tear my body apart and send the separate pieces to the four corners of the country! Just beat me to death!
> Oh God! If you strike Pak Hŭngbo with lightning,
> I'll go to the world of the dead, and on the day I see my parents, I will tell them every detail of this injustice.
> How come you aren't killing me?'
> Huffing and puffing like someone who has eaten something spicy, Hŭngbo goes back home.

1.5 홍길동전 – 허균 (*The Tale of Hong Kiltong* – Hŏ Kyun)

Translation by Anna Yates-Lu

As Kiltong gradually grew up and turned eight, his intelligence was beyond average, to the extent that if he heard one he could understand a hundred. So although his father doted on him, as Kiltong was lowborn, if he called his father 'father' or his brother 'brother,' his father scolded him straightaway and told him not to address them like that. By the time Kiltong passed ten years of age, the fact that he couldn't address his father or brother by name, and was treated with contempt even by the servants, sank deep into his bones and left him sighing, unsure what to do with himself.

'Born as a true man into this world, if I cannot follow the virtuous path of Confucius and Mencius, then I would rather learn military tactics, tie a general's seal jauntily about my waist, conquer the East and subdue the West. In this way, I would perform a great service to my country and let my name shine brightly for all ages. Is this not the greatest joy for a man? How am I so desolate that although I have a father and brother, I cannot call my father, "father," or my brother, "brother." It's enough to make my heart burst, how painful a situation this is!'

Saying this, he went out into the garden and practiced his sword skills.

It so happened that at this time his father, having come out to admire the moonlight, saw Kiltong pacing back and forth and called him over.

'What possesses you to be still awake so late at night?'

Kiltong stood respectfully as he answered.

'This humble person is out enjoying the moonlight. But I wonder, ever since all beings came into creation I thought that it is only humans that live a valuable existence, but as this humble person has no value, how can I say that I am human?'

His father guessed the meaning of his words, but acted as though he was scolding Kiltong on purpose.

'What do you mean?' he asked. Kiltong prostrated himself and spoke,

'The reason this humble person will be sorrowful all his life, is that although I received my lord's spirit and was born as a sturdy man, and have enjoyed the benefits of being born and raised by my parents, I can never call you "father," I can never call my brother, "brother," so how can I call myself human?'

As he spoke, his tears flowed down and wet his jacket. His father felt great pity listening to Kiltong, but he worried that if he comforted him he might grow arrogant, so instead he scolded him harshly.

'You're hardly the only lowborn child in a high minister's family, how dare you be so arrogant? If you speak of this again I will never let you even stand in front of me again.'

Since he spoke so harshly, Kiltong did not dare say anymore, but just lay on the ground shedding tears. Only once his father left could Kiltong return to his bedchambers and sit down sorrowfully. As Kiltong was by nature extremely talented and generous, he could not control his heart, and every night he found it difficult to sleep.

One day Kiltong went to his mother's chambers and spoke to her in tears.

'Our destinies have been entwined from a previously life, and now we have become mother and son in this life, I feel your grace deeply. But as your humble son suffers a hapless fate and was born lowly, the sorrow I must bear runs deep. It is unjust for a man to live on this earth while enduring the contempt of others, so naturally your humble son cannot contain his sorrow. I intend to depart from your care, and so I prostrate myself before you and pray that you will not worry for your humble son and take good care of your health.'

His mother was shocked at his words.

'You're hardly the only lowborn child in a high minister's family, how can you be so narrow-minded, causing your mother such pain?'

Kiltong replied,

'Long ago, Chang Ch'ung's son Kilsan was also lowborn, but left his mother at 13 and went up Ungbong Mountain to practice the Way and became renowned for generations. Your humble son wishes to emulate him and escape from the world, so please be at ease and wait for the future. In the meantime, looking at Mother Koksan's (the concubine Ch'oran) manner, I believe she sees us both as her enemy for making her lose her master's love. I fear we may meet disaster soon, so mother, do not worry about your humble son's departure.'

At this, his mother felt great sadness.

Originally, Mother Koksan had been a *kisaeng* in the region of Koksan before she became the master's concubine. Her name was Ch'oran. She was very conceited, and if anything displeased her she would go to the master to complain, causing uncountable evils in the home. She herself had no son, but after Ch'unsŏm gave birth to Kiltong and was always doted on by the master, she felt great displeasure, only wanting to get rid of Kiltong.

One day, Ch'oran came up with a wicked plot and called over a shaman, saying,

'If I want to live a peaceful life I must get rid of Kiltong. If you make my wish come true, I will repay your favour most generously.'

Hearing this, the shaman joyfully replied,

'There is a first-class physiognomist who lives just outside Hŭngin Gate, when she looks at someone's face once she knows all their past and future fortune. If you call this person over and tell her of your wish, introduce her to the master and make her speak as if she is the one seeing his fortune, the master will be fooled and decide to get rid of Kiltong. If you seize this opportunity and do it like this, isn't that a subtle method?'

At this, Ch'oran was greatly pleased and gave the shaman 50 nyang in silver pieces, saying to bring the physiognomist, so the shaman took her leave and left.

The following day, while the master was in the inner chamber speaking to his wife about Kiltong's exceptional skills, and saying what a shame it was that he was of lowly status, suddenly a woman came in and greeted them from below. The master looked at her strangely as he asked,

'Who are you and why did you come here?'

The woman spoke.

'This humble person is one who reads faces, I happened to be passing by Your Excellency's house.'

When the master heard these words, he was curious about Kiltong's future and called him over to show to the woman. The physiognomist looked at him closely and spoke in a surprised tone.

'Looking at your son's face, I see he has the features of a hero from remote antiquity, a great hero. But as his status is lacking there is no reason for further concern.'

1.6 눈길 – 이청준 (*A Snowy Road* – Yi Ch'ŏngjun)

Translated by Jieun Kiaer and Alex Kimmon

'Tomorrow morning, we have to leave.'

As I moved away from the dining table, I finally managed to force the words I'd prepared out of my mouth. My mother and my wife's spoons paused at the same time and they looked at me vacantly.

'You have to leave tomorrow morning? You're leaving so quickly this time as well?' My mother eventually put her spoon down on the table and repeated my words with disbelief.

Now, I couldn't turn back. In that case, I had to make sure I solved the problem by explaining it clearly.

'Yes. We have to leave tomorrow. I am not lucky enough to be a student on holiday. I cannot rest like this whilst others are working. Moreover, there are one or two matters which I need to take care of urgently.'

'But can't you have a few days rest . . . Since of all times you chose to come in this hot weather, I thought you might stay a few days more this time . . .'

'Do you think I have the ability to come depending hot or cold weather?'

'Should you go back that long distance so quickly? You always used to come for one day and leave at the crack of dawn . . . this time you aren't alone . . . so I thought you could rest for another night?'

'Did I not rest today? One day's rest means three days that interrupt my work. The roads are much improved but it's still a long way here from Seoul, one day here, one day back . . .'

'If only you could have finished your urgent work before you came . . .'

This time, instead of my mother, my wife gave me a reproachful look. This, of course, was not to blame me for my distracted mind. She knew that there was no urgent business.

When we left Seoul, I had told my wife that I had already dealt with all my urgent work beforehand. This time, I had first suggested light-heartedly to her that we go and see my mother for a few days since it would double as a summer trip. She was rebuking me for my change of heart and my lack of patience. She resented the heartless decision. What was clearer was that her gaze seemed to have sympathy and be begging me though for no apparent reason.

'Then if you are so busy, you should go. Would I hear of detaining such a busy person who has to undertake these matters listen to me?'

She sat and kept quiet for a while, then finally she opened her mouth again.

'I know very well that you are such a busy person, but think of your mother. It is as if my heart is sad that I can't even once prepare a comfortable bed for you after such a long journey.'

When she had finished speaking, my mother started to stuff her long pipe with tobacco with an indifferent expression. She had simply given up.

On my mother's face, there was not the same expression of resentment as my wife as she was taking the tobacco from her tobacco box. She did not show the same feelings about her cold-hearted son wanting to hurriedly leave her side.

She didn't even strike a match and her gaze, as she sat stuffing her pipe with tobacco for however long, was expressionless.

Abruptly, I felt irritation the more she simply resigned herself to this. Finally, I stood up. Then as if being pushed away from my expressionless mother, I walked out the door.

One small jasmine tree in the garden outside the sliding door had been withstanding the blazing midday sun.

———

In the middle of a bean patch which was being baked in the heat in the back garden, there was a grave covered by an alder tree. I sat under the protection of this alder tree and looked down at the bean patch. The house looked similar in shape to a summer mushroom sprouting in the marshes.

Soon I got a nervous feeling, like an unexpected wave of nausea, about a document concerning an old debt. The cause of the problem was this blasted, cramped, damp, dark one-bedroom hut. This uncomfortable feeling, similar to an old debt resurfacing, was the same thing that had caused my decision to change the initial schedule and leave a day early. However, I did not have an old debt to pay. From the outset, I had an honourable relationship with my mother, so there was no debt to her. Also, my mother had also always trusted me with everything.

'I am almost 70. Now if there are any years left for me, how long can they be?'

I watched my mother have a very difficult time chewing food properly because her teeth had completely decayed, so at some point, I made a passing remark. From the start, when I kindly inquired whether I could get her a cheap dental fixture, my mother probably thought there was no possibility and firmly declined on the spot.

2.1 소나기 – 황순원 (*Rain Shower* – Hwang Sunwŏn)

Translation by Deborah Smith – unpublished, used with permission

Note on translation: The original Korean text alternates continuously between the present and past tense, which has been retained in this translation.

Then he said, 'There's a calf over there. Let's go and have a look.'

It was a dun-coloured calf, too young to have yet had its nose pierced with a ring.

The boy grasped the halter tightly, pretended to scratch its back and sprang up easily. The calf bucks and turns in circles.

The movement made the girl's white face, pink sweater, and navy skirt, all blur together with the flowers she was holding. Like the whole thing was one big bunch of flowers. He felt dizzy, but he was too proud to get down. This was the one thing he could do which the girl could not imitate.

'You, what are you up to?'

A farmer rose up through the long grass.

The boy jumped down from the calf's back. He expects to be scolded for riding a young calf, as if he didn't know that could injure its back.

The long-bearded farmer cast a glance in the direction of the girl and said, taking hold of the calf by the halter, 'You'd best be off home sharp. There's a rain shower coming.'

Indeed, a veil of dark clouds were gathering overhead. A loud rumble seemed to come suddenly from all directions. The wind rushed past, sussurating the grass. In an instant, their surroundings became washed in a purple light.

A sound was heard of raindrops pattering on the broad leaves which covered the hillside. Heavy raindrops. The rain ran down the backs of their necks, chilling them. On the instant, sheets of rain streaked down in front of their eyes, obscuring their vision.

The hut could be glimpsed through the rain-haze. There was nowhere else for them to take cover from the rain.

But the hut's support pillars listed, and the thatch had come apart in places. The boy had the girl stand in a dry spot.

The girl's lips had turned pale. Her shoulders wouldn't stop shaking.

He took off his cotton jacket and used it to cover her shoulders. She simply turned and looked at him with her rain-blurred eyes, standing there without protest. From the bunch of flowers she had been cradling, the boy picked out those which had gotten twisted and crushed, and strewed them under her feet.

The rain began to find its way even into the place the girl was standing. There was no way for them to keep out of the rain there.

Having peeked outside, as if struck by a sudden idea, the boy ran out in the direction of the millet field. He pushed apart one of the stacks of millet, then quickly fetched another to prop up against the first. Again, he parted the stalks, and gestured for the girl to come over.

The rain didn't trickle inside the millet sheaves. But such a dark and cramped place wouldn't do for the both of them. The boy was forced to sit outside, letting the rain beat down on him until the steam rose from his shoulders.

Soft as a whisper, the girl told him to come and sit inside. He said he was okay. She told him again to come inside. He had to inch his way in backwards. The bunch of flowers the girl was holding got mangled in the process. But she didn't mind. The smell of the boy's rain-soaked body was sharp in her nostrils. But she didn't avert her head. Rather, the heat from his body was helping her shivering to subside.

The clamour of the rain on the millet suddenly stopped. The sky was clearing. They ventured out from inside the millet sheaves. Not far off, rays of sunlight streaked down dazzlingly.

On coming to what had been a mere ditch, they found the water coursing crazily, so muddy it shone red in the sunlight. There was no way they could jump across.

The boy offered his back, and the girl obediently let herself be carried piggyback. The water came up to the boy's rolled-up breeches as he waded across. As for the girl, she cried out and clasped the boy's neck, pressing herself against his back.

Before they had reached the other side of the brook, the autumn sky had cleared to a deep, clear blue without a single cloud, as if it had never been otherwise.

After this, the girl was nowhere to be seen. Though practically every day he went in hope to the brook, he never met her there.

He even searched in the playground at school, during break time. He even went so far as to steal a secret glance into the fifth year girl's class. But she was never there.

That day, too, the boy went out to the brook, fiddling with the white pebble in his pocket. And wait – wasn't that the girl sitting on the near side bank?

His heart pounded.

2.2 춘향가 (*The Song of Ch'unhyang* – Anonymous)

Translation by Anna Yates-Lu

[Narration]

'Bring a prison officer immediately!'
'Prison officer awaiting your orders, sir!'
'Listen to me. That woman was so beautiful that I asked her to be my concubine. But this treasonous wench defies me. Have Ch'unhyang declare her crimes!'
The prison officer moves forward and writes down the charges against her.
'Ch'unhyang, attend to the charges made against you. As a lowly *kisaeng*'s daughter, you disobeyed the magistrate's stern order, you scorned and insulted his dignity. For this crime, you deserve to die a thousand deaths.'
The prison officer calls over the bellman and tosses the confession to him.
'Have her sign the statement of charge.'
Ch'unhyang's whole body trembles as she holds the writing brush. She does not shiver because she is scared to die. She does not shiver because she fears the magistrate. As she thinks about dying without seeing her husband in Seoul and leaving her 70-year-old mother behind, her hands and legs shudder and tremble. She writes the characters 'one' and 'heart.'

[Slow rhythm]

Ch'unhyang throws the writing brush on the ground and sits there without a word.

[Narration]

The bellman hands the confession over to the magistrate. The magistrate reads it.
'Let's see how firm your one heart is! Officer, put that wench in a penal chair and punish her in accordance with the law.'
Ch'unhyang's delicate body is lifted on the high penal chair and tied all around. Her eyes are covered with a broadly woven cotton cloth. Her trouser crotch is pulled up high and her legs are firmly tied to the legs of the penal chair.
'Punishment officer, carry out the order!'
'Yes, sir!'
'If I sense even a hair's breadth of sympathy for her from you, you will be beaten instead, so make sure to beat her hard.'
'Yes, sir. Under your strict order, how could I go easy on this treacherous wench? I'll take out her bones in a minute!'

[Slow rhythm]

Behold the punishment officer. He brings an armful of clubs and lets them spill out clattering under the penal chair. He chooses a club. He picks up this one and gives it a swing. He picks up that one and gives it a swing. He settles on one that fits nicely in his hand.
He uses his hat to hide his face, and since the magistrate is watching having given such a strict order, he whispers to Ch'unhyang.

190   *Appendix*

'Hey Ch'unhyang. Try to endure for one or two strokes. I'll use my skill to go easy on you. Don't move an inch, or your bones will shatter.'

'Hit her hard!'

'Yes, sir!'

Thwack!

The shattered pieces of the club whistle as they go flying through the air, and fall on the stones at the edge of the courtyard. Ch'unhyang on the penal chair refuses to admit her pain. With her head spinning, she speaks.

'Let me use the word 'one' to tell you. With this one firm heart I am determined to serve only one husband. Why this one club of punishment? Hurry up and kill me!'

'Hit her hard!'

'Yes, sir!'

Thwack!

'Two strokes!'

'Is my resolve not to serve two husbands any different from the resolution not to serve two kings? How can I serve two husbands when I know the story of King Shun (舜) being served until death by his two consorts, E Huang (蛾皇) and Nü Ying (女英)? You don't stand a chance!'

'Hit her hard!'

'Yes, sir!'

Thwack!

''Ware the third stroke!'

'Our hearts that are tied together for three lives, the three rules a woman must live by, don't think of them as a March flower that can be easily plucked. Hurry up and kill me!'

As the fourth stroke lands, thwack!

'Noble Magistrate, you must know the saying that things will be as they always have been. Even if you tear off my four limbs and hang them from the four gates, you don't stand a chance!'

As the fifth stroke lands, thwack!

'You came here on a coach pulled by five horses. Please abide by the five Confucian rules. Whether asleep or awake, there is no way I can forget my husband!'

As the sixth stroke lands, thwack!

'My firmness of purpose suffuses my six organs. Even if you tear my body apart you still don't stand a chance!'

As the seventh stroke lands, thwack!

'Even if you raise a seven foot sword high and hack me to pieces with each stroke, there is no chance, it won't happen!'

As the eighth stroke lands, thwack!

'This isn't right no matter which of the eight directions you look at it from. Stop abusing your authority. Hurry up and kill me!'

As the eighth stroke lands, thwack!

'You who share in the king's nine worries and have become the head of the district office, stop this immoral act. My heart is locked firm in my body's nine chambers, even if I escape death nine times, how can I forget the old magistrate's son? You don't stand a chance!'

When the tenth stroke lands.

'Let me sing you the song of the ten strokes. Even in a tiny village of no more than ten houses there will live a loyal subject and a patriot, how could our courtesan office here in Namwŏn not house fidelity? I'm not afraid to die, but I feel sorry for my mother who only depends on me, like ten blind men relying on a single cane. If I should die now, my spirit will fly high into the sky, I will go to the window where my master lies sleeping and wake him from his dream.'

2.3 사랑 손님과 어머니 – 주요섭 (*Mother and a Guest* – Chu Yosŏp)

Translation by Deborah Smith – unpublished, used with permission

'Okhee,' she said again.

'Yes?'

'You will always, always be with me. You will always, always live with mummy. Even if I become old and wrinkled, you will always live with me. Even after you graduate kindergarten, and elementary school, and middle school, and university, even if you become the greatest person in Korea, you will always live with me, won't you? Do you love me that much?'

'This much,' I said, and spread both of my arms wide.

'How much? That much! You will always love mummy only, and study hard and become a great person?'

Her voice shook as if she was going to cry again, so I said,

'Mother, this much. This much,' and spread my arms as wide as I could.

Mother didn't cry.

'Good, good. I love Okhee so much I don't need anything else in the world. I don't need anything else! Isn't that right, Okhee?'

'Yes!'

Mother pulled me in and held me tight. So tight that I felt I almost could not breathe, but she continued to hug me tighter.

That night, after dinner, mother called me and sat me down and combed my hair. She put a new ribbon on my hair, as well as new underwear(?), new jeogori(?), and a new skirt.

'Mother, are we going somewhere?'

'No,' she replied, smiling. From beside the pungeum, she fetched a new white handkerchief, and pressed them into my hands, saying,

'This handkerchief is sarang ajussi's. Go and return it to him, ok? Don't stay long, just return the handkerchief to him and come back, ok?'

On the way to sarang, I felt something crumple inside the handkerchief, but I didn't think to (?) look at it and just handed it to him.

Ajussi was lying down, but startled up to receive the handkerchief. For some reason, he did not receive me with a smile as he usually did, but he was anxious. He kept biting his lip without saying a word.

I felt odd so I didn't sit down with him, but just returned to the an bang. Mother sat at the pungeum, thinking deeply about something. I went to sit by her side. Eventually, mother quietly began to play the pungeum. I didn't recognise the song, but it was such a sad and gentle (serene?soothing?peaceful?) melody.

Mother played the pungeum late into the night. She played and played the sad and gentle melody . . .

192 *Appendix*

2.4 시조 – 황진이 (Various *shijo* – Hwang Chini)

A translated by Jieun Kiaer

A Oh blue waters of the green mountains, don't boast of flowing so fast.

For once you reach the wide sea, it's difficult for you to reach the green mountain again
With the mountain bathed in moonlight, this good night how about resting with me here for a while?

B and C translation from O'Rourke, Kevin. 2003. 'Demythologising Hwang Chini.' In *Creative Women of Korea: The Fifteenth Through the Twentieth Centuries*, edited by Young-Key Kim-Renaud, pp. 96–121. London; New York: Routledge, pp. 109–10.

B I'll cut a piece from the side

of this interminable winter night
and wind it in coils beneath these bedcovers, warm
and fragrant as the spring breeze,
coil by coil
to unwind it the night my lover returns.

C What have I done?

Did I not know I'd miss him so?
Had I bid him stay, would he have gone?
But I did it;
I sent him away and I can't tell you how I miss him.

2.5 향가 (*Hyangga* – Various authors)

Translation by Jieun Kiaer

A

Dear Princess Sŏnhwa
Secretly married
And at night she secretly embraces
Sŏdong – her husband – then goes.

B

In the bright night of the capital,
After playing late into the night,
I come home to find four legs (in my bed).
Two are mine, but what about the other two?
They were once my beloved's, but are no more.

2.6 구운몽 – 김만중 (*The Nine Cloud Dream* – Kim Manjung)

Translation from: Kim Manjung (trans. James S. Gale). 1922. *The Cloud Dream of the Nine, a Korean Novel: A Story of the Times of the Tangs of China about 840 A.D*. London: D. O'Connor.

THE EMPRESS REPLIED: 'This is a matter of exceeding great importance to yourself as well as to the State. I must talk with you about it. General Yang So-yoo is not only superior to others in looks and learning, but already by the tune he played on the jade flute he has proven himself your chosen affinity. You cannot possibly turn him away and choose another. So-yoo has already established a special attachment with the house of Justice Cheung, and cannot cast that off either. This is a most perplexing matter. I think that after So-yoo's return, if he is married to you, he will not object to taking Cheung's daughter as a secondary wife. I wanted first to inquire what you thought of this.'

THE PRINCESS SAID: 'I am not a person given to jealousy. Why should I dislike Cheng See? But the fact that Yang had already sent her wedding presents forbids his making her his secondary wife. An act like this would be contrary to all good form. Justice Cheung's is one of the oldest ministerial families, distinguished from time immemorial for ability and learning. Would it not be high-handed oppression to force her into the place of secondary wife? I would never never do.'

THE EMPRESS SAID: 'Then what do you propose that we should do?'

THE PRINCESS REPLIED: 'Ministers of State may have three wives of the first order. When General Yang returns with his high honours, if he attain to the highest he will be made a subject king, if to the lowest he will still be a duke, and it will be no presumption on his part to take two wives. How would it do to have him take Justice Cheung's daughter as his real wife as well as myself?'

'It would never do,' said the Empress. 'When two women are of the same rank and station there need indeed be no harm or wrong done, but you are the beloved daughter of his late Majesty and the sister of the present monarch. You are therefore of specially high rank and removed from all others. How could you possibly be the wife of the same man with a common woman of the city?'

THE PRINCESS SAID: 'I am truly high in rank and station; this I know, but the enlightened kings of the past and those who were sages honoured good men and great scholars regardless of their social position. They loved their virtue, so that even the Emperor of a Thousand Chariots made friends and intimates of such and took them in marriage; why should we talk of high rank or station? I have heard that Cheung's daughter, in beauty and attainments, is not behind any of the famous women of the past. If this be true I should find it no disgrace at all but an honour to make an equal of her. Still, what I have heard of her may not be true, and by rumour alone one cannot be sure of the real or the imaginary. I should like to see her for myself, and if her beauty and talents are superior to mine I shall condescend to serve her, but if they are not as we hear them reported, then we might make her a secondary wife, or even a serving-maid, just as your Majesty may think best.'

THE EMPRESS SIGHED, AND SAID: 'To be jealous of another's beauty is a natural feelings with women, but this daughter of mine loves the superiority of another as much as if it were her own, and reverences another's virtue as a thirsty soul seeks water; how can the mother of such a one as she fail to be happy? I, too, would like to see Cheung's daughter. I shall send a dispatch to that effect tomorrow.'

THE PRINCESS REPLIED: 'Even though you Majesty should send such a command I am sure Cheung's daughter would feign sickness and not come. If she should decline there would be no way of summoning her by force as she belongs to a minister's household.'

(. . .)

SWALLOW AND WHITE-CAP MADE ANSWER: 'We are unknown people from a distant province, and though the Master has kindly looked upon us, we feared that the two ladies would not be willing to accord us a place with them so we hesitated to come. But now having entered the gates and having heard the people say that the two Princesses were blessed with the happy hearts of Kwa-jo and Kyoo-mok, and that their kindly virtues moved high and low alike, we have come boldly into make our obedience. Just at the time of our entrance into the city we learned that the Master was engaged in the Feast Grounds; so we hurried out and joined in the happy gathering. Now that your kind words are spoken to us how delighted indeed we are.'

THE PRINCESS LAUGHED AND SAID TO THE MASTER: 'Today we have a garden of flowers in the palace. Without doubt your Excellency will boast of it. It all pertains to our merits, however, and is due to us two. You must not think it due to yourself.'

THE PRINCE REPLIED: 'I was altogether defeated; no one can hope to equal General Yang in the blessings of life and good-luck. But how do blessings like these (pointing to the secondary wives) appeal to your daughters, I wonder? Please, your Majesty, ask this of his Excellency, will you?'

THE MASTER BROKE IN: 'His Highness's statement that he was defeated by me is quite aside of the mark. It is like Yi Tai-baik turning pale when he saw the writing of Choi-ho. Whether this is a happiness to the Princesses or not, how can I answer? Please ask her Highnesses themselves.'

THE DOWAGER LAUGHED AND LOOKED TOWARD THE PRINCESSES, WHO REPLIED, SAYING: 'Husband and wife are one, whether it be for gladness or for sorrow. There can be no difference in their lives. If our husband wins glory, we win it too, but if failure falls to his lot, we too must share it. Whatever makes him glad makes us glad also.'

PRINCE WOL SAID: 'My sisters' words are all very sweet to listen to, yet they are not from the heart. Since ancient times there never was such an extravagant son-in-law as this General. It would indicate that the good old laws that once prevailed are losing ground. Please have his Excellency sent to the Chief Justice, and his contempt of court and disgrace of the laws of Ste looked into.'

3.1 오우가 – 윤선도 (*The Song of Five Friends* – **Yun Sŏndo**)

Translation by Jieun Kiaer

The Song of Five Friends

If you ask who my friends are, I will tell you of water and stone, pine and bamboo
And even more gladly of the moon as it rises over the hills
What need is there to add more, other than these five?

You say the bright white clouds are clean and good, but they turn black too often.
You say the sound of the wind is clear, but too often it stops.
Is there anything other than Water, I ask, which will stay clean without end?

Flowers bloom but die quickly for any reason
Plants turn will turn yellow as often as green
I think perhaps only Stone will remain, unchanging.

Flowers bloom with the heat; leaves fall with the cold
Oh Pine! How know you not the frost and the snow?
It is by your straight roots, extending deep into the earth.

Neither tree nor grass, who made you so straight,
How is it you are hollow?
You stay green through all seasons; oh, how I like you.

Something so small floats so high, lighting all things.
Is there any in the sky as bright as you?
Though you see all, you do not speak; you are my friend.

3.2 지란지교를 꿈꾸며 – 유안진 (*Dreaming of a Good and Noble Friendship* – **Yu Anjin**)

Translation by Jieun Kiaer and Alex Kimmon

It would be good if I had a friend to speak with, who I could go and find after dinner with no hesitation if I wanted to have a cup of tea. A friend who lived close to me and wouldn't care if I didn't change my clothes or if there were a lingering smell of kimchi.

A good friend who I could put on rubber shoes and go and find on a rainy afternoon or a snowy night; a friend to whom I could fearlessly reveal my empty heart, a friend with whom I could harmlessly exchange gossip without worrying that it will get out . . . if we only share our love amongst our husbands and wives, brothers and sisters, and our children, how can we be happy? The more fleeting something is, the more we need a true friend to help us out so we can dream of eternity.

It wouldn't matter if the friend were male or female. It also wouldn't matter if they were older than me, younger, or of the same age. All that matters is that their personality is calm like clear river water, intimate, meaningful, and refreshing, and that they are mature enough to cherish art and life.

There is certainly no need for them to be good-looking, they need only be someone who is genuine, with good taste, and who can behave in a dignified manner.

Even if they were sometimes a little capricious or grumpy, it would be alright if they expressed it in a cute way, and it would be nice if they would also come out with suitable responses to my whims and unnecessary agitations; and then after a while when I'd calmed down, they would liberally offer advice in a soft and mature manner.

It's not that I want to love a lot of people; I don't even want to be acquainted with many people. In my life I just want to have a sweet and unbreakable connection with one or two people that will last until we die. Whilst travelling various countries and places, the more I saved on food and accommodation, the more I could go and see. But now there are no traces left of the amazing feelings from all those sights. If only I had properly appreciated one or two things in one or two places, they would have stayed with me for a long time.

People talk of inseparable friendships. However I don't want to trouble my friends, nor do I have the talent to be infinitely patient. I don't wish to live my life perfecting myself, and I don't want my friends to be saint-like either.

I want to live as honestly as possible, I would only want to have enough wit and intelligence to tell some lies that would be revealed on the spot for the sake of my friends' comfort and amusement.

Every now and again, I will want to eat more delicious things than my friends, though I will want to look prettier than them, but I know that that thought can soon be erased.

Sometimes, I will prefer a just-thawed stream or the cries of wild geese in an autumn reed field to my friends, but eventually I will put friendship first.

We would have the same spirit as bamboo buried under white snow, but we could be soft like wild flowers, and whilst we hate appeasements like flattery, occasionally we would wish to have the generosity that comes from living out of pocket.

We wouldn't care about fame, power, or wealth, nor would we be envious or scornful, rather we would try to find more appeal where we are as ourselves [more interested in living just as we are.]

Though we can't always be wise, even so for the sake of avoiding our own struggles, we wouldn't sell out other people. Even if we were to run into misunderstandings, we would hope to be able to silence our foolishness and audacity. Even if our outer appearance isn't pretty, our essence is beautiful.

We would talk about others' success without jealousy and seek to do what we want without competitiveness, but by fully immersing ourselves [passionately pursuing our interests.]

We would cherish our friendship and affection and avoid risking our lives through reckless bravery. So our friendship is like our affection and our affection is also like our friendship, and we avoid jazzy colours and loud sounds.

When I polish my vanity I will think of them [my friend], I'll water the flowers and open the window on a foggy morning, while I'm aimlessly looking at the white clouds in the autumn sky, I'll feel lightheaded and will suddenly miss them, and when I do they will also find me.

Sometimes they will want to cry, I also have memories and tears that could fall. We wish to be young again, but when we're old we will share carefree laughter. It's not easy for us to love tears, and we love our natural charms more than the charm we've acquired. When we eat naengmyun, we know how to slurp like a farmer, when it's steak we're more graceful than a queen, we eat up roast chestnuts like children, and when we drink tea we're more elegant than a countess.

We won't do something we're reluctant to do just to earn a few pennies, and like the paulownia tree that always keeps its melody even when it grows to a thousand years, or the apricot blossom that never gives away its fragrance even as it lives through its cold life, we will encourage each other to try and live without losing our true selves.

We won't hate anybody, nor will we dislike many people just because we especially like one or two. Although we can't produce spectacular works, we won't regret having chosen to pursue writing, and we will feel sympathy for other people's shortcomings.

If I were to buy a bunch of flowers on the road to give to them, they wouldn't scold me for going overboard, and if I cross the road somewhere I'm not supposed to, they won't mock me for being uncultured. Furthermore, even if they sometimes have sleep in their eye or red pepper powder caught between their teeth, I won't question their being a lady or a gentleman, rather I will find a kind of human composure there.

Even though our hands are small and delicate, we will become each other's pillar of support, and even when our eyes are bloodshot they will not lose their sparkle; as our vision blurs and our sight fades away, we will become the light that shines upon the other.

And then suddenly the day will come when we will wear a shroud as a wedding dress, or as a blessing. It may be on the same day, or on different days.

As time passes, all kinds of pretty irises and orchids will sprout and blossom at the place where we are buried, and we will meet again through their strong, sweet fragrance.

3.3 달밤 – 이태준 (*Moonlit Night* – Yi T'aejun)

Translated by Jieun Kiaer and Derek Driggs

About five or six days after moving to Seongbuk village, I threw away the newspapers I had been reading and said, 'Wow, this place is really out in the countryside.' I could hear the sound of a stream outside, and I even met a man called 'Hwang Sugeon' for the very first time. Even though I only shared a few words with him, I realised that he was very much a countryside-type person. I know that there are less-than-average people in Seoul. There are less-than-average people anywhere you go. But in the countryside, they seem more noticeable.

Mr. Hwang seemed very stubborn, but innocent, and really did look exactly like someone from the countryside.

One day, at about ten o'clock, he came and visited me. 'Are you delivering newspapers?' I asked him.

'Yes,' Mr. Hwang answered. 'I thought your house was over there, and I tried to find you. Why did you buy such a small house? If I knew you were coming, I would have helped you find some bigger places in the area,' he said.

I thought this was quite strange, and I looked him over. He had a big, bald head and looked abnormal to my eyes. 'Okay. Anyway, you must have worked hard to find my house.'

'No worries, that's my job.' He looked around my house and said, without my asking, 'I am Hwang Sugeon.' He smiled at me. 'You don't have a dog?'

I replied, 'I don't have one yet.'

Mr. Hwang answered me, 'You don't need a dog now, and you shouldn't get any in the future.'

'Why?' I asked.

'If you want to have your newspaper delivered, don't keep a dog,' he responded.

'Why?' I asked again.

'There's a house in the village, where the banker lives. They have a dog as big as a horse, and it's difficult for me to deliver their newspapers.'

'Why?'

'The dog bites,' he responded. I laughed, and he seemed agitated.

'I wanted to punch that animal,' he said.

'Please go home and get some rest,' I said.

Mr. Hwang responded, 'Okay, sir. Have a good night. I live close by.'

The next morning, after about nine o'clock, he came back. 'Newspaper!' he shouted.

'Why were you late today?' I asked.

'It happens often,' he said. And he started to talk about himself. He was a teacher from Samsan school, but after falling out with the other teachers he had quit his job. Now he was delivering newspapers, but only as a part-time job. At home, he told me, his parents, his brother and sister-in-law, a nephew, and he and his wife were all living together. He started to list their names, and then he reminded me that his own surname was Hwang, which can mean yellow, and his first name was Sugeon, which means tower. He mentioned that the kids teased him, calling him 'yellow towel.' In fact, a lot of the people in Seongbuk village called him yellow towel, and everyone knew that was his name.

'Don't you need to go to other houses to deliver papers, too?' I asked, interrupting.

He reluctantly left.

My family asked me why I had talked with him for so long, without a reason. But I liked talking with him. He seemed to like talking about things that don't matter, and he seemed to enjoy talking in general. After talking with him for a long time, no matter how much was said, the only thing left was laughter, and it made me feel good. So if I'm not busy, I tend to enjoy talking with Mr. Hwang.

Sometimes, we ran out of things to talk about. It wasn't because we had nothing to say, but because there were too many things to cover. But Mr. Hwang was always quicker than me at finding things to discuss. In May or June, he asked me whether I like pheasant. He also asked me whether I put the shirt or trousers on first when I wore my suit. Then he asked me what would win in a fight between a cow and a horse.

One day, I asked him what his dream was. He said it was an easy question.

'At the moment, I am an assistant newspaper deliverer. But I would like to become the main newspaper deliverer someday,' he said.

3.4 우리들의 일그러진 영웅 – 이문열 (*Our Twisted Hero* – Yi Munyŏl)

Translation by Jieun Kiaer. From Yeon, Jaehoon, Jieun Kiaer and Lucien Brown. 2014. *The Routledge Intermediate Korean Reader*. New York; Abingdon: Routledge, pp. 174–5.

Almost 30 years have passed by now, and yet, when I think back to the lonely and difficult battle I fought that year, from the spring right through to autumn, I become as desolate as gloomy as I was back then. For some reason or other, over the course of our lives we seem to keep on getting caught up in exactly these kinds of struggles, and it could be that I was feeling this way because even now I found myself unable to break free from that earlier time.

It was in the middle of March that year, when the Liberal government was in its final throes, that I left the prestigious elementary school in Seoul which I always attended with such pride, and transferred to an undistinguished school in a small town. The whole family had ended up having to move after my father, a civil servant, had fallen foul of office politics. I was twelve at the time, and had just progressed to the fifth grade at school.

Taken there by my mother on the first day, there were so many ways in which Y elementary school left me indescribably disappointed. I was used to looking at regimented rows of classrooms, which flanked the imposing red-brick three-storey main building. This old, Japanese-style cement building, with its handful of plank-board classrooms – makeshift constructions daubed with black pitch – was mean and shabby in my eyes. I was sunk into an immoderate sense of sorrow, like a young prince's grief at being abruptly struck from the succession. The mere fact of my having come from a school with 16 classes to a grade made me look with disdain on this school, which couldn't manage more than six classes. Also, being used to studying in mixed-sex classes made having boys and girls strictly segregated seem incredibly countrified.

But it was the staff room that really cemented these first impressions. The staff room of the school which I had previously attended had been as spacious as befitted a school in Seoul, and even the teachers were invariably well turned out and lively. Here, the staff room was barely the size of a classroom, and the teachers who sat there were common country bumpkins, listlessly puffing out smoke like chimneys.

The form teacher approached us on recognising my mother, who had accompanied me into the staff room. He too was far from my expectation. If we couldn't manage a beautiful and kind-hearted female teacher, I had thought at least to have one who was soft-spoken, thoughtful, and a bit of a sharp dresser; from the white drops of dried *makkeoli* splattered on the sleeve of his suit jacket, it was clear this one didn't fit the bill. He hadn't combed his dishevelled hair, never mind put any oil on it. I had genuine doubts as to whether he had washed his face that morning, or if he was listening to what my mother was saying. Frankly, it was beyond disappointing that that man was to be my form teacher. Even then, I might already have been touched by an intuition about the evil fate that lasted for a year after that.

That evil destiny showed itself when I was introduced to the class a little later.

'This is the new transfer student, Han Byeong-t'ae. Be sure you go on well in the future.'

After the form teacher's one-line introduction was over, he had me take an empty seat at the back and begin with the lessons straight away. When I recalled the kindness of the Seoul teachers, who had used to make lengthy introductions mixed with pride about new transfer students, to the extent of it being a somewhat embarrassing, there was no way that I could suppress my unkind feelings. If it hadn't been a great build-up, he could at least have informed the class about the things I had to be proud of. I had hoped this would be a help in my newly beginning relations with them.

There are a couple of things worth mentioning about that time. Firstly, in terms of schoolwork, I couldn't achieve the very first place all that often, but all the same, even at a first-rate Seoul school, I was in the top five in the class. I was quietly proud of this, as it had no small share in my relations, not only with the teachers but also with the other pupils. Also, I had uncommon skill in painting. Not to the extent of being able to sweep a national children's art contest, but sufficient to be awarded the special prize in several contests at the Seoul level. I suppose my mother emphasised my grades and art ability several times, but the form teacher paid these absolutely no heed at all. My father's job, too, might have been a help in some instances. Even having suffered a setback, even one bad enough even to drive him from Seoul to here, my father was still one of this small town's few top civil servants.

Disappointingly, the other pupils were the same as the teacher. In Seoul, when a new pupil arrived, the others would quickly flock around him during break time, and ask all kinds of questions. Are you good at schoolwork, are you strong, does your family live well, and so forth; you might say it amounted to gathering data which will form the foundation for relations later on. However, my new classmates were the same as my new teacher in having no particular interest in that kind of thing. During break time they stood a little way off, doing nothing but cast sidelong glances, and when it came to lunch time and a couple of them did gather round, their questions were nothing more than things such as: have you ever ridden on a tram, have you ever seen South Gate. My school things, which were top quality and of which only I possessed the like, were the only things they envied and marvelled over.

3.5 안민가 – 충담사 (*Song of Peace to the People* – **Ch'ungdamsa**)

Translation by Jieun Kiaer

> The king is a father, and the vassal a loving mother,
> People are like foolish children, if you love, they will know that they are loved.
> You should govern the suffering masses and feed them.
> The country will be maintained as long as the people remain.
> Ah, if only the king is as a king, vassal as vassal, and the masses as masses,
> The kingdom will be in peace.

3.6 하여가 – 이방원, 단심가 – 정몽주 (*Anyway Song* – Yi Pangwŏn; and *Steadfast Song* – Chŏng Mongju)

Translations by Jieun Kiaer

Hayŏga

How does it matter whether you live this way or that?
How is it that howsoever we live, it's as if we've become entangled in the arrowfoot vine of Mansu Mountain?
We have our whole lives to pass in such entanglement.

Tanshimga

This body though it dies, dies, and even for a 100 more times dies again
Whether it is when the skeleton turns to earth and dust that there is a soul or not
Is this something that loyal tribute to the King can ever change?

4.1 배비장전 (*The Tale of Aide Pae* – Anonymous)

Translation by Anna Yates-Lu

As he glanced by chance into the forest, he could faintly see a beautiful woman, displaying all kinds of coquetry as she taunted the spring scene. Then she took off her upper and lower garments, letting them flutter to the ground before jumping into the water with a splash. Next, playing around as she beat the water like a drum, she washed her hands, she washed her feet, she washed her belly, chest, and breasts, washed here and there, and washed her crotch, for a long time, she was bathing like this. When Secretary/Aide Pae saw this, his senses clouded and he could not stop his shoulders dancing with joy. His transformation into a lecher was complete, as he kept glancing over, his breath coming in gasps as if he was a thief being chased for stealing firewood, desperate to know the deepest depths of this woman.

'Oh! I don't know who this woman is, but she could melt the hearts of hundreds.'

But (due to his bet) he couldn't ask anyone about her identity, all he could do was swallow back his spit and bemoan his predicament.

Finally, the day grew dark, and the magistrate gave the order to hurry back to the government office. All the aides and *kisaeng*, as well as the servants, all set off together. Aide Pae had something else in mind, and pretended he had a stomach ache.

'He's already fallen under her charm.'

The other aides had caught onto his ruse and whispered amongst themselves while only giving greetings to his face.

'Rites Minister, at least get an acupuncturist to give you a shot.'

'Oh no, it's no trouble. It's not a real illness, so if I relax for a bit it will get better,' Aide Pae replied.

The other aides held back their laughter and called over Pangja, telling him:

'Since your master says his illness isn't too serious, make sure to escort him back once he has relaxed for a bit.'

Then they spoke to Aide Pae:

'We'll tell the magistrate about everything so don't worry and come back after resting well.'

'Thank you, my colleagues, for worrying about me so. I ask you to help me explain this to the magistrate. Oh, my stomach!'

All of a sudden one of his colleagues stepped forward. This fellow was mischievous without parallel. Intending to tease Aide Pae, he spoke thus:

'Don't worry about it. The magistrate seems to have guessed that you have been struck by this unexpected illness. He said that if you have a stomachache, getting a girl to rub your stomach with her hands is very effective. We'll leave a *kisaeng* with you when we go, so make sure to ask her to rub you well.'

'Oh no, my stomach is different to others,' if I even see a *kisaeng* it hurts even more, so please do not speak of this again.'

'Gee, your stomach sure is weird. You say that even hearing a girl speak causes you more pain; seeing you suffer so, as a fellow Seoulite meeting here a thousand miles outside the city, surely our affection is that of true brothers, how could I leave you here alone? It would be better for us all to head back together once you have had some rest.'

'It seems you don't know me very well. When I am ill, I must rest alone in order to recover. Even were I to stay with my brothers, not only would I not recover, in fact I would even get worse. So if you wish to save me, please go first, I beg you. Oh my stomach, I'm dying!'

'If that is truly your wish, then we have no choice but to leave you alone. After we have left, please don't think of us as heartless.'

Once his colleagues had left to escort the magistrate back to the office, Aide Pae could no longer control his desire to see the woman again.

'Hey Pangja! Oh my stomach!'

'Yes sir?'

'Since I came here it has grown faint before my eyes, I can barely see a foot in front of me. Oh my stomach, oh my stomach.'

'Seeing your lordship suffer so, your humble servant also doesn't know what to do.'

'Keep a close watch on where the magistrate is going.'

'He's heading down there.'

'Oh my stomach! Look again.'

'He's going off into the distance.'

'My stomach has stopped hurting.'

Wanting to see the bathing woman, Aide Pae went down a narrow path, between flowering plants and into the ravine. Keeping his body lowered, he tread lightly as he moved forward slowly. Then he called to Pangja in a faint voice. Pangja replied. But gradually his tone of respect disappeared.

4.2 오적 – 김지하 (*Five Bandits* – Kim Chiha)

Translation from: Kim Chiha (translated by Brother Anthony of Taizé). 2015. 'Five Bandits.' *Mānoa* 27(2): 94–104.

The third comes forward. TopCivilSerpent comes forward.

His body shaped like a rubber balloon, eyes like those of a venomous snake, corpse-like, blue, rigid flesh

With tightly clenched lips, he's obviously a clean-handed official.

Bring him any kind of sweetener, he solemnly shakes his head:

We do not like sweeteners, of course, just so, indeed.

But only look behind his back. He's wearing another face there.

He stares nimbly around on this side, stares glibly around on that,

plumply, plumply, brazenly, brazenly, so blatantly, but his teeth are quite a sight.

He's devoured so many sweeteners, they've rotted black, rotted till they've crumbled, he's obviously quite completely corrupt.

A mountain-like desk, a chair deep as the sea, straddling high and low, this fellow whose merits are big as the horn of a rat, sitting as high as the sky. With one hand, 'No, thank you.' With the other, 'Yes, yes, thank you.'

What's possible is absolutely out of the question, what's impossible is no problem at all, with piles of documents on top of his desk, piles of banknotes under his desk.

To high-ups, he's a fawning spaniel, to low-downs, he's a brutal hound; he takes his cut of public money, solicits bribes.

When did I ever do such a thing? Clouds in Heaven, be my witness!

Hostesses in swanky bars, high and low, they have no problems, do they?

The fourth thief comes forward. General-in-Chimp's his name.

In height, he's an eight-foot wall,

The line of low-ranking soldiers under his command is as long as the Great Wall,

with hairs sticking out all over his body, white rings around the irises of his eyes, a tiger's jaws, twitching nose, a short bristly beard, quite obviously an animal.

Gold, silver, nickel, bronze, brass, brightly coloured silk, and satin ribbons, his entire body is covered and wrapped in a ton of decorations.

With his black dog-legs kicking this way and that

he comes crawling out on all fours. Just look at General-in-Chimp's skills.

He fills the sacks of rice destined for his troops with sand, after taking the rice and reselling it,

serves up a hair or two from the pork and beef destined for his troops, devours all the meat alone.

When his troops are freezing to death with no barracks in midwinter

he tells them they'll warm up by working, forces them to labour all day long,

takes the wood destined for the barracks and builds himself a bigger house.

Official cars, clothing, coal, even money for snacks and wages, presents for the troops, he takes them all.

If a starving soldier gone AWOL gets caught, for discipline's sake he beats him up, locks him in.

AttentionAttentionAttentionAtEase! Attention!

He takes hefty handsome guys and serves them up to his wife as playthings,

while he has his own mistress, with whom he plays erotic war tactics in bed, engages in close warfare, uses strategies both offensive and defensive; he's huge one moment, thin air the next.

The last one comes forward. HighMinisCur comes forward.

His tongue coated white, dregs of wine sticking to him all over, he emerges

glaring eyes veiled by disgusting mucus, his left hand conducts the national

defence with a golf club.

His right hand fumblingly scrawls *production, export, construction* on a girl's breast:

Ha ha, hey, that tickles, Sir!

You ignorant bitch! How dare you say that affairs of state tickle?

Export even though people starve. Produce though nothing sells. Use the bones of those who've died of hunger to build a bridge to Japan; let's go over and greet their gods!

As he blows a broken trumpet to the beat of a fissure drum, he's thinking of the profits he can grab.

He has the use of a black sedan and in secret owns a Mercedes, but look, to show his integrity he only ever rides in a simple Corona.

From the budget he gobbles a packet, the lot; when tenders come in, he devours a great chunk, all the time chewing gum to hide any odours.

Smoking Kents, he scrawls, *Crack down hard on imported goods*, scribble-scribble on official documents, then, aha, admires his wonderful writing.

To sleek-tongued, half-deaf reporters who come running after him on hearing scandalous rumours, he replies,

How dare you talk of crime and corruption to your nation's prime minister!

Then he murmurs lines from an ancient poem praising the joys of life in the countryside before asking, What's your handicap?

Ghosts observing the peerless skills of these Five Bandits,

quite taken aback, exclaim in horror: If we're caught by them, we'll have not one bone left to call our own.

They take to their heels, scared out of their wits, which explains why nowadays so few people bother to make offerings to the dead.

4.3 닭을 빌려타고 돌아가다 – 서거정 (*Riding Home on a Borrowed Chicken – Sŏ Kŏjŏng*)

Translation by Jieun Kiaer

Master Kim had always been known as a wit.

One day he was riding his horse to the house of an acquaintance for a visit. (And, if you do not know, such an occasion calls for a respectable Korean gentleman, as host, to provide his guest with some degree of food and drink.)

Kim's acquaintance, the master of the house, had indeed arranged the sulsang, the little floor table over which upstanding Korean hosts would entertain their guests with drink and food.... But upon this table, naught but some leaves of cabbage and similar meagre greenery lay heaped.

Said the host to Kim, 'Ah, yes, you've kindly arrived. Of course, the market is quite a

And, lost for aught to say, the host went out and caught a chicken for them to share with their drinks.

4.4 허생전 – 박지원 (*The Tale of Mr. Hŏ* – Pak Chiwŏn)

Translation by Jieun Kiaer and Ben Cagan

Heosaeng lived in Mukjeok Village. If you go straight to the foot of Nam Mountain there stands, above a well, an old Gingko tree; heading for the gingko tree and opening the twig gate, his two-room thatched house wouldn't even block out the elements. But our Heosaeng liked only to read, and his wife made ends meet selling the needlework of others.

One day, this wife of his was hungry, and said in a voice mingled with tears, 'What are you doing, reading even though you have not in your whole life sat the High Civil Service Examinations?!'

Heosaeng smiled and replied, 'Well, it's just that I still haven't mastered my reading . . .'

'So, couldn't you at least work as a craftsman?'

'How could I work as a craftsman having never learned a craft?'

'So, couldn't you go into business?'

'How could I go into business without any money to invest?'

His wife flew into a rage and shouted, 'Are you telling me that even though you read day and night, all you have learned is to say, "How could I?" You can't work as a craftsman, you can't work in business, could you be a thief?!'

Heosaeng put down the book he was reading to and stood up, saying, 'What a waste. When I started, I swore to read for ten years, and it's only been seven . . .,' and suddenly headed out the door.

To Heosaeng, there was no one in town worth knowing. He went straight to UnJong Street, grabbed hold of people in the market, and asked them, 'Who is the richest in Seoul?'

There were those who said Byeon, so Heo-saeng went right away to visit Byeon's house. Heo-Saeng greeted Byeon and said:

'My house is poor and there is something I want to do but, I hope you will relinquish 10,000 coins and give them to me.'

'Okay,' said Byeon. And he immediately gave out 10,000 *nyang*. Heo-saeng left without even saying thank you. When the children and grand-children of Byeon's house looked at Heo-Saeng, he seemed a beggar. The tassel of his sash was tattered, the heel of his leather shoes fell off, he wore a withered, shabby robe, and he had a runny nose. When Heo-Saeng went off, everyone was puzzled and asked:

'Do you know that guy?'

'Of course I don't know him.'

Byeon spoke as follows: 'No, It's not for you to know him. Certainly most people who come to borrow things from others promote their own will greatly, and even though they have pride in their beliefs an unmanly light shines on their faces, and they repeat themselves again and again as a matter of course. However, his appearance is shabby but his words are simple; he moves on arrogantly and there is no look of shame on his face: he is a person who can be content even though he is not wealthy. I believe that it is no small thing he will do, therefore I too would like to test him. If I am going to give him the 10,000 coins anyway, what's the point of asking his name?'

Heo-saeng, having received 10,000 coins, went straight to Anseong without even going back to his own house. Anseong was a place where people from Gyeong-gi-Do and Ch'ung-ch'eong-Do meet, because it falls between the three southern provinces. There were shops where the merchants sold jujube, chestnut, persimmon, stuffed pomegranate, tangerine, and citrons to Hosaeng, and he sold them back at a price ten times higher. Heosaeng let out a long sigh, 'With 10,000 coins I manipulated the price of all different kinds of fruit, now I understand the state of our nation's economy.'

Next, Heosaeng crossed over to Jeju Island with knives, hoes, linen &c., and bought up all of the horsehair, saying, 'In a few years the people of the nation will not be able to tie up their hair.'

Heosaeng said this and, sure enough, before long the price of horsehair headbands jumped up tenfold.

Heosaeng met an old boatman and asked, 'Is there not perhaps some empty island abroad where a man could live alone?'

'There is indeed. I ran into a storm once and after drifting west for three whole days I landed at such an empty island. I think it must be halfway between Samun and Janggi. The flowers and trees thrive freely, the fruit ripens naturally, the animals come together and play, the fish do not frighten at the sight of man.'

He was very glad, and said, 'If you were to take me to this place, we would enjoy its riches together,' to which the boatman agreed.

In the end, they rode the wind to the south-east and arrived at the island. Heosaeng climbed to a high place, looked around in all directions, and said disappointedly, 'There can't be even 250 miles of land; what can we do here?! All we could do is become wealthy old men with this fertile soil and good water.'

'Are you speaking of who on earth you will live with, there being not a single person on this empty island?' spoke the boatman.

'Where there is virtue, the people will gather of themselves. Worry about whether there is virtue, and can there be any concern of whether there are people or not?'

At this time, thousands of robbers had overrun the Byeon mountains. They levied troops in every region and launched searches, but they did not capture many; not daring to go out and maintain their livelihoods the robbers were hungry and worried. Heosaeng sought out their mountain hideout and placated the leader, 'If a thousand men plunder a thousand coins and divide them, how many will return before each man?'

'That would be one coin for each man.'

'Do you all have wives?'

'We do not.'

'Do you have farmland?'

The robbers laughed farcically.

'Are you asking why a person with land, a wife, and children would ever become a thief, experiencing hardship?'

'If it is truly so, why don't you get a wife, build a home, buy a cow, plough a field , and live your lives like that?'

'Indeed, why wouldn't we want that? It's just that having no money we can't.'

Heosaeng laughed and said, 'Why worry about money when you can steal? I can take care of everything for you all. Tomorrow come to the sea. All of the ships flying red flags will be piled with money, so come and take as much as you want.'

Hoesaeng having made a covenant with the robbers, they all laughed at him as a crazy man.

The next day, when the robbers went to the beach, sure enough Heosaeng had come back having gathered 300,000 coins. Everyone was really stunned and lined up in front of Heosaeng.

'We will do just as master commands.'

4.5 대하 – 김남천 (*Scenes from the Enlightenment* – Kim Namch'ŏn)

Translation from: Kim Namcheon (trans. Charles La Shure). 2014. *Scenes from the Enlightenment: A Novel of Manners*. Champaign; London; Dublin: Dalkey Archive Press, pp. 35–8.

Across the street from Assistant Curator Bak's house was Yi Chilseong's house, up the street was Nakanishi's store, and down the street was the house of Kim Yonggu, a candy seller who sold sesame toffee and walnut toffee, as well as ice cream and ice pops – what he called 'real candy' – from a wooden box. Men and boys all came outside, and the old women stood in front of the reed fences by their kitchens. The white shadows glimpsed in between the cracks in the fences were the young married girls and girls of marrying age, who could not stand out by the road, peeking out from their hiding places. At Nakanishi's house, Nakanishi himself lived as a widower, so there was no one there to come out to watch. Nakanishi had first come to this village as a postman, and he later ran errands when the provincial army was disbanded and a garrison was stationed here, earning quite a profit in his first year, but now he ran a rather large general store.

Up and down the street, people gathered as they only did when there was a wedding between rich families. Those who had close dealings with the family stood by Assistant Curator Bak's side, while those who did not deal as frequently with him formed groups of twos and threes, whispering to each other as they watched the horses in the street.

The white horse that bore the groom and stood second in the procession, the stocky and sturdy brown mule to be ridden by the escort, and the small donkey in the front ridden by the one carrying the goose, had all been raised by Assistant Curator Bak. He had fed them all with his own hand: the white horse to ride on long trips, the donkey to ride to the threshing ground during harvest, and the mule to turn the mill. Standing in the middle of the road, they must have known that all eyes were upon them, for they raised their hooves, blinked their great eyes, and awaited those who would ride them.

Three rolls of white cotton fabric, which were to be given to the packhorse drivers after the wedding, were rolled out one by one; stretching from the tips of the beasts' noses to their saddles and tails, they were an opulent sight. The horse drivers stuck their horsehair whips into the back of their belts and grasped the reins tightly, and one of them stood there silently stroking his horse's head. Two heralds took their places, standing in front of the donkey ridden by Schoolmaster Gu, who was holding the goose, and carefully watched Assistant Curator Bak, waiting for the moment when their shouts would shake the streets like loud chanting, the horses' bells would ring, and the horse drivers' whips would crack down grandly on the horses' backs.

Everything was in place, but Assistant Curator Bak and Choe Gwansul, the latter serving as the groom's escort, were whispering about something inside the front gate. All eyes were fixed on them. Schoolmaster Gu and the groom, who had already mounted their animals and been waiting for some time, looked their way curiously, one holding the goose and the other holding a fan.

What they were doing was arguing about whether Choe Gwansul should take off the flat cap he was wearing and exchange it for a horsehair hat. But Choe Gwansul had no intention of listening to Assistant Curator Bak.

Up until then, there were only two types of new style, civilised hats being worn in this village. There was the hat worn by those who were students and the flat cap worn by those who weren't. Of course, not many people wore these flat caps. But Choe Gwansul perched a pair of gold-rimmed, new-style glasses on his nose, wore a pair of high-laced shoes with his black silk overcoat, and atop his close-cropped hair sat the flat cap. He'd even taken a piece of boxwood, stripped it of its rough bark, burned off the knots, and called it a new-style cane.

Never mind the rest, but if he would only take off that flat cap, or whatever it was called, sitting atop his roughly cut hair like some silly rice dish cover, and wear a respectable horsehair hat, like Schoolmaster Gu, then Assistant Curator Bak thought he might be able to ignore the new-style glasses that rubbed his nose sore or the new-style cane he like to carry around.

At first, Assistant Curator Bak thought he would just turn a blind eye to his brother-in-law's appearance, since his purpose was to send a new-style person to the bride's family, but now that the horses had gone out and he saw how his brother-in-law looked amidst all the people who had gathered, he was so plagued by unease and doubt that he simply couldn't bear it.

But the individual in question just wouldn't budge, and Bak couldn't just stand here and quarrel. When he told Gwansul to do as he wished, Gwansul twirled his moustache once and then strode out to the mule, twirling his new-style cane. He couldn't carry his new-style cane while riding the mule, so he stood by the mule and swung it futilely a few times, then quickly placed it across the mule's back in front of the saddle. At last he leaped up into the saddle, and the sunlight glinted off his new-style glasses.

'Very well, let's go,' he said, jabbing his heels into the mule's sides twice.

No sooner had he said the words than the anxious heralds raised their voices and shouted 'Ah – Ah-ha – !'

The donkey began to move forward with its short, plodding steps, while the white horse ridden by the groom swished its tail twice and began to prance ahead. The groom-to-be covered his face with his fan and stared entranced at the undulating road far ahead. The mule ridden by the escort promptly stomped its hooves a few times, then let out a noisy bray before following the horse. The animals moved forward toward Descending Immortal Pavilion, and Schoolmaster Gu's horsehair hat, the groom's black silk hat, and the escort's flat cap all danced up and down in time with the herald's cries and the ringing bells.

4.6 맹진사댁경사 – 오영진 (*The Happy Day of Maeng Chinsa – O Yŏngjin*)

Translation by Jieun Kiaer and Derek Driggs

M: Hello, is there no one? I have come back from a long journey, but I don't even see a mouse.
S: Oh, Master! I didn't know you'd already returned.
M: You fool, where is my wife?
S: Yes, she is worried about whether you were able to resolve the situation.
M: Why is she worried? Ask her to come straight away without worrying.
S: (Goes into the house and bumps into Gilbo.)
G: Oh Master! You've come back already!
M: Yes, I left Doraji village very early in the morning.
G: Your wife and the Master from Unsangol also worried about the situation.
M: The Master from Unsangol? Do you mean my Uncle? Did he come too?
G: Yes. He was also wondering how everything went.
M: Is he worried too?

G: Of course.
M: Why are they worried? Tell them that I'm coming.
G: That means that all went well.
M: Of course. Who looked after this business?
G: Absolutely. I thought so!
M: Where is Lady Kappun?
G: Lady Kappun must have went to pick up herbs with Ippun and her friends.
M: What? Did she go to pick up herbs? How careless is she? Please go and bring her back.
G: Yes.
M: How thoughtless my daughter is! I had to work hard for her so that she could become the daughter-in-law of Minister Kim.
H: You didn't say anything in Doraji village about a dowry.
M: Yes.
H: Really? Isn't it strange? Didn't you think it was odd when you received the dowry?
M: I didn't think it was a dowry.
H: What? Do you think it is something you could certainly receive?
M: Oh, Uncle!
H: This is almost like selling your own daughter.
M: I don't think so. You are too harsh.
H: If you are thinking about marrying a person of high status, just return it.
M: Uncle, you are right. But if I send it back, what will they think of me? Wouldn't it cause problems in my daughter's marriage?
H: You always talk about courtesy, but you don't actually seem to care about it in real life.
M: Alright. Can I ask you something?
H: Okay.
M: My point is, by marrying my daughter with a family of high nobility, I also want our family to receive more respect.
H: What are you talking about? Are you trying to gain power through marriage?
M: There is nothing wrong with power. I want my family to become a powerful family!
H: I don't want to hear any more from you. You received a dowry, you humiliated our family. How could our family become powerful? Do whatever you like. You already shamed my family. But I won't forgive you if you make my family a laughing stock. Ah . . . I'm leaving.
M: Uncle!
H: I don't want to talk to you anymore. If you have any problems, do come back to Unsangol.
M: Ah! He is too stubborn. I am doing what I want to do with my own daughter. Why does he care so much.

5.1 제망매가 – 월명사 (*Song for a Departed Sister* – Wŏlmyŏngsa)

Translation by Jieun Kiaer

> We have reached a crossroad
> Of life and death
> Dear sister, how could you go without saying goodbye to me?
> Just like the leaves that fall here and there
> In the early autumn breeze

We are from the same branch
But we don't know where we are going
Ah, I, shall meet you in Amitabha,
Please wait for me whilst you are in goodness and virtue.

5.2   향수 – 정지용 (*Thoughts of Home* – Chŏng Chiyong)

Translation by Jieun Kiaer, Anna Yates-Lu, Derek Driggs, Jing Yan, and Karolina Watroba

Thoughts of Home
The place where at the eastern end of the wide field
The brook flowed around and back, babbling stories of old as it passed
And the striped cow
Lowed lazily in the golden light –
Could I ever forget that place, even in my dreams?
The place where when the embers in the hearth died down,
The night-time breeze rushed through the empty fields as if riding on a horse,
And Old Father, dozing off into a thin sleep,
Leaned his head on a small, straw pillow –
Could I ever forget that place, even in my dreams?
My heart, sprouted and grown from the soil,
Longs for that blue, blue sky
In the place where I, in search of an arrow I had shot without thought,
Rustled through the dew-laden bushes, soaking myself.
Could I ever forget that place, even in my dreams?
That place where my little sister, with her black hair tucked under her ear
And glistening like the sea does at night in the old stories,
And my dear wife, perhaps plain to others' eyes –
Her feet bare all year long –
Gathered grain with the blaring sun on their backs –
Could I ever forget that place, even in my dreams?
The place where stars, scattered in the sky,
Moved towards unknowable sand castles,
And the autumn crows cawed as they passed over our humble roof,
As we sat around the flickering fire, chatting –
Could I ever forget that place, even in my dreams?

5.3   은세계 – 이인직 (*Silver World* – Yi Injik)

Translation by Anna Yates-Lu

'Ch'oe Pyŏngdo is innocent.'
'He's been dragged here unfairly.'
'What a pitiful scene.'

These words whisper their way between each compassionate-hearted soul present. But between them stands the governor, someone without even a drop of compassion in his soul. Perhaps it is because he is ashamed that his face goes red and, with his jowls drooping, he exudes composure as he sits there giving his orders, stating that Ch'oe Pyŏngdo's charges come under three categories.

What crime can be found at such short notice? Although Mr. Ch'oe spoke reasonably, the governor calls this contempt of court. He orders the punishment chair and torture instruments to be brought in, to have a punishment officer ready, as these orders drop from his lips, his underlings, flustered, and confused, bustle here and there like a boiling kettle. They bring in a punishment chair and spread out the torture instruments for Ch'oe Pyŏngdo to see, then sit him on the chair and tie him all round before starting to beat his shins with clubs. The punishment office clerk raises his voice and passes on the command to draw blood from the first stroke but the person carrying out the shin beatings refuses, putting the punishment officer in an awkward position. He puts all the strength he sucked from his mother's breast into the beatings, but like a stroke of lightning the governor declares that he is going too easy in his punishment. He lets out his anger at the punishment officer, and with the order to split Ch'oe's legs at the knee, the punishment officer inflicts such a beating with the sharp edge of a blade that Ch'oe Pyŏngdo hovers at the edges of consciousness. In this state, he is put in a large cangue and locked up in a prison cell, this cell is for solitary confinement where prisoners are locked up separately. Saying this is solitary confinement does not mean that he was being given special treatment and locked up somewhere he could be comfortable, but rather it is the case that there is a separate place for locking up rich people that have been arrested.

For what reason did they build a separate cell, and why are they arresting rich people and locking them up separately? Truly, this governor is greatly skilled at stealing the people's money. Just how many separate cells does this prison have that when the wealthy are brought here they can each be locked up in a cell of their own, and then later send people using all manners of persuasion, threats, comfort, and temptation to squeeze their money out of them.

Ch'oe Pyŏngdo is locked up in such a prison for several months, being taking for another round of beating as soon as his wounds start to heal, but Mr. Ch'oe refuses to the end to hand over his money to the governor, and so all day and all night the only sounds that can be heard are Ch'oe's moans as his wounds begin to fester, and the governor's angry gnashing of teeth. So the time passes in the prison, and the man who was captured in the depths of winter meets the new year.

During the summer solstice the rain falls, drip-drip, on your head; it is the busiest time for the village farming families. They thresh wheat and barley, and now the rice transplanting season has begun, the sound of farming songs tones out across Kyŏnggŭm village under Taekwallyŏng summit in Kangnŭng. Having eaten around five *doe* of double-boiled barley, each farmer scoops up a bowlful of raw barley liquor as a post-lunch snack. Then, dragging their drum-like bellies, they stand stooped over like the letter ㄱ; in their left hand they hold a bundle of rice seedlings, with their right hand they tear the bushel apart and plant the seedlings, gradually walking backwards as they go. But they do not feel even a little tired or in pain, and sing with joy as they work. Their song is an instant call and response with the lead singer, and as he has a natural eloquence he feeds them line by line without hesitation, what a joy it is to listen to.

    (. . .)
Yoho, yoho, plant away.
I worry, I worry, I worry about Old Man Pak's family.
The rumour has spread through the neighbourhood that the eaves of his roof are
    loaded with dried goods, and his rice bags are stacked up in great piles.

If he goes through the government office gates, he'll be saddled with a crime he didn't commit, his pockets dusted out and become a beggar.

Yoho, yoho, plant away.

Master Ch'oe from the village was an upright character, but having committed no evil deed,

He was arrested for a crime requiring the payment of thousands of pounds of rice, beaten and made to wear a cangue,

He hasn't been able to come out from prison for half a year.

Yoho, yoho, plant away.

The only son for three generations, Master Ch'oe lost his parents at a young age,

How can he not be bitter at his charges of unfiliality and disrespect to one's older siblings?

That fellow Chŏng, the provincial governor,

His ears only perk up at the sound of money, they are deaf to the sounds of resentment and despair,

Yoho, yoho, plant away.

My friends, listen to what I have to say.

If your farming gives you money to spare after keeping yourself fed and clothed, don't try to save it up,

Drink, play, and be merry.

In this world that steals everything, is it a punishment to be rich?

Yoho, yoho, plant away.

5.4 한중록 -혜경궁 홍씨 (*The Memoirs of Lady Hyegyŏng* – Lady Hyegyŏng)

From: Kim Haboush, JaHyun. 2013[1996]. *The Memoirs of Lady Hyegyŏng: The Autobiographical Writings of a Crown Princess of Eighteenth-Century Korea*. Berkley; Los Angeles; London: University of California Press, pp. 319–21.

The royal arrival was delayed somehow. News reached us that His Majesty might not reach Hwinyŏng Shrine until three in the afternoon.

The Prince again sent word that I should come to Tŏksŏng House. When I arrived, I found him drained, without his usual energy but with no sign of derangement in his face or in his voice. He was sitting with his back resting against a wall, his head lowered in a deep, meditative manner, his face devoid of colour.

I was expecting that my appearance would lead to rage. This premonition that my life might end that day had caused me to plead with the Grand Heir and to warn him. Contrary to my anticipation, the Prince said calmly, 'It looks very bad, but they will let you live. Oh, how I fear their intentions.' In deep consternation, I sat there silently, just rubbing my hands together while tears rolled down my face.

The royal procession had reached Hwinyŏng Shrine. A messenger came to summon the Prince. How strange! The Prince did not say, 'Let's escape' or 'Let's run away.' Nor did he beat anyone. Without rage, he asked for the dragon robe of the Crown Prince. Putting it on, he said, 'I am going to say that I am suffering from a disabling fever. Bring the Grand Heir's winter cap.'

As the Grand Heir's cap was small, I thought it would be better for him to wear his own, so I asked a lady-in-waiting to fetch it. This brought from the Prince a completely unexpected response: 'Your malevolence frightens me. You want to live long with the Grand Heir at your side. Since I will die today, when I get out there, you don't want me to wear his cap lest it bring misfortune [to your son]. How very well I can fathom your cruel heart.'

I did not know that he would meet that disaster on that day. I could not see how it would all end. It was the sort of thing that could end in death for all. What would become of my son, of me? And so these words, coming as a thunderbolt, tormented me. I fetched the Grand Heir's cap and gave it to him, saying, 'What Your Highness has said was indeed beyond my reckoning. Please wear this.' He refused. 'No, why should I wear what you wish to keep from me?' Could one have thought these the words of a diseased person? Oh! Why did he go so obediently? It was, I guess, all Heaven's will. Only pain and misery remain.

It grew late, and with much urging, the Prince went out. His Majesty, seated before Hwinyŏng Shrine, rapping his sword, enacted that decision. It was too cruel; I cannot bear to record the scene. Oh, grief!

When the Prince left, one could hear the fury of His Majesty's voice. Hwinyŏng Shrine was not far from Tŏksŏng House; I had someone go to the wall. He returned to say that the Prince had already removed the dragon robe and was prostrate upon the ground. I realised that it was the final decision; heaven and earth seemed to sink around me; my heart and innards felt as though they were being torn to pieces.

Too restless to stay at Tŏksŏng House, I went to the Grand Heir's residence. We hugged each other desperately, not knowing what to do.

At about four o'clock, I was informed that a eunuch had come requesting a rice chest from the kitchen. I could not understand what it meant, but I was too agitated to let him have it.

Realising that a decision of an extreme nature had been taken, the Grand Heir went through the gate and begged, 'Please spare my father.' His Majesty ordered sternly, 'You leave here.' The Grand Heir left and went to the waiting room at the Prince's residence. My state at the time was simply beyond comparison to any ever known. After sending out the Grand Heir, the sky and the earth seemed to come together; the sun seemed to be losing light, and everything went dark. I had no desire to linger in this world for even one more second. I took a knife and was about to end my life, but someone took it and I could not achieve my wish. I desperately wanted to kill myself; I looked for something sharp, but found nothing.

I went out, passed Sungmun Hall, and reached Kŏnbok Gate that leads to Hwinyŏng Shrine. I could see nothing. I only heard the sound of a sword that His Majesty was rapping and the Prince's pleas: 'Father, Father. I have done wrong. Herewith, I will do everything you say, I will study, I will obey you in everything, I promise. Please do not do this to me.' My liver and gall were breaking into bits; everything was black around me. I just beat my breast. But what was to be done? What would be of use?

With your strength and with your energy, could you not have avoided getting into that rice chest even if it was a royal command? Why did you get in? Oh, why! At the beginning he tried to come out, but in the end, he was pressured into facing that dreadful fate. How could Heaven be so cruel? There is only unparalleled grief. I wailed and wailed beneath the wall; there was no response.

Since the Prince had been stripped of his position, his wife and children ought not to have remained in the palace. Moreover, I was too fearful to let the Grand Heir stay out. I sat beneath the gate and wrote a letter to His Majesty: 'Under Your Majesty's decision, it is most discomforting for the criminal's wife and son to remain at the palace. It is all the more fearful that the Grand Heir might stay out for long, and so this person humbly begs permission to leave for her [father's] home.' I added, 'By Your Majesty's heavenly grace, this humble person begs for the protection of the Grand Heir.' I managed to find a eunuch and asked him to deliver it.

5.5   풀 – 김금숙 (*Grass* – Keum Suk Gendry-Kim)

Translation by Anna Yates-Lu

Extract 1

There was so much blood.
I hadn't even got married. But now I was defiled.
That's why everyone committed suicide.
I also didn't want to live anymore.
But I couldn't die.
No matter how much I wanted to die, there was no way to do it.
Then again, it's not like life was really living anymore either.
Those I missed: my mother, father, my siblings back home
Now
I could never return . . .

Extract 2

But then one day
'What's this? Why are my hands like this?'
(Sob)
'Why is my hair falling out?'
It was syphilis. It was only when down there was covered in sores and I couldn't receive soldiers anymore
That the comfort station owner sent me to the military hospital.
There I was given the 'No. 606 injection'
But even after a month I didn't get better.
As I couldn't earn any money the comfort station owner must have felt pressured
He got some mercury from somewhere.
He said he had got it from the army surgeon, he said to pour it into a small bowl, boil it over a flame and use the steam to heat the affected area.
Having covered my face covered and taken off my lower garments, I squatted over the bowl of boiled mercury and steamed myself. In the end the disease was cured but because of that I would never have children for the rest of my life.

Extract 3

Ever since coming out of my mother's belly, even until today, I have never once been happy.
Even my siblings, who I had missed so dearly, once they found out later that I had been a comfort woman they tried to avoid me.
And having come to Korea, I saw that even amongst themselves they didn't really get along.
I had always been jealous of seeing other families, where they all get together around the dinner table and talk and laugh . . .

With us siblings, it was more, 'You're you, and I'm me.' So it wasn't fun at all. It made me wonder why on earth I'd come here.

5.6 민요 아리랑, 가시리 (Folk songs *Arirang, Will You Go* – Anonymous)

Translation by Jieun Kiaer

1 *Are you going? (Really leaving) are you going?*
2 *(Oh me,) you are leaving, must you go?*
3 *Wi chŭngjŭlga Taepyŏngsŏngdae*
4 *However shall I live*
5 *(When it's me) you leave behind?*
6 *Wi chŭngjŭlga Taepyŏngsŏngdae*
7 *(As I see it) you shouldn't leave someone you hold*
8 *(If it be by your lover) that you're hurt, (and if you get sullen and annoyed, yet again) and you're scared to cry*
9 *Wi chŭngjŭlga Taepyŏngsŏngdae*
10 *(Letting you go) oh my distraught lover (what can I do) I'm letting you go.*
11 *No sooner gone than soon (just as hurriedly when leaving)*
12 *just as you go, you come back, oh come back. Wi chŭngjŭlga Taepyŏngsŏngdae*

Arirang, arirang, arariyo
Arirang, you're leaving over the hill.
Arirang, arirang, arariyo.
Arirang you're leaving over the hill.

You, who throw me away and leave –
Your feet will be diseased before you've gone ten ri.

Arirang, arirang, arariyo
Arirang, you're leaving over the hill.
In the clear sky there are many cold stars.
There is much hope left in our hearts.

6.1 무정 – 이광수 (*Heartless* – Yi Kwangsu)

Translation from: Lee, Ann Sung-hi. 2005. *Yi Kwangsu and Modern Korean Literature: Mujŏng*. Ithaca, NY: Cornell University East Asia Program, pp. 340–2.

Meanwhile, people who had lost their homes in the flood were sitting outside on the ground, not knowing what to do. They were becoming hungry, and starting to shiver, but they had no plans as to what to do. They could only accept what had happened, and hope for the best.

They were powerless. Though no one could stand against the violence of nature, these people were particularly powerless. They were so powerless that everything they had built up through a lifetime of hard work could be washed away by rain overnight. It was as though they had built up their lives on a foundation of sand. When the rain stopped and the water receded, they would scrape together the scattered sands, and build the foundations anew. They were like ants making a nest in the sand by digging with their weak limbs. These people who had lost everything overnight to rain and stood shivering in the rain, seemed pitiful, and yet weak and foolish too.

Looking at their faces, it did not seem likely that they would have any particular wisdom. They all looked foolish and insensitive. All they did was farm with what little knowledge they had about farming. In this manner, they might accumulate a few sacks of rotten rice over the years – that is, if God let them. If there was a flood, all of it would be washed away. They thus never got any richer, but just got poorer. Their bodies gradually grew weaker, and their minds duller. If left in this condition, they would eventually become like the Ainu people of Hokkaido.

They needed to be empowered. They needed to be given knowledge. They needed to have their means of living thereby made complete.

'Science! Science!' Hyŏng-sik exclaimed to himself when he returned to the inn and sat down. The three young women looked at Hyŏng-sik.

'We must first of all give the Korean people science. We must give them knowledge.' He stood up clenching his fists, and walked about the room. 'What are your thoughts, after having seen what you saw today?'

The young women did not know what to say in answer to Hyŏng-sik's question. After awhile, Pyŏng-uk spoke up.

'I felt sorry for them.' She smiled. 'Didn't you?' They had all grown much closer while working together that day.

'Yes, one pities them. What is the cause of their pitiful situation?'

'It is that they do not know about modern civilisation, of course. They are not empowered to make a living for themselves.'

'Then what must we do to save them . . . to save ourselves?' Hyŏng-sik looked at Pyŏng-uk. Yŏng-ch'ae and Sŏn-hyŏng looked back and forth and Hyŏng-sik and Pyŏng-uk's faces.

'We must give them strength! We must give them modern civilisation.' Pyŏng-uk said confidently.

'And how can we do that?'

'We must teach them, guide them.'

'How?'

'Through education, and through actual practice.'

Yŏng-ch'ae and Sŏn-hyŏng did not quite understand the meaning of this conversation. They thought they understood, but they did not understand with as much urgency or conviction as Hyŏng-sik or Pyŏng-uk. Nevertheless, the realities they had seen with their eyes that day gave them a real-life learning experience. Such learning could not be acquired at school, or from verbose oratory.

Everyone was nervous. Moreover, Yŏng-ch'ae had never heard a discussion of such an important question. 'How can we save them?' It was a very important question. Hyŏng-sik and Pyŏng-uk seemed very mature and impressive as they talked about this question. Yŏng-ch'ae thought about poetry in which Du Fu and Li Bo expressed concern about the world. She thought of the speech that she and Wŏr-hwa had heard five years ago, given by the principal of the P'aesŏng School. She had been young then, and had not understood the speech very clearly. Nevertheless, she remembered that the principal had said, 'Your ancestors were not as foolish as you.' She remembered that upon hearing these words, it had occurred to her that she people she encountered every day were indeed foolish. Yŏng-ch'ae thought that Hyŏng-sik's words and those of the principal shared some common points. She looked at Hyŏng-sik again.

'Right. We must teach and guide them through education and actual practice. However, who will do this?' Hyŏng-sik closed his mouth. The three women felt shivers run over their skin.

'Who will do this?' Hyŏng-sik asked again more emphatically. He looked at each of them. The young women were spiritually moved, in a way that they had never experienced before and that they could not describe in words. Shivers ran over them all at the same time.

'Who will do this?' Hyŏng-sik asked again.

'We will!' The words dropped from the women's lips in unison without their having planned it. Flames seemed to flash before their eyes. The earth seemed to shake as though there had been a great earthquake. Hyŏng-sik sat with his head lowered for some time.

'Yes. We must do it. This is why we are going overseas to study. Who is giving us the money to take the train, and money for tuition? Korea. Why? So that we can acquire strength, knowledge, and civilisation, and bring them back with us. So that we can establish a solid foundation for the people's livelihood, based on modern civilisation. Isn't that why?' Hyŏng-sik pulled his wallet from his vest pocket, and took out a blue train ticket.

'This train ticket contains the sweat of those people who are shivering in the rain, including the young man we saw. They are asking us to make sure that they are never put in such a needy situation again.' Hyŏng-sik shook himself, as though with new resolve. The three young women trembled too.

At that moment, each one of them thought about 'the work that I must do.' They seemed to have become one body and one mind, without distinctions of self and other.

6.2 삼포 가는 길 – 황석영 (*The Road Going to Sampo – Hwang Sŏkyŏng*)

Translated by Jieun Kiaer and Derek Driggs

'How long have you been here?' the man asked. Looking closely, he didn't look like a suspicious person. Youngdal thought that his unhesitant attitude was not as bothersome as it could have been. He looked about five years older than himself. In this windy winter field, he looked completely at ease. Youngdal answered with less reservation than before.

'I've been here four months. But where are you going, old chap?'

'I'm thinking about going to Sampo,' the older man said quietly, squinting his eyes.

Youngdal shook his head. 'You're going the wrong way. There's nothing there, especially in this winter season.'

'It's my hometown,' the older man said, rubbing his nose with his gloved fingers. He was already looking towards the end of the field.

He was in a completely different situation from Youngdal; he was going home, but Youngdal was going to a new place. 'Ah . . . you're going home. I see.'

The older man rose, hanging his rucksack over one shoulder, and asked, 'Are you looking for work somewhere?'

'When you first came was it because someone invited you? It's the same for everyone, isn't it?'

'I should go.' The older man climbed up the path, without looking behind him.

Once he'd reached the top of the hill, he changed his bag to the other shoulder and his body disappeared from view. Youngdal didn't have a particular idea of where to go, and he didn't have anybody to walk with. Even if they had to separate on the way, he thought it would be a good idea to walk together with another person.

He stood there thoughtlessly for a minute, and then suddenly chased after the older man. Youngdal climbed the hill, but the older man was too quick, and he was already on the path leading to the main road. The poplar trees lined the way, side by side. Youngal ran towards the man, and called out to him. 'Hey, wait!'

The man stopped and looked behind him, and then started walking slowly again. Youngdal hurried up and joined him, saying, 'Let's go together. I'm going the same direction until Wolchulli.'

But the man did not answer. Youngdal spoke to the back of his head. 'Come on! This is my first time seeing such a cold winter. Last year this time was really nice. I lived with a hostess in a room that only cost three thousand won a month, you see. Now I've got nowhere to go in this frigid winter.'

'I guess I'm used to it.' the man said.

'Do you know how far Sampo is from here?'

'It is a couple hundred ri just to the sea, and then you have to take a boat the rest of the way,' said the older man.

'How long has it been?' asked Youngdal.

'More than ten years. Even if I go there, there will be nobody left who knows me.' said the man.

'Then why are you going?'

'Just because I'm getting old. I want to go.'

They went together to the main road. The road was well made with pebbles and mud. They found it was easy to walk on. Youngdal put his cold hands in his pockets and wiggled his fingers around.

'Wow, it is so cold! I wish the wind would stop,' said Youngdal.

The man didn't look so cold, and he was well covered with a fur hat and a winter jacket. He also looked very healthy. For the first time, the man questioned Youngdal warmly.

'Have you had breakfast?'

'Not really.' Youngdal smiled. 'I barely even got up in the morning.'

'I didn't have breakfast either. It will take awhile for us to find somewhere that sells food. It's sure difficult to walk around in the winter,' said the man.

'I'm sorry for not introducing myself properly earlier,' said Youngdal. 'My name is No Youngdal.'

'Hi. I'm Jeong.'

'I do have some skills, so once I find work I won't have any problem making a living,' said Youngdal. He was trying to show Mr. Jeong that he had no intentions of relying on him.

'I know. Do you know how to use a jackhammer? I can do carpentry, welding, and cobblery,' Mr. Jeong said.

'Wow, you have many skills!' said Youngdal.

'I have been working for ten years.'

'Where did you learn all of this?'

'There are places you can learn,' Mr. Jeong responded.

'I'd like to go to those places.'

Mr. Jeong smiled bitterly and shook his head. 'You can start even now. But the place is too big.'

Youngdal looked at Mr. Jeong and Mr. Jeong looked down and walked without a word. They climbed a path and walked down together, and they reached a wild field without any houses. There were weeds all around, which were moving back and forth in the wind. The wind blew all around the river. Mr. Jeong said, 'We can only reach to Chansem village after we pass that mountain. We should cross the river to get there quicker. Do you think it is frozen?'

The river was frozen solid. Some parts were unsteady, but not slippery. The wind blew bits of ice into their faces.

'Perhaps we should have waited for the bus,' Youngdal said, out of breath.

6.3 1964년 서울 – 김승옥 (*Seoul: 1964, Winter* – Kim Sŭngok)

Translation from: Kim Sung-ok (trans. Marshall Pihl). 2008. *Seoul-1964-Winter*. Elizabeth NJ; Seoul: Hollym, pp. 10–18, 59–69.

Anyone who spent the winter of 1964 in Seoul would probably remember those wine shops that appeared on the streets at nightfall – the shops that sold hotchpotch, roasted sparrows and three kinds of wine, where the curtain you lifted to step in was flapping in a bitter wind that swept the frozen streets, where the flame of a carbide lamp inside fluttered in the gusts, and where a middle-aged man in a dyed army jacket poured wine and roasted snacks for you. Well, that was the sort of wine shop where the three of us happened to meet that night.

By the three of us, I mean, myself, a graduate student named An who wore thick glasses, and a man of about 35 or six who was obviously poor but whose particulars I couldn't figure out and, actually, had no real desire to at all to know.

The conversation started off between myself and the graduate student. When some small talk and the self introductions were over, I knew that he was a 25-year-old flower of Korean youth with the name of An, a graduate student with a major I had never even dreamt of, and the oldest son of a rich family. And he knew that I was a 25-year-old country boy, that I had volunteered for the Military Academy when I got out of high school only to fail and then enter the army where I caught the clap once, and that I was now working in the military affairs section of a ward office.

The self introductions were finished but then there was nothing for us to talk about. For a while we were just drinking our wine quietly. Then, when I picked up a charred roasted sparrow, something occurred to me to say and so, after privately thanking the roasted sparrow, I began to talk.

'An, do you love flies?'

'No, not until,' he began.

'Do you love flies, Kim?'

'Yes,' I replied. 'Because they can fly. No, because even while they can fly, they can be caught in my hand. Have you ever caught something in your hand that can fly?'

'Just a moment, now. Let me see. . . .' For a while he looked at me blankly from inside his glasses as he screwed up his face a bit. then he said, 'no, I haven't. Except for flies, of course.'

Since the weather that day had been unusually warm, the ice had melted and filled the streets with mud, but as the temperature dropped again by evening, the mud began to freeze once more beneath our feet. My black leather shoes were not enough to block out the chill that crept up from the freezing ground. Actually, a wine shop like this was meant just for people who thought they might stop for a bowl on the way home, it wasn't the place for drinking and chatting back and forth with the man standing next to you. This thought had just occurred to me when four-eyes asked me a commendable question. 'I should have expected as much from this guy,' I thought. So I asked my cold and numb feet to hold out a little longer.

'Kim, do you love things that wriggle?' is what he had asked me.

'Oh, yes, I sure do love them,' I answered with an abrupt air of triumph. Recollection, itself, can give you a sense of triumph, whether you're thinking of one that is sad or pleasant. When the recollection is sad, the triumph is quiet and lonely, but when the recollection is pleasant the triumph is a noisy one.

. . .

'What time has it gotten to be?' the listless man asked An.

'It's ten to nine,' An answered after a moment.

'Have you two eaten supper? I haven't eaten yet, so why don't we go together and I'll treat you?' the listless man said as he looked at each of us in turn.

'I've eaten,' An and I replied at the same time.

'You have your own,' I suggested.

'I guess I'll skip it,' the listless man answered.

'Please, we'll come along with you,' said An.

'Thank you. Then . . .'

We went into a nearby Chinese restaurant. After we sat down in a room, he kindly asked us again to have something. And again we refused. But he offered once more.

'Is it all right if I order something very expensive?' I asked, in an effort to make him withdraw the offer.

'Yes, anything you want,' he said in a voice that was now strong for the first time.

'I've decided to use this money up, you see.'

I felt sure the man had to have some design in mind, but still I asked for a whole chicken and some wine. He asked the waiter for what I wanted, and also gave his own order. An stared at me with a look of disbelief. It was just about then that I heard the warm moans of a woman coming from the next room.

'Why don't you have something?' the man suggested to An.

'No, I . . .' An refused abruptly in a voice that seemed sobered.

We turned our ears to the moaning in the next room that was quietly growing more urgent. From a distance came the faint click-clack of street cars and the sound, like flooding water, of rushing automobiles. And from somewhere nearby we could hear the occasional tinging of fire tongs. But we in our room were wrapped in an awkward silence.

'There is something I would like to explain to you.' He began to speak in a gentle tone of voice. 'I would be grateful if you would listen a while. . . . This afternoon, my wife died. She had been admitted to Severance Hospital . . .'

He looked searchingly at us but without sadness in his face as he spoke.

'Oh, no . . .' 'I'm sorry to hear that.' An and I offered condolences.

'My wife and I were very happy together. Since my wife couldn't have a child, we had all the time to ourselves. We didn't have a lot of money, but whenever we came by a little we'd have a pleasant time travelling around together. We'd visit Suwon when the strawberries were in season, and take in Anyang for the grapes. In the summer, we'd go to Daecheon and then visit Gyeongju in the fall. We'd see movies in the evenings and take in sows whenever we could . . .'

'What kind of illness did she have?' An asked cautiously.

'The doctor said it was acute meningitis. Though she had had acute appendicitis once and also acute pneumonia, she got over them all right. But this acute attack killed her. . . . Now she's dead.'

6.4 소년이 온다 – 한강 (*Human Acts* – **Han Kang**)

Translation from: Han Kang (trans. Deborah Smith). 2016. *Human Acts*. London: Portobello Books, pp. 55, 93–4, 122–3, 140–2.

I no longer felt 16. 35, 45; these numbers came, in turn, to feel somehow insufficient. Not even 65, no, nor 75, seemed to encompass what I was.

I wasn't Jeong-dae any more, the runt of the year. I wasn't Park Jeong-dae, whose ideas of love and fear were both bound up in the figure of his sister. A strange violence welled up within me, not spurred by the fact of my death, but simply because of the thoughts that wouldn't stop tearing through me, the things I needed to know. Who killed me, who killed my sister, and why. The more of myself I devoted to these questions, the firmer this new strength within me became. The ceaseless flow of blood, blood that flowed from a place without eyes or cheeks, darkened, thickened, into a viscous treacle ooze.

My sister's soul, like mine, must still be lingering somewhere; but where? Now there were no such things as bodies for us, presumably physical proximity was no longer necessary for the two of us to meet. But without bodies, how would we know each other? Would I still recognise my sister as a shadow?

Thinking back on it afterwards, Eun-sook could never quite remember how Jin-su had managed to persuade them. Perhaps because she didn't want to. She could dimly recall something about death itself, the various forms it might take, still disturbed her. Having seen and handled so many dead, she imagined she would have become inured to it all, but on the contrary, her fear had increased. She didn't want her last breath to be a gasp from a gaping mouth, didn't want transculent intestines spilling out through a gash torn into her body.

Had she ever had such a thing as a soul, that was the moment of its shattering. When Jin-su, rifle strap pressing against his sweat-soaked shirt, gave you all a farewell smile. But no, it had already shivered into fragments, when she would come out of the provincial office, and the sight of your diminutive frame, more like a child's than a teenage boy's, had stopped her in her tracks. Her pale-blue track bottoms, your PE sweater – and then she'd seen the gun you were clutching. 'Dong-ho,' she'd called out, 'Why aren't you at home?' She marched up to the youth who was explaining to the others how to load a gun. 'That kid is still in middle school. You have to send him home.' The young man looked surprised. 'He told me he was in the second year at high school; I had no reason not to believe him . . . we even sent the first years home just now, but he never said anything.' Eun-sook lowered her voice. 'That's nonsense. Look at his face. And you're telling me he's in high school?'

Have you known it, professor – that terrifying intensity, that feeling as if you yourself have undergone some kind of alchemy, been purified, made wholly virtuous? The brilliance of that moment, the dazzling purity of conscience.

It's possible that the kids who stayed behind at the Provincial Office that day experienced something similar. Perhaps they would have considered even death a fair exchange for that jewel of conscience. But no such certainty is possible now. Kids crouching beneath the windows, fumbling with their guns, and complaining that they were hungry, asking if it was okay for them to quickly run back and fetch the sponge cake and Fanta they'd left in the conference room; what could they possibly have known about death that would have enabled them to make such a choice?

Some memories never heal. Rather than fading with the passage of time, those memories become the only things that are left behind when all else is abraded. The world darkens, like electric bulbs going out one by one. I am aware that I am not a safe person.

Is it true that human beings are fundamentally cruel? Is the experience of cruelty the only thing we share as a species? Is the dignity that we cling to nothing but self-delusion, masking from ourselves this single truth: that each one of us is capable of being reduced to an insect, a ravening beast, a lump of meat? To be degraded, damaged, slaughtered – is this the essential fate of humankind, one which history has confirmed as inevitable?

I once met someone who was a paratrooper during the Busan uprising. He told me his story after hearing my own. He said that they'd been ordered to suppress the civilians with as much violence as possible, and those who committed especially brutal actions were awarded hundreds of thousands of won by their superiors. One of his company had said, 'What's the problem? They give you money and tell you to beat someone up, then why wouldn't you?'

I heard a story about one of the Korean army platoons that fought in Vietnam. How they forced the women, children, and elderly of one particular village into the main hall, and then burned it to the ground. Some of those who came to slaughter us did so with the memory of those previous times, when committing such actions in wartime had won them a handsome reward. It happened in Gwangju just as it did on Jeju Island, in Kwantung and Nanjing, in Bosnia and all across the American continent when it was still known as the New World, with such a uniform brutality it's as though it is imprinted in our genetic code.

I never let myself forget that every single person I meet is a member of this human race. And that includes you, professor, listening to this testimony. As it includes myself.

6.5 바리데기 – 황석영 (*Princess Pari* – Hwang Sŏkyŏng)

Translation from Hwang Sok-yong (trans. Sora Kim-Russell). 2015. *Princess Bari*. Reading: Periscope Books, pp. 1–3, 6–8, 41–2, 187.

We had a full house: Grandmother, Father, Mother, my six older sisters. Most of us had been born within a year or two of each other, which meant our mother was pregnant or nursing for practically 15 years straight. The moment one girl popped out, she was waddling around with the next. My two oldest sisters never forgot the fear that filled our house each time our mother went into labour. Luckily, Grandmother was by her side each time, acting as midwife. They told me our father used to pace back and forth and chain-smoke outside the door or out in the courtyard, but after the third girl was born, whenever our mother showed signs of going into labour, he stayed late at work instead and even volunteered for the night shift. The anger he'd been suppressing finally exploded when Sook, the fifth girl, was born. That morning, Mother and Grandmother were in the main room off the kitchen, bathing newborn Sook in a tub of warm water, when Father returned home from night duty. He opened the door, took one look inside and said: 'What're we supposed to do with another of those?' He yanked little Sook from the tub. Sook didn't cry, but just spluttered and coughed instead as if she'd swallowed too much water and couldn't breathe. When the sixth girl, Hyun was born, Jin, the oldest, wound up with a brass bowl of *kimchi* on her head as she was coming back home from the outside just as our father vented his anger by tossing the breakfast tray into the courtyard. Jin warned everyone: 'Not a peep out of any of you, and don't even *think* about stepping foot out of this room until Father gets home.'

Our father was raised by his widowed mother. Grandfather died in a war that started long before I was born. Grandmother claims he was a war hero, and that his story had even made its way onto one of the central radio station's broadcasts. In some faraway seaside town way down in the south, Grandfather had fought off a troop of Big Noses, and singlehandedly at that, as they were rolling in one of their tanks. Grandmother would often retail the story after dinner when the trays had been put away, or on summer nights when we would spread out straw mats in the front courtyard and gaze up at the stars. But, one night Father got so fed up with hearing it that he butted in, and the heroic tale of my grandfather lost its shine.

'Enough already! Stop it with your stories. That's all straight out of a Soviet film.'

'What film?'

'That film we saw in town. Don't you remember? The neighbourhood unit went to see it as a group. You're mixing it up with Father's story.'

Anyway, from what our father told us, it was probably true that Grandfather had been killed in combat on the Eastern Front. He said Grandmother was called before the People's Committee and given official notification of this death along with some extra rations in recognition of his services, and when Father went to school, his homeroom teacher had him stand at the podium while she made the students offer up a moment of silence. But Grandmother had already known exactly when Grandfather had died, and had fixed the date for the anniversary of his death so the family would know when to observe memorial rites every year. As always, she had seen what was coming in her dreams.

One day, Chilsung disappeared, and had not returned home by sunset. Grandmother saw me pacing outside the stone wall, and came out to talk to me.

'Don't worry, Chilsung is fine. I'm sure he'll be home soon. Don't tell your father, and don't let him off the leash next time.'

I squatted down in the corner of the wall. Then I closed my eyes tight and pictured Chilsung. The darkness behind my eyelids slowly paled into a milky light. I saw a road, a field, rows of cornstalks flattened in the wind, and among them, a white creature. Our little creature Chilsung was lying on his side with his legs stretched out. I opened my eyes wide.

'Grandma! I know where he is. He's in the middle of cornfield over there.' I took off running without a thought as to any danger. Grandmother followed me, first trotting, then slowing to a walk. The field was blanketed in fog.

'Slow down, girl! I told you, Chilsung is fine.'

(Excerpt continues from p. 187)

Ali and I moved into the flat the Nigerian couple had lived in, but we decided to use his grandfather's kitchen upstairs to cook. That way, the three of us could eat together as a family. As soon as I got home from work in the evenings, I cooked dinner using whatever Grandfather Abdul had picked up at the market that afternoon based on the note that we'd left for him, but it was often just Grandfather Abdul and me. As the weekend kept Ali busy, he usually took a couple of days in the middle of the week to rest during the day and work the late shift after dinner.

6.6 완득이 – 김려령 (*Wandŭgi-Punch* – Kim Ryŏryŏng)

Translation by Anna Yates-Lu

Some old man, his hair touched with white, was sitting in a wheelchair next to Tong-poo. I opened the door, intending to leave again.

'Where do you think you're going?' Tong-poo called me.

'Well, you have a guest.'

'Come sit over here.'

Tong-poo gestured towards the empty bed next to him with his chin. I went to stand behind the bed. Since it was a local hospital twin room, it was quite small, and the cold atmosphere made it stifling.

'You call yourself my only son . . .'

'It's because I'm your only son that I did this.'

'So you reported your own father's factory?'

'You treated those poor people badly, after all.'

'I treated those people completely lawfully.'

'You treated them completely lawfully while avoiding the law.'

'. . .'

'Dormitories filled with mould, sodden ramen each day, shoddy security equipment . . .'

'There are lots of places that don't even offer that.'

'There are a lot of places that offer better things than that, too. That's how you should do it.'

'Why you little . . .'

The old man grabbed the wheels of his wheelchair.

'You remember Tilo from Vietnam, right? That girl I called older sister, who you said was just like family while you made her do all of our housework as well? You know, while rolling out metal sheets for pencil cases, her finger got cut off in the cutting machine, so you sent her back to her country. Since then, I never used metal pencil cases.'

'It's not like we're some kind of charity, I can't hold on to someone who can't work.'

'Hahaha. You should have let her be treated before sending her away. Don't you think? You worked her until three of the chopped fingers were rotten to the knuckle before sending her home! Did you think I wouldn't know? This was while I was in high school. But why did you send her off without pay? Now I find out you're still acting the same these days, why on earth are you just treating foreign workers like that? Oh! Right. You always were really strong against the weak. I keep forgetting that.

'Driver Chŏng, Driver Chŏng!'

The old man called out without even turning his head.

A man, neatly dressed in a suit, came in from outside.

'You wicked fool!'

The man pulled the wheelchair the old man was sitting in and came towards the door. Our eyes met. I quickly turned my head. The two men left the ward.

'Oh God, I'm dying. You bastard, when I'm discharged you're dead meat.'

Tong-poo suddenly started groaning.

'They're saying you have a very light fracture. Just a light one.'

I sat down on the empty bed next to Tong-poo.

'Who says? I might die, you bastard.'

'So what were you doing in someone else's house. Where did you get the key?'

'Your father gave me one to look after you in case anything happened, you bastard.'

'Then what happened to me to make you come over?'

'Not you, something happened to me so I came over.'

'What happened?'

'That old goat from just now showed up at my house unexpectedly.'

'That looked like your father.'

'Yup.'

'He doesn't seem to be very well.'
'Hahaha. That old man always uses the wheelchair when he's been pushed into a corner.'
Tong-poo's laughing face looked bitter.
'Seeing as he even has a chauffeur, he must be rich.'
'Quite rich. He received all my grandfather's inheritance.'
'Then you must be rich too, sir.'
'Why, do you not like me if I'm rich?'
'I didn't like you anyway, sir.'
'I know.'
'Then why do you go around pretending to be poor?'
'You bastard, I'm not pretending, it's the truth. Can't you tell from looking at my rooftop flat?'

'If my dad was rich I could still be living in an underpass, let alone a rooftop flat. Why would you worry, when you've got a father who can sort everything no matter what mistakes you make? No matter what you say, sir, if you're not, you're not. Have you experienced having a mum who was so poor she came to another country to get married? It's so embarrassing you want to just sink down and die, but if you don't take it, you'll go hungry, so you take the things from the food bank, have you experienced that before?'

'Are you learning kickboxing with your trap, you bastard? You're speaking well.'

'You're just experiencing what it's like to be poor. You've got a nice steady place you can go back to, and in the meantime you're just playing at being poor! Do you know what it's like to be poor with nowhere to go?'

'Then does a mere teacher go to work in a Benz? If they lived in a fancy apartment complex and went golfing every weekend, would you not complain? You sure have a lot to complain about, you bastard.'

'Everyone looks down on poor people pretending to be rich, right? Rich people pretending to be poor are just as bad.'

'A kid like you who has absolutely no appeal pretending to be handsome it just as bad. To be honest, you don't even know what true poverty is. Even if your father doesn't shower you in gold, at least he gave you a place to eat and sleep without having to worry. You, you have no right to cuss me out, you bastard. Is poverty that knows shame poverty? True poverty is when you have to be happy to be able to take at least one more pack of instant rice home with you. There are families that boil up one pack of instant rice for three or four people to eat for dinner! You rude bastard, you come here on a hospital visit and don't even buy a single peach. Oh God, I'm dying.'

'You've got a rich father. Why ask me to buy it for you?'

7.1 내훈 – 소혜왕후 (*Instructions for Women* – Queen Sohye)

Translation by Jieun Kiaer and Derek Driggs

The four major achievements of women are these: first is virtue, second is words, third is appearance, and fourth is achievements.

(1) The virtue of a woman is not about being brilliant in her ability and intellect, and isn't about her eloquence. Appearance is not about being pretty. Achievement is not about being better than others. It is about being clean and quiet, right and stable, behaving appropriately, and not acting shamefully. Movement should be appropriate for setting. This is a woman's

virtue. Being able to speak appropriately, yet not speaking harshly. Thinking deeply, without making people feel uncomfortable. That is a woman's words.

Washing dirty things and wearing clean clothes, and washing frequently so as not to leave the body unclean. That is the woman's appearance. Working hard for needlework and not enjoying playing or laughing, and serving guests well with food and rice wine. That is a woman's achievement.

There are no greater achievements than these, but they are very easy to do. They depend only on one's heart. People of old have said, 'Is it difficult to achieve virtue? It is possible if you have the willingness to do so.'

Confucius said that women should not do things according to their own thoughts. There are three ways they should follow. Before they are married, they should follow their father's will. When they are married, they should follow their husband's will. When their husbands die, they should follow their son's will. They should never follow their own will.

'They should not let the commands of the family head go out of the house. Their work never ends except when eating. Women should never do anything of their own will, and should never decide anything on their own. In whatever situation, they should act only when they know everything that is going on. They should only speak when they have personal experience to contribute. They shouldn't lay about in the yard in the daytime. When they walk around in the evening, they should bring a lamp. This is the way to keep the virtue of a woman. Between husband and wife, the roles are different. Men should think of strength as a virtue, and women should think of softness as their virtue. There is a saying: 'Even if your son is like a wolf, you are worried whether your son will become soft. Even if you have a daughter like a mouse, you are worried that your daughter will end up like a tiger.'

7.2 규원가 – 허난설헌 (*Lament of the Inner Chamber –* **Hŏ Nansŏrhŏn**)

Translation by Jieun Kiaer

A few days before yesterday I was young, but how did I get to be so old?
    It's no use even saying that I think of how I passed the time happily as a child.
    In this way, telling this sad story in my old age, I choke with emotion.
    The reason that my parents suffered awfully from giving birth to me and raising me is that
    Although they couldn't wish for me to become the spouse of a high government official, they wanted me to become a good match for a nobleman. However
    It was a resentful karma of the past life, and a matrimonial relationship made by the heavens
    Like a dream I met a man who is well-known in the city, but he is a capricious man
    After going to my husband's home, waiting on him is like cautiously stepping onto thin ice.
    My innate beauty naturally blossomed after barely passing the age 15, 16
    I promised to live a lifetime with this face and this attitude
    But time passes quickly and even the creator is very envious
    The spring breeze and autumn water pass as quickly as the shuttle that weaves the thread across the loom
    My face, which was as beautiful as a flower, went away somewhere, and my visage became hateful!

Looking at this face, I wonder who could love me now?

I am ashamed but who can I blame?

Is there talk of a new *kisaeng* having appeared at the tavern where groups of several people frequently visit?

When it is the close of day and the flowers bloom, he leaves aimlessly

And with a white horse and golden whip, where on earth will he stay?

(Because I am only inside the home) I do not know near nor distant land, so how could I even know news of my beloved?

I tried to cut my emotional ties to you, but how can I have no thoughts of you?

I cannot see the face of my beloved, so I wish I didn't miss him,

Even a day is long, but an entire month is wearisome

How many times over has the plum tree in front of my quarters bloomed and died?

Why is there irritating rain all day long on long summer days, and sleet falling on the increasingly cold winter nights?

On good spring days when all kinds of flowers bloom and willow leaves are budding, even when I look at the beautiful landscape my heart is empty.

When the autumn moonlight shines into the room and crickets are chirping on the bed,

With a long sigh and tears falling in vain down my face, many thoughts pass through my mind.

Perhaps it is the case that even the ending of this cruel life would be difficult.

In retrospect I contemplated all sorts of things one by one, and wondered how I could carry on living this way?

Putting back the lantern, holding the blue *kŏmun'go* diagonally

I play a tune of the deep blue flower of the lotus mingled with my sorrow,

Like the sound of bamboo blades mingled with the night rain of the Sosang river

Like the cry of a crane at the stone posts in front of a tomb, separated for a thousand years

The hands of this beautiful woman have the same skill as in the past but

Since the room here the lotus flower pattern curtain is empty,

Whose ears will it fall upon?

I am so mournful that I feel like my stomach is in knots and has been cut again and again

I would rather fall asleep and see my beloved in my dreams,

Falling leaves in the wing and crying insects in the grass

Why did they become my enemy and awaken me from sleep?

Even if the cowherd boy and weaving girl of the heavens are blocked by the Milky Way,

They are never late and meet once a year at the Star Festival on the seventh day of the seventh month (of the lunar calendar), but

After my husband leaves what kind of obstacle is there that means

that the news of his coming and going ceased?

As I stand and lean on the balcony and look at the path by which my husband went away

The dew is forming on the grass, and I realise that (it's already the time when) the evening clouds are already passing by!

In the lush bamboo grove, the birdsong seems ever more melancholy.

People say that there are many sad people in the world,

Is there no other young woman like me whose destiny is so unfortunate?

Perhaps it is because of my husband that I am at the edge of life or death!

7.3 음식디미방 – 장계향, 규합총서 – 이빙허각 (*Recipes for Tasty Foods* – Chang Kyehyang; and *Encyclopaedia of the Inner Chambers* – Yi Pinghŏgak)

Translated by Anna Yates-Lu

From Ŭmshiktimibang

Poetry quote

> Three days after arriving at the in-law's house, I enter the kitchen,
> I wash my hands and cook a stew,
> But as I don't know my mother-in-law's tastes,
> I send a young serving girl to taste it first.

Commentary on concluding page of book

I wrote this book with great difficulty, although my eyes are getting so weak, so know of my will and follow it. Each of my daughters shall copy it out and take it with her, under no circumstances should you take this book away (from the main house), but rather keep it well so that it doesn't get damaged, and don't throw it away too hastily.

Braised young chicken

Catch a young chicken the night before and leave it hanging upside down, on the morning of the second day pluck out the remaining feathers, remove the intestines, and wash it a lot so the blood comes out. Strain very sweet bean paste through a sieve, pour in a large amount of oil, then chop perilla/beefsteak plant, green onion, and shallot into small pieces, season with raw ginger, pepper, and Sichuan pepper powder, then mix in flour and water in order to make a sauce, then add a little bit of soy sauce into the water mix. Put this in the chicken's belly, wrap it up in rice cloth, and place it on a porcelain dish, then pour water into the cauldron, and steam it in the boiling water. Let it cook until it is so soft the bones can come out, then let it cool. To make a thin sauce, sift some thick bean paste, and add various spices, add some flour sauce to make it thin, then it will taste good. When the sauce is a suitable consistency, put the chicken in and braise it.

From Kyuhap ch'ongsŏ

Introduction to the Encyclopaedia of the Inner Chambers

In the autumn of 1809, I made my home in Haengjeong in Dongho(ri). At home, in the small gaps I had between cooking food and preparing side dishes, I passed through the master's chambers by chance, and came across the old writings telling of what is needed in people's normal lives, as well as about countryside life. Taking these texts and reading whichever my hand happened to touch, this was merely a way for me to widen my knowledge and cure my boredom. It suddenly struck me that if you don't write down these wise words of the ancients, how can you prepare for the time when you forget them and they could have been helpful to your work? So, while looking at all these texts, I selected the most important and wrote them down, sometimes adding my own humble opinion. I separated this into five chapters. The first is a discussion on alcohol and food, in general how to ferment sauces and brew alcohol, as well as prepare rice, rice cake, sweet dough cakes, all kinds of side dishes, there is nothing that is not included. The second is about weaving and sewing, so it includes how to hand dry scholarly robes and court attire, as well as how to figure out sizing in order to make them. In addition, there are methods for dyeing, weaving, embroidery, and breeding silkworms, as well as patching bowls and lighting oil lamps; I have added these various methods. The third is on the joy of living in the countryside, and covers everything in general, starting from how to arrange farming tasks and how to plant flowers or bamboo, continuing into how to keep horses and cows, as well as raising chickens; it contains a rough outline of life in the countryside. The fourth is on medical know-how, and teaches the methods of prenatal education, how to raise children and how to cut the umbilical cord, as well as first aid. In addition, it includes places where the 'child evil force' resides, as well as which medicines to avoid. The fifth addresses *Sulsuryak*, and so covers how to clear the house of repressive forces, and hang up charms for avoiding bad *yin* and *yang*, and even all folk methods for chasing out ghosts. As all these areas are covered, this is to keep your distance from the lures of shamans and male shamans, etc. when faced with sudden disaster. I put great effort into writing each article, trying to keep it clear, detailed, and obvious, so that just opening the book once you can find out what you need and act accordingly. I have written the names of the books cited in small writing below each article, if it is my own humble opinion I have added the note, 'new discovery.' I have given this book the title, *Kyuhap ch'ongsŏ* (Encyclopaedia of the Inner Chambers), as it is a compilation of already completed works. However, people often say that women have no business outside of their inner chamber. Hence, a woman must not write for the purpose of spreading her ideas to other people, even if she has outstanding knowledge and special talent. [I know that] it is not virtuous behaviour [according to Korean norms], which would require me to be beautifully retained indoors. On top of that, through my denseness and foolishness I dared to think of expressing myself in writing, and wrote too many pages. In the end, the most important things you can get from this book are related to preserving health, and governing the household; these are all things that you cannot be without in daily life, so it is perfect for women to study. It is for this reason that I have gathered together these texts to give to my daughters and daughters-in-law.

Written on a stormy winter solstice day

Half-moon rice cakes

Take fine rice flour and prepare white rice cake that is softer than thimble-shaped rice cake, steam it, and beat it, until it is thick and the powder doesn't stick, coil it up in a bowl, and separate [it into smaller chunks]. Then make a hole so that the skin is really thin, and the stuffing shines through. [For the stuffing] mix red beans and honey until it is sweet, then mix in cinnamon, pepper, and dried ginger powder. If they are too small and round it looks obscene, so pay attention to their size as you form them into willow-leaf shapes. If you put it on a layer of pine leaves, the taste is especially good.

7.4 이춘풍전 (*The Tale of Yi Ch'unp'ung* – Anonymous)

Translated by Jieun Kiaer and Derek Driggs

Note on translation: Notice that the narrator's voice is often heard commenting on things or directing the audience's (or readers') attention. In the Korean text and the translation, there is no differentiation made between narration and other parts of the text. Context clues must be used to discern.

Yi Ch'unp'ung was rich, but when his parents died, he squandered his money, and his wife worked hard so their family could survive. But Yi went to Pyongyang to start a business, and borrowed money from the government Finance Bureau. But he met a gisaeng, Ch'uwŏl, and used all his money.

Look at Ch'uwŏl. She stole all of Ch'unp'ung's money and then drove him away. How sad he looks!

'I don't want to see you,' said Ch'uwŏl. She threw away her glass mirror and rebuked him with annoyance.

'Where are you going to go? If you don't have the funds to travel, please take some.'

She handed him some pennies. Look at him move. His angry heart exploding, he said to Ch'uwŏl, 'When we first met, we promised that we would not depart from each other until the river dries up. But was that vow only a joke to you? What did it mean?'

Hearing this, Ch'uwŏl's countenance changed. She said, 'You listen to me! Did you not know the reality of this life? Did you also not know the temper of the *kisaeng* Ch'uwŏl in Pyongyang?'

Ch'unp'ung decided to become Ch'uwŏl's servant. When his wife heard about this, she disguised herself as a man and went to Pyongyang together with the mayor.

As the financial administrator, she made Ch'uwŏl pay 5,000 nyang as a fine. Because of this, Ch'unp'ung received money back and returned to his home in Seoul. Ch'unp'ung's wife (back home now and without telling him what she did) pretended to be surprised, saying, 'Why were you so late? How was your business?'

Ch'unp'ung, glad to see her, asked, 'How have you been?' He gave her some money and pretended he had been very successful in his business.

Look at Ch'unp'ung's wife. She prepares food and drink, and tells her husband to partake.

Look how the fool Ch'unp'ung behaves. He rebuked his wife with arrogance. 'The food is not good and the drink is not to my taste either. In Pyongyang I had good food and good drink. Now my culinary standards are higher than before. I can't forget. I want to go back to Pyongyang.'

Throwing away the chopsticks and spitting out the food, he said, 'In Pyongyang, I ate good food with the most beautiful gisaeng, Ch'uwŏl, and now that I'm home, nothing is good. I want to pay back all the money I borrowed from the Finance Bureau and go back to Pyongyang to live with Ch'uwŏl and have good food.'

How disgusting is his behaviour! Look at how his wife reacts.

In order to deceive him, she took away his dinner and went out in the sunset. She changed back into her disguise and re-entered the gate, clearing her throat. 'Has Ch'unp'ung come?'

Ch'unp'ung looked closely and realised that this was the Finance administrator from Pyongyang. Startled, he ran outside without his shoes on and bowed low to the ground. He asked humbly, 'Your humble servant returned today, but as the time was late I planned to visit your house tomorrow. But your lordship came to see your humble servant today!'

'I was passing by, but I heard that you came back home. This is why I am dropping by.'

The finance administrator entered the house, but Ch'unp'ung couldn't enter because the finance administrator was too honourable.

'Ch'unp'ung, come in and talk to me.'

'How can I go in when your lordship is already inside?'

'Don't make excuses and come inside.'

Without knowing what to do, Ch'unp'ung entered. The Finance Administrator said, 'Have you received money from Ch'uwŏl?'

'By your help, I received the money immediately. I wouldn't have expected to receive 5,000 nyang. But by your help, I've received it all in one morning. Your grace is like a mountain.'

'Did it hurt when you were beat with the plank?'

'How could I say that was painful? It was nothing.'

The Finance Administrator said, 'Have you anything to drink in your house?'

Ch'unp'ung got up and prepared the food and drink. The Finance Administrator rebuked him, saying, 'Where is your wife? Why don't you introduce her to me? Call her quickly and make her prepare the food and drink.'

Ch'unp'ung was startled and tried to find her. But how could he?

7.5 탁류 – 채만식 (*Turbid Rivers* – Ch'ae Manshik)

Translation by Jieun Kiaer and Derek Driggs

After being treated, Taesu went to Henghwa's house in Kyebok village. As always, Hyeongbo was there already, lying down. Henghwa was fiddling with the kayageum. 'I heard you bought a house. How many rooms have you got? Do you have spare rooms?' Hyeongbo asked as Taesu entered the room. It seemed that Hyeongbo hoped to move in and leech off of Taesu when he started his new family.

'Don't worry. I've thought everything out . . .'

Taesu went into the room and took off his suit jacket, and then threw it over the kayageum where Henghwa sat. As for his hat, he put it on her head. 'Wow,' Taesu said. 'You sure are making a fuss! Am I the only one who is getting married to a high school girl?'

Henghwa remained sitting, and, without a beat, gave Taesu a sidelong glance.

'Hahaha. That's right. Lately I am just so cheerful,' said Taesu.

'Wow, I can't abide this!' said Hyeongbo. 'You have been so worried that you wouldn't be able to marry this high school girl, and now you've forgotten all about it.'

'Oh my friend, why wouldn't that be the case? I've achieved my life's dream! Don't worry. Would new love make me forget my old love?'

Henghwa interrupted sharply. 'Okay, I see. I had planned to drive up to Seoul and jump off the Hangang bridge, but I guess I'll remember what you just said and forget about it.'

'Of course, don't worry about a thing!' said Taesu.

At that moment, Henghwa was simply making a joke, but to Taesu her words were not empty. Since he had gotten engaged with Chobong, he didn't have any anxiety or worries. Up to that point in his life, whenever he was anxious or worried, he would meditate and pray. If he thought things were going to go terribly wrong, he escaped his cares by imagining ending his own life.

Despite this backup plan, at times he felt completely overwhelmed with his anxieties.

Now, he was engaged with Chobong, as he had long hoped to be, he came to a conclusion. 'Now, I can die.'

He was finally liberated from the crushing pressure of his own worries.

The final wish of Taesu's life, which was to marry the high school girl Chobong, was fulfilled, and he felt that now there was nothing left for him to accomplish. But he wanted to enjoy this life to the fullest extent until the last moment. In order to do that, Taesu felt he needed to make his days with Chobong as luxurious as possible. First of all, he would need to drink and eat a lot. He also wanted to have many women around him, so he determined to keep Henghwa around. For money, theft, fraud, and embezzlement were all okay. He would gather up as much as he could.

In order to be happy, he must not have any pain or suffering in his body.

As if he were preparing some sort of ceremony, Taesu had planned everything out. For this reason, he was really, truly happy – he was not pretending or exaggerating to the least degree.

While Taesu and Henghwa were talking back and forth, Hyeongbo was having his own thoughts. He stood up after picking up his cigarette, and joined the conversation. 'Henghwa looks alright, but she must be feeling quite upset.'

'Why?'

'Oh, because she's losing such a fine man!'

'Ha! Do you think I like him because he looks nice? No, I like him because he gives me money,' Henghwa said.

'Even when she's joking she always speaks like this,' retorted Taesu.

'Who's joking? I'm being serious!'

Hyeongbo interjected. 'Alright, alright – truthfully speaking, you will be a bit disappointed when he marries her, won't you?'

7.6 채식주의자 – 한강 (*The Vegetarian* – Han Kang)

Translation from: Kang, Han (trans. Deborah Smith). 2015. *The Vegetarian*. London: Portobello Books, pp. 36–9.

'Enough!' my father-in-law yelled. 'You, Yeong-hye! After all I told you, your own father!'

This outburst was followed by In-hye roundly rebuking my wife. 'Do you truly intend to go on like this? Human beings need certain nutrients . . . if you intend to follow a vegetarian diet, you should sit down and draw up a proper, well-balanced meal plan. Just look at your face!'

So far, my wife's brother Yeong-ho was keeping his own counsel, so his wife decided to have her say instead. 'When I saw her, I thought she was a different person. I'd heard about it from my husband, but I never would have guessed that going vegetarian could damage your body like that.'

My mother-in-law brought in dishes of stir-fried beef, sweet, and sour pork, steamed chicken, and octopus noodles, arranging them on the table in front of my wife.

'This whole vegetarian business stops right now,' she said. 'This one, and this, and this – hurry up and eat them. How could you have got into this wretched state when there's not a thing in the world you can't eat?'

'Well, what are you waiting for? Come on, eat up,' my father-in-law boomed.

'You must eat, Yeong-hye,' In-hye admonished. 'You'll have more energy if you do. Everyone needs a certain amount of energy while they're alive. Even priests who enter the temple don't take their austerities too far – they might be celibate, but they're still able to live active lives.'

The children were staring wide-eyed at my wife. She turned her blank gaze on my family, as if she couldn't fathom the reason for all this fuss.

A strained silence ensued. I surveyed in turn my father-in-law's swarthy cheeks; my mother-in-law's face, so full of wrinkles I couldn't believe it had once been that of a young woman, her eyes filled with worry; In-hye's anxiously raised eyebrows; her husband's affected attitude of being no more than a casual bystander; the passive but seemingly displeased expressions of Yeong-ho and his wife. I expected my wife to say something in her own defence, but the sole, silent answer she made to all those glaring faces was to set the pair of chopsticks she had picked up back down on the table.

A small flurry of unease ran through the assembled family. This time, my mother-in-law picked up some sweet and sour pork with her chopsticks and thrust it right up in front of my wife's mouth, saying, 'Here. Come on, hurry up and eat.' Mouth closed, my wife stared at her mother as though entirely ignorant of the rules of etiquette. 'Open your mouth right now. You don't like it? Well try this instead, then.' She tried the same thing with the stir-fried beef, and when my wife kept her mouth shut as before, she set the beef down and picked up some dressed oysters. 'Haven't you liked these since you were little? You used to want to eat them all the time . . .'

'Yes, I remember that too,' In-hye chimed in, backing up her mother by making it seem as though my wife not eating oysters was the ultimate big deal. 'I always think of you when I see oysters, Yeong-hye.'

As the chopsticks holding the dressed oysters gradually neared my wife's averted mouth, she twisted away violently.

'Eat it quickly! My arm hurts . . .'

My mother-in-law's arm was actually trembling. Eventually, my wife stood up.

'I won't eat it.'

For the first time in a long while, her speech was clear and distinct.

'*What?*' my wife's father and brother, who were both similarly hot-tempered, yelled in concert. Yeong-ho's wife quickly grabbed her husband's arm.

'My heart will pack in if this goes on any longer!' my father-in-law shouted at Yeong-hye. 'Don't you understand what your father's telling you? If he tells you to eat, you eat!'

I expected an answer from my wife along the lines of, 'I'm sorry, Father, but I just can't eat it,' but all she said was, 'I do not eat meat,' – clearly enunciated, and seemingly not the least bit apologetic.

My mother-in-law gathered up the chopsticks with an attitude of despair. Her old woman's face seemed on the brink of crumpling into tears, tears that would explode from her eyes and then course down her wrinkled cheeks in silence. My father took up a pair of chopsticks. He used them to pick up a piece of sweet and sour pork and stood tall in front of my wife, who turned away.

My father-in-law stooped slightly as he thrust the pork at my wife's face, a lifetime's rigid discipline unable to disguise his advanced age.

'Eat it! Listen to what you father's telling you and eat. Everything I say is for your own good. So why act like this if it makes you ill?

The fatherly affection that was almost choking the old man made a powerful impression on me, and I was moved to tears in spite of myself. Probably everyone gathered there felt the same. With one hand my wife pushed away his chopsticks, which were shaking silently in empty space.

'Father, I don't eat meat.'

In an instant, his flat palm cleaved the empty space. My wife cupped her cheek in her hand.

'Father!' In-hye cried out, grabbing his arm. His lips twitched as though his agitation had not yet passed off. I'd known of his incredibly violent temperament for some time, but it was the first time I'd directly witnessed him striking someone.

'Mr. Cheong, Yeong-ho, the two of you come here.'

I approached my wife hesitantly. He'd hit her so hard that the blood showed through the skin of her cheek. Her breathing was ragged, and it seemed that her composure had finally been shattered. 'Take hold of Yeong-hye's arms, both of you.'

'What?'

'If she eats it once, she'll eat it again. It's preposterous, everyone eats meat!'

Yeong-ho stood up, looking as though he was finding this whole episode distasteful.

'Sister, would you please just eat? Or after all, it would be simple enough just to pretend. Do you have to make such a thing about it in front of Father?'

'What kind of talk is that?' my father-in-law yelled. 'Grab her arms, quickly. You too, Mr. Cheong.'

'Father, why are you doing this?' In-hye took hold of her father's right arm.

Having thrown down the chopsticks, he now picked up a piece of pork in his fingers and approached my wife. She was hesitantly backing away when her brother seized her and sat her down.

'Sister, just behave, okay? Just eat what he gives you.'

'Father, I beg you, stop this,' In-hye entreated him, but he shook her off and thrust the pork at my wife's lips.

8.1 멋설 – 조지훈 (*On Beauty* – Cho Chihun)

Translated by Jieun Kiaer and Derek Driggs

The sky is growing loftier; it must be autumn. I do not know what autumn is, but the leaves have long since fallen and yellow chrysanthemums sit laughing in front of the fields. Everyone who comes here says it is autumn, and so I have no choice but to believe that it is. I've put out the candle light and I've rested my chin in front of the window, but I can't seem to think of what I should be thinking about.

What is the reason for living again? A leaf blows suddenly past on a gust of wind. Everything that is must one day change – that is what we live for, it seems.

The principles of the universe, the one true existence – tonight we call them 'beautiful' as we drink up what is left of yesterday's wild grape wine, and again we find ourselves nodding to sleep. Somehow the sound of rushing water in the mountain pass climbs high into the air, and moonlight floods through the window, open wide, illuminating the distracted forms of a book here, a wine bottle there, and my sleeping self, four limbs splayed around me.

This 'beauty' – it is called by some 'the way,' by others, 'the one thing,' or 'the one heart.' Well, whether it may be a road or a thing or a heart, tonight it is 'beauty.' The question of whether what was spoken from the beginning had any meaning or none can be answered thus: Doing what is meaningless without meaning is yet another form of 'beauty.' If the world never changes, what true beauty could there be? Such vast beauty – people on earth call it anguish, as it happens. They say it is the greatest torment.

The universe became beautiful when we became content with the universe. When we doubted the universe, it became a place of sorrow. The relationship of myself and the universe is one of servant and master – would one side do the enjoying and one become merely the object of enjoyment? It is not I who enjoys the universe, but the universe which enjoys me. My own beauty becomes sadness in one place, but in the same spot it can become joy and clarity. If we must live because we cannot die, the shouldn't we choose to find interest even where there is none?

It is written that a simple bowl of rice and wild herbs are enough to preserve a life. Is it not, then, great enough a blessing to be alive? There stands a hill from which to recite poems, there flows water in which to wash our feet; who then will fault this disorderly world? Who will say it is painful? Following the flow of one's own heart is true happiness, and by the knowing thereof true beauty can be found.

8.2 강호사시가 – 맹사성 (*Song of Four Seasons by Rivers and Lakes* – Maeng Sasŏng)

Translation by Jieun Kiaer

When spring visits nature, deep excitement naturally arises.
 While I drink makkoli [rice liquor/spirit] at the stream where I play, indeed the fresh fish are the snacks/nibbles.
 The fact that I'm able to like this [be] leisurely spending time, still is possible by the grace/blessing of my king.
 When summer visits nature, I spend the days in a thatched cottage, I have nothing to do. [Indeed] The divine river wave/current sends the refreshing winds!
 The fact that I'm able to be like this staying refreshingly cool, still this is possible by the grace/blessing of my king.
 Autumn visits nature and every fish gets fat.
 I carry a net in a small boat, flowing along the wave I throw it,
 [I'm going loading the net in my small boat; I threw the net letting it follow the waves,]
 The fact that I'm able to be like this whiling away the time, still this is possible by the grace/blessing of my king.
 Winter visits nature, the piled-up snow is more than one foot in depth.
 I wear a bamboo hat at an angle and I put my straw rain cape around myself and make it into my overcoat.
 The fact that I'm able to be like this without being cold, still this is possible by the grace/blessing of my king.

8.3 실록예찬 – 이양하 (*In Praise of Fresh Green* – Yi Yangha)

Translation by Jieun Kiaer and Derek Driggs

Among spring, summer, autumn, and winter, there is no season that does not continually shower us with benefits. But of all of these seasons, the ones which provides those benefits with the most generosity and fullness are spring and summer – and of these two seasons, the benefits of spring appear with the most beauty. Out of spring, the moment when the green leaves of Man Mountain blossom is the most wonderful. Open your eyes and gaze up at the faraway sky. The sky in May, as clean and bright as the laugh of a child; this mountain and that mountain turning greener with each passing day; this hill and that hill, bringing new wonder with each day; the bright and fragrant wind which runs through the sky, brushing through the trees as it passes. . . . Though we may claim to be poor and have nothing, at these moments we seem to have everything. Though we may feel that because our hearts are so destitute we want for nothing and hope for nothing, doesn't that wind as it runs through the sky and brushes past the trees feel as if it will bring us everything we need in mere seconds?

Today again the sky is as bright as can be, and the green enrobing the area is a level cleaner and fresher and even more alive than it was yesterday. Today, like usual, after grammar time has finished, I feel as if a great weight has dropped off of me as I shake out my clothing and climb up to my usual spot in the western grove. The place I call my spot is a stump in the middle of a pine grove, with barely enough space to sit on, but friends who pass by this way tend to call it 'my spot.' And as I tend to spend the happiest hours of my days here, I like to come back as if it's my privilege whenever I have time to spare.

Of course, I don't do this because of some highly philosophical desire to travel far away from the masses and exist in lofty solitude, or because I am particularly more ill-tempered than the average person and therefore don't like being around other people. I like to be around and spend time with people, and I am just like a regular person in my like of company. And despite all of humanity's failures, I feel that people are one of the most beautiful things in existence. And also, I feel that to become one of the truly beautiful people, a person must spend time with and cry with and laugh with and live with other people.

But at times like this – when the bright sun is clear in the blue sky, the mountains are all robed in entrancing green, and all the hills are covered up – when whispers of joy secretly seep between sky and land, tree and tree, and leaf and leaf; when the joyful song feels as if it will sonorously burst out at any moment, shaking the mountains and plains – at times like these, even if I had a friend to share a laugh or story with, I would not be able to help but to give my attention to nature, to open my ears to its song of joy.

If you think about it one way, people are constantly tied up by the world around us, forgetting that there is a sky above us, counting the money in our pockets, thinking about our positions or ranks, absorbed in our pondering about various honours or recognition. We are captured by shame or passion, we hate each other and are unable to find peace in our hearts as we despise and envy and fight each other. How small we seem, how unrefined! In the end, we look like nothing more than a blemish or a noise which distracts from the holiness and beauty and glory of nature's great harmony. At times like this, I cannot quench my desire to, if only for a moment, leave people behind; to forget about people entirely; to breathe in and feel and sing of only the grass and the trees and the sky and the wind.

At around this time, with all the green around us, our hearts gain a special strength, which gives us true joy and comfort. When I face the green nature around me, it washes my eyes, it washes my head, it washes my chest and each corner of my heart. And all of the dust and dirt to be found in my heart – my greed, my indignity, my pains, my difficulties – it disappears in the next moment, and the joyful song of the stars and the wind and the sky and the grass fills my head, my chest, and all of my heart. My bosom is green with the nature, my vision is green with nature. Things that act and things that are acted upon become one – should I call it Buddha's equal grace? – and we become free from thoughts and ideas and free from obstacles. At times like this, I forget all of my things but I become happy as if I had everything. At times like these I feel no confusion of the senses, I don't have worries and concerns, but I feel that I will always have unlimited and abundant joy and peace. At times like this I can be free from desire and free from sadness, I can overcome and uplift my heart's conflict and friction, and I can bring a feeling of harmony and order to the world that seems to make it a loftier place.

When it comes to this greenness, I have no preferences. From the lightest to the deepest shades, I love all kinds of green. But this greenness only has one short life. If the time when it first rides in on the spring wind, pouring out from young leaves, is the childhood of the greenness, than the hottest time of summer when dense leaves cast deep shadows is its prime years and old age. In childhood, there is the beauty of childhood, and in the prime of life there is the beauty of the prime of life. One cannot choose between the two. But the most beautiful part of this greenness happens around this time, the time of its youth. As each leaf emerges fully from each sprout and becomes a full leaf, it is baptised by its first taste of sunlight, and at this point it can be called the season of a new, fresh, pale shade of green. This period of greenness is unfortunately short. Some trees can last two to three weeks this way, but some don't even last three or four days before passing through this most beautiful of seasons. Though short, however, this time of greenness has no comparison. Some may say that green is a humble and meek colour, but the green of this time does not fall behind any other colour in its beauty. For example, consider the maple and larch trees at this time. If these are rare, think of the oak and the willow, and the many nameless trees and plants in the woods at this time. Look at their fresh beauty, their soft grace, and their quiet, neat scent. Is this not the height of nature's wonder? Is this not one of the great benefits of nature we should praise and give thanks for?

8.4 무소유 – 법정 (*Non-possession* – Pŏpchŏng)

Translated by Jieun Kiaer and Derek Driggs

'I am a poor begging priest. The things I can call my own are a spinning wheel and the rice bowl I used in prison, a tin of goat milk, six shabby blankets, a towel, and a less-than-grand reputation – nothing more.'

These were the words of Mahatma Gandhi to a Marseille customs officer as he spread out his belongings, on his way to attend the second round-table conference in London in September of 1931. I, upon reading this verse in Kripalani's book on Gandhi, felt extremely ashamed, for it occurred to me that I was the owner of far too many things – at least in my current position.

Actually, when I was first born into this world, I brought nothing with me. And when I have lived as much as I am meant to live and disappear from this world, I will go with empty hands. But in the course of living, this possession and that have managed to accumulate. Of course, these could all be considered objects for use in daily life. But are they truly essential to the point that I could not go without them? The more I consider this, the more I realise that things I would be better off without are not small in number.

We obtain things out of necessity, but at times those things cause us to exert no small amount of energy. For that reason, owning something may in other words be interpreted as being tied to something. When we consider that the things we obtained according to our need are actually tying us up and limiting our freedom, host, and guest get switched around and we become owned ourselves. Thus, having much is usually seen as something worth boasting about, but at the same time it carries with it another meaning: that we are actually tied to that many things.

Until summer last year, I diligently – truly using all of my energy – raised two pots of named orchids. Three years ago, when I moved my residence to Taraeheon, where I live now, a priest I know sent them to my room. Because I live alone in my residence, the only living things there were myself and those plants. I sought out and read related books for them, I asked an acquaintance who was moving overseas to send me a fertiliser called hyponech for their health. In the summer, I had to find spots of cool shade to move them to, and in the winter, shivering, I didn't raise the temperature in my room.

If I had showed this much devotion to my parents years earlier, I would surely have been labelled as a truly filial son. When spring came after I had thus whiled away for my treasured orchids, the pleasant fragrance and yellow-green blooming flowers made my heart flutter;

the leaves shone bright like a crescent moon. Everyone who came to visit Taraeheon saw my fresh orchids and loved them, without exception.

In summer last year, one rainy day I went to Pongseonsa to see Unheo Nosa. In the middle of the afternoon, the sunlight – which up to that point had been hidden by the rain storm – poured out with blinding lustre, combining with the sound of the nearby stream so that it drowned out the buzz of cicadas throughout the forest.

Ah! It was only then that the thought suddenly came to me. I had left my orchids out in the field before coming. The sunlight, which had been so brilliant just a minute before, became suddenly hateful to me. The leaves of my orchids, which were surely withering under this sun, seemed to flash before my eyes, and I could not tarry. Hurriedly, I went back to that road. As I had expected, the leaves were hanging limp. Breathing sighs of regret, I wetted the plants with water from a nearby stream until the plant looked barely alive again. But it seemed that all my strength and energy had leaked out of me somehow.

It was then that, with my whole body – deep in my heart – I felt it: that obsession is suffering. It is true. I had become obsessed with my orchids. I decided I must escape this obsession. When I was raising the orchids, I couldn't leave home even when I was meant to perform my priestly duties, and I ended up being stuck at home. When I had to leave home briefly to take care of business outside, I had to open the windows to keep the air circulating properly, and more than once I left the plants out, only to remember after leaving and have to hurry back home to put them back in place. It was a toxic obsession.

A few days later, a friend who spoke as little as my orchids came by for a visit. Without planning to, I put the plants in his arms. Only then did I truly become free from what had been tying me down. I felt to fly at the sense of liberation. For nearly three years, I had shared affection with those plants, but instead of sadness or loneliness, a feeling of lightness took place in my heart. From then on, I committed to myself that I would leave behind one thing each day. I suppose I should say that I came to understand the meaning of having nothing through those plants.

The history of mankind, in a certain sense, feels like a history of ownership. So many people seem to be simply fighting for what they want to have. In the pursuit of ownership, there is no limit and there is no day off. Instead, a person simply rolls along, wanting to gain just one more thing. Because things, in the end, do not satisfy, people begin to want to own people, too. When those people do not behave as they wish, people do terrible things, and they keep trying to own other people when they don't even have control of their own minds.

The desire for ownership is directly proportional with our understanding. It is something that occurs not only in individuals, but also in relationships between countries. We see again and again that as the confederations of yesterday stand at odds with each other today, so do the countries that have in the past growled at each other now exchange well wishes.

Ghandi said this, also: 'To me, ownership seems like a crime . . .'

He said that he would have something for himself when other people who wanted to have that same thing could have it at the same time. But that is almost impossible, so owning something for himself was something he couldn't not consider a crime. Sometimes our concept of ownership blinds us. And so we become excited, when we don't even have enough time to manage the things we have been given. But we will all, one day, return with empty hands. Even my body will be thrown away, in the end, before I leave this place all by myself. No amount of objects in this world will be able to do anything for us then.

There is a saying that only the person who gives up the most will be able to obtain the most in the end. This is a lesson for all people who feel pain in their hearts because of things. Because the paradoxical principle of owning nothing is this: when we have nothing, the whole world becomes ours.

8.5 죽은 왕녀를 위한 파바느 (*Pavane for a Dead Princess* – Pak Minkyu)

Translation from: Park Min-Gyu (trans. Amber Hyun Jung Kim). 2014. *Pavane for a Dead Princess*. Champaign: Dalkey Archive Press, pp. 185–7.

I can honestly say I worked harder than anyone, but the real world was very different from school grounds. The male employees used to say, *It's the* women *who light up our offices!* I didn't think that sexist; in fact, I think it's true. Pretty, hardworking women would brighten up anyone's day. While I didn't consider myself as someone who lights up an office, I thought I was someone who was needed. But I was wrong. As time went on, I was pushed farther and farther into the corner gloom.

Interpersonal relationships were important at the department. I worked hard to keep up a cheerful expression, engage in conversation, and, most of all, diligently complete all the tasks given me. Nonetheless, it was hard, mostly because I could feel how much my supervisors and the men at work didn't want to talk to me.

'Don't laugh, it makes you look worse,' one of them said to me once. If someone says something like that to you, that'll prevent you from ever laughing again. I mean, how could you? No one asked me out to lunch or showed any concern for me. When someone had to work with me on something, I saw the uncomfortable expressions on his face. I retreated into my shell and became someone who quietly did as she was told and nothing more. I became someone whom no one would miss.

It was worse on the store floors. I had to deal with customers face-to-face, and the employees there shunned me. Some of them voiced their annoyance and let me know I was affecting store sales. 'Get out of here!' they barked, and I spent more and more time in the parking lots and warehouses. That's where I belonged. I agree, beauty must be appreciated. I also know not everyone can be the same. What I find unfair, though, is why did the world tell us we're all equal? Why does it behave as if we're living under equal conditions? If someone is measured against a yardstick, shouldn't the yardstick be something that can be overcome by effort? No one's appreciated me for anything I've done. I've only been judged by my looks. Around the time you and I first met, I started looking for other work. In many ways, the department store was a difficult place to work in. And now I've left. I've finally left.

I can see the moon from here.

I couldn't see the moon from my room in Seoul so I haven't seen it in a while. I used to look up at the moon from my desk in my family home. My brother must be having a tough first semester at school; he fell asleep a long time ago. I'm getting sleepy myself.

I feel this letter is a lot like that moon. Yesterday, I left off saying I was sleepy; today, I'm beginning this letter by comparing this letter to the moon. I went to work this morning, and now, with the day over, I've come back to this letter. I'm only showing you one side of me, the side writing this letter. It can't be helped. People, and especially women, are like the moon. There's one side they want shown, and one side they hope will remain unseen.

There's one side that can be seen and one that's hidden.

I remember the first time I put on makeup. I was in high school. Job hunting season had begun, so our school offered a how-to class on makeup for the graduates who'd go on to find jobs soon. The teacher was only a few years older than we were. She walked around the classroom offering tips. The girls were excited. I was excited, too. I never thought I'd wear makeup, as it seemed a world far beyond my reach. But I could use the class as an excuse to try. My heart pounding, I drew on eyeliner and put on lipstick with a shaking hand. The girls fixed each other's makeup and squealed with glee. I remember seeing my face in the mirror. It looked the same, not helped by the makeup. I realised nothing could be done to change my looks, and I hung my head.

But the experience brought on a strange feeling. I saw why women put on makeup. Even if it doesn't magically grant them beauty, it gives them a new face. Women who put on makeup will gain another face. Women carry two selves within them. I remember how everyone screamed with delight after the teacher demonstrated on one lucky girl. With their fresh coats of makeup, the girls ran around the hallways and cafeterias chattering about how they weren't going to wash their faces that night, and the younger students gazed enviously at them. Women don't wear makeup for someone else. They wear it for themselves.

They want to go through life with that made-up face. Just like the moon, they only want to show one side of themselves to the world. *I don't look so bad*, says even the most unsightly woman as she leaves her house with a face full of makeup. And they keep their real selves hidden – the sides of them that can't be helped – like the dark side of the moon. When they remove their makeup, they are like astronauts returning back to Earth from a stint on the moon. I hoped makeup might help my situation, but I could only wear it under sanction of it being part of a lesson. I felt the stares. *Don't put on makeup, it makes you look worse*, they seemed to say, just like how later at work I had to endure *Don't laugh, it makes you look worse*. There was a time I thought it might just be my inferiority complex. But I felt the same stares when I had to (as part of my work uniform) wear short skirts at the department store. You know what's the most pitiful thing in the world? The obvious effort made by an ugly woman to look beautiful. The world is merciless on the pitiful attempts made by ugly women, like workers who bulldoze and set fire to housing projects to force out the evictees.

8.6 마네킹 – 최윤 (*Mannequin* – Ch'oe Yun)

Translation from: Ch'oe Yun (trans. Jung Yewon). 2016. *Mannequin: A Novel*. Victoria, TX; McLean, IL; Dublin: Dalkey Archive Press, pp. 17–20.

Will there be any news of Jini today? To be honest, I'd be just as anxious to hear any news as to hear nothing. What kind of news could there be? There's an equal chance of hearing good news, that she's safe and well somewhere, and hearing the most extremely unfortunate news. So around this time every morning, the family turns to this kind of a solution. Everyone despairs constantly, there being no clue or news, but we have as much hope as we do despair that she hasn't been found dead yet. Like a soap opera showing at the same hour every day, the soap opera of this house shows reruns every morning, each time just a little different. Only afterward can everyone go to his or her own room. You have to show that you care at least that much when someone in the family has disappeared, right?

Shark is quite dejected. It won't last long, though. I trust the blood cells of tedium, rage, and hatred going around in our bodies. They'll make us come alive again. Conch has forgotten what she has to do. Now that Jini is gone, both Shark and Conch are dithering. It's as if they've lost their jobs. That's why Shark gets angry. When he gets angry, he starts beating people and things. When he makes a scene like that, I feel refreshed as well. But I'm different. I found something to do as soon as Jini left home.

Shark has no interest or skill in anything unrelated to Jini. He always says, 'I don't want to learn anything.' He jokes around, saying, 'I'm a Jini specialist.' How much Jini gets paid for every minute of an appearance or filming, for the filming of her face and body, the nape of her neck, which is at the top of wanted lists for ad proposals, and of her hands, feet, elbows, and even her auricles … Shark is the only one who knows the price of all the particulars of Jini's body. He's been doing only this work for many years now.

Actually, Shark doesn't have the sharp teeth or the well-developed muscles of the sharks in the illustrated book of fish. He looks delicate, like a girl, with a pale face, and a thin body. But he's tall, toned from rigorous workouts, and rather good-looking. That's our weapon, bait, and asset. It runs in the family. They say that my grandfather and his brothers were all handsome. Fair is fair, they say. Once, Shark and I stole something at the market. Just for practice. We knew we were found out, so we stashed what we stole in the shop next door. But the shop owner just tilted his head and went back to his own shop after seeing us looking up at him, the picture of innocence. Shark was eight, and I was six. We know very well how to fool people. It's a piece of cake. Even now, we'll be walking down the street, and we'll wink at each other and steal something. We don't do it all the time, but we do it for a thrill every now and then. We never get caught.

Shark is scary when he gets angry. He turns viciously on his family, like someone off his medicine. Not because we're family. He says he's against those primates called humans. Still, he said a few days ago, 'Jini's going to come back on Mom's birthday. So make sure to set the table for a birthday feast!'

For the first time in years, my mom was going to have a feast thrown in her honour. Shark threatened us so we wouldn't start dinner before he came home, but he came home very late at night. We were all starving to death, but we waited without eating. Jini didn't come – there wasn't even a phone call. When it was midnight, Shark kicked the table, knocking it over. My mom didn't even get to touch her own birthday feast when it had been so long since she'd had one. I can't really imagine Jini forgetting my mom's birthday. I've seen Jini cry many times because of my mom. She cried like a wounded animal moaning because she couldn't talk. Whenever I saw her crying, I thought, 'She's beautiful even when she cries.' So I would let her cry. That's the way it is – life is no big deal. It's like a gift that comes with a purchase. Some of them you like, but some of them you just can't stand.

There's a tacit understanding between Shark and me. Sometimes, we meet downtown and go into a hotel. And we take off our wordly shells and comfort each other, lying still with our flesh rubbing against each other. Because we're pitiful. Because we're primates that have stopped evolving. We order expensive room service, and make a toast to Jini, who's made such pleasure possible. If people who knew we were brother and sister saw us, they'd jump to conclusions and point fingers at us. But we're not interested in what people might think. When we want is simply the comfort of our flesh. We can momentarily forget the tedious affairs of the world as we relish in our own soft, resilient flesh. That's the only time when Shark is soft. We become children and fall into a deep, long sleep, side by side.

We meet in this way and do business. I make sure to modify our tacit contract. Shark keeps a record in a little notebook. Through many negotiations, I've increased my share to include Jini's hands, nape, and hair. The income from those parts of Jini's body becomes mine. I've earned quite a sum this way. Saving money without any particular aim, that's my hobby. I don't spend it on anyone, not even myself. Shark says that I'm just one of the many money collectors everywhere. Shark, of course, has a monopoly on Jini's whole body, feet, face, arms, and so on, which are the most popular with advertisers. At any rate, he's in charge of arranging the contracts, collecting the down payments, increasing revenue, and taking Jini to shoots and interviews. He even supervises the household expenses and Conch's salary. We like transparent, precise dealings. When I open my eyes, Shark is always gone. That's the way it is. We understand each other, but we don't have much to say to each other.

였[다니] / 으시 / 우니 /리라
?[음이]?
좋아
에게
음[기]
을
을 수 있었
[하고자]?
까에서
있[다고 했어요   자네의
때에는
자기 스스로
~~맡아야... 하며~~
~~다니 (시)~~
~~되더이야~~
알(고 는)
에도
할(가 받)
-임 subox